Human Behavior in the Social Environment

Human Behavior in the Social Environment

AN ECOLOGICAL VIEW
Second Edition

Carel B. Germain
and
Martin Bloom

Columbia University Press   New York

Columbia University Press
Publishers Since 1893
New York   Chichester, West Sussex
Copyright © 1999 Columbia University Press
All rights reserved

Library of Congress Cataloging-in-Publication Data
Germain, Carel B.
Human behavior in the social environment : an ecological view /
Carel B. Germain and Martin Bloom. — 2nd ed.
p.   cm
Includes bibliographical references and indexes.
ISBN 0–231–11140–1
1. Social psychology. 2. Environmental psychology.
3. Developmental psychology. 4. Family—United States—
Psychological aspects. 5. Minorities—United States—Psychology.
6. Social work education. I. Bloom, Martin, 1934–   .   II. Title.
HM251.G3497   1999
302—dc21   98–37513

CONTENTS

ACKNOWLEDGMENTS

To Carel and Bill Germain, for enduring words and memories.

To Gretchen Stark Went, MSW, the complete reader.

To my students over the years, from whom I have learned much, in particular, Steve Block, Jack VandenHengel, Pam (Pearlingi) Wright, H. A. Musser, Harry Almond, Robin Woods, Felix Borges, Jennifer Clement, Regina Dyton, Lauren Gibson, and many others whom memory hides from memory.

To my colleagues: Frank Reeves, Diane Drachman, Barbara Pine, Waldo Klein, Francine DeFranco, Jan Lambert, Joan Andreoli, Virginia Starkie, Bruce Parkhurst, for various forms of welfare to work, but free of any guilt over what I did with their aid.

A special thanks to Lois Bloom for her words on words, to Robert H. Bloom for his words on torts, and to Anne R. Gibbons for her lines through words.

With love and appreciation for the human and humane behavior throughout this grueling labor of love—my family: Lynn; Bard and Vicki; Laird, Sara, Paul, and Elizabeth.

PART I

The Person and Environment Configuration

The academic course human behavior in the social environment (mercifully abbreviated HBSE) is full of surprises. If you had taken this course at the beginning of the twentieth century, you would likely have received lectures in sociology dissolved in a tincture of moralistic concern because social work was still tied to the scientific fountainhead from which it sprang (in the form of the Conference of Charities) after branching off from the American Social Science Association in 1874 (Klein and Bloom 1994). By 1920 when a handful of bona fide schools of social work had been established, you would have had lectures in medicine and psychiatry because this new profession was still smarting from a pronouncement by a distinguished physician (Abraham Fechner) that social work was *not* a profession because it lacked a theoretical foundation. By 1940 your HBSE class would likely have been mostly on psychoanalytic theory—in spite of the Great Depression and the enormous socioeconomic factors affecting the nation.

By 1960 there would have been a major corrective emphasis on groups and communities, along with the older concern for individuals, partly because the field itself began to expand and workers in groups and communities wanted students to have basic information on these topics. Social workers were also much involved in the civil rights movements of the 1960s, which brought in new interests in the social environment, power, conflict, and social justice. By 1980 who knows what you would have had. Because no brand of HBSE was demonstrably "better" than another, each school could pick its own and argue for accreditation from the Council on Social Work Education, and there were many to select from: behaviorism, cognitive theory, general systems theory, social systems theory, communication models, field theory, to say nothing of psychoanalytic models that were being roundly criticized as sexist, racist, and classist. Other models were emerging at this exciting, if chaotic time, including the predominant orientation of this book: the ecological model used as metaphor rather than formal theory (Germain 1991, 1994b).

The book you are reading focuses on the first decade of the twenty-first century. It is still ecological in orientation, but as Germain foresaw, HBSE content is going to be quite different from what the previous century had constructed. In place of the "dual, yet one-dimensional" focus on HB and SE, this course will be transformed into "a multi-dimensional focus on 'diverse persons in diverse environments.' " This new HBSE is strengthened by new concepts and stronger research findings on human and environmental diversity that are derived from the biological, social, and behavioral sciences and from social work itself.

Carel Germain died in 1995, and a year later I was invited to write this revision. Fortunately, I had her recent publications (Germain 1994a, 1994b; Germain and Gitterman 1995; Germain 1997) and her notes on the future to guide the construction of this twenty-first-century text. So what you are to read is a blend of Germain's admirable scholarship with my own ideas as they developed, somewhat in tandem with hers. There are several principles of this revision you should understand. First, no one book can contain all the bio-psycho-socio-cultural-economic-political information you will need. This text provides a starting point for searching for information.

Second, there is no shortage of good materials that describe advances in biology, psychology, and sociology. But few methods interrelate all this information in a comprehensible fashion for students in the applied social sciences: simple and clear enough to remember for practice (at whatever level or brand the student chooses), but strong and sound enough to provide reasonably clear visions of multiple dimensions of diverse peoples and environments. Tightening up Germain's ecological model and screwing up our courage to grasp it—rather than screwing up Germain's model and tightening our minds to be able to grasp only a portion of it—will be a major task of this book.

Third, many readers of this book have encouraged me to continue the extraordinary work Germain began and have offered many suggestions (some of them contradictory) on what ought to be changed. I accept all these ideas, even the contradictory ones, because this is exactly what the real world is like. In this book, do not expect to learn one party line; rather, expect to develop for yourself a framework containing the multiple perspectives of others and the diverse settings in which these people and environments have transactions with each other and change one another as they are themselves changed. This is a complex task, and yet we do this every moment of every day by making sense of our world and moving toward various life goals.

An Ecological-Configural Model

If we believe that everything in the world is related to everything else, we need a road map to help us see these connections in a systematic way, lest we get lost in a forest of details and overlook some important components. Here is one road map:

I suggest that any significant social event, such as making a friend, having a child, talking with a client about a significant problem, retiring from a job, and so on, is the product of several kinds of forces acting on the people involved. One set of forces strengthens the individual, the support of some group, and the resources from the physical environment, while another set of forces increases personal limitations, social stresses, and environmental pressures. Clearly, the second set reduces the chances for the first set to achieve its goals. If you like a person very much but that person is from some outgroup such as a different ethnic group or a member of the same gender as you, in a racist and homophobic society you will experience forces that pull you back from establishing this friendship. However, if you also have supportive relationships such as understanding parents, tolerant friends, and access to locations where diversity is celebrated, you will experience forces pushing you toward establishing this friendship. What you do may be seen as the result of these pushes and pulls. Indeed, all of life is filled with pushes and pulls of various degrees of intensity. Social services may be seen as an additional force that clarifies these various pushes and pulls and perhaps contributes new energy, helping clients achieve the goals they seek within their contexts. Here is a formulation of these various forces pushing and pulling on any significant social behavior (Bloom 1996):

	Individual strengths	+	Social supports	+	Physical/environmental resources
Any significant social behavior is some function of:					
	Individual limitations	+	Social stresses	+	Physical/environmental pressures

Therefore anytime we consider significant social behavior, we should analyze these six factors for what they contribute to the particular situation. Sometimes all will be involved; other times, only some will be. But our unit of study will always include people in environments.

We have to specify the subsystems or components of these major factors, such as the cognitive, affective, behavioral, and physiological attributes of individual strengths and limitations; the various kinds of social groups, from small primary groups like families and peers to large organizations and communities; and possibly the differences between built and natural environments. The devil is in the details of this formulation, and as we assess any situation as the basis for professional helping, we will consider all these ingredients. It is as if we have a cube with six faces (three strengths and three corresponding limitations), any of which may predominate in some given situation. If we neglect to consider any of the six, the cube will collapse and we may be overlooking an important factor in the behavior and life situation of clients. If we routinely consider what, if any, relevance each of the six facets of the cube holds for a given situation, we are less likely to overlook an important feature and are more likely to thoroughly analyze a complex life situation. We offer this formulation as a checklist for thinking about what goes into any significant social happening for individuals or groups.

In part 1, we review components of this configural formulation: chapter 1 presents the ecological point of view, a new language and perspective for viewing our everyday world. Chapters 2, 3, and 4 examine large groups as contexts for human behavior, while chapters 5 and 6 focus on small groups. The physical environment is discussed throughout these chapters in appropriate places, especially in chapters 1, 2, and 3. The individual is the reference point throughout this book—the *person* in these various *environments*. However, additional discussion of the person in a genetic and biological context is the subject of chapter 7.

I

The Ecological Perspective

This first chapter presents the ecological perspective as the general framework for the rest of the text. This ecological perspective is intended to provide a rationale for considering and possibly incorporating specific theories and research findings into one's own theoretical foundation for professional practice. We consider some central concepts bearing on personal structures, development, and functioning in social and physical environmental contexts, details of which are expanded upon in the following chapters.

Outline

Introduction

The Social Ecological Perspective: Basic Assumptions
    Assumption 1: Person:Environment Unit of Analysis
    Assumption 2: General Tendency toward Adaptation
    Assumption 3: Factors That Facilitate or Impede Adaptation
    Assumption 4: Flow of Life Events
        Coping with stress
        Coping: Two appraisal questions
        Defending against stress
    Assumption 5: The Transacting Configuration
The Social Ecological Perspective: From the Perspective of the Person
    Concept Set 1: Person:Environment Fit (Structural concepts)
        Goodness of fit
        Adaptedness and adaptation
        Maladaptation
    Concept Set 2: Life Course Development
    (Developmental concepts)
        Growth (maturation) and development

Introduction

Rashomon is a poetic tale of love and death from medieval Japan in which the same event—the death of a young husband—is interpreted in a court of law from the point of view of the wife, a bandit, and the ghost of the dead man. (Remember, this is a fairy tale.) The incomparable director Akira Kirosawa created a cinematic gem from this story that brings the enigma directly and inescapably to us. The narrator of the story, a woodcutter who happened on the scene after the death occurred, tells how each witness in turn describes the murder (suicide) that he or she *admits* having committed, all using the same set of facts. There is even a feminist version of the story that directly involves the narrator himself. All this leaves us, the audience, wondering which if any version is true.

What is the truth of a life or of any significant incident in a person's life course? This question is of vital concern to social workers and other helping professionals who have to sort out the confusing mass of interacting events so as to help clients help themselves within the multiple contexts of their lives. In art as in applied social science, we cannot escape viewing the person and the environmental contexts as inseparable. More formally phrased, the National Association of Social Workers saw the purpose of social work as being to facilitate personal development-inducing and environment-ameliorating transactions (cf. Gordon 1969). The Council on Social Work Education defined the purpose of social work as the promotion, restoration, maintenance, and enhancement of the functioning of individuals, families, households, social groups, and communities (Curriculum policy statement 1992). To do this, social work students learn some basic elements of the social, behavioral, and life sciences, not as an end in itself, but in order to be able to apply this basic knowledge to solve the enigmas of modern life, which are in no way less complicated than *Rashomon*.

The multiple stories that a client and collaterals (family, employers, etc.) tell helping professionals are variations on *Rashomon* and require a sensitive openness to the facts and the multiple meanings attached to them. When we work as professional helpers for others, we use a variety of tools to guide us with some degree of efficacy, because ultimately we must facilitate the kinds of changes the client (and society) wants, and to develop problem-solving skills for clients to adapt themselves, their environments, or both to life changes. In this book, we offer a conceptual perspective to make sense of the complexity of life and to help clients adapt more effectively. Instead of millions of words describing some life situation (which would still be incomplete), we offer these few hundreds of words of a theory that can be used with any human context, to give some sense of coherence while we help clients construct useful approaches to deal with their world. The theoretical framework that we use in this book is the *social ecological perspective*.

Ecology studies the relations between organisms and their environments. In this book, we use the phrase "social ecology" as a metaphor to facilitate our taking a holistic view of people and environments, neither of which can be fully understood except in the context of its relationship with the other. That relationship is characterized by continuous reciprocal exchanges, or transactions, in which people and environments influence, shape, and sometimes change each other.

At first glance, the notion of transaction seems simple. Yet it is quite complex and is made more so by the fact that our language and our education from elementary school on are generally geared to *linear* or simple cause-and-effect thinking. Relationships between individuals and their environments can indeed be linear; that is, a cause may precede an effect. One element is then understood to influence or change the other at a particular moment or in particular circumstances but is not itself changed. Such linear causality, useful in understanding some simple phenomena, is less useful in understanding the complex situations with which social workers and other helping professionals are involved.

Transactional relationships, in contrast, are reciprocal exchanges between entities, in which each changes or influences the other over time (Bandura 1986). Whereas in linear relations one entity changes the other, in transactional relations both entities are changed. Whereas linear causality is one-directional, proceeding from an observed or assumed cause to an observed or assumed effect, transactional causality is *circular*. It is like a loop, in which an event or process may be a cause at one point and an effect at another in the ongoing flow around the loop of sociocultural, psychological, and biological processes. This significant difference in the two kinds of thinking about human phenomena has an impact on how we view causality in people's life issues, how we act to help, what kinds of social work research are needed, how environments can be made more responsive to people's needs, and how we teach and learn the knowledge and theory, the values, the ethical principles, and the skills of social work.

Rooted in the notion of transaction, the ecological perspective points to theoretical systems that provide a useful understanding of human beings (at all levels of organization from the individual to collectives of various kinds and sizes) and their environments. Thus biological, physiological, intellectual, emotional, social, cultural, and physical environmental knowledge are required for the theoretical foundations of social work.

The Social Ecological Perspective: Basic Assumptions

In this section, we describe the overall theoretical framework that we call the social ecological perspective. This succinct and abstract statement is elaborated on in various sections of the book as applications of the general metaphor to specific person:situations. First, we begin with some fundamental assumptions. We use the various terms below (indicated in italics) so as to distinguish different aspects of a common process. We then recombine these terms as we develop the overall theoretical perspective.

Assumption 1: Person:Environment Unit of Analysis

We begin with a fundamental assumption regarding what it is we are looking at as we discuss human behavior in the social environment: namely, that the appropriate unit of analysis for an applied social science (such as social work, counseling, community psychology, social psychiatry, public health, and others) is the person:environment complex. We most nearly understand a human situation to the extent that we know what relevant people bring to and receive from specific situations in given periods of time. Remove any of these factors from the formulation and we lose a significant aspect of social reality.

Assumption 2: General Tendency toward Adaptation

Actions to ensure survival of the species are built into the organic evolution of *Homo sapiens* as with all living things. Even though human beings have replaced organic evolution (i.e., genetic mutation and environmental selection) with cultural evolution (i.e., changes in knowledge, technology, and social organization), we can still assume the general actions people take with regard to themselves and their environments are survival-oriented. Gross survival has been replaced, in most nations, by more subtle adaptations to the highly varied social and physical environments. "*Adaptations* are continuous, change-oriented, cognitive, sensory-perceptual, and behavioral processes people use to sustain or raise the level of fit between themselves and their environment" (Germain and Gitterman 1995:817).

The ongoing goal of adaptation is called *adaptedness*, which is defined in terms of some level of goodness of fit between the parties involved, ranging from a favorable to a minimally adequate level. Let's analyze the following situation to illustrate this point: A child (assisted by the parents) gets ready to go to school for the first time and the school agents (teachers, principal, maintenance workers, etc.) get ready to receive and respond appropriately to that child and his or her classmates. Consider the mutual adaptations that this involves.

The child has a variety of *needs, rights, capacities,* and *aspirations* (goals) as he or she enters the school situation. Among these are the need (curiosity) to know about people and the world, which the school is supposed to satisfy through its teaching. The child has a legal right to public education, as well as certain responsibilities when receiving this right, such as coming to school on time. The child has various capacities, such as language skills, motor skills, and intellectual skills. And the child has learned certain familial or cultural aspirations, such as going to college and getting a good job, for which school is a necessary path to their accomplishment. All these needs, rights, capacities, and aspirations reside, as it were, within the child, and are what the child brings to the interaction with the school situation. A child may have different degrees of needs, capacities, and aspirations—legal rights to public education are assumed to be equal for all—and these differences will mean different kinds of interactions at school. What we see is one child who in effect is the sum of these needs, rights, capacities, and aspirations. The child may not be able to articulate any of this, but the parents or the state (in the form of laws requiring individualized goals of education) may be able to do so.

Schools, likewise, are complex partners in the person:environment interchange. School situations will vary both in arrangements of the built and natural *physical environment,* as well as in the *sociocultural arrangements* of which teachers, classrooms, playgrounds, principals, support staff, and parent volunteers are components. Having greater or fewer numbers of experienced teachers, clear or uncertain educational goals, appropriate or inadequate amounts of resources needed to deliver the program, and so on are all combined in the resulting sum of physical and sociocultural arrangements that is "the school."

The child and the school (as resulting accommodations of the factors composing them) interact. We believe there is a general tendency for each party to this interaction to seek a goodness of fit or positive adaptedness vis-ß-vis themselves and the other party. In effect, each party gives to, and receives from, the other as part of a mutual dynamic process where each necessarily involves the other: teachers teach pupils and pupils learn from teachers. When the process works well, there is a favorable exchange, which we term *goodness of fit.* Children learn a great deal that propels them into the adult world with satisfaction and success; teachers are pleased with their efforts to convey information in meaningful ways. When the process works with only bare-bones adequacy, children learn enough to get by, and teachers manage to get through the lesson plans one day after another.

This mutual dynamic process can be problematic in many ways—such as when a child has disabilities that make learning in the conventional mode more difficult or the school is inflexible in accommodating children with different cultural lifestyles and behaviors. Some of these interactions may lead to setbacks for the plans of one or another party, and indeed, the child may drop out of school or the school may expel a student. These are unfavorable adaptations that generally lead to social and personal problems in a society that increasingly requires education and skills for adequate economic participation and reward.

Society changes continuously. President Clinton's efforts to make two years of college available to anyone able to master it may change the basic entry level of education, from high school graduate to junior college graduate. Should this occur, many young people will have to readjust their plans about education and employment, just as many colleges will have to prepare for larger numbers of students. The goodness of fit between young adults and society will have to be renegotiated, both on an individual and a collective level.

Adaptation is a continuing active process; we attempt to understand this flow of events in the professional context by obtaining verbal snapshots, as it were, stop-time observations representing the client's ongoing life situation. Think about what your client narrated to you last week—itself a series of such snapshots—as compared to what the client has said today that indicated adaptation or renegotiation with aspects of his or her life situation, seeking a better fit between this person and relevant environments.

Assumption 3: Factors That Facilitate or Impede Adaptation

Persons and environments contain structures and functions (happenings) that may affect adaptation in a positive or negative way, that is, the positive structures and happenings may facilitate adaptation, while the negative ones may impede it. Living consists in planning and acting so as to increase the former relative to the latter. For the most part, individuals and families can adapt to conventional environments on their own, except in times or conditions of special needs, pressures, or limitations. Other times, certain life stressors are often beyond the ability of most individuals to change them. For example, consider a working-class school district where all the entering pupils used to speak English; demographic changes occur so that now most speak Spanish or Southeastern Asian languages. If the school system is unresponsive to these changes, students and teachers will experience many frustrations until the cultures and lifestyles of both parties are understood. The school system might employ bilingual speakers to help translate language and culture in both directions. Small groups and neighborhoods might collaborate to celebrate cultural holidays and to share foods and traditions thus making everyone more comfortable with each other's ways, even as the children are going about the business of learning English and the dominant culture.

Still other stressors, such as structural unemployment, poverty, inflation, and bionuclear dangers are societal in nature and causation, and require societal solutions, as well as serving individuals and families as needed. Individuals and small collectivities may enter into coalitions for political action that will affect at least the more tractable societal stressors. For social workers, societal and institutional stressors become the subject of social policy analysis and legislative advocacy.

Assumption 4: Flow of Life Events

As schematically presented in figure 1.1, we assume a general flow of life events that are perceived by people as negative stressors or positive challenges (or some mixture of the two). That is, life events are perceived as potentially harmful (stressors) or potential helpful (challenges), based on past experiences and the present face value of the situation. While these perceptions may or may not be correct, we deal with the life events as we perceive them. We list these concepts here and describe them in more detail later in this chapter.

Those life events that are perceived as predominantly *stressors* evoke a stress response, arousing various physiological or psychological symptoms or both. We may begin to feel uncomfortable or think unhappy thoughts, perceiving that these life events will be problematic for us and may be beyond our capacities and resources to resolve.

The perception of stress leads people to respond in different ways. First, people may *cope* with the stress, which we define as the use of conscious tactics that enable a person to deal with some problem. Second, people may *defend* against the stress, using tactics the person may not even be aware to enable the individual to deal with the problem, even if only temporarily and to a partial degree.

Coping with stress. Coping expresses a person:environment relationship, and it is transactional and perceptual in nature. Two major functions of coping are

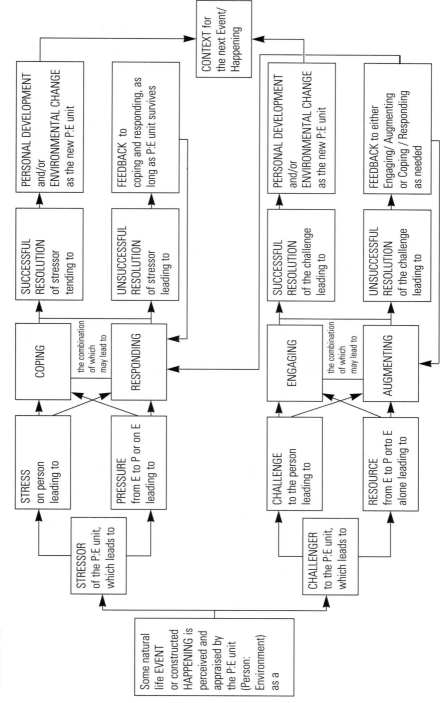

FIGURE 1.1

(1) problem solving—what is the problem/stressor and what needs to be done to deal with it? and (2) regulating the negative feelings aroused by the stressor (Coyne and Lazarus 1980). These are interdependent functions inasmuch as each is a requirement of the other, and each supports the other. Progress in problem solving leads to the restoration of self-esteem and to more effective regulation of negative feelings generated by the stressful demand. Progress in managing feelings and restoring self-esteem frees the person to work more effectively on problem solving.

Coping: Two appraisal questions. First, the person asks what is the presenting problem (and by definition of a person:environment problem, how adequately am I dealing with it). And second, what (more) can be done about it—by the person, the environments, or both. If the ordinary coping efforts are not successful, then a feedback process would inform the person, and extra coping may be initiated by calling on additional personal or environmental resources. If this coping is successful, then the stressor—usually a problem involving a hurt or loss or the threat of same—is resolved. Personal benefits and positive environmental changes may accrue from this circular loop of events, which becomes the changed person:environment unit facing the next life event. If, ultimately, a person and all the additional resources he or she can command cannot cope with some overwhelming stressor, then the person may have a persistent handicap; in other cases, where no substitutions are possible, the person may die.

Defending against stress. Sometimes, in the case of severe stressors, such as a serious spinal injury from a driving accident, the person may temporarily block out some aspects of the situation and some of the negative feelings that inevitably emerge, so as to deal with immediate tasks. Such defensive denial may serve a useful purpose on a *temporary* basis (Lazarus 1984), but eventually the reality of the situation must be faced. Defending against stress may become maladaptive when rigid, unrealistic patterns of past responses are used without adequate thinking and in spite of unproductive feedback. In some situations, denial may be maladaptive from the outset. Alcoholism and other chemical dependence will not yield to denial, even in the short run, since it blocks the initiation of problem-solving efforts to relinquish dependence. Resorting to drugs to defend against painful life stressors misfires and leads to further stress in other areas of life, including health, economic and employment status, and family life.

Those life events that are perceived predominantly as *challenges* evoke an *exhilaration response*, with various appropriate physiological, psychological signs, or both. One may feel "up" for the event, ready in body and mind to deal with it and relishing the opportunity. When people life challenges with exhilaration, they may be said to be *engaging* those events. We introduce this term, engagement, so as to have a distinctive label for acting with regard to positive challenges; it is parallel to the term coping for stressor situations. When a person engages a challenge, two general questions are asked: What is possible for me to do with the presenting opportunity? and What can be done to attain these goals—by the person, the environment, or both?

When the engagement proves to be successful, the challenge is met and usually results in personal development for the involved person, or positive changes in the environment, or both. For example, Bandura (1986) describes an increase in perceived self-efficacy when the individual masters some specific situation (see appendix 2). These changes in perceived self-efficacy will influence events in new but similar situations. When a challenge is not successfully engaged, there may be a disappointing loss of opportunity but the status quo ante persists.

Family, friends, service providers, and professionals may all contribute as part of the social environment to the success of people's efforts to adapt to some event, especially when they need more resources than they themselves can ordinarily provide.

Helping professionals offer a *continuum of services,* from primary prevention, through treatment, to rehabilitation. *Primary prevention* involves (a) *preventing* predictable problems; (b) *protecting* existing states of healthy functioning; and (c) *promoting* or enhancing desired goals. *Treatment* involves a range of services addressing existing, often acute, problems but increasingly, chronic problems as well. *Rehabilitation* involves attempting to resituate people who have received treatment back to the level where they were functioning before the illness or problem occurred. (See relevant discussions of these practice modalities in the 1995 *Encyclopedia of Social Work.*)

Assumption 5: The Transacting Configuration

To understand any life event, we must put it into the full person:environment configuration, that is, we must consider all the relevant systems and subsystems that may play a part in the mutual adaptation. This includes subsystems of the person, such as the person's biological, affective, cognitive, and behavioral status, and subsystems of the environment, particularly the primary and secondary groups, culture, society, and the physical environment. Each of these may, in the particular circumstance, be important in influencing the person:environment transaction. The task of the social ecological perspective is to provide an approximate tool to grasp this understanding. We offer figure 1.2 as a configural checklist—examples of the kinds of systems that may be relevant to events in a client's life situation.

These assumptions form the basis for selecting the three major sets of interrelated concepts that comprise the social ecological perspective. These sets of concepts involve structural, developmental, and functioning considerations. By *structural considerations*, we refer to the persistent set of relationships emerging over the course of time between two or more communicating persons. For example, newlyweds learn the roles of husband and wife that will become relatively persistent in their marital situation through vast numbers of conversations and actions. By *developmental considerations*, we refer to the distinctive structures that emerge over usually long periods of time. For instance, that married couple conceive a child and take on a new status as parents in a three-member family, a new social structure that takes many months to evolve. When the child is ready for school, the family takes on yet another structural feature that incorporates school functions as part of family dynamics. By *functioning considerations*, we refer to the significant patterns of everyday actions, such as the physical and psychological communications that occur in lovemaking, or the behaviors, verbal and nonverbal, that take place when the child is read the ritual bedtime story. Obviously, these are interrelated terms, with ongoing functioning generating the structures at any given time period, which give way, through further communicating and behaving (i.e., functioning) to new developments in these persons and groups.

The Social Ecological Perspective: From the Perspective of the Person

Concept Set 1: Person:Environment Fit (Structural concepts)

We use the colon in the person:environment formulation to signify a holistic or unitary system as the object of our analysis, not persons or environments separate from one another. To understand this person:environment unity, we present several sets of concepts used metaphorically from the science of ecology to construct a working tool that seeks to describe, explain, and predict

FIGURE 1.2. Basic Concepts of the Social Ecological Perspective

Concept Set #1 [Person: Environment Fit— Structural concepts]	Concept Set #2 [Life Course Development— Developmental concepts]	Concept Set #3 [Functioning under Stress and Challenge— Functioning concepts]
PART I: CONCEPT FROM THE PERSON-SIDE OF THE FORMULATION		
Goodness of Fit	Growth(Maturation) and Development	Life Events
Adaptation and Adaptedness		Life Stressors Stress Coping
Maladaptation		Mastery/Defeat Feedback loop Personal development/
Diverse Social and Cultural Contexts		Personal deterioration
		Challenges Exhilaration Engaging Mastery/Nonmastery Feedback loop to Engaging or Coping Personal development:
PART II. CONCEPTS FROM THE ENVIRONMENT-SIDE OF THE FORMULATION		
Physical Environment Natural Built	Temporal Behavious Biological time Psychological time Social time	Territoriality Spatial Behavior
Social Environment Pairs, Small Groups Families, Neighborhoods, Enclaves, Communities, Organizations	Cultural time	Interpersonal Spacing Crowding and Isolation
Culture Values Norms and roles		
PART III. POSITIVE PERSONAL DEVELOPMENT: POSITIVE ENVIRONMENTAL CHANGE		
Relatedness	Self-Direction	Competence Self-Esteem

transactional aspects of individual and collective human behavior in sociocultural environments.

Goodness of fit. A goodness of fit between the needs, rights, capacities, and aspirations of individuals or groups, on the one hand, and the qualities of their sociocultural and physical environments on the other involves some degree of meshing, which may be described as favorable, minimally adequate, or unfavorable. A *favorable* goodness of fit would promote continued growth and development of the involved persons while sustaining or enhancing the environment. The *minimally adequate* goodness of fit would be enough to support at least one party without offering much support or growth for the other, although it would not absolutely harm the other. The *unfavorable fit* would not be sufficient to support either of the parties involved and might detract from or be harmful to one or both.

Adaptedness and adaptation. We have earlier assumed that all people, following the cultural version of the biological impulse for survival of the species, tend to adapt their actions and environmental changes in ways that would optimize a goodness of fit. Of course, not all people or environments achieve this favorable fit; we examine this later in light of person:environment transactions, particularly personal limitations and certain environmental conditions (discrimination, oppression, social and technological pollutions). The central ecological concept is *adaptation,* which refers to human beings actively striving through life for the best person:environment fit possible between their needs, rights, capacities, and aspirations, on the one hand, and the qualities of their sociocultural and physical environments on the other. When the fit is good, we can speak of a positive *adaptedness.* When the fit is not good, for whatever reason and to whatever degree, then people may actively decide to change themselves or the environment or both. Such changes are termed *adaptations.* These may be internal (physiological or psychological) or external (social or cultural). Adaptations may be directed to changing oneself in order to meet environmental opportunities or demands, or they may be directed to changing the environment so that physical and social settings will be more responsive to human needs, rights, capacities, and aspirations. Or both.

The term "adaptation" should be distinguished from the notion of "adjustment," which connotes a passive accommodation to the environment or status quo, even if that environment lacks health-supporting, growth-promoting qualities. For example, people may adjust to a noisy, noxious city even though it may have detrimental effects on themselves and their children. A series of studies by Bell et al. (1990) linked living place (high-rise apartment houses), noise (from traffic on nearby freeways), and school performance (children living on the lower floors have poorer reading test scores, are more distractible, and show a lack of persistence on cognitive tasks, than children living on higher floors).

What makes the critical difference in respect to the active (adaptation) or passive (adjustment) distinction is whether or not the individual is in control of the decision-making process or is controlled by either internal or environmental forces. A person who chooses to be passive, as for example submitting to the unreasonable demands of a sick child, is actively adapting as he or she thinks best at that moment. A parent who chooses not to give in to a child's temper tantrum is also actively adapting.

Another type of adaptation involves the search for new environments and includes moving, migrating, religious conversions, and the like. Here, the issue of activity versus passivity is connected not only to whether the new environment promotes a better person:environment fit but also, in some circumstances, to whether the person is moving toward something or away from something else (Hartmann 1958), that is, whether a life issue is managed by actively grappling with it or by passively avoiding it (Lazarus and Folkman 1984). A move, for example, can be either active or passive, depending on whether it is an attempt to avoid a predicament or to search for a better fit. Determining which is operative or uppermost in a given situation requires that many pertinent factors be considered in the assessment process. The content and direction of adaptations are shaped by personality, resources, experience, the nature of the social environment, and culture.

Maladaptation. Adaptation and maladaptation are the end points of a continuum. Sometimes the interaction of person and environment will be such that the fit is not well satisfied. Perhaps the person receives less than he or she needs or wants, or perhaps the environment is stretched so far as to be unable to provide required supplies. Or both. Either the person or the environment aspect of the P:E unit can compensate to some degree for deficits in the other. This is the critical practical reason for working with the person:environment unit. However, when the net effect emerges—such as a frail but lively aged widow who has minimal financial resources—there may be an overall unfavorable fit in the person:environment unit—she may have to accept inferior quality accommodations at a county poor house as her only recourse. It is to this that we apply the term maladaptation, without implying that either the people or the environments are necessarily at fault. The causes of the maladaptation require investigation and usually the solutions involve changes in people and the environment.

Concept Set 2: Life Course Development (Developmental concepts)

People grow and develop over time; this is not in dispute. However, whether these changes are built into the structures of people and sociocultural arrangements and whether there are inevitable stages of development that are universal and thus predictable for all people is a matter of great dispute. In this book, we take a *life course perspective* on human development. This involves a conception of bio-psycho-sociocultural development of people at every age that is nonuniform and indeterminate. This position contrasts with traditional life cycle models in which life stages are conceptualized as sequential, universal, and predictable. Stage formulations by S. Freud, E. Erikson, J. Piaget, L. Kohlberg, and others still guide numbers of helping professionals; their theories are briefly summarized in appendix 1. However, different conceptions of human development incorporate more of the diversity of real life in individual, social, and historic time. The microsocial theories of A. Bandura, B. F. Skinner, and others are briefly summarized in appendix 2 and elsewhere in this book, while macrosocial theories of E. Durkheim, K. Marx, and M. Weber and others are briefly summarized in appendix 3. We suggest that human development is a lifelong occurrence and varies with all kinds of social, cultural, and personal changes as they interact with one another.

However, many empirical regularities in psychosocial development can be usefully studied and applied. For example, research has informed us that truanting behavior and opposition-to-authority behavior in first-graders are predictors of delinquent acts in adolescence (Robins and Wish 1977). This empirical correlation is not based on any model of universal development; it is merely a useful empirical regularity that provides teachers and others with an opportunity to reduce the likelihood that events will lead to the predicted untoward outcome. Changing truanting behavior in first-graders may be easier than changing later delinquent behavior.

Stage models were usually developed within narrow experiential limits—often emphasizing Europeans or Euro-Americans, males, or the middle class. Social work professionals serve a broad array of clients and thus need to know about functioning and development of diverse groups of people. Stage models usually do not consider changes in laws and sociocultural conditions that influence how people develop at particular times and places; this time-bound and culture-bound characteristic has led to charges that stage models do not adequately consider the development of women or minorities and thus provide poor guides to practice with these people in particular.

Growth (maturation) and development. It is helpful to distinguish human growth from human development. *Growth* or *maturation*—we use these terms interchangeably—involves the emergence of genetic potential as a bundle of preprogrammed changes in structure, function, and development. While there are great individual differences among people in maturation—such as the early or late sexual maturation that may cause concern to the persons involved who are ahead of or behind their peers in these obvious characteristics—still, the patterns of such changes (such as girls maturing earlier than boys) are relatively fixed and uniform for all human beings. We also know that historical changes, such as the general improvement in nutrition, has lowered the average age of sexual maturation over the past several hundred years, while it has also added inches to average height.

We know *about* when infants will be able to hold up their heads (3 months), reach for objects (6 months), sit erect (8 months), crawl (10 months), stand (12 months), and walk unaided (15 months). Poor nutrition or illness may delay these events, but good health and proper diet will not speed them up dramatically. The order of these motor maturational events is practically universal. Speech involves a number of physical parts that also mature over time, but speech is stimulated by the social environment, which greatly reduces the preciseness of our predictions about it. We know approximately when children begin to use single words (around 12 months), combinations of two or three words (sometime between 18 to 24 months), or in sentences (between 2 and 3 years) (L. Bloom 1975, 1991). However, the ranges of time when language develops are highly diverse; even within one family, one child may speak much earlier than her or his sibling.

As we consider behaviors that are increasingly under the control of the social and cultural contexts, we find still wider variations and less predictability. This is the domain of *development* that we define as usually progressive and cumulative changes in the structure, thought, personality, or behavior of a person, which are the function of both biological growth and environmental experiences. Complex development such as intelligence, creativity, and various social skills are strongly influenced by the social and cultural contexts. However, we discuss current thinking and research in chapter 7 on genetics and biology because the critical discussion on the relative influence of nature versus nurture continues apace (Albee 1983; *Journal of Primary Prevention* 1996; H. Johnson 1996). In a practical sense, that is what we can currently *do* about this nature/nurture interchange; we mainly act in the environmental world to affect desired changes but we must be alert to significant biological and genetic information that opens up new modes of environmental action.

Concept Set 3: Functioning under Stress and Challenge (Functional concepts)

This third set of concepts requires explanation beyond our earlier discussion, in order to link the various elements together in a coherent package. Essentially, we describe two strings of concepts—one starting from the predominant presence of stressors, the other from the predominant presence of challenges. Figure 1.1 presents these strings of concepts.

Life events. We use the term *life events* to refer to all the stimuli that impinge on people and environments. An event takes on meaning (such as being predominantly a stressor or challenge) in connection to the parties involved; one event may be perceived as a positive experience by one person, a negative experience by another, and a mixed or neutral experience for a third party. A life event may change in its meaning to a person depending on subsequent events.

Stressors. We use the term *stressors* to indicate a major category of life events that causes problems for persons or environments or is perceived as causing problems. Germain and Gitterman describe *life stressors* as involving life transitions, events, and issues that disturb the level of the person:environment fit or a prior state of relative adaptedness (1996:9–14). There are *external life stressors*, usually in the form of a harm or loss, or the threat of a future harm or loss. These would include job loss, interpersonal conflict, and difficulties in moving through ordinary life transitions. There are also *internal life stressors*, such as illness or bereavement. Both represent a disturbed and disturbing person:environment fit.

Stress. A person's psychological and physiological response to the stressor is called *stress*. People experience stress when some external or internal life event impinges on them and they do not think they have personal and environmental resources deal with it adequately (Lazarus and Folkman 1984). The untoward physical and psychological responses in us, such as a queazy stomach or a feeling of anxiety, makes very clear to us (operationalizes) the meaning of stress.

Coping and defending. Once these thoughts or feelings are recognized as stress, then two sets of questions appraising the situation are likely to be asked: First, how am I (currently) doing with the presenting problem? And second, what (else) is to be done about it—by the person, the environment, or both? Coping involves both person and environment aspects.

When coping is effective, the perceived stress is resolved. Some new personal energy, environmental energy, or both applied to the stressor has mastered what had previously been perceived as exceeding one's ordinary personal and environmental resources. Coping occurs over time; that is, coping may be an ongoing activity for renewable stressors and resulting stress. Other times, the stress may be permanently resolved. As we discuss in greater detail, when people cope effectively, the experience adds to their repertoire of behaviors and their feelings about themselves as problem solvers triumphing over life adversities. Some of these resulting feelings may be momentary pleasures, while others may build self-structures of various kinds such as increased self-efficacy (Bandura 1986), general self-esteem, competence, and self-direction.

When coping is not effective, then the stress is likely to increase and lead to physical, psychological (cognitive and affective), and social dysfunction. When stress is great enough for a long enough period of time, the reactive systems of the person and environmental supports may break down, and the person may die (Selye 1976). Stresses in one area of life may spread, which means borrowing energy from these others areas to solve the problem in the initial area. This may then cause problems in other areas of that person's life.

Risk factors and protective/promotive factors. Another set of terms used in public health and primary prevention fields describes similar events in people's lives, which may offer new insights into the social ecological perspective. People may be described as having *risk factors,* traits that have been known in other people who shared them to lead to identifiable problem behavior. For example, a sexually active individual faces some risk of AIDS, depending on the conditions involved. Hulley and Hearst provide specifications for certain kinds of risk defined in terms of empirical outcomes of people engaging in specific behaviors. If the sexual partner is HIV seronegative, with no history of high-risk behavior, and uses condoms, then one sexual encounter leads to a 1 in 5 billion risk of contracting AIDS. However, if the sexual partner's HIV serostatus is unknown but the person is in a high-risk group (such as homosexual men, intravenous drug users, etc.) and does not use condoms, then the risk increases dramatically to 1 in 50,000 encounters. If the sexual partner is HIV seropositive and does not use condoms, then if there are 500 sexual encounters, the risk of contracting AIDS is 2 in 3. This kind of person-in-environment risk information is very powerful and needs to be communicated to relevant audiences in effective ways (1989:63).

Risk factors have been identified for a wide range of behaviors, from cigarette smoking (about five minutes shorter life span for each cigarette smoked, among other associated risks [Elder et al. 1993; Windsor et al. 1993]) to the specific drinking patterns of pregnant women (increased risk for fetal alcohol syndrome in their offspring [Alcalay, Ghee, and Scrimshaw 1993; May and Hymbaugh 1989]) and associated risks for mental retardation. We also have normative information about groups who are at risk for various kinds of untoward outcomes, such as pregnant women who smoke or men who have unprotected sex with men. This kind of knowledge about group characteristics and behavior can be a powerful tool both in attempting to influence collective health and educational policies, and in trying to change attitudes and behaviors of groups of involved individuals (Coates 1990).

In addition to risk factors, we also know something about *protective factors*, those conditions that appear to enable people to avoid the identified risk. We know even less about what might be termed *promotive factors*, those that positively move people toward good health and happiness. However, it is through the use of protective and promotive factors that we can conceive of the strengths of people and environments that may eventually make progress in helping to reduce predictable problems as well as to enhance possible goals (M. Bloom 1996).

Challenges. The second string of concepts regarding reactions to life events begins with the concept of *challenge*, by which we refer to experiences that have the effect of increasing the goodness of person:environment fit. These are growth- and development-promoting experiences. We generally consider public education as stimulating children to learn, to think, and to develop; thus school lessons and experiences would constitute potential challenges to youngsters.

We emphasize that challenges may involve some tensions—students will have tests (which are supposed to "challenge" their eager, inquiring minds); adolescents will begin to explore potential sexual partners (albeit with the delicious tensions of dating); adults may consider changing jobs at various points in their lives (weighing the possibilities of gain against the probabilities of loss, all in connection with the tensions involved in making such major life changes). However, it is important to recognize that these challenges provide a great deal of the zest in life, that being under some pressure wonderfully focuses the mind, that having deadlines concentrates our energies to get the job done. Thus there are many occasions when life events lead to challenges, defined as experiences where we believe that we have the personal and environmental resources to master the events in question and to benefit from the experience. Successful challenges promote growth or development; unsuccessful challenges may lead to coping with the unresolved challenge or may lead nowhere.

Stressors and challenges are relative terms; the identical event may be a challenge to one person, a stressor to another. It may even be perceived differently by the same person at different times. A person initially judges a life event as a stressor or a challenge based on a preliminary reading of the situation in light of past experience—is it harmful or helpful? The person acts on that initial judgment by following the stressor or challenge string of events until new information changes the meaning of that life event.

We assign the term stressor or challenge only after we see how the person:environment unit has responded to the life event. Sometimes, the person:environment unit can turn what appears to be a highly stressful event into a wonderfully challenging one that promotes positive development and positive environmental change. Other times, a wonderful challenge somehow becomes so complicated as to constitute a stress that requires coping to solve the problem.

Feedback loops. We have described the above terms mainly in linear terms—it is easy to do so, compared with holistic presentations. However, introducing feedback loops emphasizes that the transactions between life events and person:environment units go in both directions. First, consider the feedback mechanisms that take place when a person attempts to use available personal and environmental resources to deal with a perceived stressor. Conventional responses are first tried. If they do not succeed in resolving the problem, that information is fed back into the person:environment system so as to generate more energy or more resources, from either the individual or from resources the individual can request or commandeer from others. These feedback loops continue until the problem is solved—or until the person:environment unit collapses.

Second, what begins in one string of responses to life events may leap over to the other string of events. If an apparent challenge becomes more difficult to master than anticipated, then the person may take a problem-solving mode in increasing personal energy or environmental resources, which is coping. Likewise, if something appeared to be scary and beyond one's control, such as being put on a two-wheeler for the first time, and if one is fortunate enough to have a good experience in riding the bicycle, this initially stressful situation becomes exhilaratingly challenging and wonderful.

Third, adaptive changes in either person or environment are stored as structural changes in the person:environment goodness of fit, and will be called upon again under similar circumstances. This kind of feedback is what helps construct new personal self-structures as well as new environments. When such new personal or environmental structures are in place, they in turn affect the environment (and self) in a way different from before. Some of these transactions occur rapidly; others occur more slowly; all have the potential to change the person:environment system. The child is now riding her bike, which means new concerns for the parents, greater freedom for the child, more income for the bicycle repair shop, and so forth; many repercussions stem from this one event.

Positive Personal Development: Positive Environmental Change

Some important positive outcomes of adaptive person:environment relationships are personal qualities even though they depend, in part, on the environment for their development and maintenance. These are labeled (1) relatedness, (2) competence, (3) self-direction, and (4) self-esteem. Germain and Gitterman identify these four as desired outcomes of all practice, in addition to whatever other goals of practice given individuals or groups may have (1996:14). These four terms refer to potentialities in the human species that depend for their release and continuance on the properties of people's past and present environments. (We see corresponding versions of these four terms at the collective level in chapter 2.)

These personal attributes appear to be interdependent; each derives from and contributes to the development of the others. While these personal attributes take different forms in various cultures, we assert that the attributes themselves appear to be free of cultural bias. For example, every human society seeks to prepare its members for competent adult performance in its valued social statuses and roles. What constitutes competence may vary across cultures but as a desired outcome of socialization, competence is probably universally relevant. Even within our own society, competence may be defined differently by different groups.

Relatedness

The structural concept of person:environment fit necessitates a sense of *relatedness*, which refers to the hypothesized innate capacity of the human being at birth to form attachments with other human beings. Bowlby (1973) sees attachment as a biological and social imperative built into the genetic structure of the species over evolutionary time because of its survival value. That is, attachment behavior in the infant, such as crying and clinging, and caregiving behaviors on the part of the parent ensured proximity between infant and caregiver as protection against predators in the evolutionary environment. Evidence is accumulating that human relatedness, whether innate or not, exhibited through attachments and social affiliations is essential for optimal functioning throughout the life course (Parkes, Stevenson-Hinde, and Marris 1991; Rutter 1981; see also a critical work in a related area, Eyer 1992). Relatedness appears first and remains central. It will continue to be enhanced by the development of the other three concepts, just as it facilitates their development.

As a person:environment unit adapts to the circular pressures from each component, new forms of relatedness may appear over time. From parents to siblings and relatives to peer playmates to authoritative adults like teachers and bosses people relate as part of social living. When they have problems relating, we see maladaptation of various degrees, some of which may need the services of helping professionals or nonprofessional support groups. Social affiliation refers to informal networks of kin, friends, neighbors, and others that often serve as positive support systems, protecting the person against life stress or enhancing the coping resources for dealing with it. We return to this form of relatedness when we discuss the environment-side of the equation.

Competence

White (1959) introduces the term *competence* as involving an innate desire to have an effect on one's environment in order to survive. However, competence depends on the environment for its release. Because child-rearing practices vary widely different children will get more or less of the feedback that tells them that they are (or are not) able to have an effect on the environment. As experiences of being effective in influencing one's environment accumulate, the young child develops a sense of competence, of being able to influence and control the environment, to explore it, and to learn in it and about it. In youth and adulthood, social and physical environments may provide for the continuing development of competence or may hamper its further development and even stifle the innate motivation. This is the reason that many children growing up with institutionalized racism, entrenched poverty, deficient public schooling, inadequate health and housing, and little opportunity for suitable employment develop little sense of personal competence. Furthermore, not having a sense of competence or various environmental resources leads to further stagnation. Blame-the-victim thinking picks out a single point—such as a single parent collecting child welfare benefits—in what is, in truth, a complex circular process. For instance, the lack of adequate day care at affordable prices that prevents the parent from working to support the child, which in turn, forces the person to seek welfare.

Self-direction

The concept of *self-direction* connotes taking responsibility for managing one's life while respecting the rights and needs of others. It is the power to make choices, reach decisions, and engage in socially effective action on behalf of the self and the collectivity. However, it is important to note that personal power and the freedom to be self-directing are very much functions of where one is located in the stratified social structure of society. That is, one's social position influences one's access to options, choices, and resources, and to opportunities for making decisions and taking action about one's life, the well-being of one's family and cultural group, and so on. Poor and oppressed people have little control over these forms of powerlessness, and consequently have fewer opportunities for self-direction.

Self-esteem

One important component of self-concept is *self-esteem*, which refers to positive feelings about oneself acquired through experiences of relatedness, competence, and self-direction across the life course. "A high level of self-esteem is intrinsically satisfying and pleasurable" (Germain and Gitterman 1995:818). One's self-concept begins to build in infancy through identification with and incorporation of the caregiver's perceptions, expectations, and affirmations of oneself, and through successful experiences of eliciting from the environment responses appropriate to one's needs. Later, in toddlerhood, the self-concept is reinforced by experiences in exercising one's beginning independence with the caregiver's approval and pleasure, as in eating, playing, exploring, walking, and talking. Self-esteem and self-concept are subject to greater opportunities and greater threats as children move into social larger circles where their personal and cultural characteristics will be appreciated or rejected by others. Both self-esteem and self-concept continue to develop over the life course. Sometimes people may be their own severest critic; overly harsh perfectionistic self-evaluation can diminish self-esteem or undermine the self-concept. Low self-esteem is often associated with depression, inadequacy, and inferiority. On the other hand, some self-critical awareness is a type of information one uses for self-improvement and social sensitivity. We should also distinguish this general concept of self-esteem from the more focused concept of self-efficacy, one's belief that one can perform a particular action based on prior mastery of similar acts, vicarious learning from others, or persuasion by authority figures (Bandura 1986).

In addition to these four concepts, we connect the social ecology perspective with a growing movement in social work called the *strengths perspective* (Cowger 1994; Saleebey 1992, 1996). This point of view seeks to counter a pathological perspective that sees social work through the lens of sickness and—no surprise—sees dysfunction at every turn. There is sickness in some people, of course, but there is also strength in everyone, and we draw on these personal strengths (and environmental resources) in order to facilitate adaptive changes in clients. In practical terms for this book, the strengths perspective encourages us to present a positive side to each person:environment situation, as well as to be aware of the negative, problematic, or limiting side.

The Social Ecological Perspective: From the Perspective of the Environment

Heretofore, we have been emphasizing the person-side of the person:environment unit because of the tyranny of linear writing. We have many times referred to the environmental contexts such as the physical and social environments and culture, but we now expand this discussion, looking, as it were, at the same landscape as previously discussed, but from the perspective of the environments.

Expanding Concept Set 1: Person:Environment Fit

When we consider the major structural concepts with regard to the environment-side of this formulation, we have to take into consideration topics that are not often addressed by helping professionals, such as the physical environment, the social environments, and culture. Yet these factors often play significant roles in human events and must be considered as part of the environmental formulation. We discuss each of these concepts in turn, and then consider other functional and developmental concepts.

The physical environment. Physical settings comprise the natural world of plants, animals, and geographic and climatic features, and the built world of urban, suburban, exurban, and rural layouts; city squares and village greens; dwellings and other structures in which human activities take place (like work, play, experiences with the sacred, etc.); aesthetic and utilitarian objects of all kinds; and media, transportation, and electronic systems, as well as physical space and certain structures of time. Obviously, the breadth and depth of the physical environment as a setting for human behavior and development is extraordinary. To ignore it in one's calculations for helping clients may be a major mistake.

These kinds of physical environments in general provide the space within which human behavior and development occur, the boundaries beyond which they may not (easily) go, and the physical things that represent obstacles or facilitators with which much human activity has to be concerned. The physical environment acts as a stimulus for some forms of human activity—a serene lake may be the stimulus for swimming, fishing, contemplating, or water-skiing; a stormy sea may evoke other possibilities. In the specific situation in which clients find themselves, helping professionals should get a sense of the meaning and use clients' physical environments have to them.

Is distance from possible jobs, social services, religious activities, and so on a part of the problem? Is the presence of a nearby divided highway, a series of dark streets, or boarded-up houses a difficulty? Does the presence of personal artifacts, home self-improvement wallpaper, or a tiny garden stubbornly existing in an urban environment have special meaning for an older client? Is the location of one's home near to the children a priority in the client's judgments when thinking about Sun Belt–relocation? We don't know the relative weights these positive or negative environmental factors hold for clients unless we explore these issues with them.

We do know that those fortunate enough to experience mountains, seashore, sagebrush, or wheat field countryside may gain a sense of serenity and wonder that is intrinsically nurturing. Some of these may even be peak experiences (Wuthnow 1978; Maslow 1971). Dubos (1968) believes that some of the ills of civilization are due to our disregarding our relationship to the world of nature from which our biological and psychological equipment evolved. We tolerate conditions such as technological and social pollution that we have created but that do not fit our evolutionary needs. But as a species we have perhaps lost our essential connectedness with the natural world.

The social environment. Social settings comprise the world of other human beings. Its components include pairs or dyads (two-party systems such as friends or couples); families; neighborhoods, enclaves (Abrahamson 1996), and communities; natural groups and social (formed) networks. The social environment also includes formal organizations, such as systems of health care, education, and recreation; workplaces; religious organizations; political and economic structures at local, state, regional, national, and international levels; and social space and social time.

There is a potential ambiguity when the term "social environment" is used to describe systems like families, groups, neighborhoods, organizations, or communities, because under some circumstances these systems may also be target groups receiving social services. They are then not environments in the strictest sense, but need to be viewed as embedded in their own larger social and physical environments. But of course they may be the environments for other smaller target groups, such as a parents support group composed of selected workers in one factory or a factory seeking help from the community to prevent its being closed down. Thus social environment and targeted service groups are relative terms.

Communities and organizations are physical and social settings simultaneously. Continuous, complex transactions take place between physical settings and social life. Physical settings and arrangements shape the nature of social arrangements and the interactions that occur in them. A classic example is the mental hospital whose janitorial staff placed chairs against the long corridor for ease of cleaning. Patients sat side by side with little interaction until the chairs were rearranged in circles or small groupings more congenial to conversation. In turn, physical settings and arrangements are shaped by social patterns, needs, and goals. Separate changing rooms, as dictated by society and culture, preserve the modesty of the two genders of bathers whose skin-tight fashions leave little to the imagination. Such reciprocal relations, together with the influence of culture on both physical and social settings, must be kept in mind in consideration of human development and functioning—especially as we seek to change some behaviors and preserve others. For example, problems of access for children and adults with physical disabilities appear mainly in the physical setting, but they act to limit participation in social settings as well. If all public and private buildings had ramps as well as stairs, gaining access would be as natural for people with disabilities as for those without. If we add some cultural dimensions, such as stereotypic responses to gender, ethnicity, or age issues, we would likely see yet other forces complicating the question of access. For instance, some children with disabilities could play on those wonderfully attractive jungle gyms if ramps were included and ladders were arranged horizontally *overhead* so children in wheelchairs could pull themselves up the ramp hand over hand (Shaw 1987). Problems of equal access continue, sometimes for lack of imagination, despite the passage of relevant federal legislation such as the 1990 Americans with Disabilities Act.

Culture. One useful definition of *culture* suggests that it is an integrated pattern of communication among a people with a common history, language, and place that results in common values, behavior patterns (lifestyles), and expectations that are transmitted across generations. Another classic anthropological version defines culture as the totality of socially transmitted behavior patterns, arts, beliefs, institutions, and all other products of human thought and effort that are characteristic of a particular population of people. These are very general definitions, although they provide some direction in understanding the particular variations in the diverse subcultures that helping professionals face, but perhaps less direction in knowing what a given member of that cultural group will be like.

Included in the concept of culture are value orientations and the norms governing behavior; knowledge, technology, and belief systems; language; and the meanings attributed to objects, events, and processes, including the uses of and the responses to time and space. Values and norms are described in this section; the other aspects of culture are presented in later chapters.

Values are relatively stable preferences regarding goals and acceptable means to be used to attain them (Rokeach 1973). The content of values include assumptions about the world, expectations of the self and others, and attitudes toward life events and processes. Values are derived from life experiences, planned and unplanned. The saying "Do as I say, not as I do" is almost totally wrong as a method of teaching values to children, who learn their values by modeling and reinforcement (Patrick and Minish 1985). Values are internalized early in life as part of the ways of behaving; they are not a set of abstract rules per se. These values then shape our thinking, perceptions, feelings, and behaviors. For example, values underlie and justify the gender-typed roles that many people assume are "natural." Another set of experiences could just as well generate values that justified egalitarian gender roles. Values are not right, true, or perfect; they are just relatively stable preferences regarding goals and acceptable means used to attain them that one learns within one's local culture.

Norms and roles are interrelated terms: *Social roles* involve sets of behaviors that are expected of a person in a given social position. *Norms* are sets of affective expectations that develop around roles in given social contexts. In effect, these norms involve a given group's awareness of the positive and negative sanctions related to acceptable or nonacceptable ranges of behaviors in that role. Thus norms become rules of social behavior about what is proper, customary, and desirable behavior for a given role holder in a given context. It is exceedingly easy to observe the misbehavior of others using our own set of norms (or normative standards), wherein these others tend to fall short of *our* norms, even though they may be performing splendidly in their own.

Expanding Concept Set 2: Life Course Development

Temporal behaviors. Time, like physical and spatial aspects, is an important dimension of both physical and social settings. Growing and development take time, as does learning. One must have time for solitude and time for interaction, as well as time to develop ways of coping with stress and engaging challenges. For everything there is a time. Actually, the experience of time has biological, social, psychological, and cultural dimensions. Like other forms of life, human beings have certain biological rhythms, or what are often called *biological clocks*. We are aware of some, such as respiration and pulse, while others are outside our awareness. All have been entrained in human beings over evolutionary time in consonance with rhythmical aspects of the physical environment. Hence some rhythms are entrained to day and night, or twenty-four-hour cycles (circadian rhythms), and others to monthly, seasonal, and annual planetary cycles. Many of our ways of life in contemporary society, such as long airline flights over a prolonged period, as well as night or rotating shifts in workplaces, are life stressors. They violate biological rhythms, cause physiological and perhaps psychological stress, and may lead to dysfunction, unless people carefully adapt to these changes.

Social time refers to such matters as standard and daylight time; hourly, daily, weekly, semimonthly, or monthly pay periods; rental and leasing arrangements; work shifts and vacation schedules; organizational hours of service; travel schedules; and so on. *Psychological time* refers to differences in how the passage of time is experienced, depending on age, feeling states, and physical and mental condition. Time's passage is experienced by children as slow, stretching out endlessly, and by the elderly as accelerating rapidly. The elderly also tend to reckon time in terms of nearness of death, instead of how much lies ahead, as is the case with children and young adults. People who are physically ill and in pain may experience short durations of time as long, so that it is hard for them to wait for attention or service.

Additionally, *cultural* attitudes toward time are often reflected in the language. In the English language, the clock "runs," but in Spanish, the clock "walks." American Indians begin their celebration ceremonies when the time is right, not with a clock but when the spirits move them. These different views about time also influence conceptions of punctuality, the sequence and pacing of events, and the rhythms of family life. English tenses build the linear structure of past-present-future into the language. Other languages may not use tenses at all, thus imposing a different temporal structure on their users. Speakers of English rely on spatial metaphors to describe time: time flows like a river; it unrolls like a carpet; it lies ahead or behind us; it is long or short. By contrast, some other languages use temporal metaphors to describe space: a village, for example, lies so many sleeps away from another one.

People develop temporal behaviors reflective of the biological, psychological, social, and cultural dimensions of time, and these behaviors become part of the social environment. Like spatial behaviors, they may be used to regulate togetherness and separateness, intimacy and distance, in social relations in community and family life, as in the meshing of work-and-family schedules in a two-breadwinner family.

Expanding Concept Set 3: Social Functioning under Stress or Challenge

Territoriality. In social ecology, *territoriality* becomes important because it represents one kind of marked pattern of social dominance or control over possessions. Whether human territoriality is like territorial behavior in animals, which is genetically programmed, is still open to question. Nonetheless territoriality is evident in observable patterns of behavior in individuals and collectivities. People display feelings of possessiveness toward space and objects. They mark spatial territories with nameplates, signs, doors, locks, and fences. They use uniforms and badges, gestures, threatening verbal and non-verbal behaviors, bells and buzzers, and in-group language and jargon to defend their physical or psychosocial space (Bloom, Wood, and Chambon 1991).

In Altman's (1975) analysis, territoriality can be a positive means of regulating social interaction, helping to reduce conflict and distorted communications in groups and between individuals. Territorial behaviors are important means of defining the individual or group identity. They also provide important cues to others, help to make statuses and roles clear and explicit, and thus stabilize social organization in families, organizations, and communities. In upper-middle-class apartment buildings, for example, the residents tend to keep control over their shared territories of lobby, garage, laundry, stairwells, and elevators by employing doorkeepers, television monitors, and maintenance personnel. In many public housing projects, however, the residents have no control over who enters their shared spaces, and they live with a sense of constant danger. The blocking of their territoriality affects the family's lifestyle and its transactions with the environment (Newman 1972; Cose 1994; P. Hall 1988).

Spatial behavior. Not only are people influenced by physical settings in various ways, they also actively use their physical environments for living, working, playing, therapy, and so forth. Also, people use certain behaviors in different physical environments that then become part of the social environment, such as a "library voice" for normally loud, chattering teenagers; quasi-nude dress on hot summer days at home of the button-down or power suit set; or demonstrative behaviors at a professional football game for the normally sedate businessperson. These spatial behaviors are commonly used by individuals and collectivities to regulate social intimacy and distance. They serve to define and maintain status and role expectations, as well as authority and decision-making hierarchies in families, communities, and organizations. They include verbal, nonverbal, and territorial behaviors.

Privacy is defined as the selective control of access to oneself or to one's group by others, not merely aloneness. It is viewed as an interpersonal boundary process that regulates levels of social interaction for an individual or a collectivity. Regulation takes place by means of various spatial behaviors such as territoriality and interpersonal spacing.

Interpersonal spacing. In his classic work on the anthropology of space, E. T. Hall (1966) developed the concept of personal distance, one of several zones of social space. *Personal distance* can be understood as a kind of protective imaginary shell in which one is encased. Cultural differences in the size and shape of this imaginary shell can distort communication and social interaction. What is regarded as proper distance for intimate relations and for impersonal relations differs across cultures: Latinos prefer smaller interpersonal spacing than North Americans. The differences can distort social interaction as the North American retreats from the Latino's advancing closeness. A Greek person gathers information from the way people use their eyes and look at her or him, but in the Navaho culture, one's eyes must never meet those of another person. Most New Englanders stay out of other people's olfactory range and avoid breathing on anyone, while Arabs have great difficulty interacting with others without being enclosed in their olfactory cloud (Dubos 1968).

Maladaptive flight-or-fight responses connected to the personal distance zone can also be observed. People described as "schizophrenic," for example, may display flight responses to physical closeness, resisting even eye contact. They may also be unaware of other people's personal spatial boundaries and may intrude on others in unwelcome ways (Sommer 1969). Some evidence exists that persons prone to violent behavior have large spatial shells, misperceive intrusions into them as hostile actions, and react with fight responses (Kinzel 1970). In addition to differences in personal distance related to personality factors, there appear to be age differences (De Long 1970), gender differences (Moos 1976), and differences due to physical states (Spinetta, Rigler, and Karon 1974).

Crowding and isolation. Crowding and its opposite, social isolation, are experienced when the processes of interpersonal spacing and territoriality do not function effectively. *Crowding* results when a person's demand for space exceeds the available supply or when the amount of social interaction is greater than desired. Crowding is an unpleasant psychosocial state regardless of the number of persons present in the setting, but it does not necessarily lead to untoward actions like increased crime or violence (Freedman 1975). It is different from *density*, which is the ratio of people to space. Density may or may not be experienced as unpleasant and stressful depending on one's personality, one's culture, and who the other persons are. One may feel crowded at any level of density, even when it is as low as one other person.

Social isolation occurs when space is in excess so that one is more distant from others than one wishes to be. This is perceived as an unpleasant state. The amount of social interaction is less than is desired. Again, social isolation appears to be unrelated to density since one may feel painfully alone in a crowd, depending on the quality and quantity of those who are present (Perlman and Peplau 1984). When others are not available or are lost through separation or death, or when one is fearful or otherwise unable to reach out to others, profound loneliness and social or emotional isolation may result (Weiss 1973, 1984). Rook (1984) summarizes the personal and social environmental interventions aimed at preventing and treating social isolation, including such prevention techniques as social skills training so as to meet interesting people, or treatment techniques such as environmental network building, group assertiveness training, or individual cognitive-behavioral counseling.

These various structural, developmental, and functional concepts are to be viewed in reciprocal transaction. When interpersonal spacing and territoriality are successful, the desired level of either privacy or social interaction is achieved. If boundary regulation by spatial behavior is ineffective, crowding is experienced when one desired privacy; isolation or loneliness is experienced when one desires social interaction. One may interpret these experiences as stressors or challenges and use appropriate methods to address them. Loneliness and social isolation are widespread in our society and are often a major problem for those using social work services. Therefore they are examined further in later chapters.

In general, physical and social settings, as well as the culture, are context variables in human development and functioning throughout the life course. They provide security and shelter, symbolic identification, and opportunities for social contact, pleasure, growth, and feedback about the consequences of one's action. They can also be sources of pain, stress, and conflict. And through processes of internalization, environments and culture become "part" of the person's self-concept. Their properties, functions, and influences, as well as their interplay, are therefore part of the theoretical foundation of social work. Their operations through the life course of individuals and collectivities are considered in later chapters.

2

Society, Culture, Community, and the Physical Environment as Contexts

The largest contexts for person:environment transactions are the society, culture, the community, and the physical environment. This chapter discusses each of the macrosocial contexts, beginning with a case study of their interrelationship in the gay community of San Francisco. Society is built on a basis of law, and this chapter discusses how the legal system permeates all social relations. Cultural differences require that social workers have a sensitivity to their clients and their own cultures. A case illustration of the use of culture (or subcultures) to activate social change with regard to migrant workers is given. The impact of the physical environment is discussed in several places in this chapter (as well as in chapter 1). Finally the various attributes of community are considered as possible stressors and challenges to people.

Outline

Physical and Social Settings in Community Life
    Human Habitat
    Spatial Stressors and Spatial Challenges
    Temporal Stressors and Temporal Challenges
    Social Niche: Immigrants and Other Persons New to the Country
Social Pollutions: Racism, Sexism, and Other Isms
    Racism: Individual, Institutional, and Cultural
    Sexism
    Able-ism (disempowerment based on disability)
    Homophobia

Introduction: The Gay Community in San Francisco

San Francisco contains a number of distinctive enclaves that provide much of the flavor, excitement, and notoriety of this cosmopolitan city. In particular, the Castro and Mission Districts, located roughly east of Haight-Ashbury and south of Chinatown, Nob Hill, and the notorious Tenderloin, contain high concentrations of gays and lesbians respectively. Abrahamson describes the history of these areas, making the point that these districts constitute distinct enclaves—"concentrations of residents who share a distinctive status that is important to their identity" and "specialized stores and institutions that provide local support for the residents' distinctive lifestyle." He goes on to note that the geographic place becomes a "calling card," symbolizing the lifestyle identities of the residents of the enclave (1996:13).

About twenty-five years ago, San Francisco became a magnet for many kinds of people interested in exploring alternative lifestyles in a relatively open atmosphere (in contrast to most of the rest of the nation) and beautiful surroundings of the bay area and California in general. Between 1969 and 1978 nearly 30,000 gays moved to San Francisco, and by 1980 about 5,000 gays were moving to the area every year (Shilts 1987:15). Homosexuals dishonorably discharged from the military landed there and stayed—rather than returning to the uncongenial heartland. The hippies congregated in Haight-Ashbury, bringing along gays and lesbians in the process. The large number of bars, bookstores, discotheques, and bathhouses drew people seeking excitement and stimulation, including other gays and to a lesser extent lesbians. As the traditional factories moved out of the Castro District, leaving a depressed housing market, more affluent and educated gays moved in because of the congenial cultural climate and its pleasant physical environment. Sexual freedom and experimentation were the norms during the 1970s and much of the 1980s. Today, the Castro District is a largely middle-class environment, with renovated Victorian homes and a profusion of professional and business people in an openly gay community. The medieval saying that "city air makes free" has a special meaning in sunny California.

Even so, homophobia was alive and well in America. Gays and lesbians were widely oppressed with physical force, social ridicule, and legal injustice; they responded often by leading closeted lives until one day (27 June 1969) police raided a gay bar, the Stonewall Inn, in New York City's Greenwich Village where to their own astonishment the gays—an " 'army' of middle-aged homosexuals, transvestites, teenage male prostitutes, and a few lesbians and some passersby"—fought back (Abrahamson 1996:108). This Stonewall revolt became a rallying point for gay and lesbian groups around the country. Gay and lesbian people became more open about their lifestyle and fought for their civil rights, and as has often been the case of such struggles in this country, after considerable opposition and snail-like movement, there was a glimmer of the dawning of tolerance (in some parts of the country). At the 1978 Gay Freedom Day Parade in San Francisco, 375,000 people were in attendance (Shilts 1987:16).

Then came the 1980s and the emergence of a new enemy of humanity: AIDS. And San Francisco (specifically the Castro District) was its epicenter (Shilts 1987). This was true in part because of the particular way the HIV virus was spread in relationship to the gay lifestyle that often included impersonal (i.e., no long-term commitment), frequent (large numbers of partners pairing up in accessible places like local bathhouses), unprotected anal and oral sex that increases the probability of contracting HIV infections leading to AIDS. The death rate shot up; few gays did not know men who were infected and, after a latency period of years, who died from opportunistic painful illnesses.

Shilts's sensitive reporting of AIDS-related events, from before 1980 to about 1987, gives an intimate portrait of the lives and deaths of many participants. First, a brief background sketch of the gay liberation movement of the 1970s: The explosive openness of gay life had spawned bathhouses and sex clubs where people could freely express their sexual desires. Shilts reports a Denver study that found the average bathhouse patron having 2.7 sexual contacts a night, with attendant rates of sexually transmitted diseases—relatively easily controlled by medications. Across the country, bathhouses were big business, a $100 million industry often run by gay political leaders.

Other politicians and health officials were aware of the growing power of gays in the life of San Francisco and tried to show sensitivity to the gay community and its rough sexual antics; the gay community also brought in great wealth to the city (Shilts 1987:19–21). The gay community in New York never was as well organized or as politically powerful as in California (27). But this political power had its downside, as the inevitable conflict arose between the civil rights of a formerly repressed group and the public health recognition that bathhouses were sensual conduits to HIV infection and AIDS. After a considerable period of tiptoeing around the issue and distributing brochures on safe sex, the issue of closing the bathhouses was raised publicly, which produced organized gay resistance (promoted by powerful bathhouse owners). Other gay leaders who supported closing the bathhouses (since there were no reductions in disease-transmitting behaviors) were reviled by fellow gays, even as the numbers of deaths grew steadily in every corner of the Castro District, and indeed, the world. Then, on 9 October 1984, the bathhouses were officially closed; the expected storm of protest did not occur but gay leaders wondered whether this would start a backlash on the civil rights of gays.

An atmosphere of fatalism infected the gay community, especially when cries for service met little response from the local, state, and federal governments—that is to say, from "society." From President Reagan on down, there was very little encouragement to study the problem or to support treatment for the "gay disease." Even with the realization that AIDS affects heterosexuals as well as homosexuals, the sexually innocent as well as the sexually active, aid was very slow in coming. When the popular movie star Rock Hudson died of AIDS, public sentiment began to turn the corner. The AIDS quilt project emerged in San Francisco from a gay and lesbian alliance, publicizing and humanizing the statistics with stories and mementos of individual victims stitched onto large patches of cloth that formed quilt that was acres in size.

Gay agony and criticism notwithstanding, society was in fact responding, albeit in various ways, some homophobic, others rational attempts to address the epidemic. Shilts (1987) reports on the early and continual efforts of researchers and medical people to discover the cause of this fatal malady and to get help to its victims. Much of this research received minuscule support from the conservative government of that time, and researchers were often barred from professional arenas.

By the mid-1980s the need for preventive research was recognized. A model program in San Francisco produced extraordinary changes and bears careful study (Coates 1990:60–63). This program involved a multidimensional transmission of information about AIDS; stimulating individually oriented motivation ("I, too, can become infected"); skill training in performing safe sexual acts that were still pleasurable; modification of peer and subcultural norms away from high-risk sexual behaviors; and changes in policy, legislation, and use of mass media. In three years time, from 1985 to 1988, the percentage of gay and bisexual men engaging in high-risk sexual behavior went from around 35 percent to about 3 percent of men surveyed (averaging responses regarding anal insertive and receptive behaviors). The epidemic rates for new cases of AIDS in the San Francisco area came tumbling down. At first. Then, after some years of relatively low rates of unprotected sex, during which time the community coalition sponsoring the AIDS prevention program ended, new younger people came to the Castro and were not a part of that initial public health and the gay community effort. And the community rates are once again rising, as the complex transactions among society, culture, and community continue.

Societal Contexts of Human Behavior and Development

Society, sociologists tell us, is a group of people with a common and distinctive culture, who occupy a particular physical area, who have a feeling of unity among them, and regard themselves as a distinguishable entity (Theodorson and Theodorson 1969). In fact, each of these attributes has to be qualified to make the definition fit the wide array of human groups to which it is applied:

1 The group of people usually is large, such as the more than 1 billion Chinese, but some societies are quite small, like the few hundred peoples in some preliterate groups in Third World areas.
2. A society does have a common culture, but it may also have many subcultures, such as does the United States of America, so that members of that society may belong to several cultures simultaneously. Their values may not necessarily be congruent.
3. Societies are usually located within a given political area, but some may not be, such as the Kurds who have no exclusive political homeland but live in the several adjacent countries of Turkey, Iran, and Iraq.
4. The feeling of unity may vary by marked degrees, from the alienated citizen to one fully involved and patriotically committed to the society.
5. Regarding oneself as a member of a given society presumes some degree of understanding and motivation. Oppressed citizens may

have little to gain from regarding themselves as members of a given society or at least of the dominant structures of that society.

As important as these characteristics are, others are equally necessary to consider:

6. Society itself is composed of interrelated roles, positions, and norms. We address many of these in this and later chapters, such as the community, organizations, small groups, and families.
7. Overlapping this sixth aspect of society are the numerous institutions necessary to meet basic human needs—institutions such as health, education, the family, and many others.

In a sense, the Castro District is a small society (an enclave) within many larger societies, like nested boxes within larger boxes. Enclaves do not have a political structure that encompasses the cultural and social lifestyles. They are usually part of larger political units, even though, as was the case with the Castro and Mission Districts, they wielded considerable political clout when they organized. In this chapter, we emphasize the societal and communal nature of the ways people can come together to live their individual lives in relative peace and harmony (or controlled aggression and hostility).

"Society" is such an abstract term we may be inclined to ignore "it"—whereas we necessarily engage many of its vital components:

1. The legal structures, from the federal constitutional level, to the state statutory level, to local ordinances, along with the parallel courts and legal functionaries—sheriffs, police, jailers, probation officers, and so forth
2. The political structures, which also have a wide but interrelated order, from the federal government (and through it, to the international "community"); to a "region" (usually including several states); to individual states and their county units, metropolitan areas, local service units, and rural areas
3. The economic structures, from multinational corporations existing perhaps temporarily in one nation, but more permanently in cyberspace and trading in the international market (thus with no necessary connection to any one nation), to national companies large and small to the networks of supportive businesses (such as transportation and communication) that move the basic elements of these abstract economic entities, down to the mom-and-pop shops of the immediate neighborhood

The same kind of analysis may be made for educational, religious, welfare, and other social structures.

The main point of listing these continua of organizational units in the various institutional areas is to show that a fairly extensive enumeration reveals a continuous fabric or network of societal units coexisting and often interacting, sometimes effectively, sometimes in conflict. Society, in the most general sense, is a special collectivity made up of a "comprehensive social system" of smaller entities interrelated and in continuous transaction to keep the whole emergent entity—that is, society—alive (Theodorson and Theodorson 1969:398). As the "fabric" of society is woven and worn by many people in many contexts, it may begin to unravel and show holes or gaps where some other social unit is needed to mend the cloth of society. This process of weaving and wearing out of the social fabric is an important part of a sociological analysis of society.

One could talk about "world society," composed of all peoples—the 6 billion of us; "international society" consisting of the family of nations; "western society," which currently consists of Euro-American nations, and so on. But for practical purposes in this book, we speak of "North American society," including the United States and Canada, and in some contexts, Mexico, as the major focus of attention on a large-scale society influencing individuals and groups. However, except for some major laws and federal organizations that influence individual, family, community, and state actions—and all the hundreds of connective tissue organizations and entities through which "society" is made manifest—we emphasize the influence of state and local societal units.

Before leaving society in this general sense, we have to point to the apparent shift in social service policy and planning that occurred during the Clinton administration in the mid-1990s, which changed "welfare as we know it" from a system that supported large numbers of persons on various kinds of public assistance funds without being successful in moving large numbers into productive areas of society, to a new system whose goals seek to replace welfare with work, but whose ramifications may generate enormous social disruption during the transition period. This change is a change in societal level thinking and planning, which will have vital implications for all the service professions, as we discuss in various chapters throughout this book. It will also have implications for particular programs conducted at the state level, such as primary preventive services with regard to AIDS or training programs for persons involved in welfare-to-work plans.

The general movement of funding in this welfare reform is to put both money and responsibility back into the hands of the elected officials in the states, and thereby, to local governments, where there are many competitors for increasing limited funds. Private businesses will also try to participate in the running of state-level program, not only using computer systems for accounting purposes but also to enforce limits set on various services, such as through managed care in the health sector. These national changes hypothesize that local governments and decision makers are closer to the local problems and therefore presumably closer to more sensitive and effective solutions. Professional helpers need to rethink and reorganize their service efforts to aid these local units in considering the options before them and to help them plan how to spend money and resources wisely—rather than only denouncing the social revolutionary change and the transitional chaos is it likely to create. For example, how popular will it be for states to assign scarce funds to AIDS prevention or welfare-to-work training? Given the long history of lack of effectiveness in reducing welfare needs and increasing significant long-term well-being for large numbers of people, we suggest the need to work toward making the national hypothesis come true, while at the same time attempting to deal with the many likely casualties in the process.

Law and the Legal Context of Society

Although laws exist physically on the printed pages of thick books, the product of authorized legislative bodies, executive implementations, and judicial interpretative and corrective decisions, in fact "law" is an intangible net that covers the body politic, lacing it together, for the good of many citizens and, sometimes, to the detriment of others. We see this, for example, in the application of public health laws with regard to citizens' rights to use bathhouses versus the public safety in reducing the spread of AIDS.

What is this law? The English Common Law, from which much of our own laws are derived, comes from age-old rule-making agents such as church laws or the judicial precedents established in various local settings in attempts to resolve disputes peaceably. These local customs and procedures are codified to form a body of formal rules reflecting the norms of dominant parties in society at that time. New decisions would amplify or modify the common law, but rarely would they make major changes in it. The emergence of new diseases like HIV-AIDS (Shilts 1987), as well as recent technological and scientific advances, especially with regard to conceiving life, preserving it, and ending it, have put great pressure on the ancient common law whose principles are being adapted as well as possible to these new questions. In 1997 the Supreme Court ruled against doctor-assisted suicide, while reminding society of the importance of humane palliative care for the terminally ill. As Chief Justice Rehnquist (1997) wrote for a unanimous Court: "We have also assumed, and strongly suggested, that the due process clause [of the Constitution] protects the traditional right to refuse unwanted lifesaving medical treatment." This statement speaks as much to AIDS victims as to any other terminally ill persons.

The judicial structures evolved as part of the system of checks and balances worked out in the U.S. Constitution and its amendments, which contain the broadest and most general principles of law. From these flow the particular laws or statutes generated by the various federal or state legislatures. When cases are brought before the courts, these bodies interpret whether the laws or statutes conform to the letter and the spirit of the Constitution and other laws that follow from it. They also interpret whether administrative regulations that direct particular role holders to perform certain actions are legal. These administrative regulations are of vital importance to helping professionals because these are the instruments that directly touch the lives of people in their service.

Statutes (from federal or state legislative bodies) and ordinances (from counties or communities) are categorized into codes that represent the current body of law for a given jurisdiction. Each jurisdiction interprets its own laws, but should one party to a case disagree with the local decision, in some cases that party may appeal the case to higher courts, and ultimately, to the Supreme Court, the highest court in the land. Typically, each state has some form of the three layered court system like the federal courts: a supreme court, courts of appeal (appellate courts), and district trial courts. Depending on the size of the community, there may be other divisions at the trial level, such as traffic courts, family courts, and so forth.

Crimes are divided into categories as well. Felonies are the more serious crimes, such as the violent crimes of murder, assault, rape, armed robbery. The serious nonviolent crimes include theft and burglary, forgery, and the so-called victimless crimes, like gambling and prostitution. Felonies are punishable by jail sentences of a year or more, or large fines, or both. Misdemeanors comprise the category of lesser offenses, like traffic violations; these are subject to fines and short jail sentences, but also directives to attend educational sessions on topics that might alleviate the cause of the misdemeanor, a kind of preventive approach in the judicial arena.

One of the enduring value conflicts in criminal justice involves the question of law and order versus freedom from excessive interference in one's personal activities. Both are important to a democratic society; it is how they are balanced that is the critical issue. For example, bathhouses in the Castro District were places where casual sex partners could be easily found. Thus they became one public area where HIV transmission was likely to occur in high numbers. But bathhouses were legitimate establishments, and while they might participate in educational campaigns and have suitable protective equipment, still they were a high-risk area. So, should bathhouses be closed down (for public health reasons) or left open (for individual freedom issues)? After considerable controversy, the Castro bathhouses were closed down, but the issue remains.

A series of U.S. Supreme Court decisions in the 1960s and 1970s combined to increase the rights of individuals in relationship to the police and the courts. Accused people had to be informed of their right to remain silent and warned that their statements might be used as evidence against them, and they had to be told that they had the right to receive an attorney's counsel when criminal charges were being made, at public expense if necessary (the Miranda rule). The 1961 decision in *Mapp vs. Ohio* recognized the rights of individuals in all states and municipalities; it held that the amendments to the federal Constitution applied to other jurisdictions as well.

Eternal vigilance is the price of liberty and its foundation of social justice. While considerable progress has been made in establishing due process under the law, many questions remain: Justice appears to depend on one's social characteristics, as well as one's criminal acts. For example, in one classic study, 9 out of 10 persons arrested on felony charges were male, nearly 8 out of 10 were under the age of 30, and three-quarters belonged to ethnic minorities (Zeisel 1982). Even within ethnic groups at that time, blacks constituted 53 percent of arrested felons, while Hispanics accounted for 23 percent and whites 24 percent (Silberman 1978). By the mid-1990s 1 in every 3 African American males between the ages of 20 and 29 was involved with the legal system, either in jail, on probation, or on parole. These grossly disproportionate figures have driven many scholars to look for causal explanations—from the biological drives of young men to the sociocultural explanations of frustration and oppression among minorities. No one answer on causality appears to be fully satisfactory.

However, some progress has been made in the area of the primary prevention of juvenile delinquency. For a discussion of empirically effective and promising methods, see Howell, particularly part 2. The researchers' analysis of the empirical literature suggests some methods of primary prevention have proven effective—such as reduction of class size for kindergarten and first-grade classes, cooperative learning, tutoring, classroom behavior management techniques, parent training, marital and family therapy, and youth employment and vocational training programs *with* an intensive educational component. Evaluation of other prevention methods shows no effect or negative effects on risk and protective factors, such as humanistic and developmental instruction strategies; nonpromotion of students to the next grade; peer counseling; special educational placement for disruptive, emotionally disturbed, learning-disabled, or educable developmentally disabled elementary school students; and youth employment and vocational training programs *without* an intensive educational component. Some promising programs that have not yet received adequate empirical support include after-school recreation, youth service, restriction on the sale, purchase, and transfer of guns, metal detectors in schools, community policing, and neighborhood block watch. More research is needed in this area, as everywhere. But more *use* of available research knowledge would be appropriate too. There are likewise bodies of knowledge on primary prevention of other content areas (M. Bloom 1996).

Cultural Contexts of Human Behavior and Development

Culture refers to shared lifestyles, customs, habits, skills, technology, arts, science, religion, values, political behavior, language, and history that characterize a particular group of people at a particular time and place (Barker 1987; Ponterotto and Pedersen 1993). Culture supplies meaning and zest to civic life, empowering individually weak people to be collectively strong, and integrating large numbers of people on the basis of a lifestyle and a collective history (including a shared language, religion, and sometimes, victimization) rather than formal legal relationships. The vibrant and supportive gay culture in the Castro and Mission Districts in San Francisco was a primary attraction to the thousands of people who settled into these areas and the thousands of others who visit.

Culture is such an inclusive term that there appears to be very little that it does not include, but for practical purposes helping professionals should recognize how the culture of clients and others affects and is affected by social services. To this end, we offer the following table that connects culturally sensitive practice with the basic steps in the problem-solving sequence.

TABLE 2.1. **Culturally Sensitive Professional Practice
with Individuals and Families**

Steps in the Problem-solving Sequence	Culturally Sensitive Considerations
Step 1. Identify the problems and strengths of both client and situation.	1. Begin where the clients are in their personal, social, and cultural contexts as they affect the clients' problems and strengths. Empasize strengths; be aware of problems. 2. Use bilingual or bicultural workers or others experienced with the cultures involved, when possible. This may involve spending more time getting to know one another, rather than moving directly to the problem or challenge. 3. Use acessible locations and appropriate methods of communication, maintaining client dignity at all times. Use surnames and other culturally appropriate forms of address. 4. Admit one's own cultural limitations, when neccessary, in asking for assistance in. determining how to help the client.
Step 2. Identify alternative theories of behavior, and empirical and practical options.	1. Recognize that any theory must be modified by cultural considerations, as when young female workers may not be acepted as authorities by older male clients or by people from cultures where women do not ordinarily hold positions of authority. Be prepared to adapt, such as having an indigenous older male as aide to the professional. 2. Clients may have folk theories about their problems and roles that should be integrated with modern scientific methods as far as possible.
Step 3. Identify short-and long-term goals as part of decision making.	1. Help clients formulate goals in terms of the multiple cultures in which they live. Acept client goals, unless laws and good practice dictate otherwise. Be careful of one's own biases as you try to facilitate

TABLE 2.1. *(continued)*

Steps in the Problem-solving Sequence	Culturally Sensitive Considerations
	client goals within the clients' way of viewing the world and its dynamics.
	2. Work to empower the powerless by helping them develop personal skills needed to perform socially valued roles. Assist others in similar circumstances to join together in seeking their rights, to the extent the culture tolerates collective action.
	3. Be alert to individual differences within a cultural context. Don't culturally stereotype.
Step 4. Implement and concurrently evaluate the process and the outcome of the helping action.	1. Work with clients' strengths, available social support groups, and physical environmental resources, rather than trying to remidiate deficits and limitations only.
	2. Show respect for clients at all times and do not use techniques that blame the victim. However, do not ignore clients' contributions to the problems. Understand them through historical, social, and cultural perspective, as well as through psychological analysis of the present situation.
Step 5. Terminate when a goodness of fit between client and environment has been achieved and when personal and situational resources have been built in to maintain these goals	1. Termination should be discussed early as the appropriate outcome when clients have reached their goals within the cultural definition of a good solution. No new problems should emerge when the initial problem/challenge has been resolved.
	2. Leave clients with a sense of self-competence and a network of sociocultural supports as provided with the clients' culture, so as to be able to deal with new issues.

Migrant Workers: An Example
of Cultural Change Strategies

In addition to these cultural understandings with individual clients or small groups, cultural ideas may be used in large-scale social services. Allen (1986) provides some cultural practice principles in services to migrant farm workers that illustrate this point. Allen uses an ecological perspective in which multiple levels of social system structures and forces are studied and appropriate measures employed to orchestrate multiple movements toward the desired goals of all persons and groups involved. Migrant workers, who traditionally move year-round with the crop seasons, typically lack even the most elemental basics of life, such as a fixed abode (or any sense of place in their lives), decent health care, and basic education for their children. They usually receive low (piecework) income and no fringe benefits, have no cushion against untoward natural or social events that are endemic to farming culture, and face constant pressure to get the harvest in as soon as possible.

On the other side are the employing groups with their farms ranging from large- to small-scale. Equally buffeted by natural and social events, they have need for many hands during short periods of the year and cannot afford to hire full-time field hands. As economy measures, they supply only the bare essentials, as do all their competitors. If one employer undertook to provide better facilities, this would add to his or her costs without any perceptible improvement in productivity, and this employer would soon be out of business. (But see the discussion of mill-owner Robert Owen, in chapter 3, to the contrary.)

The two cultures of migrant worker and seasonal employer appear locked in conflict. What would be a gain for one would be a loss for the other. Yet Allen describes a method of cultural change practices that appears to overcome this dilemma. He makes the following points: Cultural change principles state that one should involve all the people in decisions affecting them—both workers and managers. Adopt a no-blame-placing approach and a mutually beneficial solution for both parties involved. Clarify both the immediate objectives and the long-term goals so that every change effort can have a clear focus. Show the connection between individual enhancements and organizational success; one cannot attain one without the other; changes have to be personally fulfilling as well as organizationally desirable. All these principles would fit comfortably within the social ecological perspective (1986:94–101).

Allen goes on to suggest that we need to tailor any change to all the local cultures involved, again, both workers and employers. There must be a focus on multilevel change strategies—a whole package of interrelated changes—because changes in one area will affect all the other ecological components. He recommends developing a positive outlook and the creation of a sense of community, that is, a shared fate in which the positive efforts of each party contribute to the well-being of all others.

With the migrant worker example, Allen describes some specific issues the workers raised—very low wages with no fringe benefits, no toilet facilities in the fields, poor educational opportunities for children, no social services, and many chronic health problems. From the employers' view, turnover was very high, the quality of work was indifferent, and productivity was relatively low.

Readers may observe the high levels of distrust and antagonism on both sides, each justified according to their cultural values, and the larger societal system in which they both worked. The cultural change effort confronted these values directly and the organizational structures that maintained them. By careful analysis of the situation, Allen and colleagues modified the existing cultural systems, from the ways individuals worked, to the creation of work teams, and worker-employer meetings to define and monitor levels of productivity and worker satisfaction. Weekly worker-team meetings were initiated to monitor productivity and income objectives, as well as to discuss changes in housing and sanitation. Step-by-step mutually related changes were initiated and monitored that moved both groups toward their interdependent short-term and long-term goals. They were in place for five years by which time Allen could report: "Annual worker income had quadrupled and turnover had reduced drastically. Instead of migrant camps, an 85-home model community had been developed," with social service programs, a library, and a homeowners association (1986:104). Thus with a careful analysis of the common and distinctive cultures of opposing groups, it may be possible to make such connections so as to mutually benefit both parties involved. (See also Albee, Joffe, and Dusenbury 1988; Orlandi 1986; Schilling et al. 1992).

Community Contexts of Human Behavior and Development

The term *community* denotes many things. The people of the world are coming to be viewed as a global village or community; social workers consider themselves a professional community; a university is often described as a community of scholars; people communicating through the electronic highway on a regular basis with one another may also be a kind of community; a group of people from many parts of the country sharing one special characteristic such as deafness may be considered a community (Wax 1995); and a rural village, an urban neighborhood, an ethnic enclave, or a large residential district in a city may all be termed communities. The last four examples are attached to a place or a particular locality, and it is that which singles them out as the principal focus of this section.

People tend to live in localities where they are in physical proximity to one another. They display locality relevant behaviors (Warren 1963); they depend on common social structures and services; they may share similarities of interest and concern; they may even think of themselves as belonging to a community. This belief, shared and acted upon in synchronized ways by large numbers of people in the locality, is what is meant by sense of community—a feeling of being a part of some group in some place by sharing common interests and activities (Chavis, Stucky, and Wandersman 1983). Some communities manifest a psychological and perhaps a cultural or a social component in addition to locality base. A locale-based community presents to its members a physical setting in which primary group relationships, institutions, and organizations are created and re-created.

As in the Castro and Mission Districts, what is often seen in urban life is communities within a community, much like a set of nested boxes, one within the other. Depending on the focus of observation or the level of analysis, the practitioner may work with the residents of a tenement, an apartment house, a city block, a housing project, or a neighborhood, each of which may view itself as a community within the larger community. Community social workers may serve the community as the client unit. Other social workers may consider the community as the environment in which individuals and families live and are served.

Before the Castro and Mission Districts became residential localities for gay and lesbian peoples, they constituted a kind of nonplace network community that provided a safe if temporary communal haven where individuals might make contact with other gay and lesbian people. These nonplace network communities share some of the functions, structures, activities, common sentiments, and reciprocal supports that other communities do. For gay men in the early days of the Castro District and in other parts of the country that lack a physical place for a gay community, bars, coffeehouses, restaurants, social and educational groups, churches, bathhouses, and gyms serve as the sites of nonresidential urban communities of this vulnerable group (Moses and Hawkins 1982). The gay bar is the community's major site where gays can eat and drink together, dance, and find sexual partners. The absence or presence of a particular physical environment is critical in the social and cultural lives of people.

Nonresidential lesbian communities are structured quite differently. The bar is less important, and the personal community that enables lesbians to relax with others who share the same lifestyle and to enjoy a strong network of support is more important (Moses and Hawkins 1982). The function of a lesbian community is to serve as an extended family or support network that provides approval, a sense of continuity, emotional and financial support in times of stress, shared experiences, and a common history and culture. Lesbians are more engaged in lesbian culture and community than gays are in gay culture and community, possibly because lesbians are more apt than gays to view this lifestyle as something more than a sexual orientation. The gay and lesbian communities may join together in rallies, marches, and projects such as the AIDS quilt, and in organizations such as the National Gay Task Force, but for the most part they function as separate communities (Moses and Hawkins 1982).

Living in a rural community may cause problems for gay and lesbian people because of their greater visibility in a place where everyone knows everyone else and because of the conservatism of rural communities, which tend to be unaccepting of differences. The social isolation of gay and lesbian people may be great under these rural conditions where they may live at great distances and have few congenial recreational sites or social activities where they can congregate (Moses and Hawkins 1982).

Five Functions That All Communities Serve

Warren offered the classical functional view of communities as they influence the functioning and development of their members (1963:9–11). Specialized communities, like those in the Castro and Mission Districts, would express these in functionally equivalent ways; for example, while some lesbian and gay families do raise children to be good citizens, the socialization function can also be served in acquainting teenagers or young adults who have "come out" publicly as homosexuals to become good citizens in this special community.

1. Production-distribution-consumption refers to local participation in producing, distributing, and consuming those goods and services, access to which is deemed desirable in the immediate locale. This

function is carried out by small and large businesses, schools, churches and temples, governmental units, health and welfare services, systems of housing, and so on, which directly or indirectly influence this function.

2. Socialization is the process by which the community's institutions, especially the family and school, transmit prevailing knowledge, social values, and behavior patterns to its individual members.

3. Social control is the process through which certain community structures influence the behavior of its members toward conformity with its norms. This function is carried out by the police, courts, schools, families, religious organizations, and social agencies.

4. Social participation is provided by religious organizations, recreational systems, voluntary organizations, and informal groups of many kinds.

5. Mutual support is provided by primary groups such as family, friends, neighbors, and other affiliations and by formal systems such as health and welfare organizations.

Community Attributes

Over time, people living in communities experience, to varying degrees, positive outcomes in their transactions that relate to the outer environment and to their inner environments among their neighbors. We speak metaphorically when we say these outcomes include the emergence of community identity, the competent community, the self-directed community, and human relatedness. As we explain in the following sections, we mean that individuals share common experiences and grow to have common feelings and beliefs (social norms) and to perform expectable actions (social roles). We do not mean that communities have identities in the same sense that an individual has an identity; rather, we speak of common patterns of identities of people who live in the same community.

Residents' sense of community. Members of homogeneous, self-aware communities, such as American Indian reservations and Canadian Indian reserves, and those formed by ethnic, religious, lesbian and gay groups, and others manifest *communitas,* which may be translated as sentiments of solidarity that are based on similarity, intimacy, and reciprocity. These lead to a strong sense of the shared community. Metaphorically, this could be discussed as community identity. Such a sense of community is not inevitable; people living in close proximity but lacking a sense of shared interests and concerns do not have this sense of shared community even though they in fact share such locality based services as water, sewage disposal, and fire and police protection.

People residing in various kinds of congregate or close quarters living (such as a public housing project, a nursing home, group homes for the mentally ill, and the like) may be considered by outsiders to be a community, whether or not the members of those facilities consider themselves to be a community.

In today's rapidly changing society, people frequently move in and out of local communities, without necessarily forming the relationships with others to provide the basis for evolving a sense of community. Communities experiencing rapid change, like boomtowns or districts where the young migrate to better jobs while the elders stay behind, also may undergo a breakdown in a shared sense of community. Time is required for newcomers and longtime residents to develop a new sense of community identity based on recognition of and pride in the community's fresh and rich diversity. Without a sense of community, people living in this locale will find it difficult to develop commitment to the commonly defined needs and goals.

The competent community. The competent community is one whose members manifest a collective capacity for dealing with the wide-ranging needs and challenges in communal life. Cottrell (1976) defined this collective competence as the ability of the community component parts to "collaborate effectively in identifying the problems and needs of the community; achieve a working consensus on goals and priorities; agree on ways and means to implement the agreed-upon goals; and collaborate effectively in the required actions." As an ideal type, the competent community values and seeks to mobilize the active participation of all members in matters that concern them individually and are pertinent to the collective well-being. Members help to maintain connections with the community's larger social, economic, and political environments so that needed resources can be located, obtained, and used, and they seek to acquire the technical skills for maintaining connections and seeking resources. The competent community is also concerned with achieving and maintaining internal strengths, as defined by the residents, through developing and nourishing mutual aid and natural support systems. Residents develop skills in managing intergroup conflict and in building or restoring mutual concern and respect among all parts of the community.

The self-directing community. Communities are always part of larger societal organizations and are influenced by political, economic, and social factors outside their boundaries. So a fully autonomous community has probably never existed. Rather, we speak of a self-directing community as one that strives to maximize its beneficial connectedness to the outer environment—obtaining needed resources and selling valued supplies—while maintaining its internal strengths—being a competent community whose residents have a sense of their own interconnectedness.

Pinderhughes's (1983) transactional conception of disempowerment suggests that weak connections to the larger environment or its failure to provide needed resources to a community entrap the members and set in motion a malignant process by creating powerlessness in members of the community. The more a denial of resources and services renders residents powerless, the more these residents are hindered from meeting their own and their families' needs and from organizing to improve the community. The more powerless the family is, the more its members are blocked in their attempts to acquire skills, to develop self-esteem, and to strengthen the family, and consequently, to contribute to the health and strength of the community. This process is an example of the circular causal loop described in chapter 1.

The issue of community self-direction parallels issues of empowerment, and it is illustrated in the determination of American Indian leaders and parents to see that their children are reared in Indian families.

> Most American Indian groups, for example, in Nevada, Washington State, and Minnesota, and Alaska native groups have taken over and are now administering their own social service programs. . . . The cornerstones of these successes were self-determination and opportunity rooted in tribal control. Indian people, working through tribal social service agencies and tribal courts, more quickly identified solutions to child-welfare problems in the rich resources visible to them in the lives of their people. Historically, these strengths have been wasted by non-Indians, who ignored or misunderstood them. (Blanchard and Unger 1977)

Without such self-direction, a community is in danger of internal disorganization or of external tyranny and social neglect.

Human relatedness. The sense of community, the competent community, and self-direction of a community all rest on human relatedness, the sense of belonging and being "in place." Relatedness is the essence of community. It is the base of *communitas,* or the reciprocal relationship involving caring for and being cared about. Many communities transcend the harshness of their conditions by the operation of their natural support networks (Stack 1974; B. Valentine 1978; Myerhoff 1978a); their shared pleasure in music, language, laughter; and their shared commitment to religion, social clubs, or other affiliations—that is to say, their common culture (Valentine and Valentine 1970; Draper 1979; Mizio 1974; Moses and Hawkins 1982). A community laced with natural support systems is more likely to be a community whose members have a firm sense of identity, competence, and self-direction. Readers should note the parallels between individual and collective levels of these 4 factors, as described here and in chapter 1: Social workers' practices in neighborhoods, organizations, and communities seek to establish among their residents a social relatedness, a sense of community, a competent community, and a self-directing community. To the extent that social workers and others can accomplish these objectives, for individuals and for community groups, the residents may form a more positive adaptedness with their environments.

Physical and Social Settings in Community Life

Two concepts from ecology, when applied metaphorically, are useful in considering the physical and social settings of communities. These are the human habitat and niche (Germain 1985).

Human Habitat

In ecology, habitat designates where organisms are physically found in a living community. In the case of human beings, both the physical and the social settings of the community, workplace, school, and so on, constitute the human habitat. Physical settings such as dwellings, buildings, rural villages, and urban layouts must support the social settings of family life, interpersonal life, work life, spiritual life, and so on in ways that fit the lifestyles, age, gender, and cultural patterns of the residents. The human habitat must provide a physical environment capable of supporting the full range of human needs and interests as they evolve biologically and culturally, including appropriate access to physical (and social) settings for the community's aging and physically disabled populations. The same physical setting may support multiple social functions.

In poor communities, dwellings may be in poor repair, be infested with vermin, contain lead paint and asbestos fibers, or be otherwise dangerous to the health and well-being of children and adults. While residents may be dissatisfied with their slum housing, they may nevertheless be satisfied with their immediate neighborhood because of the supports it offers as a social setting, something that may be broken up in urban renewal projects and high-rise public housing. Homeless people have neither a physical place that is safe and comfortable nor a social setting that is supporting and affirming. This becomes one of the greatest threats to life, human dignity, and a personal sense of self.

Spatial Stressors and Spatial Challengers

There are various kinds of spatial stressors and challenges in the human habitat (Ittelson et al. 1974). Newman (1972) used the spatial concept of territory to help explain the prevalence of crime in high-rise housing apartments and the lack of defensible spaces. Crime takes place in semipublic spaces such as lobbies, stairwells, elevators, and grounds where surveillance by tenants is not possible. Boundary markers are not present, and intruders cannot be recognized as such, so these spaces become indefensible. Newman proposed architectural design (such as garden apartments) that would stimulate a sense of community among residents. The human scaling of low-rise apartments is less institutional and rigid than high-rises; people can become involved with one another in neighborly ways. But for the interim, he advocated the creation of intermediate territories, such as a play facility for young children on each floor. Such a facility is apt to bring families out to use it and may lead to a shared effort to maintain the facility's security for children by screening intruders.

Cotton and Geraty (1984) present a fascinating case study in constructing a goodness of fit between a physical environment and specific mental health service goals. They discuss how clinical concepts were translated into architectural and design features for a psychiatric unit for children ages 4 through 12 who have serious problems such as suicidal behavior, stealing, and school adjustment difficulties. For example, one goal was to provide spaces that represent a continuum of external controls and can be adapted to the needs of individual patients and groups of patients as they fluctuate in their capacity to use internal controls (Cotton and Geraty 1984:629). To attain this goal, the planners had to resolve the dilemma of providing a safe (controlled) environment versus one that offered freedom and openness as a stimulus for healthy development. So they had locked doors (control) made of Plexiglas (openness). There were no doors for the kitchen on the unit (openness), but the drawers were locked (control). The quiet rooms were designed to be safe (with tamper-proof screws, carpet that was glued to the floor, and the absence of ingestible, sharp, or throwable objects) but also warm and cozy (warm colors, cloth hangings on the walls). Each small component of the therapeutic environment as well as each broad feature of that setting was carefully considered by all relevant parties for multiple uses that expressed both control and freedom.

Clearly, this care is not taken in most current architectural planning and designs. Otherwise, we would not build housing, roads, and workplaces where and how we do. For example, Bell et al.'s (1990) series of studies linked living place (high-rise apartments), noise (from traffic on nearby freeways), and school performance (children living on the lower floors having poorer reading test scores, are more distractible, and show a lack of persistence on cognitive tasks). Events in space may be stressors or challenges; it is necessary that community workers and others keep watch on built environments to reduce the harm they may be doing and to promote healthy growth and development, based on available information. Bell et. al. propose the concept of *place identity* to refer to the physical-world socialization of the child who comes to learn who he or she is not only by the continuous transactions between child and caretakers but also by means of the continuous experiences with space and physical objects in space (clothes, toys, beds, chairs, and such) that make up the substratum of existence. Place identity is a component of self-identity. Children living in dilapidated housing in slum neighborhoods are probably incorporating some of these negative physical props into their sense of self, even when family, school, and church are trying to instill a sense of pride.

Temporal Stressors and Temporal Challenges

In addition to spatial sources of stress and challenge, there are stresses and challenges related to temporal events. Violation of biologically based temporal rhythms, culturally based orientations to time, or psychologically based needs for time that are the effects of temporal arrangements of the community's institutions will also be stressful. Going with the temporal flow may be satisfying and constructive, such as eating only when hungry, taking advantage of natural light (daylight savings time) to conserve energy, celebrating seasonal changes to bring together members of the far-flung clan. Rigidly fixed hours in community service facilities may not fit the social needs and opportunities of families with child-rearing, caretaking, and work responsibilities. On the other hand, the tradition of family weekends and extended vacations may provide the incentive to keep going in a work-a-day world. Like spatial behaviors, temporal behaviors are evoked by a community's physical settings and contribute to the operation of its social settings.

Social Niche: Immigrants and Other Persons New to the Country

In ecology, niche designates the position a species occupies in the biotic community's web of life. In the case of human beings, the social niche is used as a metaphor for the status or social position occupied by particular persons in the social structure of the community. Hence, the term is related to issues of power and oppression. What constitutes a growth-supporting and health-promoting social niche is defined differently in various societies and in different historical eras. In our society, most people assume that a niche is shaped by a set of rights, including the right to equal opportunity (DeLone 1979). Yet today, millions of children and adults worldwide are forced to occupy niches that do not support human needs and goals—often because of gender, age, color, ethnicity, social class, sexual preference, mental or physical disablement, or some other personal or cultural characteristic devalued by society.

Many communities are laced with such marginal or destructive niches as "deinsitutionalized patient," "hard-to-place dependent child," "hard-core unemployed," "school dropout," "migrant laborer," "old woman," "AIDS patient." These and similar social niches are shaped by political and economic structures and by systems of education, health and mental health care, the welfare system, and the mass media, among others. Such social niches violate society's professed commitment to social justice, cultural diversity in communities, and enhanced quality of life for all people.

Social workers need to be aware of additional social niches in some communities where so-called new arrivals of various racial, ethnic, and national origins are living. We have only indirect information on the numbers of persons involved. The 1990 U.S. Census lists about 19.7 million foreign-born people residing in the United States, which is about 12 percent of the entire population. Recent immigrants come from Asia, the West Indies, Central America, the Middle East, Eastern Europe, and Africa—everywhere but Western and Southern Europe where the vast majority of earlier immigrants originated. Within these areas, are many further distinctions; Asians, for example, include Filipinos, Chinese, Vietnamese, Koreans, Japanese, Asian Indians, Cambodians, Laotians, and Pacific Islanders. The U.S. Department of Labor estimates that immigrants will represent 22 percent of new workers in the labor force by the beginning of the twenty-first century (Drachman 1996:118), workers whose taxes will go toward the support of retired people largely Euro-Americans (Ozawa 1986). They occupy a particular status or niche that leads to numerous stressors and few challenges. For example, early in the studies to identify sources of AIDS, immigrants from Haiti were named as one risk group, which led to many associated problems for these immigrants. Let's define some basic terms.

Refugees are persons who apply to come to the United States from another country because they fear persecution because of race, religion, political opinion, or membership in persecuted groups in their home countries. (*Asylee* are like refugees except they apply for asylee status from a U.S. territory.) For instance, many in the Southeast Asian groups came to this country because of special war-related circumstances. As Christopher (1994) notes, "Since 1975, 200,000 Lao have been resettled in the U.S. [as a result of America's military involvement in Indochina]." Hsia and Hirano-Nakanishi (1989) report comparative figures of families living below the poverty line (1980 data): U.S. families (9.6 percent); Vietnamese (33.5 percent). Cambodian (48.7 percent), Hmong (62.8 percent) and Laotians (65.9 percent). Corresponding rates of mental health needs reflect these economic conditions.

Unlike the immigrant who usually has time to prepare for the relocation to the new country, refugees often are forced to leave quickly and are not able to take many possessions. Thus refugees receive a broad package of relocation assistance, financial aid, medical care, English language training, employment counseling, and job placement services for 18 months, together with the same services that U.S. citizens receive, such as Supplemental Security Income (SSI), Medicaid, and food stamps (Drachman 1996:122). After one year of residence in the United States, refugees may apply for immigrant status.

An *immigrant* is an individual lawfully granted permission to reside permanently in the United States (Drachman 1996:125). One can apply for this status in different ways, each connected with different kinds of benefits. Privately sponsored immigrants come with some person or organization guaranteeing economic support for the first three years of the immigrants' residence in this country. Benefits are somewhat more restrictive than for citizens. Those who move to immigrant status from refugee status are eligible for the same services as U.S. citizens. A *temporary resident* is a person who has legal permission to live and work for a set period of time in the United States, such as a student who attends a U.S. university. After that time period, the person must either return home or apply for permanent resident status (Drachman 1996:126).

Undocumented persons (sometimes referred to as illegal aliens) are people with no current authorization to be in the United States. They may have entered illegally, or they may have stayed beyond their temporary nonimmigrant status (such as students or tourists). They are subject to deportation and are not eligible for federally funded cash assistance programs and many other social services (Drachman 1996:126–127). The numbers of undocumented persons in the United States are unclear; estimates reported by Drachman range from 2 million to 6 million people, numbers that have generated the most recent anti-immigration sentiment and state propositions seeking to end basic health, education, and welfare services to these people and their children. (Children born in the United States, even to undocumented people, are considered U.S. citizens with all rights and responsibilities thereto.) This is producing some extraordinarily difficult issues for the helping professions and society at large.

There are two types of émigrés—people who have fled their countries on emergency bases—with different labels signifying different statuses and eligibility (or noneligibility) for services. A *parolee* is a person admitted into the United States based on considerations of the public interest or under emergency conditions. (There is no connection between this immigration status and the like term in the criminal justice system.) *Entrants,* such as Haitians and the Mariel Cubans, entered illegally but were given special considerations because of conditions in their homelands. These "special considerations" were not necessarily pleasant or successful, as many people were restrained in prisonlike holding camps for long periods of time until decisions could be made on an individual basis.

All these new arrivals to America face difficult stressors of relocation, but especially illegal or undocumented persons, most of whom come from Mexico. They can safely seek only irregular or part-time work, and they fear applying for welfare, Medicaid, and food stamps, lest they be reported to the Immigration and Naturalization Service for deportation.

Social Pollutions: Racism, Sexism, and Other Isms

Pollution may take several forms. Physical pollution involves contaminating a clean area, making it dirty and less usable, as in the Chernobyl nuclear accident or in the U.S. Love Canal incident (Gibbs 1983). Social pollution involves social actions that make some aspects of social resources inaccessible to some (vulnerable) people, generally through the purposive use of power. In the sense we use this term, it would include racism, sexism, classism, ageism, able-ism (disempowerment based on disability), homophobia, and anti-intellectualism and anticreativity. Technological pollution refers to (physical) contaminations, (social) inaccessibilities due to technological innovations, or both. The fascination of a "star-wars technology" removes energy and resources for a "war-on-poverty technology."

Racism: Individual, Institutional, and Cultural

There are typically individual, institutional, and cultural forms of social pollution. For example, individual racism includes detrimental actions individuals take toward other individuals and groups based on prejudicial attitudes and beliefs about those individuals or groups in favor of one's own group. Institutional racism involves detrimental actions that role holders in organizations take, knowingly or not, that disadvantage some denigrated group, regardless of individual merits, in favor of one's own group members. These practices would include formal and informal policies, procedures, and practices in community housing, schools, workplaces, health care, social services, and so on. These processes produce negative outcomes for people of color relative to those for whites. They encourage among whites passive, acquiescent, and ineffective responses to inequality. Institutional racism may be associated with high infant mortality rates, high morbidity rates, low life expectancy among, and high unemployment rates, especially among minority youth actively seeking work. Cultural racism involves detrimental actions based on prejudicial values denigrating a given cultural form in favor of one's own culture and allowing the advantages and privileges of society to be dispensed differentially. All three forms of racism create community environments in which people of color must live and establish a circular loop that may trap some of them in powerlessness (Barbarin 1981).

Sexism

Sexual inequality based on gender differences is a major life stressor. Male dominance and privilege subordinate, devalue, and oppress women in family, work, and community life. Since the 1960s the feminist movement has achieved progress on the road to gender justice. Changes have occurred in gender ratios in some occupations, professions, and workplaces; elementary and secondary schools' curricula; political roles and voting patterns; the civil and legal rights of women; sexual reform, reproductive health care, and new social services for battered women and rape victims; family life and family roles; and the legitimation of women's natural closeness and affiliation with other women through proclaiming sisterhood (Lerner 1971). Despite valiant efforts, however, little change has been achieved in the portrayal of women in the media, pornography, and advertising. Even where changes in laws have been attained, the community institutions that should support them still lag behind (for example, equal pay for comparable work, adequate child care arrangements for working mothers, and adequate law enforcement against violence toward women).

"Male domination and female subjugation are the two interlocking arrangements promoted by sexism" (Humphreys and Nol 1997:273). Documentation of, and organized reaction against, sexism is discussed many places throughout this book. In addition, Humphreys and Nol go on to recognize that even though men generally possess power, status, and dominance in a patriarchal society, they also face gender-based stresses. There are the stressors of always being assumed to be task-oriented, unemotional, inexpressive— when men as well as women have equal needs to be integrated with others, to experience the richness of emotional possibilities, and to express (and receive expressions of) warmth and affection from others (including other men).

We describe sexism as a cultural prison, with men and women on opposite sides of the prison bars, yet imprisoned by the same set of stereotypes. Men who "defy the (patriarchal) script" by engaging in nonsexist actions (like showing care and concern for others in a helping profession) face various stressors from other men—but also from nonfeminist women. Both men and women experience the guilt and discomfort from awareness of gender oppression, albeit from different sides of the bars of that sexist prison and with grossly uneven societal rewards. The individual and collective efforts toward egalitarianism remain a primary mission of all helping professions regardless of what individual cases or groups are being served.

These effects of sexism on women, as well as on men, are examined in later chapters. For now, it is sufficient to note that stereotyped male roles in the family appear to be changing slowly among younger adult men in some communities—perhaps, in part, because of modifications of the socialization of male children that began in the early 1970s within educated middle-income families. The beginning change may also be due, in part, to the recognition among some younger men of the emotional and physical costs of competing for success in the workplace, which deprives them of time with their families and the pleasure of bringing up their children. (See the discussion of feminist theory in appendix 2.)

Able-ism (disempowerment based on disability)

Persons with disabilities face major life stressors from discrimination in the community that creates destructive, unjust differences in the resources and life conditions of the millions of people involved. Asch and Mudrick provide some relevant numbers:

> The 1990 U.S. Census estimated that 22.4 million people in the United States age 16 or older have a disability—that is, a work disability, a mobility limitation, or a self-care limitation (McNeil 1993). Data from the 1990 National Health Interview Survey (NHIS) of people living in U.S. households suggested that there are about 33.8 million people with disabilities that impose major limitations on activities or limited an important activity (LaPlante 1992). If the estimated 2.3 million people with disabilities who are living in institutions were included, the total number of people with disabilities reported by the NHIS would increase to 36.1 million, or approximately 14.5 percent of the U.S. population (LaPlante 1992).   (1995:753)

American society has permitted the assignment of a stigmatized niche and a deviant role to people with physical or mental impairments and has frequently excluded them from the mainstream economic, political, and social processes of the community. Gliedman and Roth (1980) showed how the characteristic medical-model approach to persons with disabilities magnifies the problems they face and obscures the societal forces and responsibilities that are often more important to their functioning. These authors proposed in place of the medical model an approach that views individuals with disabilities as an oppressed minority group, not because of a shared culture but because "society exposes most of them to a common set of socially produced hazards" (1980:4). Their oppression imposes a social identity on an otherwise heterogeneous group of children and adults who happen to have a physical or mental impairment. Able-ism results in prejudice, job discrimination, and destructive stereotypes and myths that exaggerate the true limitations of many disabling conditions and minimizes the strengths of these people (Hockenberry 1996).

The independent living (IL) movement among the physically disabled is a powerful and empowering influence in the lives of many physically handicapped persons, as well as a major force in societal change in public attitudes and in reducing environmental barriers and social obstacles. Some contemporary writers view disability as "the by-product of social and physical environments that do not accommodate people with different functional abilities" (Asch and Mudrick 1995:752). Rejecting the sick role and the impaired role for the physically disabled, the IL movement declares that "the disabled do not want to be relieved of their familial, occupational, and civic responsibilities in exchange for a childlike dependency" (DeJong 1979). Society needs contributions from all its citizens with potential, including those people who have disabilities.

People with disabilities, like all people, should be viewed in a person:environment context. Disabilities are located as much in the physical and social environments as they are in the person, particularly with regard to modes of adaptation. (To put all the responsibility onto the person with disabilities to adapt to the world is another form of blaming the victim.) The IL movement emphasizes the importance of living arrangements, consumer assertiveness regarding rights and entitlement, outdoor mobility, and out-of-home activity. It sees self-care as a less important outcome since assistance from a human helper does not necessarily mean dependence but may actually make employment, for example, more feasible.

A major piece of legislation, the Americans with Disabilities Act of 1990 (ADA), has moved this issue a giant step forward. It prohibits discrimination in employment (of firms with 15 or more workers), public accommodation, public services, telecommunications, and transportation on the basis of disability by public and private sector employers, businesses, and service providers (Asch and Mudrick 1995:758–759). Yet other policy issues remain, such as the provision of adequate and affordable health insurance for people with preexisting conditions and the work disincentives present in current income support programs such that people with disabilities lose all benefits once they have earned more than $500 a month. For further discussion of the ADA in relation to poverty, see Kopels (1995).

On a value matter, disability rights groups argue that life with a disability can be as worthwhile as life without a disability. However, this position leads some from the disability rights groups to argue against abortion after prenatal testing reveals a fetus with a major genetic problem. This value position may trouble social workers who favor the mother's rights in such cases.

Persons with mental disabilities have not fared as well in this society. The mentally disabled include the "mentally retarded" and those with Down syndrome and other mental conditions such as severe epilepsy and severe psychiatric disturbances. The conditions may be genetic or congenital in origin, or they may be the result of accidents, disease, or toxic materials affecting the brain and the nervous system, which may be the result of environmental pollutions harming otherwise healthy individuals. The mentally retarded also include those who were malnourished or seriously deprived of environmental stimuli over a very long time in early infancy and childhood without later enrichment (cf. Levenstein 1988; Barnett 1993).

The phrase "mentally retarded" is being critically reassessed. Mental retardation is defined by what are seen as arbitrary criteria in a limited context (usually public schools). Moreover, it has a discriminatory effect, and it is being replaced by the term developmental disability, which strictly speaking, refers to all physical and mental impairments that appear before the age of 22 years and are likely to continue indefinitely.

Disempowerment is created by community attitudes that stigmatize those with mental disabilities and their families, and prevent the establishment of group homes for children and adults, the recruitment of foster homes, the development of coordinated services and respite care to support the family's wish to provide home care, and the provision of appropriate educational and vocational training. Such disempowerment is a severe lifetime stressor added to the multiple stressors created by the disorder itself.

Begab (1974) pointed out some time ago that we currently knew enough to prevent half of what he termed mental retardation. This includes methods to ensure planned, safe, and healthy births to parents willing and able to raise children is a wholesome manner. It includes use of screening methods like amniocentesis, chorionic villous biopsy, or ultrasound for appropriate decisions regarding the birth process (Schild and Black 1984). It includes screening tests for newborns like the Brazelton Neonatal Assessment Scale, which has the additional psychological benefit of stimulating the parents' understanding of and raised levels of interest in their child (Brazelton 1973, 1986). It would involve designing the physical environment to stimulate the growth and development of children with or without disabilities, such as raised sandboxes and a variety of enclosures that become "defensible spaces" (Shaw 1987), or a flower garden for people without sight with well-defined foot paths, touchable and sniffable plants, and informative voice messages activated when a person is near by. It would include various programs that seek to stimulate the development of those children showing delays, as well as those who are not. Children's museums have many and varied hands-on experiences for children who enjoy participating to whatever level of ability they have at a given age. All these we know how to do as preventive, protective, and promotive modes of adapting to the challenge of disabilities as well as of abilities.

Interestingly, far less systematic concern and fewer organizational supports are available for the gifted and talented, whose potential contributions to the nation is enormous. Renzulli (1973) pointed out long ago that we are wasting large untapped sources of human intelligence and creativity among individuals in lower socioeconomic levels, particularly among minority and disadvantaged groups. Recent thinking about giftedness has expanded the meaning of the term to include the logical-mathematical, linguistic, musical, spatial, kinesthetic, interpersonal, or intrapersonal aspects (J. W. Gardner 1984). This means the potential number of persons who may show high levels of these various abilities, if given suitable societal and community encouragement, is 3 to 5 times the number of recognized gifted people in the past (Hallahan and Kauffman 1994). In an age of international competition, this is a fact that has to penetrate the social agenda.

Homophobia

Homophobia is defined as an irrational fear or hatred of homosexuality or homosexuals. This is a belief system that supports negative myths, misconceptions, and stereotypes about gay and lesbian people, and leads to discriminatory actions by individuals, institutions, and cultures. Thus homophobia is a major life stressor for the estimated 1 to 10 percent of the U.S. population who are gay or lesbian; the exact percentage is a matter of considerable dispute (Gluckman and Reed 1993; Berger and Kelly 1995). Discrimination in various employment practices has been reported across 21 studies at a rate between 16 and 46 percent of gays and lesbians surveyed (Badgett and Lee 1995). Gay and lesbian people live with constant stress arising from deprivation of human and civil rights in the threatened loss of their work, housing, friends, and family, including their children. Yet as life in the Castro and Mission Districts of San Francisco illustrates, it is possible for people not merely to endure but, as William Faulkner stated in his Nobel Prize acceptance speech, to prevail.

3

Complex Organizations as Contexts

This chapter continues our exploration of the macrosocial contexts of human behavior and development. The large-scale organization plays an important part in the lives of every citizen, young or old, male or female, majority or minority. In order for helping professionals to make the best use of complex organizations, they must understand the nature and functioning of these many-faceted social settings. We begin in the early nineteenth century and end with questions about the future of our corporate society in the twenty-first.

Outline

Introduction: Utopian Dreams and Realities in a Nineteenth-Century Cotton Mill

At the beginning of the Industrial Revolution in eighteenth- and nineteenth-century England, captains of industry were building new social environments that would become grist for horror scenes in Dickensian novels and Marxian socioeconomic diatribes. Large numbers of workers were needed to run dangerous machines in the crowded unsafe factories for long working hours at very low pay and with no benefits. They lived in dismal crowded houses near mines and factories, with little in the way of sanitation, schools, medical services, or the like. If the workers didn't like the conditions, they could quit and starve, because there were plenty to take their places, and there were no other places to go. Over the preceding century, the enclosure movement fenced in land for sheep herding, which had the effect of evicting large numbers of serfs who had farmed pieces of land around the villages in which they lived. It had become more profitable to raise sheep and supply raw materials to the new factories than to engage in agriculture.

Old medieval relationships, such as those between master and apprentice, dissolved in the new social structures. No longer, for example, did the foreman in the factory have responsibility to educate his many youthful employees. It was an ugly scene. Some tried to rationalize these major socioeconomic changes in society by emphasizing the sanctity of work—a combination of laissez-faire capitalism, the Protestant ethic, and later, social Darwinism. They made statements like these: "Change is inevitable. Change is good. The effort to stabilize is death. It's death for the economy. . . . It's destructive to the society" (Gilder 1996:37). "What's happening . . . is that people in this country are starting to come to grips with the fact that the point of business is to make a profit. Profit, gentlemen, is not a dirty word" (Dunlap 1996:37).

In the course of events, a few people became very wealthy, while many sank into poverty and degradation. Among these new industrialists was Robert Owen (1771–1858), who rose to become owner of a set of mills (by dint of talent, hard work, and by marrying the original owner's daughter) and who saw a completely different vision of industry and society. Although he may have been the most effective critic of the new nineteenth-century capitalism, it must be firmly emphasized that Owen's mills were very profitable, which was the first test of his ideas given the ethics of the time. But Owen's was a very different kind of industrial vision from all the others (Butt 1971; Morton 1969).

Owen was guided by a philosophy that a person's social environment strongly influences his or her character. So, he redesigned his mill town's social and physical environments to shape the character of his workers and their families—in this he shared the vision of religious reformers—as well as to make a profit. As a very strong hand at the head of his factory and the town built around it, he had his lieutenants and their workers follow his orders so as to achieve sobriety, productivity, and worker contentment at the mill, and civic contentment in the mill town.

Very briefly, he set up manipulative devices in the factory to encourage hard work—something like a token economy. He also created workmen's insurance systems (and forced workers to contribute a few pennies to their own insurance), established shorter working hours, and decreed that child workers be removed from the mills (a radical idea at the time, since children's tiny fingers could fit between the strings of thread on the machines to make tiny knots as needed). In his mill town, he had pleasant new housing built for his workers and set up nursery schools (the first ever) where children played with real tools, not toys. (He also instituted music and gym classes; it took the educational establishment many decades to catch up with his ideas.) He established a central store where quality foods and goods could be purchased at a discount (a food cooperative principle for which he was an acknowledged innovator, and later, a patron saint). He removed all forms of punishment in the community, but added some manipulative devices for his paternalistic ends (e.g., he gave prizes and public praise for clean homes at a weekly voluntary inspection). His workers and their families were probably the best paid, supported, and voluntarily manipulated in all of England—and he achieved all this while making a handsome profit. He might have spread his reform gospel even further, except that he vigorously eschewed organized religion and estranged himself from the political powers. Owen came to the United States late in his life to set up a utopia at New Harmony, Indiana, under the direction of his son and others, but it proved to be unmanageable. Nonetheless, his ideas continue to challenge us, as we shall see.

The Rational Bureaucratic Model and Formal Organizations

For the most part, we are born, live, and die in various organizations—hospitals, schools, churches and temples, factories and offices, recreational settings, and the like. It is important to understand this organizational context of life for its applications to the practice of social work, because most social services are also delivered through various organizational means. But it is also necessary to understand organizations and their influence on individual and group behavior because clients also spend their lives involved in these formal, complex bureaucratic organizations.

Bureaucracy as a phenomenon and as a concept evolved in the nineteenth century as a consequence of industrialization and urbanization. It was a way of organizing collective efforts to achieve greater productivity, efficiency, and profits through rational methods of management—and correspondingly with little concern for the needs of workers or environments. The new social arrangement spread to other areas of life, including the emerging charity organization societies. So-called scientific philanthropy bureaucratized almsgiving by the use of management methods borrowed from industry and sought to solve welfare problems rationally and to control duplication of services and fraud (e.g., collecting charity from several different organizations who didn't know what the others were doing) (Googins and Godfrey 1987; Hodson and Sullivan 1995).

Max Weber (1864–1920) gave the classic expression to the concept or ideal type of bureaucracy—where "ideal type" means an exaggerated set of characteristics, not necessarily a wonderful set of ideas, which any real organization only approximates to some degree. (See also, appendix 3.) The bureaucracy was a large-scale, formally organized collection of people, whose work was highly differentiated and coordinated into levels of necessarily well-trained workers, forming a hierarchical chain of command—the classical pyramidal organization chart. This bureaucracy was characterized by a centralization of authority and emphasis on impersonal procedures, which could be performed by any knowledgeable worker—thus making workers expendable. It emphasized rationality in solving the organizational task and impersonality mixed with equality in treating all clients equally and by the book (i.e., the manual of procedures). Records were to be kept in duplicate, and procedures were to be written down (leading to a flood of paperwork and records, which become "red tape"—a term derived from the tape used to tie English government documents that was an impediment to their use). (See also Bendix 1960.)

Formal organizations are created to achieve specific objectives and to solve problems that arise, both external tasks and internal integrative functions. As an organization develops, much planning is needed to deal with these external and internal concerns. Such planning brings complexity in its wake. Administrators must be hired to oversee operations, set priorities, and manage resources. They must coordinate the efforts of personnel who carry out specialized tasks. Policies, rules, and procedures are originally designed to ensure uniform quality of services; equitable, fair treatment of all clients and staff; and efficiency of operations—all in support of problem solving and goal achievement. Because of their nature, however, rules and regulations may become more rigidly interpreted over time, so that the original intent of the bureaucracy is transformed into maintaining the status quo, rather than serving avowed goals, a process known as goal displacement.

Nonetheless, formal organizations of all sorts are the dominant form of social arrangements in the modern world, from industry, government, education, the military, medicine, and probably social services as well. Today, many people may have had a negative experience with various bureaucracies, wherein their individual needs and strengths were given low priority compared to their categorical statuses. (You may be a kindly, wise, busy person in your ordinary life, but in a hospital, you are merely the appendectomy in room 318.) Cost effectiveness and financial accountability were originally the prime organizational norms (Hage and Aikin 1970). They are probably still the dominant motivators of organizational activity, but the larger social environment has imposed various (usually government and occasionally industry-wide) regulations and community expectations. Political liberals and conservatives attempt to convince the voters of the wisdom of having more or less regulation over various areas in their lives, everything from cigarettes as vehicles to addictive drugs to control of public land use for private gain. Consequently, we see broad swings back and forth with regard to governmental regulations of industries.

Community expectations are an entirely different kind of social force—compelling organizations to be "good corporate citizens" in their own community. This may involve an organization giving time off to individual workers to perform some specific community service, such as tutoring in the schools, or to have the whole organization undertake a local project such as sponsoring an arts program or an athletic team. These are done to earn the good will of the community, with the possibility of attracting customers in the future. For some of these community service activities, social workers might be appropriate planners and implementers, thus involving the economic sphere more directly in the health, education, and welfare areas.

Some organizations, especially in the social welfare fields, may involve contradictory features, such as the bureaucratic structures with highly defined job specifications versus the relative autonomy that helping professionals need in exercising professional values, knowledge, and judgment. This is especially true as increasing areas of social and medical services are subject to managed care organizations, where bureaucratic efficiency may conflict with professional service principles. Such conflicts may involve increased staff turnover and burnout, when workers face large caseloads, poor working conditions, fixed salaries, and limitations on professional judgments and actions. These matters may affect practice adversely, reduce the quality of service to the community, and damage staff well-being. Since they tend to be more prevalent in large-scale public services, they play a part in some practitioners forsaking the public bureaucracies that primarily serve the poor and seeking positions in private agencies. This is a serious problem for the community, the profession, and society.

The Human Relations Model: Informal Systems in Formal Organizations

It soon became obvious that bureaucracies were more than formal organizations; many informal systems (such as primary groups of coworkers) emerged within bureaucratic structures. These informal systems are networks of interpersonal relationships created by people who work together over time. The bureaucratic model had no formal place for individual or primary group interests or needs. The informal group structure is a way of meeting these needs. It is shaped by the personalities—attitudes, motivations, personal goals, professional commitments—of the members and reshaped in the give and take in the interpersonal work arena. What emerges is a small subculture within the organization, as an adaptation to the stressors and challenges of organizational life. And significantly, these informal systems may facilitate or impede the tasks of the larger organization.

The human relations model evolved through the work of many researchers and theorists. Provocative research by Roethlisberger and Dickson (1939) (the famous Hawthorne studies—where added social attention to workers, regardless of content, led to higher productivity) showed the importance of the informal but real relationships workers had with each other, which never appeared on the organizational charts. Norms on how fast one should work and other matters limiting or promoting productivity were set by informal groups reacting to bureaucratic goals and the formally structured procedures by which to achieve them. Coch and French (1948) found that workers who participated in goal setting and the tasks of group decision making were more productive and had higher levels of job satisfaction. This core idea was expanded in the writings of Likert (1961) who emphasized that the role of effective leaders was to promote open communication at all levels of the bureaucracy and to maximally involve workers in the whole process, which necessitated the sharing of power and the reducing of the hierarchical structure—other themes that could not be represented on the traditional organizational charts (Hodson and Sullivan 1995:196–198).

There were efforts to humanize the workplace in the late nineteenth century, efforts that were to culminate in various forms of occupational social work. Interestingly, businesses continued to lead the way for this humanization (Googins and Godfrey 1987; Masi 1984). "Social secretaries" were hired by businesses to watch over the well-being of the large numbers of young women employees who worked in factories—although the motivating purpose was to maintain these workers as productive cogs in the business system. The U.S. form of early welfare capitalism included some of the features of Owen's Scottish experiments decades earlier and were often just as paternalistic.

With the rise of industrialism, new forms of worker association were needed to counterbalance the enormous force that employers could bring to bear on individual workers. In the middle ages guilds supported specific craftsmen and their families, and some early and unsuccessful attempts were made to bring large numbers of new factory workers together in solidarity. But in the late nineteenth and early twentieth century, first special craft unions (AFL) and then general unions (CIO) emerged to face hostile employers and antiunion legislation. Great cycles of successes and failures marked the early as well as the later history of unions, especially with prounion legislation starting in the 1930s. Googins and Godfrey (1987) note that at no time in U.S. history was more than 30 percent of the workforce unionized; it is considerably lower today. The 1996 *Statistical Abstracts* reports the median weekly earning of various groups: unionized and nonunionized, men and women, and whites, blacks, and Hispanics. These are best viewed as a table to observe the median weekly earning figures, as of 1995, which vividly reveal the differences in pay that different categories of workers receive.

TABLE 3.1. Median usual weekly earnings, by various types of workers

	Union Members	Not Represented by a Union
Full-time workers	$602	$447
Male workers	$640	$507
Female workers	$527	$386
White workers	$621	$466
Black workers	$503	$348
Hispanic workers	$499	$311

Source: Statistical Abstracts, table 684, p. 438

Specific union activities on behalf of their members' wages, working conditions, job security, health benefits, and pensions have had repercussions across the entire occupational scene, although not to the same extent as in unionized settings. However, clearly these benefits do not reach women workers or minority workers to the same degree.

As the early unions resisted paternalistic efforts of employers in favor of broad-based wages and benefits, social secretaries were replaced with impersonal personnel departments, and U.S. business went out of the business of welfare capitalism. As equipment and operations became more sophisticated, the required level of education and training rose, and more skill in recruitment and training were needed.

U.S. history is also marked by cycles of economic prosperity and depression, as well as peace and war. When such combinations of events occurred to produce shortages in trained laborers, businesses began to offer nonfinancial benefits or indirect financial benefits on top of the direct salary or wage. These fringe benefits have become about 25 percent of the wage dollar and represent a very large portion of organizational expenses (Herzberg 1982:56). However, it is important to note that these fringe benefits are an important part of what workers expect from the economic system that is not covered by federal or state governments, so in effect, the business world is underwriting a significant portion of the welfare-and-well-being system. As fringe benefits are reduced an, obvious question arises: What other parts of the social system will cover these diminishing services and benefits for workers and their families. In a larger sense, the systemic question is the optimal balance among organizational productivity, individual well-being, and national enhancement.

A new start at this question emerged in the 1940s when businesses concerned with the specific problem of alcoholism in the workplace began to take a "tough love" approach to make employees face the drinking and work-related problems: shape up or be fired (Googins and Godfrey 1987). By the 1970s a broad-spectrum approach began to emerge, employee assistance programs in which individual workers and their problems (now including family-related problems outside the workplace) were connected with relevant occupational social services. In the 1980s a second-generation of broad-spectrum programs began, emphasizing mental wellness as well as physical health and emotional problems. Naditch (1985) documented some encouraging effectiveness data on an industry-based wellness program. Such industry-related health promotion programs began to coincide with health and wellness developments as specialized businesses and the enlarged spirit of recreation nationally.

In general, informal groups (and family groups outside the workplace) are well recognized as important influences on workers as well as on the organization and its productivity. Books on the social organization of work take primary and secondary groups into account, even though they have yet to incorporate culture and diversity issues into an overall picture (Hodson and Sullivan 1995).

Social Service Organizations: Ecological Variations

Clearly, social service agencies are not typical bureaucratic organizations because their "product" is service to clients with needs or with potentials, that is, under conditions of treatment services or primary prevention services, and often take place in not-for-profit situations (Patti 1980a, 1980b; Brilliant 1995). So we can expect some important variations on the Weberian and Likert models. The ecological or open systems model of Katz and Kahn (1978) views the organization as a social system composed of units interacting within a constantly changing environment. This view emphasizes the external task functions along with the internal integrative functions as part of an overall system seeking to maintain balance in a dynamic context over which the organization has only limited control. Various subsystems of the organization focus on one or another themes in seeking to contribute to the overall balance of the whole.

This ecological perspective clarifies the special nature of social service agencies where the service component is delivered by professionals trained to make autonomous judgments, supported by various technical, maintenance, and managerial subsystems to provide the wherewithal to deliver this service. As the level of available resources decreases (in current political and economic contexts) and as the boundary limits are set on kinds and amounts of service (under managed care), social service agencies are going to have to adapt their professional services to what is going to be supported by the agency and society (Patti 1980a, 1980b). This will likely lead to new ways to provide social support for persons in need and to help clients help themselves.

Staff of a social service organization must be familiar with the demographic characteristics of the community, including distribution patterns of age, race and ethnicity, religion, gender, family forms, and socioeconomic status. They must keep up with rates of unemployment and plant closings in a metropolitan community (Hurst and Shepard 1986), farm foreclosures in a rural community, and the community's epidemiological data on physical illness or disability, emotional disorders, and rates of mortality and morbidity by age and race. Services and programs can them be shaped to fit community needs and cultural orientations to the greatest degree possible in order to be effective and optimally used, and to elicit more positive than negative attitudes toward the organization and its staff and services.

The organization's spatial and temporal arrangements are important for access and utilization—especially by the poor, those with disabilities, and working parents. Public transportation, parking space, easy physical and social access, and flexible office hours are important to potential users of services. Most agencies have not yet promoted community members' involvement in policy and program development that goes beyond token membership on advisory councils and the like. It is difficult for social service organizations, just as it is with commercial organizations, to share power with either workers or consumers. Yet this can be an effective way to secure community acceptance and to increase rates of utilization.

Social support, whether formal or informal, is transactional, mediated by what the person does and how receptive she or he is to the efforts of others, the behaviors of those others, and the environmental context (Coyne and Holroyd 1982). Hence, social support expresses a person:environment relationship. Empirical questions of whether a support system's impact is positive or negative, what meaning it has for the community, family, or individual being served by the social worker, and whether the focal unit is receptive and able to use social support are part of the process and content of social work assessment. In addition, some people may lack the requisite social skills or receptivity to others that would allow them to use a support system. For example, the absence in early life of warm, responsive, affirming interpersonal experiences is thought to lead to later difficulties and fears in relating to others. Others may be subject to personal orientation or cultural proscriptions that interfere with the use of formal support systems, even in the face of need.

Social support systems are not necessarily always prosocial. They may exert a negative impact occasionally or consistently, in which case a system may be viewed by clients and social workers as an object of change. A young mother, for example, may feel criticized and unsupported by her social network. An organization may be unresponsive to the cultural norms and values of the community it wishes to serve or to its own workers. In their operations, informal and formal systems may arouse stress instead of reducing it, may interfere with coping efforts instead of supporting them, and may undermine the individual's or the collectivity's sense of competence, relatedness, self-esteem (self-concept), self-direction, and construction of reality (worldview or meanings). A formal or information support system may also be temporarily unable to be supportive because of a high level of stress within the system itself, environmental pressures, or the focal person's conflicted relationship with a supportive figure.

Consider unemployment. Sales (1995) describes the variety of means by which blue-collar workers and their families survive short and long periods of unemployment. Individually, such workers feel considerable anxiety, while they and their families begin to experience financial hardship, which sets in motion a chain of losses—depleted life savings, reductions in life style, increased social stresses and their physical and psychological sequellae such as physical and mental health problems, and so forth. However, workers are embedded in various friendship, familial, organizational, community, and societal networks, which may provide some sources of support during these difficult times of unemployment. Unemployment insurance and means-tested programs provide pivotal support for the unemployed, which in the United States means receiving generous but time-limited support. (In other countries, such as the United Kingdom, Germany, and Australia, unemployment benefit support is relatively generous and continues indefinitely. This structural difference appears to lead to very different effects on the unemployed of these nations, compared to the United States.) When the time-limited benefits run out, the pressure on unemployed workers and their families is further tightened. Private charities provide only limited support. However, various combinations of family and friends' help, borrowing, use of savings, and other household earnings remain an important source of financial assistance throughout all periods of unemployment. The longer the time unemployed, the greater the vulnerability to this major life crisis. For instance, "long-term unemployed workers, sometimes labeled 'discouraged' workers, may need special programs to maintain their work identities" (Sales 1995:491). We can see the complex ecology of relationships in unemployment among individual workers, their families and friends, the former employer, private charities, and various levels of the local, state, and federal government, both initially and over longer periods of time.

New Capitalism and New Well-Being in the Twenty-First Century

The more things change, the more they stay the same. In the May 1996 issue of *Harpers' Magazine*, there was a debate on where capitalism was taking America in the twenty-first century. It is interesting to read this debate among the then–U.S. Secretary of Labor (Robert Reich), a major conservative-capitalist theorist (George Gilder), a vigorous capitalist well-known for his successful "restructuring" of several large companies while laying off thousands of workers (Albert Dunlap, also known as "Chainsaw Al"), and other representatives of labor and liberal thinking. We can almost imagine Robert Owen, Karl Marx, Max Weber, and Rensis Likert sitting around this table. We will paraphrase portions of this debate because it identifies significant strengths and problems with American society presently, but also for the future.

By most indicators of economic progress, the last 30 years have been very successful, and in the last few years, the Gross National Product (GNP, the total monetary value of all goods and services in the country for the past year) has been rising, while unemployment and inflation were low. "The median wealth of American households about doubled, from $24,000 to $48,000 in real terms [between 1976 and 1993]. Per capita personal income went up by almost a third; there were some 31 million net new jobs created" (Gilder 1996:40).

Yet there is widespread anxiety about the state of the economy and one's own place in it. If things are so good economically, then why are people feeling so bad about their personal economic status? Secretary of Labor Reich made these comments:

> As the median male wage began to decline in the late seventies, American workers developed a number of coping mechanisms. The first one was for women to go into the workforce in great numbers . . . [so as] to prop up family incomes. The second coping mechanism, which emerged in the eighties, was for people to have smaller families . . . because they couldn't afford larger families. And then that coping mechanism was exhausted. In the late eighties, the third coping mechanism was to work longer. . . . We saw a lot of people take on second, even third jobs. (1996:41)

Thus people in general had to work harder and longer just to stay in place, and with downsizing in all kinds of industries, even industries that are doing well economically, everyone seems to feel vulnerable.

So what is the implication of having a powerful economic machine that is not also making citizens happy or even tranquil? This debate raises the fundamental question about the nature of a "good society" (Reich 1996:37). What Robert Owen was facing in the mid-nineteenth century, what Marx was critically describing at a somewhat later time was unbridled capitalism. "The business of America," said President Coolidge, "is business." Yet there is more to society than profits. Secretary Reich points out that we want a society in which most people have a chance at a high standard of living; that we want a society that has a moral character (Robert Owen here thumps the table with approval); that we want a society where there is trust among people and a deepening sense of what it means to be a human being (Karl Marx stirs at this paraphrase of his ideas). What we have is a society where we have beautiful cars and houses but are afraid to leave them unattended, let alone feeling personally vulnerable. We have lost tranquility in the rush toward profits, and we have overlooked the deadening costs of this lack of tranquility (1996:37).

Is there an answer to this dilemma? Perhaps Ronald Blackwell (chief economist for a leading labor union) came closest to a vital clue when he discussed his union's experience with the Xerox Corporation, which resisted the temptation to downsize when it lost a major portion of its market share in the late seventies. Instead, they retained their experienced workforce, recognizing in them an invaluable if intangible resource. The company realized that knowledgeable workers wouldn't make a creative contribution to their employing organization unless they felt involved and secure in their livelihood. It was very difficult for Xerox to give up any power by giving security (Likert nods with understanding), but they did it and received the bonus of enthusiastic workers whose interests and ideas were aligned with those of the company. Eventually they regained their share of the market (1996:43). Layoffs are, therefore, not the only road to economic success. Other options can mean economic success with security and with a sense of social responsibility.

Capitalists would counter that trying to soften capitalism with job security programs is like the European social welfare system, which has resulted in very little economic progress. Yet this is a critical point: shall we let the economic system expand freely but let the society fall apart, or should we work toward a balance between economic advancement and social tranquility? We now have a high GNP and a high standard of living—especially for chief executive officers of large organizations, who in the United States earn on average 120 times what the average worker earns, versus Japan where the average CEO earns only 16 times what the average worker does. It may be time to address that expanding economic system by improving social tranquility.

Cultural Patterns of Informal Systems in Four Major Groups

Not only are there informal groupings within formal organizations, there are various informal systems that workers bring to organizations, as well as to communities and society, from their own cultural backgrounds. We examine these additional informal systems among blacks, Hispanics, American Indians, and Asian and Pacific Islanders, but first we have to clarify some frequently confused terms.

Race is an old anthropological classification dividing humankind *(Homo sapiens)* into several broad categories based essentially on physical characteristics like skin color, shape of the nose, lips, head, and so forth, stemming from heredity. In fact these physical characteristics are not strictly exclusive to any category; rather, the categories are formed by clusters of physical characteristics that are statistically more frequent in one group rather than another. For example, darker skin is more predominant in one group, a distinctive eye shape more distinctive to another group, and so on. Race as a biological component is no longer widely accepted as a scientific concept. It has had a long and ugly history and is still used in lay language, as in the term "racism," an ideological or value term that assumes one's own racial or ethnic group— hence the broader term "ethnocentricism"—is superior to others and that is often taken as the basis for prejudicial attitudes or discriminatory actions against those other groups. The U.S. Census uses race to refer exclusively to American Indians and Alaskan Natives, Asian or Pacific Islanders, and black and white people. Hispanics are not a racial category, but are categorized as an ethnic group.

An *ethnic group* is primarily a cultural entity. Members of this group have a common cultural tradition and define themselves as distinctive from others in the same society. They may have a distinctive language, religion, and lifestyle, but the primary factor is the group members' sense of identity with one another as a distinctive group. Jackson (1985) argues that groups may have different degrees of ethnicity: for example, Hasidic Jews are highly distinctive ethnically from others; Orthodox Jews are moderately distinctive; and Reform Jews (or Jewish Americans) may be considered to have low levels of ethnicity, of distinctiveness from other Americans.

A *minority group* is any racial, religious, ethnic, sexual orientation, or gender group in a community that is a target for prejudicial attitudes, discriminatory behaviors, or both. This nontechnical term can be used with people who in fact are a majority in numbers (such as women), or who are not a formally organized group (such as gay or lesbian people). Jackson (1985) adds that a minority is a vulnerable or disempowered group with limited access to roles and activities central to the economic and political institutions of the society. Not all authors use these terms in the same way, so read carefully to determine what is being said about minorities, ethnic groups, or races.

Given an understanding of these terms, we now turn to four cultural patterns of informal systems, the nature of which is informed by ethnic characteristics and ethnocentricism. We believe that a more nearly complete understanding of these four ethnic networks is enhanced by recent scholarship in the strengths orientation, finding particular traits that seem to provide these groups with adaptive and survival skills within an oppressive society.

Black Networks

Daly et al. ask: What coping strategies have enabled African Americans not only to survive in a discriminatory society, but to achieve against all odds (1995:240–242)? Their answer involves a discussion of the Africentric orientation to problem solving at the individual, family, and community systems levels. The Africentric orientation views humanity in a collective sense, which gets expressed as shared concern and responsibility for the well-being of others, rather than as an individualistic enterprise. Daly et al. speak of an African social perspective that focuses on universal charity and codes of conduct that give dignity to people regardless of their station in life (241). The Africentric orientation accepts emotions (and the expression of emotions) as equal to cognitions as ways of experiencing the world; spiritual awareness is as acceptable as a pragmatic orientation to the material world. The heritage and experience of African Americans, including the devastating impact of historical discrimination, strengthens this ethnic group.

Daly et al. also discuss African cultural survival and coping strategies at the organizational level (1995:243–244). Mainstream organizational theory can be described as focusing on productivity and efficiency, using materialistic achievements as criteria of success, and viewing workers' families as potential interferences with corporate matters (Schiele 1990). In contrast, Schiele suggests that the Africentric perspective emphasizes cooperative group support and preservation rather than raw productivity, and a communal view of sharing work tasks and making consensual decisions rather than extensive division of labor and hierarchical structures. Daly et al. cite research that suggests these features are part of organizations with African American managers.

Hudgins (1991–1992) updates Robert Hill's classic 1972 monograph on the strengths of black families, which was written in response to the 1967 Moynihan report that described the "black matriarchal" households and the "tangle of pathology" in them. Hill discussed five specific strengths—strong kinship bonds, adaptability of family roles, strong work orientation, high achievement orientation, and strong religious orientation—that enabled blacks to survive in an often hostile and oppressive environment. Hall and King (1982) restated Hill's five strengths in terms of practice-oriented interventions: kin-structured networks, elastic households, resilient children, egalitarian households, and steadfast optimism. Hudgins uses the 1990 Census data to provide an updated review of these matters.

"Family" means extended family in the context of the black tradition. Census data show that about the same numbers of blacks and whites live alone. However, more blacks than whites live with relatives (about a 2 to 1 ratio); more whites than blacks live with a spouse (also about 2 to 1). So preoccupation with "nuclear families" (mother, father, and children living in one household) leads to a misunderstanding of the black tradition in America. A "single-parent [mother] head of household" is a misnomer because it doesn't reflect the fact that many of these women have an extended kin-structure that is part of their family and that may provide male role models for children and a loving supportive context.

Role flexibility involves family members performing both traditional and nontraditional gender-types family roles. Older siblings take care of younger ones; males do household chores; females work outside the home, which is not surprising given the high rates of unemployment for black men as well as their disproportionately high rates of incarceration. Census data suggest that black husbands of employed and unemployed wives spend a little more time on household tasks (including child care) than do white husbands, a median of five hours versus three hours. These data continue to recognize the fact that women, black and white, spend considerably more time on household tasks than men, but the data offer support for the assertion that black households tend to be more egalitarian than white households.

The strong work and high achievement orientation in African American families is also documented by Hudgins from census data. Nettles and Pleck (1994) provide a broader perspective on these matters. Resilience in the face of aversive sociocultural conditions requires that we identify not only the many risk factors faced by blacks—such as health and life-compromising behaviors, employment, police involvement, and so on—but also the protective factors—such as individual resilience, factors in the family environment, and features in the school and community ecologies. To give a few examples from the extensive discussion by Nettles and Pleck: The rough life in the ghetto produces kinds of behavior that middle-class suburbanites find disconcerting, such as hustling, and yet these behaviors may be adaptive competencies for survival in these ungentle places (167). Most studies report that blacks have self-esteem comparable to whites at all ages; the source of self-esteem for black youths comes from the communications with significant others (family, peers, and teachers) who have the doubly complex task of protecting youth from negative and racist images, while building up self-esteem (163–164). Racial pride may stimulate positive coping strategies. Overall, the picture is mixed. Hudgins notes that there were significant increases in black women completing high school between 1970 and 1989 (from 32 to 65 percent), and college (4 to 12 percent). Yet school dropout remains high among black youth, even as education is seen as a major pathway out of lower-income occupations. Religion has an impact on almost every aspect of black life, Hudgins asserts. He notes that religious beliefs and activities were at the core of the most competent black families, and were less important to the least competent black families (1991–1992:16). Churches have welded families to the community and have a long tradition of providing child care, emergency food, and limited financial aid. Hudgins cites evidence that when poor black youth participate in churches, youth groups, and athletics, their chances of moving out of poverty tend to improve. In general, Hill's "five strengths" perspective is a useful device to analyze the progress of African Americans, as well as to note problems (such as continued growth in single-parent households) for the future.

Hispanic Networks

Delgado (1995) and Delgado and Humm-Delgado (1982) analyzed natural support systems in Hispanic communities, in particular Puerto Rican and Chicano communities. These systems comprise:

1. The extended family, including those related by blood and marriage, as well as friends and special neighbors within ritual kinship systems of reciprocal support and obligation.
2. Folk healers. In Puerto Rican communities these include four types: the spiritist and the *santero*, who focus mainly on emotional and interpersonal problems, and the herbalist and the *santiguador*, who focus mainly on physical ailments. "In Mexican American communities, the *curandero*, a fifth type, is the primary folk healer" (Delgado and Humm-Delgado 1982).
3. Religious institutions that serve as support systems for individuals in crisis. These include the traditional Catholic Church, as well as the smaller missionary societies and Pentecostal churches that reach out

to new arrivals on the mainland and to persons experiencing serious problems.

4. Merchants and social clubs. These fulfill both formal and informal roles in a culture-specific framework. The most common are the *botanicas,* which provide herbs and healing paraphernalia; the bodegas, neighborhood grocery stores that also meet a variety of social needs; and the social clubs, found predominantly in Puerto Rican communities, which are hometown clubs that provide recreation, orientation for newcomers, and linkages to housing, employment, and other social institutions.

Queralt (1984;1996) observed that while Cubans, Mexicans, and Puerto Ricans are more alike than different, sharing similar versions of the Spanish language and of Catholicism, they vary in their demographic characteristics, cluster in different areas of the United States, have different immigration histories, and belong to diverse cultures. For example, on the average, Cuban Americans are twelve years older than Puerto Ricans and Mexican Americans. Their personal income is larger than that of the other two groups but substantially lower than that of the general U.S. population, despite the stereotype of their prosperous condition. More than 50 percent of the 1 million Cuban immigrants live in Dade County, Florida (the Miami area), while smaller Cuban communities are found in New Jersey, New York, California, Illinois, Texas, and Puerto Rico.

Cuban immigrants have come to the United States in large numbers only since the Castro regime attained power. Those in the earliest group tended to be of the upper and upper middle class. However, each successive group comprised more people of lower socioeconomic, educational, and occupational status than the previous one (Queralt 1984). Progressive discrimination by the larger society accompanied these shifts. Cubans came to this country as political refugees and tend to have a more conservative outlook than Puerto Ricans and Mexicans, who came seeking better jobs and living conditions, and hence have a greater interest in liberal activism than do Cubans. Puerto Ricans and Cubans lack the Indian ancestry of many Mexicans because the Indian populations in Puerto Rico and Cuba were all but wiped out by the Spaniards, whereas the highly advanced Indian populations of Mexico were subjugated but could not be annihilated by the conquistadores (Queralt 1984).

The *santero* and *santera* are described by Queralt as important supportive figures in Cuban communities. They are consulted for various folk illnesses, such as the evil eye, fainting spells, lack of energy, and obsessive thinking.

Santeria is a religion centered on the worship of gods and derived from a melding of Spanish Catholicism with the religious beliefs of African slaves brought to Cuba by the Spanish colonists. It is believed that *santeria* beliefs and practices, such as the sacrifice of sheep and chickens and lavish dinners offered to the gods, are widespread in U.S. Cuban communities (Queralt 1984).

Primarily because of the lack of jobs in their own country and the presumed availability of jobs in the United States, large numbers of Mexicans cross the border (often at great risk). Martin and Midgley (1994:19–20) report that "prior to the Immigration Reform and Control Act of 1986 (which offered legalization to certain illegal immigrants), Mexicans were believed to account for an estimated one-half of all illegal aliens residing in the United States." These illegal entries cause large expenditures for education, nutrition, health, and social control in affected states, especially California, Florida, and Texas. Yet the federal government does not seem able to reduce the millions of people coming to this country illegally, even though large sums of money are spent on border control. This reflects the desperation of illegal aliens seeking a livelihood. However, Massey and Singer (1995) also note that there is a substantial return flow of aliens back to Mexico, as well as changes in legal status after entry. This issue of illegal aliens is likely to remain a major social concern in the next decade.

American Indian Networks

In a consideration of informal systems of tribal and family networks among American Indians, important differences among a population of some million individuals must be kept in mind. There are 13 different language groups (and 200 mutually unintelligible languages), 130 major tribal groupings and an undetermined number of subgroupings, and different levels of sociocultural development among American Indians (Carpenter 1980; R. G. Lewis 1995). Despite these differences, common value orientations concerning the importance of tribal and family networks prevail. Blanchard and Unger (1977) observed, "Indian people derive their identity from relationships to their families, relatives, tribes, and land base. Blood and clan ties are the strongest relationships between individuals. Every Indian person has the benefit of these two relational systems, and the responsibilities of persons to each other are as strong and binding in either." Of tribes, Wilkinson (1980) wrote: "A tribe is a collection of families in which everyone has accepted duties and obligations to different people, and people operate in that kind of context. . . . A tribe is certainly nothing less than a big self-help organization that is designed to help people and meet the psychological, spiritual, and economic needs of its members."

Yet American Indians face significant problems. For example, Bereuter (1992) cites U.S. Census reports indicating that 24 percent of all Indians living in Indian communities or on reservations lack adequate shelter. In contrast, the national estimate of homelessness is about 6.4 percent. Pressler (1993) notes that, compared with the population as a whole, American Indians suffer from higher rates of many alcohol-related problems such as suicide, homicide, accidental deaths, and particularly fetal alcohol syndrome (the primary known cause of preventable mental retardation). Social work researchers such as Schinke, Schilling, and Gilchrist (1985) are attempting to prevent some of these problems using the strengths of American Indians in their own behalf. However, this remains a difficult problem in a complex social ecology.

Asian and Pacific Islander Networks

Vast differences exist in the history, culture, religion, language, and appearance of Asian, Southeast Asian, and Pacific Island Americans. The resulting complexity is increased by intragroup differences across generations, social classes, urban-rural origins and settlement, and the presence or absence in North America of family, extended family, and community support systems. These differences are overlaid by differing conditions of immigration or experience as war refugees, and for more than 110,000 Japanese Americans (two-thirds of whom were citizens), internment during World War II—now recognized as a violation of constitutional rights. The most populous Asia American groups are Chinese (from the mainland, Hong Kong, Taiwan, and Vietnam), Japanese, Korean, East Indian, Lao, Lao Hmong, Cambodian, Thai, South Vietnamese, Filipino, Guamanian, Samoan, and Hawaiian. There are many others, but in smaller numbers. Asian Americans are the most rapidly growing segment of the population. Ozawa (1997) notes that in 1995 Asian Americans were only 3.5 percent of the population, but by 2050 they are projected to constitute nearly 10 percent. Mogelonsky (1995) observes the rapid growth in particular subgroups: Asian Indians numbered 815,000 in 1990, up 111 percent from the 1980 figure. With much smaller absolute numbers, the Pakistani and Bangladeshi populations in America expanded even more rapidly, about 5 to 10 times in the same time period. And for reasons associated with the war in southeast Asia and subsequent immigrations, Cambodians and Hmong people living in America made enormous increases in their populations.

Most groups live in ethnic communities and isolated ethnic ghettos, although some people from China and Japan, and those from India are financially advantaged and may live away from urban enclaves. These three groups, in particular, are plagued by positive myths and stereotypes of the "model minority," educational achievement, and financial success (true only of some). Such stereotypes overlook the realities of poverty, discrimination, high rates of physical illness and emotional disturbance, substance abuse, and poor services and low utilization rates that prevail among Asian and Pacific Americans. As O'Hare reports on the conditions of children in particular:

> Historically, immigrants have lower income and higher poverty rates than nonimmigrants. The difference is very marked for Asian and Pacific Islander children in the United States. . . . For Asian-American children as a group, the poverty rate for the foreign born (27 percent) is more than twice as high as the poverty rate for those born in the United States (13 percent). . . . A very high percentage of children in some Asian subgroups were born outside of the United States. Over half of all Cambodian (57 percent) and Laotian (56 percent) children were foreign born. Over 40 percent of Hmong (44 percent), Vietnamese (45 percent), Indonesian (41 percent) and Melanesian (40 percent) children were foreign born.   (1995:4–5)

The Vietnamese, under centuries of Chinese domination, display many Chinese cultural patterns, including Confucianism, Taoism, Buddhism, and traditional Chinese medicine. Interpersonal relationships are highly valued, regulated, and hierarchical yet reciprocal. Lao Hmong not only differ from other Asians, but also from other Laotians. "Hmong culture is uniquely structured in corporate kinship groups. . . . The patrilineal clan system of the Hmong dominates their social organization, serving as a primary focus for their culture as a whole by tying together social, political, economic, and religious aspects of behavior" (Tou-fou 1981:79).

Below the clan is the branch, persons who share the same distant paternal ancestor and are important sources of help, and below the branch is the extended family, which is the most important unit. (It is discussed in chapter 6.) In America, the Hmong try to live next door not only to other Hmong, but to their parents, children, and close relatives, so that all may thrive. Cooperation among a number of families helps the whole group to become self-sufficient.

With respect to all Southeast Asians coming to America from such systems of identification with family and community, Wong wrote: "Enhancement of community systems through community development and community organization activities improves individual and family support systems. Through social action, refugees learn ways to make their voices heard, to empower themselves, and to attempt to solve systemic problems in refugee programs" (1981:202). As in other cultural groups, religious personages (in this instance, Buddhist monks) often serve as significant natural helpers, and mutual aid associations (collectively among Southeast Asians or individually within Vietnamese, Cambodian, and Hmong communities) promote health and reduce the stress and loneliness of refugee life in America. However, the value placed on family and mutual aid networks is sometimes unrecognized by agencies and professionals, so that social services may violate cultural norms and patterns.

Pacific Islanders are less known to other Americans than the Asian groups, even though Guamanians and Hawaiians are U.S. citizens, and Samoans are U.S. nationals. Little research and few specialized services have been directed their way. Yet they suffer from the same general barriers and problems as the Asians. Far from home in an industrialized mass society, the islanders band together for social survival. The primary group of friends or families provides social roots and an affirmation of cultural heritage and identity: "The various Islander peoples have their own clubs which [offer] social activities and economic assistance to members, but mainland family and friends remain the chief source of support for new arrivals" (Munoz 1976).

In light of the great significance of informal support systems to all people, social work services, policy, and practice need to be directed to strengthening and sustaining them. Services that draw on social networks in community life have greater cultural congruence than traditional services and are apt to be more effective. Considering the rich diversity of history, language, and culture among the new and older groups of Americans described here, social workers engaged in cross-cultural practice with individuals and collectivities require cultural sensitivity, culture-relevant knowledge, and a bicultural training on an experiential basis (Pinderhughes 1979). Those who serve a particular cultural group must become thoroughly familiar with the specific value orientations, norms, patterns, and sociocultural history of that group.

Dana (1981) specified three dimensions of cultural differences between middle-class white Americans and the four major groups of Americans of color that affect the utilization of services:

1. The meaning of emotional distress and physical symptoms within personal experience and the cultural milieu: Similar symptoms either

do not merit similar interventions in different cultures or require supplemental preventive and interventive efforts, such as spiritists, *curandero,* medicine men or women, or herbs.

2. The manner in which a group's worldview shapes feelings and perceptions about the self and society: Americans of color "typically experience less personal power, feel less control over their own lives, and they may also feel that they should not be directly responsible for themselves or experience greater control over their own lives" (Dana 1981:353–54).

3. The function and importance of family and community: Extended-family structures have a wide range of influence over individual lives. However, the central value of autonomy in white middle-class America is not part of the cultural heritage of these groups. Thus potential for generational conflict exists in the families and communities of all newcomers to America, as the children take on its values, norms, language, and teenage behavior, including autonomy and self-direction. Cherry and Redmond (1994) report on such a conflict in recent Afghan immigrants, an ordinarily abstemious Muslim group, in the face of an alcohol-saturated culture. The themes in this new report are similar for each group of immigrants trying to adjust to a new society and culture.

4

Schools and Work Sites as Special Contexts

We single out two social environments that play an especially important role in the behavior and development of individuals—schools and workplaces. In this chapter we provide the particulars of these two institutional settings, as we recognize the continuing state of tension framed rawly in such questions as "Are schools in America any good" and "Are our businesses losing out to the Europeans and the Asians?" We have asked these questions since our country's founding and probably always will. But in the twenty-first century, these questions may be intricately related.

Outline

Occupational accidents
Occupational disease
Drug use at the workplace
AIDS and the workplace
Job loss

Introduction: Full-Service Schools, A Case Study in Innovation

By definition, social institutions, such as families, educational institutions, or economic institutions, are created to solve persistent collective problems or challenges, such as to perpetuate the species, educate the young to take their place in society, and provide the wherewithal by which a society can sustain itself, respectively. When we clarify the details of these broad collective tasks, we discover people have found many ways to engage in sexual activities that lead to creation of new persons, many ways to provide necessary societal skills to young people, and many ways to arrange economic systems. What is prescribed as the "right" way for one group may be proscribed by another group, or even by the same group at another time.

In our own time, we have lived through major societal adjustments, such as the collapse of the Communist economic system in the former Soviet Union, and major changes in family forms in our own country (as discussed in chapter 6). Equally important are the population projections that inform us about the growing proportions of minority peoples in U.S. society: In 1995 whites constituted about three-quarters of the total U.S. population, but in 2050 the projections are that whites will constitute slightly more than half (52.5 percent) of the population (Ozawa 1997). This means that after the middle of the twenty-first century, the "minorities" are likely to become the "majority." Less visible, but no less important, are changes taking place in the educational system as it attempts to adapt to the enormous changes in family and society. Yesterday's deft institutional solution has become an unwieldy instrument today. What is on the horizon for tomorrow?

Dryfoos (1994, 1997), Zigler and Styfco (1993), Zigler, Kagan, and Hall (1996), and Comer et al. (1996) have provided us with some images of schools to come in the twenty-first century. First, there will be new problems with which we will have to deal, described as the "new morbidities"—the victims of unprotected sex, drugs, violence, and depression—in contrast with the old morbidities of malnutrition, chronic diseases, and personal hygiene problems. Massive poverty creates new challenges: "More than fourteen million children—22 percent of all children—live in families below the poverty line . . . [including] those children living in mother-only households [which] have become the most deprived of all, with more than 55 percent living in poverty" (Dryfoos 1994:2).

Zigler and Styfco (1993) and Chadiha (1992) describe bleak employment prospects of large numbers of youths, especially minority youths, whose unemployment rates are somewhere between double to triple those of majority young people. As discussed in chapter 3, work experiences are a major contributor to human behavior and the conventional values of society. What, then, is the lesson for minority youths who are unable to enter the legitimate workforce with well-paying meaningful jobs? As our society ages, that is, as an increasing proportion of people enter the retirement years who have to be supported by a decreasing proportion of people currently in the workforce, we are going to be forced to consider how well- or how ill-prepared are the new workers (Ozawa 1986).

Yet out of this dismal social scene some important ideas and experiments offer hope to reclaim disadvantaged young people who will, eventually, become major contributors to the retirement funds for advantaged older people. Dryfoos suggests the term *full-service schools* to describe an institutional innovation that may meet some of the needs created by the social conditions described above. Full-service schools bring together education, health, mental health, and various employment and welfare services. The following is our abbreviated version of Dryfoos's idealized full-service school, where everything that might be needed in a particular community is available under one roof, the product of collaboration among many separate agencies, government, and free enterprise:

- Quality education provided by the schools through effective basic skills, individualized instruction, team teaching, technological (computer) supports, cooperative learning, parental involvement, and effective discipline
- Support services provided by community agencies through health, mental health, and dental services; individual and group counseling, substance abuse prevention and treatment programs, sex education and family planning, health promotion; social skills training; comprehensive health education; family welfare services; housing and food services; cultural activities; recreation (especially after school and

on nonschool times); mentoring; and child care (for students who are parents and for parents who are working)

- Economic training through vocational training programs, job skill training, interviewing skills for young applicants, career information, apprenticeship programs (especially in connection with private enterprise), assistantship programs (especially for the gifted and talented to work with individual scientists and artists [Renzulli 1973]).

These services provided at the updated little red schoolhouse sound beyond belief, but Dryfoos provides a broad sampling of schools in various social and cultural settings around the United States that have taken some of these items and adapted them to their local situation. For example, in Washington Heights, New York, a "settlement house in a school" was created for a poor Hispanic neighborhood, in part because of the cooperation between the school system and the Children's Aid Society, a nonprofit organization. By a set of fortuitous circumstances, this community was given the opportunity to design a new institution with "education as its centerpiece" in combination with health, employment, housing, welfare and cultural aspects (Dryfoos 1994:107). Here is what they did.

The building opens at 7:00 a.m. and runs its various programs until 10:30 p.m., including weekends and during the summer. In the morning, there is a Latin band and recreation, along with breakfast served to about 8 percent of the student body. Classes during the weekday run alongside the family resource center, where people can get help with public assistance, employment, housing, immigration, crisis intervention, drug prevention, and adult education, serviced by social workers, paraprofessionals, and volunteers. A small number of parent volunteers are on a stipend program learning to become dental assistants, secretaries, and the like. A health and mental health clinic is next to the family resource center and offers a wide range of services, from dealing with minor injuries and illnesses to the provision of primary care for the children (backed up by a community medical clinic). An after-school program offers tutoring and other activities. One adult education program is particularly interesting: teaching Spanish to local police; the "teachers" are students and parents.

Another example of an operating school-based health center is from the Child and Family Agency of Southeastern Connecticut. This program is described by Calvert as a wide range of integrated primary medical and mental health services, including:

Physical Health Care Services: General and sports-related physical examination; screening for health problems; diagnosis and treatment of acute illness and injury; diagnosis and management of chronic illness, in conjunc-
tion with the student's primary care provider; immunizations; comprehensive health promotion and education; diagnostic testing (e.g., dip stick
urines . . . rapid strep); prescription and dispensing of medication for treatment; referral for clinically complicated and specialty services that are
beyond the scope of this school-based health center; parent education;
classroom presentations; and consultation to school staff.

Mental Health and Social Services: Assessment and treatment of psychological, social, and emotional problems; crisis intervention, counseling, and
referral as appropriate (e.g., for suicide risk; family violence); short term individual, family, and group counseling, and referral when appropriate; substance
abuse prevention education, risk reduction, and early intervention; identification of, and outreach to, students at risk (i.e., risky lifestyles; behavioral "red
flags"); psychoeducational and support groups focusing on issues prioritized
by school administrators and special services staff, faculty, and students (e.g.,
anger management, conflict resolution, self-esteem, depression, loss, sexual
harassment, healthy lifestyle choices); advocacy and referral for concrete services such as child care, housing, legal aid, and employment; parent education;
classroom presentations; and consultation to school staff.   (1996)

Dryfoos's (1994) book is filled with examples of specific innovations carried
out in schools around the country. In each case, a local community is attempting to understand the unique set of sociocultural as well as developmental
stresses and challenges facing children and their families, and to make structural changes in the community schools, helping agencies, and places of
future employment to accommodate these needs, just as the educational system is attempting to help children and parents fit better into the realities of
their contemporary world. There are beginning to be pieces of encouraging
evidence. For example, she writes: "Scattered evidence suggests that school-
based clinics have had an effect on delaying the initiation of intercourse,
upgrading the quality of contraceptive use, and lowering pregnancy rates, but
only in programs that offer comprehensive family planning services" (135).

The Educational Institution: Formal and Informal
Experiences in Sociocultural Contexts

First, we must distinguish between the formal and informal aspects of education. As with all formal organizations that are designed to address particular

classes of problems and challenges, we will observe various educational structures, functions, and developments, along with a variety of informal groupings that emerge as formal structures operate on a day-to-day basis. Viewed historically, each formal structure that emerged to become conventional practice did so by challenging the previous structures that were unable to adapt to societal changes. So, formal structural mechanisms to "learn by doing" came to replace those based on rote memorization, as the societal need for flexible and innovative citizens became clearer.

Informal structures turn out to have enormous power over educational experiences. For example, Lippitt and Gold (1959) examined the informal social structures and mental health profile in 39 elementary school classrooms. This classic Lewinian field study provided the scientific knowledge base on which later applied action programs were based. First they discovered a social power structure (who can get others to do what he or she wanted?), an affective structure (who likes or dislikes whom?), an expertness structure (who is perceived to be able to do things well?), and a coercibility structure (who has the capability to use physical coercion?). Their analysis showed a high correlation between power and affect structures, and between power and expertness (although this correlation was not as strong). The children seemed to be making discriminations about one another such that either being liked or being perceived as experts is a path to social influence. Over the course of the school year, these stratifications tended to remain quite stable; those who have power or who are liked tend to retain these attributes.

Moreover, when these observations were correlated with mental health functioning (such as behavior problems, problems in school adjustment, or emotional adjustment), Lippitt and Gold (1959) found that those who had low positions in the social structure of the class had higher levels of mental health problems, both the inner emotional difficulties and the outer (interpersonal) ones. Interestingly, in related research, it was found that children who are in low positions in the social structures of the classrooms tended to use more primitive defense mechanisms when faced with conflict than those children high in the classroom social structure who used more mature defense mechanisms. Lippitt and Gold conclude that this combination of classroom structural forces and personality behavior patterns maintain a circular destructive process: low evaluations from others and lack of effective interpersonal skills leads to unrealistic and ineffectual behaviors toward others, which in turn brings further negative evaluations.

Later applied research by Aronson and Bridgeman (1979; Aronson 1995) used this Lewinian field perspective by creating *interdependent* learning situations in the classroom where each child has a piece of the puzzle that requires cooperation for its solution. These authors report that children came to learn that each classmate was a necessary member of the group-learning task and each had a contribution to make. Children in such a situation learn to like each other better and to develop a greater self-esteem than do children in traditional (competitive) classrooms. And no less important, teachers preferred to use these interdependent techniques. Aronson (1995; Aronson and Bridgeman 1979) and others went on to apply this research model to the reduction of prejudice by getting children to recognize individual strengths in place of their own group stereotypes.

The formal structure of schools as we know them emerged over time. As Melvin notes, "The political necessity which gave rise to public education was the self-preservation of the modern society. Education is the cement which binds the social whole into the coherence it needs to carry on its affairs" (1946:257-258). There were three approaches to education in the American colonies: the private teacher, no free schooling in the South; parochial schools in New York and Maryland; and the real pattern of public education in America in New England where the law of 1647 instituted the principle of free universal education (Melvin 1946:266-268). The little red schoolhouse was the name of the early elementary school in this country, one that still persists in some backwoods areas today. Then, as now, the pattern of education was defined by local control. Elementary school graduates could read and write at a basic level, and this was adequate for the education level of the workforce in the nineteenth century.

High schools, and their predecessors, the Latin Grammar school and the academy, existed early in this country—Boston Latin School was founded in 1635—essentially as preparation for the university. Although the high school was a tax-supported institution, it long served mainly the wealthy few or those brilliant and worthy hard-working students who could likely get through college. In the depression of 1929, when young people couldn't find work, they went to high school not to prepare them for college but to seek practical knowledge and skills suitable for employment. Vocational schools blossomed, and academic high schools gradually reduced their elitist orientation and substituted sciences and modern languages as more appropriate for the contemporary world. At midcentury a high school degree was considered the minimal schooling necessary to enter the workforce; less than a quarter of the population went to college.

As we enter the twenty-first century, we may be seeing another historic change in basic level of education. President Clinton's call to make at least two years of junior college financially accessible to every qualified student suggests that the ante is being raised. Society in the electronic cyberspace future needs citizens who are well-prepared in mind and body to be effectively tuned in and turned on.

Let's consider the ecological perspective on education. Clearly young children have to be readied for a formal educational experience in a specialized school structure by learning from parents some basic skills (speech, self-control, assertiveness, cooperation, etc.) that are part of ordinary socialization. On the other hand, the school system has to be readied to receive and educate children, especially types of children for which they may not have experience in the past. One in every 7 children of school age speaks a language other than English at home (Escamilla 1994), and in New York City public schools teach children in 10 different languages (Headden 1995). Schools likewise have to be readied to receive demands and resources of society, such as changes in technology that in effect require part of the curriculum to include computers so young people will be ready for the twenty-first century or the changing climate with regard to tax-supported public services including education for huge numbers of children, many of whom have not been well served by our public educational institutions in the past. The person:environment fit always involves a two-way transaction, and in this case multiple environments are involved as well (school, technology, and the changing nature of work and society).

There is a small movement toward home schooling, instigated by parents who for various reasons believe the available schools (public or private) are inadequate, unsafe, or inappropriate with regard to certain value training and believe they can do a better job educating their children at home. Exact numbers are unknown, but from a third to a million children are estimated to be receiving home schooling (Spaid 1994; Kaslow 1996). Kaslow (1996) reports that an estimated 80 percent of parents who are conducting home schooling are fundamentalist, born-again Christians with big families. All states have statutes or case law that condones home schooling and policies to check on the adequacy of the overall instruction. The effect of isolating youngsters from their peers during the years of home education is unknown, although presumably they associate during nonschool times. Home schooling is also a challenge to public schools: how can its instruction, educational climate, and other features be made more congenial to these parents, while at the same time protecting the values of free, universal, and democratic education, embodying the constitutional requirement for the separation of church and state?

Some observers believe schools must enhance their contribution to the community by serving also as community centers for (1) after-school and vacation-time play, study, and other activities for all children, especially those who return to unsupervised homes after school because their parents work; and (2) evening educational, cultural, and civic programs for parents and other community members, especially in poor neighborhoods.

School social workers can make important contributions to achieving the needed reform. The ecological nature of the school makes it a potent site for social work programs, services, and child advocacy to help (1) prevent negative educational and socialization outcomes among children with a range of vulnerabilities, (2) promote personal capacities for successful learning and socialization for all pupils, (3) restore adaptive social and educational functioning in situations where a good child-school fit is absent, (4) facilitate needed policy and procedural changes, and (5) encourage parents' participation in school policies and educational matters. For social workers engaged in policy formulation and analysis and in research, school systems are an important arena for policy and program development and for studies that will contribute to a public understanding of the need for structural change in public education.

Extra-Familial Sources of Child Socialization

Day care: Formal and informal arrangements. To understand the context of day care, we must review some demographic characteristics of mothers, fathers, and employment. In a time long past, when men went out to work and women stayed home to care for the children and, as needed, the elderly, there was little concern for *day care,* meaning a situation where the children are cared for in the home or homelike setting, usually by experienced but not professionally trained workers. As dual employment has increased, female workers-homemakers continue to spend much more time tending to the children and the housework than do their working husbands. Moreover, as the number of single-parent families has increased—now representing about 17 percent of households with children (U.S. Department of Commerce 1994), most of them mother-child households—these families are more likely to be in poverty. In 1993 the poverty rate was 9 percent among married couples compared to 46 percent among 8.8 million female-headed families (*Economist* 1995:28-29). Thus the challenge of combining work and child-rearing continues to arise for most adults but under new circumstances from times past. Couples are having fewer children and are waiting longer until they have their first child. At the present time, women tend to continue their participation in the labor force even with young children. In 1992 70 percent of mothers with children one-year old or younger were working, a dramatic increase over previous decades (U.S. Department of Commerce 1993:400). Cattan (1991) argues that a lack of affordable child care has prevented some mothers from working outside the home.

When mothers choose (or are forced by circumstances) to go to work, they have some options. They can work part-time, perhaps with the full-time worker, relative, or friend taking over some child care duties ; they can work full-time but with different work shifts so one parent is home with the children while the other is working; or they can try to work at home (see Hodson and Sullivan 1995:85-86). A major event takes place when both parents (or female-headed households) work full time and when early child care is performed in another person's home or in some organized child care facility or school. After age 6, the public school becomes the major source of child care. About a third of preschoolers go to other homes and another quarter attend child care facilities or preschool (Hodson and Sullivan 1995:86). What effects do these changes have on children?

Many studies suggest that high quality day care does not damage preschool children and may even enhance their development provided such care begins after age 24 months (Gamble and Zigler 1986; Schweinhart and Weikart 1986). Brazelton (1985, 1986) believes that the longer the parent who is the primary caregiver can remain at home with the new baby the better. But he recommends not returning to work until the baby is well into the fourth month of age. By that time, parent and infant have learned much about each other, and the reciprocal attachment may be in place. (The age at which attachment is formed is quite controversial. See Bowlby 1969, 1973; Rutter 1979a, 1981; and Eyer 1992.) Also, by that time, the mother is apt to be more ready to share her baby with another caregiver, and the baby is ready to relate to a new caregiver. Other "good" times for returning to work are when the baby is 9 to 10 months old or when it is 18 months to 2 years of age.

Although Brazelton (1986) focuses on the mother, he believes the father also should have a period in which to have the same learning experience with his baby even if he is not the primary caregiver. Brazelton therefore supports the need for paternal leave for those fathers who wish it. By interacting with and learning more about their new baby together, the parents reinforce each other's nurturing capacities.

Finding an acceptable substitute caregiver is a conflicted task for many working parents because of guilt feelings and anguish over leaving the baby.

Brazelton believes the best solution is a paid sitter in the parents' own home (not an option for low-income working parents or most solo mothers), provided the sitter is capable of (1) being responsive to the baby's signals and needs, (2) being pleased with her or his development, (3) feeling connected to and noncompetitive with the parents, and (4) being supportive of their role. Brazelton's second-best alternative is family day care provided by a mother with a child who takes in several other children. This is an especially good solution because by the end of their first year, babies are able to enjoy, play with, and learn from one another. Brazelton suggested talking with the other parents for their appraisal of the caregiver and observing her during mealtimes, morning leave-taking, or evening reunions.

As difficult as the decision may be to place one's child out of a home setting, Brazelton believes a good day care center can be rewarding for both child and parents. It provides appropriate experiences for the child and becomes a community for working families. The support of the other working parents is important to the parents' well-being, especially since grandparents tend to be less available now because of their own work or geographic distance. Brazelton included criteria for evaluating a day care center that are also useful guides to the social worker whose client faces this task, including having adults who can relate individually to each baby, with enough energy to assure sensitive care. There must be safety and stimulation in the environment; appropriate ratios are one adult to three infants, or one adult for every four toddlers. Training of caretakers and supervision for quality control are also vital (Brazelton 1986).

Early childhood education. Quality preschool programs are effective vehicles for primary prevention and growth promotion for children living in poverty. By facilitating later school achievement, the programs enhance children's self-concept, feelings of worth, and sense of competence, which support continued learning. An example is Head Start, established in 1965 for low-income children (Zigler 1985; Zigler and Valentine 1979; Zigler and Styfco 1993). Amid great enthusiasm and perhaps insufficient pilot testing, the program quickly evolved to be a 2-year preschool for 3- and 4-year-olds. Each program, tailored to meet the needs of an individual community, had to contain 6 major components that represented the broad goals of Head Start: (1) health (each child gets a complete medical examination with follow-up treatment); (2) nutrition (Head Start centers provide at least one hot meal and one snack every day; some programs train parents how to prepare well-balanced meals at home); (3) education (including planned learning experiences and the development of self-confidence, with special reference to the needs of the ethnic groups in the community); (4) parental involvement (opportunities are created for involvement in all phases of the program); (5) social services (coordinating the needs of individual families with services provided in the community); and (6) mental health services (helping both parents and staff become aware of ways to foster the emotional and social development of children (Richmond, Zigler, and Stipek 1980).

There were also some associated experimental projects like Follow Through (providing nutritional and health care, social and psychological services, and special teaching assistance to children during their early years of elementary school); Parent and Child Centers (helping parents learn about the needs of their children and about supportive services available in their community); and Home Start (providing Head Start health, social, and educational services to children and parents at home, rather than at a center). Other effective programs dealing with young children took different forms, such as Levenstein (1988) involving in-home toy demonstrators who in effect taught parents how to play with their children using age-graded toys and books, and Shure and Spivack (1988) who taught preschoolers (and other age groups) how to problem solve more effectively, a skill that has widespread impact on children's competent social interactions.

Because of the large numbers of persons involved in a nationwide program, an evaluation of the total Head Start program is difficult to obtain. Early studies focused on objective measures such as IQ scores and grades, and found gains in Head Start children, but these gains diminished when they reached higher grades in school. There were few studies of any of the other important goals mentioned above. Later research has been more supportive across a wide band of factors. The Perry Preschool Program in Michigan involved a 25-year longitudinal study of a group of low-income black children at high risk for educational failure. A randomly chosen experimental group received an enriched version of Head Start, following a Piagetian model. Results indicate a number of positive outcomes including better school achievement in reading, language, and arithmetic (Barnett 1993). Experimental students in this project showed less need for special education classes, less unemployment after school, fewer arrests by age 19, and fewer births by age 19. As Schweinhart and Weikart state:

> The major cost of the program was the initial investment of about $5,000 per participant per program year. Major benefits to taxpayers were reduced costs of about $5,000 per preschool participant for special education programs, $3,000 for [reductions in] crime, and $16,000 for [reductions in]

welfare assistance. Additional postsecondary education of preschool participants added about $1,000 to costs.

Participants were expected to pay $5,000 more in taxes because of
increased lifetime earnings resulting from their improved educational
attainment. Thus total benefits to taxpayers amounted to about $28,000
per participant, nearly six times the initial cost of the one-year program or
three times the cost of the two-year program. (1986:100-101)

Carmody (1988) reports that minority teenagers' scores on the Scholastic
Aptitude Tests (SATs) and American College Testing improved in 1988 for the
third year in a row, while overall scores remained substantially the same.
Blacks and Mexican Americans made the largest SAT gains. Large 10-year
increases were also scored by American Indians, Asian Americans, and Puerto
Ricans. There are still gaps in minority/majority academic scores, and still too
many graduates of the impressive Perry Preschool Program who commit
crimes, have unwanted babies, and live on welfare. Even high quality programs are not yet a panacea; we have much work to do to reach all young citizens in need, but we have some important foundation knowledge.

Beginning school experiences. Every society prepares its youth for the adult
roles considered necessary to its functioning and survival. Schooling represents learning and socialization processes that usually take place outside the
family in a special, formalized setting and, in the case of public schooling, is
provided by the community. Starting school is a momentous event for both
child and parents. For children school is a new and unknown world that they
are excited about and eager to enter, although a few children may be initially
reluctant to leave the safety and protection of home and family. For parents,
school represents the first real exposure of their parenting abilities—via their
child's behavior—to a major community institution. Developmental delays
and behavioral disturbances are often first recognized by the school personnel.
Parents may hold positive expectations about the new transition of school
entry for the child and themselves, or they may be fearful of the school's judgment of their parenting or their child's abilities and deportment.

In addition, parents may have concerns about their child's exposure to values, norms, and lifestyles that vary from their own personal, religious, and
social-ethnic values. The caretaking parent may welcome the relief that school
entry can bring or may dread the "loss" and loneliness. Poor, handicapped, or
minority parents may have had unhappy learning and social experiences in
their own schooling and may fear similar experiences for their child. For these
and other reasons, first-time school entry is an important life transition for all

families with children, and in most instances, it is a smooth and even a happy one. To ease the transition, some school social workers conduct "early prevention" programs, such as discussion groups for parents whose children are beginning school, as well as transition programs for youngsters entering junior high and high school (Felner and Adan 1988).

The school is an extension of the family in terms of its educational and socialization functions, but it differs from the family in some basic ways. The school relates to children on the basis of organizational function and what the child does and achieves, while family members relate to one another on the basis of who one is in terms of kinship, age, and gender. Role relationships between teacher and student are relatively formalized and impersonal—less so in kindergarten and the primary grades—while relations in the family are highly personalized and affectionate. School life is pervaded by a competitiveness in which the child's performance is continually compared to that of peers by the child, the teacher, and others, while family life is not ordinarily conceived of as an arena of competition among the members, although competitiveness may develop between siblings or even between the adult partners. Regular and systematic evaluation is part of the school experience but not of family life. Middle class norms of punctuality, promptness in completing assigned tasks, and compliance with rules are emphasized to a far greater degree in school than in most families.

Coming to terms with these differences is part of the child's adaptive task in the transition to school life—and indeed, life in the larger community beyond home and neighborhood. They represent preparatory socialization for adult roles in bureaucratic work settings that are formalized, hierarchical, competitive, and achievement-oriented, and in which worker performance is evaluated. Sometimes this conformist bureaucratic mold is in conflict with parental values, which leads some to turn to home schooling. One major consequence when schools are not able to keep students from dropping out is that these students—predominantly minority students—miss out on knowledge acquisition, social experiences, and cognitive development, and are not as well prepared for adult working life.

Current Issues in Education and Educational Reform

Every era seems to have its national commissions to investigate current problems. Education has had its fair share, such as the 1983 National Commission on Excellence in Education, which produced a strong negative report, *A*

Nation at Risk. In 1990 the National Commission on the Role of the School and the Community in Improving Adolescent Health made a report in which strong concern was expressed about the adolescent health crisis in our nation, which has important economic implications: "For the first time, young people are less healthy and less prepared to assume responsible places in our society than were their parents. This situation is especially worrisome inasmuch as society is more complex and competitive than every before" (Consortium 1994:270). The authors of this consortium report present a constellation of risk factors for adolescent antisocial behavior, which includes factors at various levels and contexts that summarize a large volume of research:

1. Individual level: . . . early and persistent conduct problems; alienation and rebelliousness; attitudes favorable to drug use or crime; early onset of drug use or crime;
2. Family environment and interactions: poor and inconsistent family management practices; family discord and conflict; drug behaviors and substance abuse-supportive attitudes of family members; parental criminality; low bonding to family;
3. Peer and social interactions: peer rejection in the elementary grades; association with drug using or delinquent peers;
4. School experiences: academic failure; low degree of commitment to school; and low expectations for performance by school staff; and
5. Community contexts: laws and norms favorable toward problem behaviors; availability of substances; extreme neighborhood deprivation; and neighborhood disorganization. (271)

Furthermore, they review research on enhancing promotive factors, again looking at studies at different levels or contexts:

1. Attributes of the individual: resilient temperament; positive social orientation and activity level; accurate processing of interpersonal cues; good means-ends problem solving skill; an ability to evaluate alternative actions from both instrumental and affective perspectives; the capacity to enact behaviors that accomplish desired outcomes in interpersonal or social situations; and a sense of self-efficacy;
2. A supportive family environment: bonding with adults in the family; low family conflict; supportive relationships;
3. Environmental supports: [social groups and institutions, such as schools and families, which] reinforce and support coping efforts and recognize and reward competence. (272)

The consortium sees the "school as a base" in generating programs that work to address both these risk and protective factors (1994:278-295; see also

J. Hawkins 1997). In reviewing the research literature in the area of school-based efforts, they are cautiously optimistic, and they review a group of well-known studies, including Shure and Spivack (1988); Elias and Clabby (1992); Weissberg, Jackson, and Shriver (1993); Botvin and Tortu (1988); and Comer (1988; better represented by his recent work, Comer et al. 1996). These research and demonstration projects have successfully addressed reducing risk factors and encouraging protective factors on a relatively small scale. But as a knowledge base, they are a solid beginning point for schools of the twenty-first century in affecting the physical, psychological, and social health and well-being of our children and youth.

The Economic Institution: The Work Site as Context for Human Behavior and Development

Baumer and Van Horn summarize the costs of unemployment: "As unemployment spreads, crime, family disintegration, spouse and child abuse, and physical and mental illness also increase. The victims of unemployment lose more than their jobs; their health, property, and hope for the future are also at risk" (1985:276). There is no question we have to earn our living by the sweat of our brow, but the ways in which we do this are a very telling story about human development. Work, as Karl Marx described it, is divided into two major camps that have historically been in intrinsic conflict, those who control the means of production and distribution—the *bourgeoise* whose brows merely perspire—and those who do not—the *proletariat* who have to sweat just to keep food on the table. In fact, the world of work is enormously more complicated, but it is useful to have this underlying perspective as a beginning point. (See appendix 3 on macrosocial theories.) Marx's distinctions led to conceptualizations of *social class,* ways of classifying people according to commonalities in economic circumstances, educational experiences, and prestige statuses (positions in society). The familiar distinctions among upper, middle, and lower classes may be briefly and roughly summarized as follows:

The *lower class* is characterized by lower incomes, education levels, and prestige. Upper-lower and lower-lower further distinguish persons within this class, where the upper-lower include the respectable workers and families, while the lower-lower tend to be on welfare or hold low-paying part-time jobs when available. Sometimes the terms "hard core poor" or "underclass" are used for lower-lower class peoples (Auletta 1982).

The *middle class* is roughly characterized by middle incomes, education levels, and prestige. In U.S. society with its pretense to egalitarianism, some 80 percent of the people believe they are in the middle class. Upper-middle people may include well-educated and prosperous professionals, while lower-middle people include white-collar workers, skilled laborers, and sales people. Miller and Swanson (1958) emphasized another distinction between the old and the new middle classes. Roughly, the old entrepreneurial types are represented by small business people, farmers, and independent professionals—autonomous risk takers in an unpredictable world. The new middle classes include those who are part of large-scale organizations that organize their personal as well as work lives—cooperative people in a predictable world of a known division of labor.

The *upper class* includes people with money, power, and authority. The lower-upper classes have "new" money (and no inherited wealth) along with a "new" family name that has not been recognized for generations as prestigious. Upper-upper people have "old" (inherited) money and a prestigious family history. Perhaps a distinction can be drawn between the new upper-uppers (the ultra-rich) who made their hundreds of millions by having a brilliant idea and resources to pursue it at the right time and the right place, and the old upper-uppers whose families have had big money seemingly forever. M. Lewis (1996) notes that these new rich are different from the old rich, who had been our model of the leisure class with their conspicuous and enviable consumption. The new rich, says Lewis, are working furiously hard and are engaging in inconspicuous consumption, relatively speaking. For example, Bill Gates is spending about $30 million on his futuristic home; that amount is about .002 of his estimated total financial worth, whereas for most of the rest of us, our home represents a more sizable proportion (perhaps on the order of 10 to 20 percent) of our total worth. We'll leave the rich to their own peculiar forms of misery as we pursue other social concerns.

Dimensions of the Person:Environment Work Situation

In the work environment in general, two major factors must be considered by all players: organizational productivity and worker satisfaction. On a formal level, if an organization is to succeed, it has to yield a product with some degree of efficiency, or else its institutional purpose will not be fulfilled. Products may be of the tangible sort—for instance, a certain number of sellable widgets—or of the intangible kind—such as a professor lecturing to her class, the minister giving a sermon or visiting the sick, a social worker counseling clients on problem solving.

Satisfaction involves a cluster of factors that have to do with the way workers feel about approaching and carrying out the tasks they were hired to do, the contexts they do this in, and their payments. As we have seen in chapter 3, there are organizational factors but also small group factors that influence satisfaction and productivity.

We can probably observe satisfaction in performance and nonperformance (e.g., absenteeism, vandalism at the work site, job turnover). However, the empirical correlation between job satisfaction and productivity is relatively low, although it is consistently positive (Iaffaldano and Muchinsky 1985). Moreover, it goes in both directions. Feeling satisfied about salary and work conditions may lead to increased productivity, and increased productivity may lead to feeling good about one's job. On the other hand, when workers are satisfied, they tend not to have high rates of absenteeism, vandalism, and turnover. Yet, any one of these correlations (not causal statements) has to be qualified with other relevant factors, for instance, alternative opportunities or expanded family needs as related to job change.

Unemployment is a continuing problem for all nations, especially in times of economic slowdowns; in America, about 10 million people lose their jobs annually (Caplan et al. 1989:759). Yet, even when there is stable economic growth, the unemployment rate stays around 5 percent—making such good economic news a hollow victory for those persistently unemployed. This situation further disguises the fact that unemployment rates for some youths and disadvantaged groups remain very high even in times of economic growth.

Moreover, unemployment has ripple effects across a wide pond. Vinokur et al. summarize epidemiological literature documenting that unemployment produces significant deterioration in mental health and well being, such as risks of depression, anxiety, and decreased self-esteem and life satisfaction, as well as contributing to other adverse effects, such as poor physical health, suicide, and child abuse. However, these authors point to the optimistic fact that "when unemployed persons regain employment, they also regain their previous levels of mental health and well being" (1991:213).

In their long-term study, they created a jobs program for coping with job loss (Caplan et al. 1989; Vinokur, Caplan, and Williams 1987). The Michigan group conceptualized an experimental preventive service in terms of the process involved in motivating continued job seeking (of quality jobs), along with inoculation against setbacks in the job-seeking process. Prior research indicated that a worker's spouse plays a key role in developing attitudes and expectancies regarding the value of job seeking (Vinokur and Caplan 1987).

Of the 1,087 persons recruited from the Michigan state unemployment offices, eventually 606 persons were placed in the experimental group, and 322 in the controls. However, only about half actually participated in the eight three-hour training sessions, a fact that is considered in the data analysis. The others apparently chose to work out their employment status on their own. In the course of the training sessions, small groups were formed to brainstorm or problem solve with regard to some case examples, including phone meetings between sessions. Training was given in using social networks to obtain job leads and to use "buddies" within the training group and outside of training sessions.

As hypothesized, the experimental program produced higher rates of reemployment for participants than for controls, as well as higher monthly earnings and lower rates of job change. A follow-up study several years later also suggests a strong cost-benefit outcome: a large net benefit to these participants and the state and federal government programs that supported this project (Vinokur et al. 1991; see also Vicary 1994). This suggests that embedding the microsocial dynamics of an unemployed person, the family, and work buddies in a macrosocial and economic situation of job loss and a retraining program can lead to positive results for individuals, families, and organizations—and thereby for society itself. Sensitivity to the ecology of unemployment and reemployment increases the opportunities for such successful results. It is the ecological conceptualization that provides the overview of such sophisticated programs—a model for social work practice as well.

The Family and the World of Work

Social workers sometimes overlook the influence of work and the workplace on the lives of individuals, families, and communities (see *Journal of Primary Prevention* 1994). Yet the family and the workplace interpenetrate each other for good or for ill. What goes on in the family may support or interfere with job performance; what goes on in the workplace may enrich or interfere with family life. Failing to take into account the influence of work can lead the practitioner to errors in assessment and intervention. For example, what is defined as marital conflict may have its origin in job stress that needs to be ameliorated if the conflict is to be resolved. Or the strengths indicated in a woman's work history, if they are explored and affirmed, can be enlisted in helping her bring order into what may be a chaotic personal life.

A second-year social work student wrote:

> My client is an elementary school teacher who is clinically depressed and on lithium. I was ineffective, trying to treat her by talking about childhood, marriage, kids. After our class discussions and the readings, I started talking with her twice a week about work—a subject we hadn't touched on in our three months together! We learned that her work feeds into all her negative feelings about herself: her low self-esteem, lack of confidence, feelings of incompetence, and lack of self-direction. She and I are now doing well, and she is thinking about securing an M.A. in teaching reading, which would lead to positions that would allow her more control and autonomy at work. It would be simplistic to say that it's a cure or even that work is the only element in her depression, but it's an important key to working with her.

Wetzel (1978a, 1978b) demonstrated that the antecedents of depression may be found in the environmental features of work that interact with features of the personality. Her study of working women supports her hypothesis that women socialized to a dependent orientation are vulnerable to depression if their job requires them to be assertive and self-directing. Conversely, women having an independent orientation are vulnerable to depression if their job does not provide an opportunity for self-direction, major problem solving, and decision making. In each instance, the person-job fit is poor. Wetzel pointed out that, to a lesser degree, the same relationships hold true for the family as an environment. For example, a woman who is socialized to an independent orientation, and whose partner maintains rigid control over the family budget and other major decision areas, is more likely to be depressed than a woman with a dependent orientation in a similar partnership. However, the woman with a dependent orientation whose partner expects her to manage finances or participate in major decisions is more likely to be depressed than a woman with an independent orientation in a similar situation.

Person-job fit may be good until it is upset by family processes such as divorce or serious illness or by community processes such as a change in day care arrangements. Or the fit may be poor to begin with, as in Wetzel's examples. Occasionally, the fit is too encompassing, so that absorption in the work role engulfs the person's family roles and reduces the quality of life for family members. In other situations, the person-job fit is good, but the family-job fit is poor. For example, the uprooting of corporate families may be difficult for the spouse and the children, as important social ties are left behind and the sense of place that forms part of one's identity is lost. The worker, however, moves into a new ready-made network of coworkers and the demands of the new position and so may not be aware of the stress for the spouse and the children.

Families that face the periodic absence of one parent, often the father, due to such work as long-distance trucking, submarine service, and frequent business travel have the special tasks of dealing not just with the father's absence but with the father's return. Borders reported a new clinical category devised by a psychiatrist called the "intermittent husband syndrome." It was said to be found in wives of oil riggers, military and diplomatic service personnel, and others. One woman was quoted as saying, "I can't keep on making this transition, at two-week intervals, from being completely dependent on him to running the whole show by myself" (1980:B12). This so-called clinical disorder is manifested in such symptoms as headache, moodiness, and uncontrolled weeping. Such psychologizing appears to be an example of blaming the victim, who is said to require psychiatric treatment for what is actually an environmental stressor.

In sharp contrast to this approach is a preventive social work program for U.S. Navy submariners and their families (Gerard 1985). It is a psychoeducational group program designed to help submariners and their family members cope successfully with the stressor of periodic separations of five to six months' sea duty followed by reunions. The program provides information on and opportunities for the discussion of the emotional, practical, and social role changes involved. It seeks "to reach people affected by stressors before they define themselves as suffering from those stressors. to make the private experiences of anxiety, loss, family friction, and stress feel normal and bearable rather than unexpected and pathological" (Gerard 1985:85). The program is supplemented by individual consultation if desired.

Work as a Developmental Force

The world of work has a significant impact on the development of all family members, not just the working member(s) (Felner et al. 1994). The socioeconomic status of the working parent(s) (in combination with ethnic or racial factors) influences the child's access to education, health facilities, and adequate nutrition. It determines the nature of the child's physical environment, including housing and neighborhood, and it influences the kind of child-rearing practices and peer relations that the child experiences (Hoffman 1984). The schoolchild soon perceives the segregation of occupations by race, class, and gender, the concentration of males or females in certain occupations, and the gap between the earnings of whites and people of color and between women and men in U.S. society.

Although some barriers are coming down, limited access to male-dominated occupations and professions and upper-level positions, together with the lack of job-protected maternity leave and unequal pay for comparable worth, continues as a life stressor for most working women. For the first time since records began being kept in 1979, the U.S. Bureau of Labor Statistics reported in February 1988 that full-time working women earned 70 percent of what men earned in 1987. The figure was 62.5 percent in 1979. Even so, this is still less than the percentages reported for women in many other Western countries. And the total ratio hides some important subgroups. In 1993 "most young women graduating from high school and going straight into the workforce can expect to take home paychecks that are 25 percent smaller than [those of] their male counterparts" (Milgram 1994:389). In 1995 the median earnings of year-round full-time male workers was $31,496, while female workers earned $22,497, or about 71 percent of what their male counterparts earned. The difference is greater at executive, administrative, and managerial levels: women earned only 66 percent of what men earned in 1995. It is smaller at the professional level: women earned about 70 percent of what men earned in 1995. Female administrative support (clerical) workers received 77 percent as much as did male clerical workers (U.S. Department of Commerce 1997:432). Additionally, "Educational improvements for blacks [during the 1980s] were offset by lower earnings at the same educational level, higher rates of unemployment and underemployment, and a much larger share of female-headed families" (Rosen, Fanshel, and Lutz 1987:24). Unemployment rates for Hispanics fell between those for whites and blacks but were closer to the black rate. These discriminatory processes affect children's motivations and their life chances.

The nature of the parents' work affects the lives of all family members. For the infant, it makes a difference in the time and energy available to the parents for pleasurable interaction with their child and the resources they have for adequate infant care. It makes a difference in the life of the schoolchild as she or he becomes aware of the above-mentioned racist and sexist (and ableist) processes and of who works and is paid for it, and who works but is not paid for it (as in homemaking, child rearing, care of elderly family members, and the unpaid work responsibilities of the spouses of clergy, corporate executives, politicians, small business operators, farmers, and physicians).

Working parents are important role models for their children. Studies show that the daughters of working mothers are more likely to want to work, to plan to work, and to have higher career aspirations than the daughters of non-working mothers (Moen 1983). Moen added that since fathers take a more active role in child rearing when the mothers work, the gender-typed socialization of boys and girls may diminish, and the development of independence and achievement in girls may be facilitated.

The world of work also affects adolescents in direct ways, since some teenagers work part-time while in school; others not attending school look for work; and still others are engaged in occupational or career planning. For young parents, work can be a major source of challenge, socialization, and continuing growth and development, or it can be a severe life stressor. For example, parents who work but receive too little to support their family learn that they are neither needed nor valued by society. Underpaid work creates severe problems for families and interferes with developmental processes throughout the life course. Underpaid work is most often the lot of people of color, migratory laborers, and those who perform the "dirty," unskilled but necessary work of society.

And finally, retirement from work roles affects the aging family in various positive and negative ways, including reduced income (see chapter 13). For all family members, not only the working members, then, the world of work is a developmental context of singular importance and a potent force in family life.

The Workplace as a Social Environment

As a social setting, the workplace is often an arena where friendships are made, thus expanding the worker's and the family's social support network and enhancing their relatedness. When jobs are lost, many workers report losing their network of friends at a time when emotional support is needed most (Vinokur et al. 1991; Vicary 1994). The presence of informal support systems has been found to ameliorate the health effects on blue-collar workers of stress generated by job loss due to plant closings, with differences noted between rural and urban workers (Hurst and Shepard 1986). In the city, the men lived all over town, so the plant itself conveyed a sense of community and social support. When it closed down, this sense of "community" was lost. But in the small rural town, the inhabitants were the major source of the sense of community and of social support. When the rural plant shut down, the community was still intact, and the social interaction among the former workers continued.

Although many workers experience supportive relationships at the workplace, others find their relationships with workmates, supervisors, or supervisees difficult because of job stress or because of personal and interpersonal factors such as anxieties, ambivalences, problem attitudes toward authority and control, high performance expectations held by oneself or others, and the sexual harassment of working women by male supervisors or coworkers (the reverse is thought to be rare). Sexual harassment is a severe psychological stressor still experienced by many working women despite laws to prevent it (Roscoe 1994).

The Workplace as a Physical Environment

The spatial and temporal aspects of the physical setting affect the social environment of the workers. For example, the work site may or may not be accessible by public transportation and may or may not provide such amenities as parking spaces, lunch facilities, areas for privacy as well as social interaction, rest areas, or child care facilities—all of which help mediate work-generated stress. Temporal characteristics such as irregular hours, overtime, night shifts, rotating shifts, travel requirements, and take-home work, in the case of professionals, can be major stressors. They violate the worker's biological needs and limit the amount of energy and social time for family activities and responsibilities. Also, many women and men in managerial and professional employment work long hours, while blue-collar workers often hold down two jobs in order to support their families. These various temporal arrangements can have adverse consequences for the mental and physical health and social functioning of the worker and the other family members.

Safety, Health, and the Workplace

As a physical setting, the workplace may create health problems that are a major source of severe stress to workers and their families, undermining the developmental potentials of all members. The extent of injury, chronic disease, disability, and death caused by the workplace makes it one of the most dangerous of human environments.

Occupational accidents. The rates of accidents due to fire, explosion, electrocution, unsafe machinery, falls, moving and lifting equipment, and so on are still high. The Occupational Safety and Health Administration (OSHA) established in 1970, estimated that from 1955 to 1984, more U.S. workers were killed in the workplace or died from occupational disease than in any modern war. In the years from 1990 to 1994, the number of workers killed on the job decreased (from about 10,000 to about 5,000), while the number injured or disabled by an accident on the job varied from 3.9 to 3.2 million each year—it was 3.6 million in 1995 (U.S. Department of Commerce 1997:437.) These are minimum estimates, since many workplaces pad their safety records and disguise job accidents. We should note that off-the-job fatalities are about seven times higher than on-the-job fatalities.

Different occupational groups have different rates of fatalities. Mining (30 deaths per 100,000 employees 16 years and over) and agriculture (24/100,000) have the worst rates, followed by construction (16/100,000) and transportation/public utilities (13/100,000). The lowest rates of fatalities are in the fields of manufacturing (4/100,000) and services (2/100,000) (U.S. Department of Commerce 1997:437). Correa (1991) reports that agricultural workers constitute only 3 percent of the workforce, but they suffer more than 10 percent of work-related deaths. Wilkerson (1988) cited a 1988 report of the National Safety Council that 1987 saw 1,600 adults and 300 children killed in accidents involving farm equipment, and 160,000 more adults and 23,000 children disabled. Of all on-the-job deaths, 95 percent occur among males, who represent only 52 percent of the labor force. Discrimination is also present in the workplace.

> More than any other group, black men die from personal injuries on the job. Because of the racist structure of the labor market, black men work in some of the dirtiest, more dangerous job situations in this society. For example, a disproportionately high number work near open hearth furnaces and in industries that produce toxins and contaminated wastes. Davis (1977) has shown that blacks face a 37 percent greater chance of suffering occupational injury and a 20 percent greater chance of dying from a job-related injury than do whites. (Gary and Leashore 1982:57)

Occupational disease. Occupational accidents are far easier to control than health hazards because the latter are more difficult to recognize, and their consequences may not appear for many years. Approximately 100,000 die of industrial disease each year; 340,000 more are disabled by it; and about 390,000 new cases appear annually, according to estimates made by the U.S.

Public Health Service. Other estimates of yearly deaths from occupational disease are far higher, ranging from 200,000 to 300,000. Miners, construction and transportation workers, farm workers, and blue-collar and lower-level supervisors in manufacturing and industry suffer the bulk of occupational disease. The expression, "mad as a hatter," comes from the historic fact that people who made hats used mercury in the process, which led to their madness.

White-collar workers, executives, and professionals are not exempt from occupational hazards. Dentists have high rates of nervous system disorders, leukemia, and lymphatic cancer, as well as the highest rate of suicide of any professional group. They are being studied for the possible effects of contact with X-ray, mercury, and anesthesia. Administrators have higher rates of cardiac disease than do scientists and engineers. Operating-room personnel have several times the number of defective newborns and higher miscarriage rates than other women. Beauticians are said to have high rates of cancer and of cardiac and respiratory disorders.

In 1973 OSHA listed more than 12,000 toxic materials in workplaces, including harmful fibers, dusts, gases, heavy metals, chemicals and their vapors, and radiation. With the continuous development of new industrial technologies, new substances appear at the rate of about 3,000 a year (Stellman and Daum 1973). The effects of some are immediate, but the effects of most will not be known for years. Not until 1985, for example, did OSHA set standards for the carcinogens benzene, formaldehyde, and cotton dust. In January 1989 OSHA put new limits on 164 substances, including grain dust and gasoline fumes, and strengthened the existing limits on 212 other substances. Until these new regulations were promulgated, the agency had issued limits on only 24 substances in the previous 17 years. Toxic materials enter the body through the eyes, the ears, the mouth, and the skin. In some instances, materials and fibers unwittingly carried home on workers' clothing have resulted in the contamination of family members.

Although some improvement has occurred, OSHA has insufficient resources for the enforcement of laws and standards regarding safety and health at the workplace. In 1988 it had only about 1,125 inspectors to cover 4 million workplaces on a regular basis (Trost 1988). Since it is currently able to conduct 70,000 inspections a year, it would take 60 years to inspect all existing workplaces just once. Also, setting standards for workers' exposure to potentially dangerous materials takes years. Since 1987 the agency has been pursuing a more aggressive policy in industrial record keeping in matters of health and safety. Since 1985 chemical industries have been required to inform workers about toxic substances present in the workplace. In 1986 the requirement was extended to manufacturers and importers, and in 1987 to all non-manufacturing industries under the jurisdiction of OSHA.

During the first half of this century, the Women's Bureau and the Children's Bureau in the U.S. Department of Labor reported regularly on the occupational health of working women and the effects of working during pregnancy on the health of mother and newborn. But these studies ended a half century later and there were no major health studies of working women until recently. Now there are a number of important studies, such as the long-term Nurses' Health Study, which has been following 115,818 women for a period of 14 years; this study has called into question the then-existing "overweight" guidelines—the risk of heart attacks was greatly increased in women who were at the high end of weight recommendations (Redefining "overweight" 1995). Other studies are addressing questions about estrogen and the health of older women, nutrition studies, exercise studies, and the like.

With the introduction of new technologies and new substances, a conflict has arisen between concern about equal opportunities for women and concern about protection from special health risks for pregnant women and their expected infants, such as miscarriage and birth defects from exposure to radiation and to toxic substances. Also few companies restrict the work of men whose partners are trying to conceive.

In their study of 54 Massachusetts electronic and chemical industries in which workers were exposed to toxic substances hazardous to reproductive health (out of a total sample of 198 companies), Paul, Daniels, and Rosofsky found that some policies overprotected women workers. Policies restricted them from work that does not represent a significant threat specially to women as a class. "For instance, one company restricted all women from any heavy lifting. . . . Women only (including pregnant women, women of childbearing age and all [other] women) were restricted from work with lead and radiation even though these exposures may present a risk to adults of both sexes as well as the conceptus" (1988:40). In contrast some restrictive policies were "under inclusive" on the assumption that only pregnant women were at risk.

> Pregnant women and women trying to conceive were restricted from work with glycol ethers, which are also strongly implicated as male reproductive hazards. In sharp contrast, none of the 54 companies with glycol ethers in use had policies or practices that restricted men from work with these substances. While such policies may protect the health of pregnant women in the short run, they cannot address the risk posed to the reproductive health of men and women before conception. (Paul, Daniels, and Rosofsky 1988:40)

A different, yet in some ways similar, issue has arisen in connection with proposals for gene screening at the workplace in order to determine the presence in workers of hereditary hypersusceptibility to the toxic effects of hazardous substances. Those who support the idea believe it will protect workers from illness and death through guiding employers' placement of their personnel in safe jobs. Those who oppose the idea believe it is racist, antilabor, an invasion of privacy, interferes with free choice, and is a means of outright or, at the least, de facto discrimination. Some suggest it is being supported by industry as an alternative to cleaning up the workplace.

Drug use at the workplace. Other kinds of health problems at the workplace are alcoholism and illicit drug use. Gray reports conflicting data on whether drug use is more prevalent in some occupations that in others (1995:801), but Anderson notes that while there are more current drinkers among white-collar people, the blue-collar jobs are at greater risk of alcohol dependence—such as workers in food service (particularly bartenders and food servers), fishers, forestry workers, machine operators, construction worker, and laborers (1995:207).

According to the National Institute on Alcohol and Drug Abuse 1 in every 6 workers is impaired by alcoholism or the abuse of illicit drugs (*NIDA Capsules* 1988). Sixty percent of the nation's top firms now have alcohol and drug abuse programs, reporting a reduction in accident claims, workers compensation claims, and health-related absences. By 1985 more than 11,000 corporations had established employee assistance programs (EAPs) for referral and counseling for familial, personal, and drug-related problems. Many are staffed by social workers, and some are operated by hospital social work staffs. Family service agencies also contract with industry to provide counseling under a company's EAP.

Fine, Akabas, and Bellinger (1982) described the social and structural characteristics of work sites that induce or support the norms and values of "cultures of drinking" on the job (as in the construction industry, or in the routine, prolonged liquid lunches of managers and professionals, often sanctioned by company policy). Such cultures create an occupational endorsement of drinking and protect or hide the vulnerable problem drinker and even exacerbate the disease of alcoholism in those afflicted. These authors described interventions that industrial or union social workers can use in helping to modify such drinking cultures.

AIDS and the workplace. About 1 million Americans are believed to be infected with HIV, the virus that causes AIDS; approximately another half million cases of AIDS have been reported, and while there may be a long latency between being infected with HIV and the appearance of AIDS, still, most of these people are of working age—from late teens to the sixties (Greeley 1995:11-12). As a new health problem at the workplace, AIDS raises many issues to be faced by employers, workers, customers, and patients. Because of the extreme variability of the disease across patients, no single answers can yet be given. The issues range from the legality of firing employees with AIDS or terminating workers who refuse to work with, treat, or serve people with AIDS, to the ethical issue of whether employers should advise workers, customers, or patients that they have an employee with AIDS. Gradually, many of the legal questions will be resolved by the courts, but it is likely that ethical issues such as the patient's right to privacy and the public's right to know will remain. For now, potential conflict exists (in such occupations as food handling and such workplaces as hospitals) between protecting the applicant or employee with AIDS or AIDS-related complex from discharge, deprivation of insurance, or other discrimination, and the legitimate business concerns and health interests of other employees (a growing concern of unions) and the public.

According to Banta (1988), the number of legal challenges of employer decisions by workers with AIDS is small, perhaps because of the reluctance of workers to declare their condition publicly, the absence of statutes, and the desire of many employers to reach equitable solutions. On the other hand, a gay rights lawyer reported that job discrimination against AIDS patients and those who are carriers of the AIDS virus is prevalent in New York City: "People are fired, asked to take the antibody test, ostracized to lower posts, or not allowed back after a hospital stay" (James 1988). In contrast, exemplary AIDS health and information programs for the workplace have been developed by some employers.

Discrimination is also believed to be rampant against employees with cancer, heart disease, and other disorders who wish to return to their job or who are applying for a job after surgery or other treatment. No federal laws protect all workers from discrimination based on health, although federal workers and others paid from federal funds are protected by the 1973 Rehabilitation Act. That legislation was originally designed to protect only persons with physical disabilities, but it is now extended to certain diseases. Additionally, a number of states have enacted laws protecting private-sector workers against discrimination because of illness. The recent legislation protecting workers with pre-existing conditions may have a major influence on discrimination against workers.

Despite the extent of occupational mortality and morbidity, few educational programs of any of the health care professions, including social work, include the issues of occupational health and safety in their curricula. The possibility that many illnesses coming to the attention of social workers in health care, union and industrial settings, family services, and so on are occupational in origin is therefore not considered. However, some sixty occupational health clinics have now been established across the country, mostly at university medical centers. In some of them, new roles are developing for social workers as the skilled gatherers of pertinent work history and workplace data, as workers' compensation advocates, and as collaborators with labor organizations, lawyers, and government officials.

The ecological nature of the workplace makes it an important site for industrial social work services, program development, advocacy, and research. Social work contributes to occupational health and safety, occupational disease clinics, union welfare programs, community support activities of business and industry, corporate programs in management and organizational development, and employee assistance programs, among other possibilities.

Job loss. At the societal level, the economic-industrial structure affects both family life and community life. Lack of work arising from job loss due to plant closings, corporate takeovers, and major layoffs—known euphemistically as downsizing or right sizing—as well as chronic unemployment and the steady loss of unskilled jobs since the 1960s have grave economic, emotional, and social consequences for the worker and all family members and for communities where unemployment is widespread.

Having less seniority, young adults with growing families are vulnerable to job loss when the local or national economy is in trouble. New economic forces are now causing many skilled and professional persons in middle adulthood to lose their jobs as well. Another position, especially at the same level, is not easily found despite laws against age discrimination. Little is known, however, of the impact of job loss or chronic unemployment on women workers, an area that awaits study. Beginning in February 1989, federal law requires employers with 100 employees or more to give their workers 60-day notification of plant closings. It also provides federal aid to the states for job training and counseling services for workers as well as for displaced homemakers and others without a place in the occupational structure (Vinokur et al. 1991; Vicary 1994).

Job loss followed by prolonged or permanent unemployment is a nonexpectable development in family life, triggering emotional turmoil in even well-functioning families. The sense of competence, self-esteem, and self-direction is damaged not only in the worker member but also in the other adult family members and the children. Hence the quality of relatedness in the family, and between family members and their social worlds, may also be strained or even damaged. If a new job is not found soon, the average family also faces economic problems (Sales 1995). Many do not earn enough to have savings, and those that have savings may soon exhaust them. The family may face a severely reduced standard of living, loss of its home or its rented dwelling (because the rent is now beyond its means), ultimate impoverishment, and even homelessness (Zigas 1993). The worker's feelings of guilt, rage, shock, despair, and shame may not be easily assuaged by supportive family members, who may gradually succumb to their discouragement and fear. These, in turn, increase the worker's negative feelings, which then increase the family's, in a recursive loop (Hurst and Shepard 1986).

Individual efforts to cope with this major stressor and the feelings it arouses affect how the family reorganizes itself. For example, widespread job loss and unemployment are associated not only with higher rates of suicide, physical illness, depression, and infant mortality but also with increased rates of substance abuse and family violence (Brenner 1984). These maladaptive attempts to cope with the stressor intensify the pain felt by all family members. Also, the children and teenagers in the family may act out their anxiety in troublesome ways, ranging from lowered academic performance to antisocial behaviors. The various maladaptive coping efforts by the adults and the children interfere with the family's needed transformation of its structure and, if not halted, can lead to family disorganization and even dissolution.

Fundamental changes in the family's structure and processes are required. The family's social reality and image of themselves as individuals and as a family are severely threatened by the loss of work, income, and status. Family loyalties, relationships, communication, role allocations, transactions with the environment, and worldview are all affected. As the tension mounts to a crisis point, the family may draw on its self-healing processes, of which the members may have been previously unaware.

In so doing, the family begins to restructure its internal world: role assignments may need to shift, so that another adult becomes the wage earner or one or both undertake job training. Others may reach a creative solution such as beginning a small business that requires little start-up money or undertaking a career change. Routines of daily living, including the use of time and space, may need to be adjusted to accommodate new demands imposed by the stressful event. The parents will need to strive for open communication between each other and with the children. Efforts to draw all the family members into the restructuring process in age-appropriate ways may be required to help the children actively manage the difficulties during the period of reorganization.

Similarly, the family's view of its external world may need to change in response to economic and industrial realities at the societal or community level. Certain expectations of the parents for themselves and for the children may need to be placed in abeyance, at least temporarily, and other, more limited goals may have to be adopted to give a more positive meaning to the struggle for reorganization. The family must also restructure its relations with the environment: a move to another location may need to be carefully weighed. Financial counseling and job counseling may be helpful. Reaching out to network connections for emotional support and for assistance in job finding is necessary. Public assistance following the expiration of unemployment benefits may be required. And perhaps the school will need to be made aware of the child's home situation, so the teacher will handle the child's upsets constructively. These last three changes may first require the resolution of conflicted issues such as shame and damaged pride.

In making these or other changes in their internal organization and in how they view and use their environment, the family creates a new paradigm and worldview oriented to a new reality that enables it to survive intact and even to improve its position. Without such changes, the family may become more and more demoralized and even disorganized, so that meeting the developmental needs of the members become extraordinarily difficult or impossible.

5

Small Groups as Contexts

The social world is arbitrarily divided into various kinds of persisting social relationships, from the interpersonal to the small group, larger groups (such as organizations), and culture. This chapter focuses on small groups as contexts for human growth and development. We consider some basic aspects of groups—their structures, dynamics, and developments. Then we discuss various kinds of psychosocial or educational groups and more briefly, treatment groups, social action groups, and administrative groups that operate within organizations to accomplish tasks.

Outline

Introduction: The Good Behavior Game

Most adults are on their good behavior most of the time, but it's difficult. There are so many temptations, so many antisocial impulses striving for expression, so many possibilities that would probably strike some people as "bad" even though we might think they were absolutely splendid. So have some sympathy for young children who are being civilized, who spend years of involuntary servitude in schools doing as their various taskmasters demand, who are, in a word, learning to be "good." Recently, in a number of public school first-grade classes in Baltimore, something new was added to the task of learning to be good (Howell 1995:64). Kellam and Rebok (1992) and Kellam et al. (1994) designed, delivered, and evaluated a behavioral classroom management technique called the Good Behavior Game to children from low- and middle-income residential areas, including neighborhoods varying in ethnic backgrounds. Forty-nine percent of the children in the study were male, and 65 percent were African American. In these classes, the teachers measured students' levels of aggression and disruption before starting the Good Behavior Game. This preintervention measure is called a baseline and is the reference point to compare changes at the end of the project. In each participating class, three teams were constructed; each contained equal numbers of disruptive and aggressive children, along with the less problematic ones. Then the teacher introduced the Good Behavior Game.

Each time a team member engaged in any disruptive behavior, the whole team received a check mark on the chalkboard. At the end of the game, just 10 minutes long at first, teams with fewer than 5 marks against them earned a reward. (Notice that these are not competitive games as such; any team can win by keeping its members from getting too rambunctious. Notice too that behavioral theorists might raise the point about this emphasis on bad behavior, since conventional behavioral wisdom says to "catch people being good, and reinforce the good behavior" is more helpful in the long run than emphasizing bad behavior. See appendix 2 on operant reinforcement.) By the end of the 1-year project, the Good Behavior Game was increased gradually to a maximum of 3 hours long. At the beginning of the project, game periods were announced and tangible awards were given immediately when the results were announced. As the project continued over the semester, the teacher began the game unannounced and provided less tangible rewards, such as getting an extra recess. Moreover, teams that won (by having fewer than 5 check marks) most often during the week received a special reward on Fridays.

The researchers used a true experimental design to evaluate program effects. Some schools in 5 urban areas in Baltimore randomly received the Good Behavior Game as their intervention, while others received an intervention involving mastery learning instruction or no intervention at all—the latter group was a pure control group. Now the researchers could compare the changes that took place in each of the 3 groups from baseline to the end of the project. These results are quite interesting and potentially important for preventive services. After 1 year, the students in the Good Behavior Game were rated as significantly less aggressive and shy by teachers and peers in comparison to the control students. The largest program effects after 1 year were found for the most aggressive students. (Compare similar results found in the Shure and Spivack [1988] studies in Philadelphia, when using an interpersonal problem-solving training program.) So it appears that by simply creating teams in classrooms and giving teams marks for bad behavior, we can bring about improvements in some basic social skills. Furthermore, by inference, we may project that reducing aggressive behavior in first-graders may have the effect of preventing later antisocial behavior (cf. Robins and Wish 1977). Surely more research is needed, including following the graduates of this program for years until they go through adolescence. But this is a most interesting idea for future programming. What is going on here? Is it telling individual children to be good that is making them act this way? Probably not, otherwise, we would have had a heavenly population by now, given all the centuries that children have received Great Lectures on Morality, in Sunday schools or their equivalent. The underlying assumption of this study suggests that influencing group structures, dynamics, and development will have a powerful effect on the behavior of members of that group. This assumption supplies the motive for this chapter.

Group Structure

You may not literally be able to see the group structure but you will be able to observe the ways a certain cluster of people are interacting with each other over time, from which you can make inferences about the set of persisting rules that each appears to be following vis-ß-vis one another. These relatively stable patterns of interpersonal behaviors and expectations about behaviors constitute the group structure. Some theorists are concerned about the connection between the relationship of a member's thoughts and feelings about the group and the group structure itself. For example, a misperception about the presumed common values of a group may cause problems for one of its members. Moreover, one person may belong to several groups, each with its distinctive sets of values; how the individual resolves these differing expectations to form his or her own unique personal identity is another complex matter. We'll return to these points when we discuss group dynamics.

We'll discuss some of the major structural features of groups—social roles, norms, subgroups, and size—because these will provide some understanding of the various types of groups described later in this chapter.

Social Roles

A *social role* is a pattern of behavior organized around the specific rights and duties belonging to a defined position in a social structure. A given person fills that role by behaving in ways the person and the other members of that social structure believe he or she should behave. This person is said to occupy a defined position in some social structure, such as a "student" or a "teacher," and thus acts according to his or her understanding of how any person should act in the same position.

Clearly, the way a person defines the rights and duties will differ in some measure, and we can expect variations in how Joe occupies the student role versus how Jane interprets that student role, even though both consider themselves students. Over time, these different interpretations on how to fulfill the rights and duties of a defined position may lead to differentiations in the social structure itself, such as emerging leadership positions. This may be because the person has unique talents valued by the group or because that person has acted in ways the group needs. Jane may move into a role of frequently answering the teacher's questions or raising new issues, which is one task or problem-solving function of being a student. Joe may move into a role of frequently cracking jokes in an attempt to reduce the tensions generated in class discussions, which is a kind of integrative or socioemotional function of being a member in that class. It is possible that Jane or Joe might both answer questions and crack jokes, but it is more difficult to serve both group functions at the same time and requires more talent from the individual to do so.

Of course, one person will likely hold many roles in a complex social system—child, student, spouse, parent, worker, friend, colleague, citizen, to name only the most obvious. Role demands of one may very well conflict or inter-fere with the role demands of another, which requires the role holder to nego-tiate and accommodate the multiple demands. This would constitute interrole conflict. However, it is also possible to have conflicting demands within one role: should I do X or Y, both obligations of my position, when I have time and energy for only one? This would be intrarole conflict. (Think of the full-time working wife who has to figure out how the household shopping and cleaning will get done, when she and her husband had formerly treated housework as woman's work—that is, woman's work for a person who wasn't employed for pay outside the house.) There is another kind of multilevel conflict that occurs between a system's role holder and any person who comes into contact with that system, such as when a tired clerk snaps at a customer and hurts the cus-tomer's feelings. The resolution of this kind of multilevel exchange is to disen-tangle the different levels: the customer should try not to take the offense per-sonally, as it really reflects a system-level problem (overwork and momentary lapse of self-control), and not a problem in the individual. In general, conflict between and among people is probably built into the human condition. As Markman et al. (1988) point out with regard to marital conflicts, it is not so important whether a couple have disputes or not, as it is how they resolve their disputes. There are better and worse ways to reduce conflict and promote coop-erative interactions, as we discuss in the group dynamics section.

When new patterns of behavior emerge, there is a corresponding change in specific rights and duties belonging to what is a new position in the group, which members of the group now begin to recognize. There is a chicken-egg dilemma as to which comes first: new patterns of behavior leading to an emer-gent role or new role demands and the emergence of new behaviors to fill them. Probably both occur simultaneously. This is a serious issue, as when an inexpe-rienced candidate for office wins; will the new person influence the role signifi-cantly or will the office influence how the person fills it? Even when the group is less structured, like a new marriage, the same question emerges: how will the personality of the newlyweds influence their new roles, and how will this new social group influence the people who are members (and sole constituents)?

Norms

A *social norm* is a standard of behavior that is defined in terms of the shared beliefs and expectations of two or more members of a group with regard to what is appropriate in some particular context. When the norm is accurately understood by all members of that group, then it functions as a set of rules for regulating the behavior of these members. Violation of the norm often produces a group reaction, possibly a sanction for "inappropriate" behavior in that group. In a positive sense, norms guide members toward "appropriate" behaviors and may reward them for what the group members believe should be done. For instance, a sports team may have norms that encourage the players to work together and "try harder." Norms "exist" apart from the members of the group and can be transmitted to new members, even as old members leave. And while norms tend to be relatively persistent, they can change when current members decide as a group to do things in a different way. For example, a street gang may take up the police department's offer to use a new sports facility as an alternative activity to gang rumbles (fights).

Subgroups

As groups increase in size and complexity, it becomes difficult for all members to participate and to have equal influence on the activities of the group, and so groups tend to form *subgroups*. Sometimes these subgroups are formed according to shared interests or talents; other times they reflect the needs of the group. In all cases, the division of labor in the larger collectivity begins to be performed by these subdivisions of the whole—and for the whole. Some of the subgroups may perform particular task functions, such as a program committee, while other subgroups may perform internal tasks to keep the group running smoothly, such as a grievance committee. These are subgroup level functions that correspond to the individual tasks and integrative functions described above.

Subgroups differ in terms of permanence. Obviously, there can be "standing committees," but temporary coalitions can also emerge to attain a particular goal that all members of the coalition share—even if they can't stand one another under normal circumstances—and that requires cooperation. For example, conservative Republicans may come together with liberal Democrats on a proposed legislation to prevent child abuse. The conservatives and liberals share the same goal, even though the former sees this as protecting the sanctity of the family, while the latter interprets this legislation as providing greater opportunity for children to grow up in a wholesome manner. There is enough of a shared interest that the two sides can work together (temporarily) for this one goal. Whether these parties could work together on future issues depends on the experience with this one and what general values are activated. However, coordination among subgroups becomes a critical issue as division of labor expands.

Group Size and Composition

It is interesting that the formal attribute of size appears to produce some distinctive possibilities regarding collective problem solving and mutual satisfaction (Simmel 1950). Let's first assume that the people involved have about the same degree of power and status, as when neighbors come together to try to resolve neighborhood conflict or when campers meet for the first time in the shared tent and have to figure out how to be tentmates for a week. Simmel hypotheses that the dyad (2 people in a relationship that is significant to them) is the most fragile of groups, but it can generate intense feelings and intimacy. The relationship in dyads may be diffuse, with no clear roles for each to follow, or it may be very precise in who is to do what, or anywhere in between.

The triad may reduce the intensity of the relationships by dividing the affect among the three members. However, a third member may exploit the differences between the other two members for his or her own benefit. Such an emergent coalition (2 against 1) may add new sources of strain, especially for the minority member. There may be further role differentiation, but the overall structure may still remain diffuse, with each member doing any and all role functions.

The 4-member group permits several forms of coalitions to form. Three against 1 presents great pressure on the one, while 2 against 2 presents difficulties in solving group problems. However, with 4 members, there can be more division of labor and a sharper definition of norms and sanctions. The 5-member group permits a majority/minority subgroup coalition, along with further division of labor and clearer norms and sanctions. Some researchers have suggested "ideal" sizes of groups for various purposes. Slater (1955) suggested that groups with 5 members were effective in dealing with complex mental tasks that required sharing of information. Osborn (1957) suggested groups with 5 to 10 members as being most effective for brainstorming groups. Others suggest the size of 5 to 7, small enough to allow everyone to talk, but large enough to have sizable minorities in coalitions (3–2 and 4–3, etc.); large enough to generate a goodly variety of ideas for problem solving, but small enough to be a satisfying group experience because members can participate more fully and feel a sense of ownership of what the group decides.

Larger groups have more opportunities for division of labor, coalition formation, and both productivity and conflict, as we saw in the discussion of organizations in chapter 3. What are coalitions in small groups may become informal groups in organizations, a kind of persisting coalition that begins to have strong influences on organizational productivity and worker satisfaction

All this discussion assumes that participants of groups are relatively equal in power. But in many circumstances, they are clearly not: adult parents and small children compose groups of unequal power, as do clients and workers, students and teachers, and many others as well. How do the characteristics of group members affect the structure and functioning of groups? Davis (1979) experimented with mixed-racial groups and found what he termed the "psychological majority" to occur with black members when they had 3 or 4 members out of 10, while white members preferred to have a distinct majority for them to feel comfortable.

If one forms a group composed of Latinos of different ages, their ages may indicate their arrival in the United States at different time periods that also reflect differences in values and level of acculturation (Queralt 1996:320). So if one assumes homogeneous values in forming a group, this assumption may not be valid in such a Latino group. Forming treatment groups with Asian Americans may lead to another set of problems because as part of their culture they may be reluctant to discuss personal feelings with strangers. Also, Asian American women who have arrived recently may find it difficult to take the initiative with men in a group (Queralt 1996:320).

The gender of group members also plays a part in how women act in groups, given the sexist orientation of many people in America. Older women may perceive themselves as lower in status than men and may resist taking the initiative when men are in a group. They may act more deferentially toward men in the group, and thus not assert themselves in any leadership roles. Younger women (or more active feminists of any age) may change all these gender-based observations. Thus in composing groups, social workers would probably do well to have an equal balance of men and women. Queralt notes that "groups balanced as to the sex of their participants have a positive effect on men; specifically, in such groups men become more personable, less competitive, and less aggressive and controlling" (1996:318).

Group Dynamics

Kurt Lewin (1951) created a scientific study of persons in groups. The main ideas from his field theory are so widely accepted today that it is difficult to reconstruct how astonishing they were more than a half century ago, when they were first met with incredulity, then stubborn resistance, and finally, grudging acceptance because of the clarity of his conceptual thinking and the soundness of the empirical research that demonstrated various of his ideas. His fundamental principle stated that human behavior was a function of the person and the environment, and that one had to consider the interaction of person and environment to understand any significant human event. Sound familiar? There are some differences between Lewin's view of the environment (usually a phenomenological view) and that of contemporary social work, but the spirit of this interactive unit of analysis is identical.

Group dynamics was the label given by Lewin's students to a new kind of applied social science, namely, the systematic study of actions and interactions of the group on its members and of the members on each other (that is, on the group). Contemporary ecological thinking essentially applies this dynamic perspective to all aspects of the human drama, from individuals, primary groups, secondary groups, communities to society and culture. Lewin probably would not disagree in principle, although he would be appalled by the looseness by which these dynamic ideas were tossed about.

Germain (1995) clearly intends her ecological perspective to be used as a metaphor, I believe, in honor of the standards of scientific construction that Lewin established. Social ecology is not a theory in the technical (i.e., Lewinian) sense, that is, specific and testable predictions cannot be logically derived from its statements. However, it can still serve a heuristic function of alerting students to the interdependence of all things and what this means in terms of a scientific-based practice (Germain and Gitterman 1995).

Group dynamics involve the study of several major group processes, including communication, leadership, decision making, cohesion, and morale. Today we are still concerned with these central processes in groups, but we have evolved from field theory to balance theory (Newcomb, Turner, and Converse 1965), systems theory (Buckley 1968), social ecology (as in this book), and a large array of theoretical positions that derive, in spirit, from Lewin's work—sometimes without due credit being given to the originator of these ideas.

Communication

We briefly describe a social communication perspective in appendix 2. Messages and metacommunications are sent to a receiver who processes the information in the context of prior experiences and expectations, and then responds with messages and metacommunications to the original sender who likewise processes these in the context of prior experiences and expectations. Communication cycles add to the experiences and expectations of the other parties in the mind of the receiver/sender; these become the norms of behavior for the roles people play in any given social group. Thus the social world is imported into the individual world, and responses by multiple individuals shape the social world.

The process of learning to speak one's native language is an especially important kind of communication, as we discuss in chapter 9. The learning of a professional language is no less important for social work students, as it involves active listening and planful communication directed toward attaining client goals (see Germain and Gitterman 1995 for a fuller development of the practice principles emerging from the ecological perspective). If one conceives of this communication interchange as part of a larger group and sociocultural dynamics, then one has made the connection between Lewin's ideas and the practical training derived from it (and other theoretical sources).

Leadership

A great deal of effort has been given to the study of leadership—and followership, communication channels between leaders and group members, the bases of power between and among persons in groups, and the like. The theoretical notion of a field of forces operating among persons in a group is useful as a guide to current thinking about leadership roles—whereas the older (non-Lewinian) notion of specific leadership traits that determine who is leader have not been supported by research. Leadership appears to be a mutual interactive relationship whereby needs communicated by group members are addressed by actions of certain members, which in turn, shape the needs communicated by the group in seeking to attain some goal. Leaders emerge out of the interaction of group processes and personal characteristics that fit at that time and place. Informal leaders may change as needs and resources change, whereas formal groups often elect or appoint their leaders, who stay in office for a set period of time in hopes that the leaders adapt effectively to changing conditions. Groups can be constructed, as in skills training groups, so that the social worker acts as leader of the group so as to solve common external problems (perhaps the members are abusive parents who are required to get parenting skills by court order) and problems common to the group itself (possibly dealing with conflicting personalities within the group). But even within constructed groups, specialists emerge under various conditions—such as the jokester who relieves tensions building up in the group, the scapegoat who gets blamed whenever the group is having problems, even the silent member who may be taking ideas from the group but who contributes little to the group process.

This conception of group leadership fits well with feminist conceptions of egalitarian relationships, where specialists emerge to help the group perform needed tasks, but the connections between facilitator and member is quite different from the hierarchical boss ordering subordinates to perform certain tasks because *he* has the talents to be leader, whereas the subordinates lack these talents. This conception of leadership also fits some of the modern organizational styles as discussed in chapter 3 (Likert 1961).

Decision Making

This third major area of group dynamics follows from the communications among members and leadership functions. Eventually, the group must decide what it is going to do and who is going to do it. Decision making relates directly to the task and integrative functions of groups, solving problems or challenges to move the group toward goals or to make the group work together more smoothly.

An important part of making decisions that facilitate group problem solving is to get the members to act in coordinated ways to accomplish a goal. For example, a social worker leads a parent skills training group, which requires participation from the members in the form of role playing and the like that presumably help the actor as well as the audience experience some challenging situation. But what if some members don't want to participate? What influence does the social worker as leader of this group have over its members? French and Raven (1959) speak about various bases of power (or influence over people to do what the leader requests, even when they do not wish to do so). The leader can give positive rewards to the cooperative members, from tangible gifts to intangible symbols like compliments; the basis of this power is on being able to mediate rewards. The leader can, in principle, cause pain (such as informing the judge that a given child-abusing client has not been cooperating in his or her education in parenting skills). The judge is the party with the legitimate power (granted by the state) to legally inflict pain; the social worker is in a sense the agent of the judge, using coercive power. The social worker may convey some knowledge about effective parenting techniques and thus exhibit what French and Raven describe as expert power. If the social worker is also personable and likable, the clients may do as he or she requests because they admire that individual and want to be liked by the worker; this is termed identification power.

Clients may use their own form of reciprocal influence attempts, even though they do not have the upper hand in this example (because of the legal requirement that they attend training sessions). However, they can attempt to ingratiate themselves to get more rewards, or they may subvert training efforts to reduce perceived coercion, and so forth. Power and its reciprocal are complex ingredients that occur throughout the time a group is problem solving or making decisions. Obviously, a person may have more than one basis of power in influencing another. Consider a mother who is trying to instruct her daughter in the rules of safe bicycle riding—the possibilities of influence based on reward, punishment, expertness, legitimacy, and identification are all present.

Cohesion and Morale

The strength of the forces attracting a member to a group is termed *cohesion*. There are various bases for this attraction—something like French and Raven's bases of power. Cohesion is the glue that holds the members together; it is a psychological glue because the group has to have value (positive attraction) for the member, and this is a state of mind for the individual. When a social worker sets up a voluntary group, what keeps members attending? A member develops strong positive feelings about the group (its goals and activities that achieve what the individual wants), wants to remain in that group (possibly for its high status and related symbols), and comes to like the other members.

When these cohesive feelings are shared by most or all of the group, then a positive group morale emerges, a positive feeling of "we-ness." An important part of this cohesiveness is an agreement with the norms and roles of the group and enactment of this agreement. Such agreements also act as pressure toward conformity with the group norms—this could be a positive or a negative result, depending on the group's values. Cohesiveness is a major measure of the healthy functioning of a group over time, as we see in the following discussion of group development.

Group Development

Groups change over time, as innumerable collective actions and reactions occur that make changes in the structure and dynamics of groups. These changes may be gradual or sudden, planned or unplanned, positive or negative in results, but eventually many quantitative changes appear to lead to qualitative changes. That is, the group structure and how it functions become different. The group remains a cohesive entity, but a changed one. There are some new goals and objectives as the group moves toward a developmental change.

None of these changes are inevitable, and there are no universal stages of group change, even though theorists have proposed some phases (Tuckman and Jensen 1977). Others have conducted research that suggests certain problems or challenges seem to be the central focus of a group at different stages of its development (Bales 1950, 1955). Both stage theories and developmental focus ideas have found their way into group work practice as suggestive notions of how the group comes to be formed, how it gets organized to deal with its task and integrative functions, how these activities cause stresses among group members, and how resolution of these tasks produce good feelings among members who then may terminate or continue as a group (see Brown 1991 for a discussion of social group work practice).

First, let's examine short-term developments. Lewin studied group change in which a change agent brought about the desired change. This kind of movement involves unfreezing a given system of roles and norms, then moving the group to some new set that is presumed to be more effective in achieving their goals, and finally refreezing the new norms and roles in place (Lewin 1951). We looked at an example of this in the work of Allen (1986) in chapter 2, when migrant workers and farm owners were enabled to reach a more effective ongoing employer-employee relationship.

Long-term developments may be illustrated by mission statements of companies and universities, and the elaborate efforts made by staff to work toward accomplishing these global objectives. Families have long-term goals, although they are rarely as specific as organizational mission statements. For example, a family may wish to provide for its children as they go through the school system, then to college, and then as they enter the workplace and possibly form families of their own. These long-term plans require many short-term cycles that move the family one step closer toward their long-term goals. Each step of the way becomes a change in the structure and functioning of the family, for example, providing encouragement for young students to study, saving large sums of money for tuition at college, and providing advice as the young adult takes his or her place in the world. We discuss these tandem changes in the later chapters of this book, recognizing that each represents developmental changes in the structure and functioning of the family and its members over time to one another and to the external events that impinge on the way the family and its members function.

Types of Groups

People are so completely socialized and social that it is inconceivable to consider human nature without embedding it in the many social contexts that make up life as we know it, from the classrooms in the Good Behavior Game project to the homes and neighborhoods where these children lived to the larger community where the teachers, researchers, and funders lived—and from which they imposed their middle-class values onto a "good behavior" game. Social scientists have categorized various portions of this social world for convenience of study, but ordinary citizens walk through this complex maze of social statuses, roles, organizations, norms, sanctions, and the like with little apparent difficulty. Even young children learn how to behave differently at school (particularly when sanctioned behaviors are so clearly identified as in the Good Behavior Game) and at home (during versus after the grandparents visit), at church or temple and at the ballpark. Yet there are problems and challenges in living in groups, as the high divorce rate, group conflicts, and institutional racism document. In this section, we describe how we distinguish portions of the social context and suggest how this knowledge may be used in developing strategies for action.

Four sets of persisting social relationships are important to human existence. The first type involves interpersonal relationships, which includes the many forms of 2-person groups—a marital couple, a parent and child (viewed separately from the rest of the family), a tutor and tutee, a relationship between old friends in which each is a confidant of the other, a worker-client relationship, and so forth. In each of these situations, ongoing communications have taken place such that each has knowledge and expectations of the other, and his or her part in that relationship. Clearly, some of these interpersonal situations are natural (in the sense that people create the relationships themselves without outside help—like friends) while others are formed or constructed (in the sense that some agency has brought the people together for specific purposes—like a client and social worker).

A second type of social context involves primary groups, those ubiquitous small groups where members hold diffuse role relationships to one another and meet frequently on a face-to-face basis to accomplish some purpose (Brown 1991). Included under this heading would be families, peer friendship groups, small work teams (such as a platoon of soldiers or a team of workers on a project), certain types of therapy groups, and a neighborhood enclave in which every one knows everyone else (and their business). What is important to helping professionals about such groups is that these are the contexts through which members receive various forms of assistance from the others and provide assistance to them as well. They exert powerful influences on individual members, and thus become another point of entr¥e, should we need to aid an individual member or the whole group.

Primary groups can also be natural or constructed. We devote chapter 6 to a discussion of the family, the primary group par excellence. In this chapter we consider the other primary groups. Following Brown's (1991) general model, we distinguish four types of groups: (1) psychosocial/educational groups whose main focus is on providing support, socialization, entertainment, education, or some combination of these, (2) treatment groups whose primary task is to facilitate behavioral and social change within the group and its members, (3) social action groups, which seek community change, and (4) administrative groups that operate within organizations to accomplish tasks. We give major attention to the first of these types of groups in this chapter.

A third type of persisting social relationship involves the secondary group or large-scale organization, which we discuss in chapter 3. These are all essentially constructed groups, some of which are designed by helping professionals for a range of service needs. For example, schools can establish Good Behavior Games as part of the overall curriculum that is supposed to prepare children to take their place in a complex society.

The fourth type of persisting social relationship illustrates the function of culture, as discussed in chapter 2. Cultural relationships, artifacts, and processes probably emerged out of small natural groupings but became institutionalized in language, art, foods, dress, and the like as groups became more numerous and more extensive. For example, migrant workers from Hispanic backgrounds share a culture that helps preserve their lives and their lifestyles as they move from crop area to crop area, merging and separating from other migrant workers.

Psychosocial/Educational Groups

Social networks. Social networks consist of relatives, neighbors, and friends, each of whom serves different functions (Litwak and Szelenyi 1969). Relatives or kin have a permanent commitment and so are appropriate providers of long-term resources, such as help during a period of unemployment (Sales 1995). Neighbors are nearby and are best able to provide short-term services and help in immediate emergencies, such as transportation. Friends, who are unlikely to have permanent commitment or to live nearby, are best able to help in matters requiring guidance, perspective, affirmation, emotional support, and feedback. Associates, such as coworkers, coreligionists, and others, may provide some short-term tangible services and degrees of emotional support; they may also be part of the person's natural helping network as described below.

Social networks serve as coping resources for dealing with life stressors and challenges. They facilitate mastery of the twin tasks of problem solving and management of feelings by providing various degrees of information and advice, emotional support, tangible aids, and selected actions. It is important to note that social networks function in both primary preventive and ameliorative situations. With primary prevention, there are the three associative functions of preventing predictable problems, protecting existing states of healthy functioning, and promoting desired goals. With amelioration, there is treatment of acute and chronic problems, as well as the rehabilitation after treatment has proceeded as far as it can go.

There is extensive information on the value of social networks. Let us give a few examples from different domains. The long-term, prospective Alameda County study (Berkman and Syme 1979) of 7,000 adults of different ages found a significant relationship between deaths from all causes and a low social network index (the number of close friends and relatives and how often they were seen each month). McKenry et al. (1990) studied 157 adolescent mothers (about three-quarters of whom were black) and found that general social support—defined by contacts with friends and relatives, religious activities, group memberships, and telephone contacts—reduced their depression at the birth of their child and 1-year postpartum. Zambelli and DeRossa (1992) report on a bereavement support group for schoolage children. Self-help groups have been developed successfully for the homeless (Marin and Vacha 1994). While there is evidence that unrelieved stress can lead to physical dysfunction, it is not yet equally certain that social support makes a difference. All that can be said so far is that social support does moderate the effects of stress and that it does appear to be positively related to health.

There are also a variety of tools to conceptualize and evaluate changes in social networks. Hartman (1978) developed an ecomap related to both formal and informal supports, in which the conflicted or nonconflicted nature of the relationships and the direction of energy flow in the connections can be shown. The ecomap is a powerful tool in social work assessment and intervention, as it helps individuals or families visualize their relationships with informal and formal support systems in a way that talking about them cannot convey; notes changes in these relationships through the passage of time or as a consequence of life events and transitions; and helps clients reach decisions about any changes they believe are needed in their present support systems or about engagements with new ones.

Figure 5.1 illustrates an ecomap. Clarice is a 26-year-old single white woman who operates a small business she recently purchased, which is fraught with financial and personnel problems. She feels empty and lonely and is continually fatigued. Suffering from chronic anxiety, she has expressed the fear that she is going "crazy." The ecomap reveals few informal or formal supports. Only one relationship shows reciprocity; the rest are conflicted for different reasons. This reciprocal relationship is with a good friend, described as the one normal person in her life. Her former boyfriend has a college degree but works at an unskilled job. He is pressuring Clarice for reconciliation. Her one employee has been a friend. This young woman often fails to show up for work and, when she is there, makes many errors. Clarice cannot bring herself to fire this person because she fears hurting her.

Clarice's parents are divorced. Her father is described as a "jerk." Her mother is described as possessive and demanding, but dotes on her daughter's young children from an earlier marriage. This doting is difficult for Clarice as she felt neglected as a child by her mother. Clarice also feels hurt and rejected by her half sister. Her grandparents died about 12 years ago. They were loving and supportive, and she misses them very much. Inquiring about the cause of death brought out the family history of diabetes. Her aunt is now severely ill with the disease, and her brother, Clarice's uncle, died of it. Clarice worries about being diabetic herself.

Natural helpers. Pancoast (1980) and Collins and Pancoast (1976) have described natural helpers as central figures in a social network or in a neighborhood who have gained recognition for their unique wisdom, resourcefulness, and caring qualities. They have achieved centrality by "playing key helping roles

FIGURE 5.1. Ecomap for Clarice

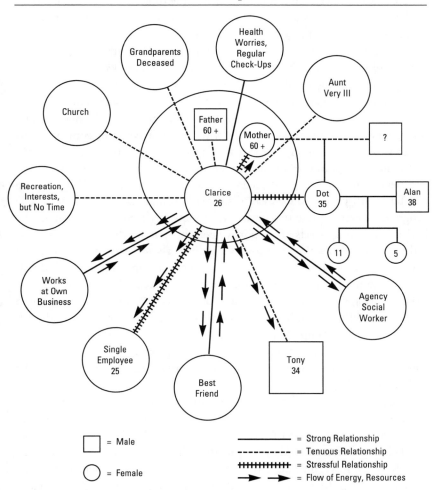

and by matching resources to need" (Pancoast 1980:114). They have numerous and rich relationships with others in the network. They may link people together who were previously unknown to each other, and they may help coordinate the efforts of others to assist someone in the neighborhood. Not every network has such a central person, but Collins and Pancoast have demonstrated how, in those neighborhoods where a natural helper is present, she or he can provide preventive support to families at risk for child abuse and neglect.

Natural helpers are often crucial in the successful management of disease suffered by chronically ill individuals and in the provision of essential respite to their families. For example, Strauss and Glaser (1975) found that strategies of illness management require the assistance of family and friends and also, at times, natural helpers who may be acquaintances or strangers. All these helpers, termed "agents" by the authors, fulfill different tasks. Some act as rescuing agents (saving a diabetic individual from dying when he or she is in a coma); protective agents (a wife agreeing to warn her husband, suffering from cardiac disease, when she senses his oncoming fatigue before he does); assisting agency (helping a kidney patient with home dialysis); or control agents (helping a patient comply with dietary, medicinal, or other regimens). We might add transportation agents, grocery-shopping agents, and so on.

Friends can also be "good medicine," as a major study by the California mental health promotion bureau discovered (Roppel and Jacobs 1988). The program objectives were to inform the citizens of the whole state about the health-promoting effects of supportive personal relationships, both for physical and mental health, to encourage individuals to invest more time and energy in their personal relationships, and to create opportunities for individuals and communities to come together to strengthen relationships. Using a mass media approach, they distributed public service announcements and a 64-page booklet containing appealing pictures, poems, exercises, and such encouraging friendship. Later research studies provide evidence that the friendship message successfully reached a large proportion of the California audience, and many of the program components were continued locally at the end of the project.

Patterson and her colleagues studied rural natural helpers ranging in age from 16 to 83 in two rural communities in the Midwest and New England (Patterson and Brennan 1983; Patterson et al. 1988). They found that rural natural helping is characterized by reciprocity—that helpers provide help to their friends, neighbors, and kin, and they themselves have been helped by those same individuals. Men tended to be doers, for example, performing farm and garden chores in the case of illness. Women tended to be facilitators, inviting emotional expression and encouraging the person's own thinking and doing. Some women and men used both styles, especially older women. For the most part, rural helpers and recipients share similar worldviews, have known each other for a long time, and often grew up together. Helpers displayed almost total spatial and temporal accessibility. They tended to reach out when they saw the need, and not wait to be asked.

Recognition is now being given to companion animals as significant natural helpers in physical illness and emotional disturbance, offering patients attention, affection, and physical contact. Pets have been used in the treatment of psychiatric patients and to relieve the loneliness of elderly persons and others. Horseback therapy is used for seriously physically disabled children, including those with muscular dystrophy, paraplegia, spina bifida, and cerebral palsy. Programs for bringing pets from animal shelters to visit patients in hospitals, nursing homes, and geriatric facilities are spreading (Curtis 1981). In addition to the services that dogs, cats, and monkeys perform for blind, deaf, and paraplegic individuals, pets of all kinds are reported to have a beneficial effect on the 1-year survival rates of coronary heart disease patients (Friedman et al. 1988).

Self-help groups. Self-help groups have skyrocketed in numbers in the past few decades. There are more than 6 million groups such as Alcoholics Anonymous (AA), Mothers against Drunk Driving (MADD), and the like. Self-help groups may be characterized as being self-constructed groups, generally without a professional creating or running the resultant group. The members themselves provide various degrees of specialized knowledge about the topic at hand, and provide the empathy, genuineness, and warmth of a natural helping system (Maguire 1991). As a member of the Crib Death Parents Group said, "I have much less guilt and I don't feel like a curiosity anymore. . . . I realized that I'm not the only person in the world who has experienced the unexplained death of a child." The rapid expansion of self-help reflects the readiness (always present, but until recently neither recognized nor acknowledged) of people in all segments of society to solve their own problems in concert with others like themselves.

Self-help groups may include several subtypes. First, are those groups that come together in order to manage a personal shared life issue and to bring about desired personal or environmental change. Such groups may be initiated by lay individuals, or professionals may being the members together at the outset. Groups may function entirely without a professional, or they may have a professional as consultant while members retain control of policy, resources, and the ongoing meetings.

Katz (1993) notes that self-help groups proliferated because individual professional helpers and therapy groups were not meeting a collective need. Or the topic of the group may be one on which professionals have had relatively little success, such as addiction, chronic mental illness, and sexual offenses. Further, under the elitist medical model, once a client's active disease has been resolved as far as possible, it becomes the responsibility of the client, family,

and friends to provide the follow-up care—something that is highly important to the client but of relatively low interest to the health care specialist. Katz
also points out the antagonism that some professional helpers extrude as they
find nonprofessionals taking over some of their "territory," and doing very
well at helping solve problems and providing comfort. Justice reports that
strong social supports enable participants to bolster their immune systems to
prevent illness (1987:127–140).

A second subtype of self-help group includes those oriented toward social
change rather than personal coping. These groups educate the public, raise
funds for research, and lobby for needed legislation on behalf of a class of
individuals (Spiegel 1982). Generally, these groups focus on local concerns
such as preventing the destruction of a local landmark to the promoting a new
bus route for the elderly and disabled. Probably this kind of group sprang
from mutual aid societies of bygone ages that offered various kinds of assistance in times of illness or provided burial services for its members. Some of
these groups started out as small, informal units geared to peer support and
experiential learning. As they grew in size, and as longtime members became
less interested in personal concerns and more interested in social change
beyond the locale in which they originated, the groups took on some characteristics of formal organizations, such as hierarchial decision making and specialized roles and functions (see chapter 3). They may also connect with like
organizations in building a statewide or national association—at which point
they are no longer primary groups as discussed in this chapter.

A third type of self-help group is the resource-exchange network, such as
local food co-ops, day care co-ops, neighborhood improvement associations,
and groups that help members explore new interests and learn how to be self-
directing for greater fulfillment, such as feminist groups (Lenrow and Burch
1981), retired persons teaching in "senior universities," and the like. This type
of self-help group involves the exchange of tangible goods, intangible services,
or both. There are barter groups—"you cut my lawn and I will type your
paper"—and labor exchanges, which involve the circulation of services among
a group of persons through a credit system—"I earned credits for reading to
a blind student, and I want to use these credits to pay for someone else to wash
my windows." In communities where money is scarce or in devalued communities, these kinds of resource exchanges may be a very important structural element that could be promoted by helping professionals. For example,
baby-sitting exchanges arranged with student-parent groups or the provision
of supportive services for current AIDS victims that would enable a recent
HIV positive person to stockpile credits for his or her future assistance.

Through group processes the members are gradually empowered by gaining information and rediscovering their own capacities. This is another example of the circular causal loop of community-family-friends-individuals transactions identified by Pinderhughes (1983) and discussed in chapter 1. As resource-exchange networks grow, they may become mutual aid societies where the exchanges have to be put on a more formal basis because of the size and nature of the group.

Self-help groups and mutual aid associations not only fit the worldview of various cultural groups in pluralistic North American society but also are a significant force for the empowerment of impoverished or devalued communities. No matter what the groups may later accomplish, most start out from a disempowered position. They lack needed resources, social respect, opportunity, or all three. Through group processes the members are gradually empowered by gaining information and discovering their own capacities. As the individuals and the group are empowered, the community itself gains in power in the circular causal loop mentioned above.

Treatment Groups

We briefly describe treatment groups, as they are not a usual part of normal development, although they may be very useful in periods of acute stress or to prevent predictable problems. The main purpose of treatment groups, Brown notes, is personal change through therapy (1991:47). Group treatments have group changes as their main purpose, such as in family therapy where changes in all members (not just the identified client) are likely goals in order to resolve the presenting and evolving problems. Either kind of group may make use of the group per se as a vehicle for the change or may simply employ the group setting as a convenient way to deal with individuals on an individual basis.

Reflecting the newer ideas about the nature of group leadership, Brown states that "treatment groups are most effective when group members are able to share leadership, either by offering support to others, by providing information, or by offering feedback to those in the group about the meaning and effects of their behavior." He goes on to discuss when the social worker (group leader) should encourage this shared leadership role and when he or she should become more directive: "A therapeutic relationship based on caring, respect, and empathic listening should be fostered, although group workers may become more directive if members with many deficits cannot assume indigenous leadership" (1991:48).

Social Action Groups

Again, we provide only a brief introduction to the topic of social action groups. In this instance, a small group may be organized to address large issues that affect considerable numbers of people (including many not in the present group). The efforts of social action groups, like the early social work reformers, are directed toward perceived social problems and (sometimes) suggested solutions, for example, the status of the poor, unhealthful or nonexistent housing, poor quality of public education, lack of health insurance, and harm being done to innocent people in the changes in welfare laws.

Like any social problem, a concern first has to come to public awareness as to its seriousness and its extent; then it has to be put on the social agenda for seeking a solution; and then preventive or ameliorative actions have to be taken, with some quality control as oversight. We discuss in chapter 2 the activities (or inactivities) of various groups in attempting to make people aware of the AIDS epidemic and the various implications in attempts to prevent its spread. Some groups were specifically formed to lead in the social action, while others were "borrowing" time and energy from their other duties to make people and decision makers aware of the seriousness of the problem.

When the problems are large scale, social action groups may have to form collaborative arrangements with groups seeking similar ends. Coalitions among friendly (or even once-unfriendly) agencies requires additional time and energy to make the cooperative effective. Conflicts emerge, related or unrelated to the task at hand, and some energy and time are lost addressing these conflicts. But there is an economy of scale, and when the problem is large and long lasting having an organizational unit that can mobilize proportional energies over long periods of time is useful.

Administrative Groups

Briefly, an administrative group is used to coordinate and facilitate other groups, usually within one large organization, or in the case of social action groups, across organizations dedicating part of their efforts to a shared cause. The purpose of administrative groups is to facilitate the task of the collaborative effort while they see to the integrative functions of coordinating several different groups. Usually, the administrative group's entire effort is directed toward the one shared cause, while the member groups have this and other tasks to be served.

Member groups may have formed themselves into a collaborative effort, or the administrative group may have acted to bring various groups on board a specific shared effort that no one of them could do on its own. The member groups may be committed to the shared task to a large degree or small degree—but large enough to join and contribute. It is difficult to gain as much cooperation from the individual representatives of the group members as the administrative staff believes is necessary, probably because of the divided attention the individual representatives have. They probably continue some of their old duties and suspend others while they take on new (usually temporary) duties. This puts role strains on them, and these strains accumulate for the administrators of the collaborative effort. Clearly, this administrative group needs the backing of all the relevant members of the component groups, as well as of the administering organization.

Less formally, various organizations may form a working team to address a specific issue. Brown notes that members of the team may represent different specialties, but each contributes to the overall goal. "There may be a coordinator who maintains responsibility for the functioning of the team, but the leadership is usually shared" (1991:56).

6

Families as Contexts

While we have all experienced life within one kind of family or another, the term "family" is a center of controversy, with the differences of opinion having important policy, practice, and personal significance. This chapter considers the variety of definitions that abound, and then addresses family functions and family forms to illustrate why we have so many definitions of what is a family.

Outline

Introduction

What Is a Family?

Family Functions

Family Forms

    Nuclear Families—One Provider

    Nuclear Families—Two Providers

    Solo-Parent Families

    Blended Families

    Extended Families

        Spanish-speaking families

        Black families

        American Indian families

        Asian American families

        Communal families

        Lesbian and gay families

Family:Environment

Introduction

The justice of the peace who married them in two brief back-to-back ceremonies thought they were a particularly attractive set of couples, Betty and
Bill, June and Jim, and regretted that their families and friends weren't there
to witness the happy events. The four young people drove back to the city and
to the house they were buying together, since no one of these young yuppies
could afford to do so alone. They had been living together in a seedy apartment building for about a year before they decided to get married and buy the
house. During this time, they had long philosophical conversations on the
state of society and had come to recognize that they shared some common (or
rather, uncommon) values, and they began some discussions about the future
that none of them would have predicted from what they had known about
themselves and their partners.

Hand in hand, Betty and Bill, and June and Jim, happily opened the front
door of their new home. Once safely inside, Bill and Jim when to one set of
rooms, while Betty and June went to another, to consummate their official
marital status, one which gave them numerous fiscal and social advantages,
even though these came with a price that many young couples did not have
to pay. The homosexual couples shared the housework and the various
expenses and had vibrant discussions over their occasional common meals
together, but they also led very happy private lives with their partners. Betty
and June wanted to have children, and while Bill and Jim were not especially
eager to become parents, they willingly obliged their housemates. Soon there
were two infants at the house. Some rearrangements were made to give the
women more room and to outfit the basement as a play area; these arrangements were willingly made, and the men participated in avuncular fashion
with considerable enthusiasm. In fact, Bill was quite a taskmaster when it
came to teaching and modeling moral values. "Kids have got to see values in
action in order to learn good values," he asserted. "You can't just lecture kids
to do what you say, and not do what you do." (Patrick and Minish [1985]
would concur in these judgments of how altruistic values get conveyed to children.) "Thank you , Janice, for sharing your truck with Ben," Bill said when
the situation offered the opportunity.

When preschool arrangements were made, Ben was identified as Betty and
Bill's handsome son; Janice was the beautiful daughter of June and Jim. No
questions asked. (Have you ever been asked to produce your wedding certifi-
cate to prove you were married?) Unfortunately, the work Jim was doing was
in an industry that had sharp downturns, so Jim was forced to look for a new

job in another city. He commuted back home frequently at first, then with less frequency as costs and involvements in the new location took precedent. Bill was quite depressed at first, but became more involved with the children and eventually with a new friend, Ricardo, who moved into the house. Four-year-old Janice thought Ricardo was the cat's meow and fawned all over him—much to his amazement and delight. Ben eyed him with suspicion, but eventually was won over because Ricardo had a wonderful set of woodworking tools that he let Ben use, under careful supervision. June and Betty were so pleased at how the children were developing; they continued to make plans for summer vacations (to visit grandparents who eventually if gingerly got used to their grandchildren) and to get advanced degrees (first, one of them, then the other, so they would always have at least one full-time income) in order to have more options in employment. So life in this busy two-family household continued in its merry if unconventional way.

What Is a Family?

The family is the most intimate and influential environment in which human development takes place, yet there is much controversy over the exact meaning of the term. In times past, the family was commonly regarded as a group of persons related by blood or legal marriage, living together, and cooperating economically and in child rearing. As recently as 1974, Ball pointed out that this definition rules out childless couples, unmarried cohabiting couples, same-sex partners with or without children, one-parent families, and some extended families where the kin are fictive—"pretend relatives" or ritual kin, such as the *compandrazos* of Hispanic cultures, or in any ethnic group and across socioeconomic status, parents' good friends known as "uncle" or "aunt" to the children.

Among all groups sometimes an older person and a younger person (and perhaps the latter's child) may live together yet be unrelated and not have sexual encounters with each other. Kellam (1975) empirically distinguished dozens of distinct compositions of families living in the Woodlawn area of Chicago. The U.S. Biennial Census has to have a fixed and abstract definition of family and household so as to count the numbers of groups of various sorts and to compare these results over time. Here is how the census defines these terms:

> The term "family" refers to a group of two or more persons related by birth, marriage, or adoption, and residing together in a household. . . .

A "household" comprises all persons who occupy a "housing unit," that is, a house, an apartment, or other group of rooms, or a single room that constitutes "separate living quarters." A household includes the related family members and all unrelated persons, if any, such as lodgers, foster children, wards, or employees who share the housing unit. A person living alone or a group of unrelated persons sharing the same housing unit is also counted as a household.

Hartman and Laird present a definition of family that may be useful in capturing two major categories of families. The first is the biologically rooted family of origin, into which one is born, which may include adopted members and fictive kin. This is the "family of blood ties, both vertical (multigenerational) and horizontal (kinship), living or dead, geographically close or distant, known or unknown, accessible or inaccessible, but always in some way psychologically relevant" (1983:30).

The other category is the current family constellation (structure) in which people have chosen to live. This family

> consists of two or more people who have made a commitment to share living space, have developed close emotional ties, and share a variety of family roles and functions. This family may consist of a middle-aged married couple whose children are reared; two elderly sisters, one a widow and the other a spinster, who share an apartment in a retirement community; a group of biologically related and unrelated adults and children who have formed a group of communal family in which a range of commitments exist and in which instrumental and expressive roles are shared.
>
> (Hartman and Laird 1983:30)

It may also consist of a same-sex couple with or without children from a prior marriage of one or both partners. This definition would encompass the Bill-Betty-Jim-June-Ricardo-Ben-Janice group described above.

In their definition Hartman and Laird took "a phenomenological stance in saying that a family becomes a family when two or more individuals have decided they are a family, that in the intimate, here-and-now environment in which they gather, there is a sharing of emotional needs for closeness, of living space which is deemed 'home,' and of those roles and tasks necessary for meeting the biological, social, and psychological requirements of the individuals involved." They go on to note that the future may view these many emerging family forms as functional adaptations, or solutions to the problems and challenges of the changing environment, rather than blame-the-victim problems in and of themselves (1983:30, 31).

Family Functions

Most students of the family include in its functions some of the following: the legitimation and regulation of mating and sexual relations; the procreation of children and child rearing; the socialization of all members into gendered (or nongendered) roles and other social roles valued by the society or cultural group; economic maintenance and household management, including the division of domestic labor; structures for authority and decision making about major and minor choices in family life; the transmission of the culture, including language, norms, value orientations, and belief systems; and the provision of connective links to the larger environment needed for the optimum development and functioning of all members throughout the life course.

Given the variations among cultures and subcultures, the accelerating rate of social change, and the emergence of new theories and knowledge about the family, it is unlikely that wide agreement will be found on any one of the above items or on desirable additions and deletions. For example, the assumption that the procreation of children is a definitive function of the family no longer holds, given the growing number of young couples choosing not to have children at all. Among families with children, the function of early child rearing is being increasingly shared with community day care facilities as mothers of infants and of children under school age enter the labor force in growing numbers. "More than 10.5 million American children under the age of 6, including 6.6 million infants and toddlers under the age of 3, have mothers who work outside the home. Another 18 million children 6–13 years of age have working mothers" (Alexander 1992).

Some functions were lost over time to other social institutions, although some were later reclaimed. For instance, early in the twentieth century, the family lost to the formal health care system its function of birthing and of caring for the ill and the dying. In recent years, some families have reclaimed these functions: more births take place at home or in homelike settings with family members often present, and many terminally ill patients die at home.

Sometimes a lost function is replaced by new ones. An interesting example of this is education. The nineteenth- and twentieth-century laws on compulsory education and the publicly supported school system practically ended the family's formal role in educating children. Recently, there has been a resurgence in some families educating their children at home (but under strict state laws). Estimates of numbers involved in home schooling differ but range from 350,000 to 500,000 (Kaslow 1996; D. Hawkins 1996). Parents may also take part in formal contacts with the schools and informally through parent-teacher associations.

As discussed previously, school systems are facing many pressures with reductions of resources, particularly in economically impoverished areas. Comer (1988; Comer et al. 1996) has demonstrated that it is possible to energize families, schools, children, and the community to invest in quality education. His model project involved two poor schools with 99 percent black student body and achievement and attendance rankings near the bottom of New Haven city schools. "There were serious problems with attendance and discipline. The staffs were discouraged; their turnover rate was 25 percent. Parents were dejected, distrustful, angry, and alienated" (Comer 1988:44). What Comer and his colleagues found was a profound sociocultural misalignment between home (poor, black) and school (middle class, white). Children from these families are likely to enter school without adequate preparation or the social skills for negotiation and compromise, reflecting the historical background of slavery and postslavery that disadvantaged generations of blacks. However, Comer notes that schools remain the hope of alienated black families, in spite of their structural rigidities in responding to underdeveloped or differently developed students.

Comer's project suggests that the key to academic achievement is "to promote psychological development in students, which encourages bonding to the school. Doing so requires fostering positive interaction between parents and school staff, a task for which most staff people are not prepared" (1988:46). So Comer set up a governance and management team of a dozen people led by the principal and composed of elected parents and teachers, mental health specialists, and a member from the nonprofessional support staff—all stakeholders in the outcome. This team made decisions on general academic and social programs, down to specific procedures that were causing problems in the school. Parents were paid to be classroom assistants; teachers and parents had potluck suppers, book fairs, and other social gatherings that fostered good school-home communications. Special programs were constructed as needed, such as a Discovery Room for turned-off students; a Crisis Room was set up for children who were temporarily out of control. "With each intervention, the staff was becoming increasingly sensitive to concerns of developing children and to the fact that behavior problems result mainly from unmet needs rather than from willful badness—and that actions can be taken to meet these needs" (Comer 1988:48).

Comer's program produced significant academic, attendance, and behavioral gains, going from the bottom to near the top of the charts within a half dozen years. Cauce, Comer, and Schwartz (1987) used an experimental–control design involving randomly selected students in carefully matched schools and reported that those who experienced the School Development Program were significantly higher in language, work study, mathematics, and overall mean grade equivalent, compared to those who did not have this experimental intervention. Other studies showed improvements in self-concept, classroom and school climate, attendance, group participation, and attitudes toward teachers (Comer et al. 1996). A few years later, the project left the schools with its program fully integrated into the social and academic structures. Since that time, Comer's work has been used in more than 50 other settings around the country, all suggesting the need to made solid connections between family and school.

The problems schools now face have a familiar historical ring. Great waves of immigrant and refugee families have often come to the United States—we are indeed a nation of immigrants. These immigrants have always faced a bewildering array of language, cultures, and demands—and most have succeeded in mastering these challenges. Immigrant parents may learn the language and customs of the new country from their children, although this may lead to family conflicts because of the power it gives children over their parents. Another kind of family conflict may emerge when the mores from the old country conflict with the mores of the new country. For example, Cherry and Redmond (1994) describe the situation of recent immigrants from Afghanistan where the elders followed abstemious Muslim practices, while their children had to face an alcohol-saturated American culture and all the peer pressures to drink. It is difficult to resolve such conflicts. Children inevitably learn from their parents, grandparents, and great-grandparents—often the custodians of the family's history, cultural values, traditions, and rituals—just as the older generations may have to learn something about the new host culture from their younger family members. Another example is child-rearing practices; when immigrants to a new nation use old culturally accepted techniques (such as leaving one's infant in the care of a young sibling), they face the fact that the new nation's laws consider such actions as maltreatment, and they will be subject to police action. Survival as an immigrant in a new nation may involve preserving the core values and actions of the old culture and dealing flexibly with the peripheral ones, but only when the laws of the new nation are not violated. Immigrants have to conform to the laws of the new land.

Whatever functions a particular culture assigns to its families, an arrangement of statuses and roles is needed for carrying out those functions and their associated tasks. Such arrangements are referred to in this book interchangeably as the family's organization, form, or structure. Probably the most striking feature of American families today is the remarkable variety of their forms. The next section describes several prevalent family forms as we enter the twenty-first century.

Family Forms

Nuclear Families—One Provider

Until quite recently, many clinicians and students of the family assumed that a new type of two-generation family, consisting of two parents and their children, had begun to spread with the start of the Industrial Revolution in the early nineteenth century. It was further assumed that before then, agricultural or peasant families tended to live in extended-kin households. Most also believed that by the twentieth century, the family consisting of father-breadwinner, mother-homemaker, together with one or more dependent children, was the dominant structure in the Western world. This so-called nuclear family was assumed also to be separated from kinfolk by distance, upward mobility, or norms of autonomy and independence. The nuclear family structure was presumed to be the dominant and "normal" form by social scientists, human service professionals, the media, other social institutions, and the American public.

Myths abound in these assumptions. First, contemporary historians of the family have discovered that the nuclear form prevailed in England and western Europe long before the onset of industrialization. Probably it was only the wealthy and powerful who lived in large, extended households. The nuclear form was brought to America by the first colonists. The assumption that agrarian Americans lived in extended-kin families is unfounded, although it is true that at times an elderly, infirm parent might move back to the home or farm of an adult child. This arrangement was not frequent because the life course was much shorter than it is today. However, extended-kin networks currently serve as support systems to many so-called nuclear families. Even when geographic distances are great, contact is maintained by telephone and rapid transportation facilities. It is said that today many of us are housed in nuclear units but live in extended networks.

Second, the nuclear unit has been steadily declining in number and percentage of total families. The proportion of "traditional" families went from 35 percent in 1980 to 23 percent in 1991 (Barron 1992). "More than 40 percent of today's young adults [in the United States] spent at least some time in a single-parent family by age 16" (Zill and Robinson 1995).

Third, while the nuclear family was prevalent even before industrialization, few such families then or later represented the idealized form of father-bread-winner and mother-homemaker. The fact is that in agricultural societies, women and children performed farm labor along with the father. Changes in the social order due to industrialization and urbanization meant that many poor and working-class wives and mothers worked in cottage industries or outside the home in sweatshops, domestic service, factories, and offices instead of in the fields. In middle- and upper-class households created by industrialization, however, many wives and mothers were freed from labor inside and outside the home. Instead, they were expected to be the source of emotional support for the other family members and to make the home a refuge from the outside world. The nuclear family, or father-breadwinner and mother-homemaker. was a reality only in these classes. "It was only in the 1920s, for the first time, a majority of children were born to male-breadwin-ner, female-homemaker families" (Coontz 1996:40). In the 1950s, after many economic and social ups and downs, American society reached the highest percentage of male-breadwinner, female-homemaker families—60 percent—and it is the most atypical decade in our history of American marriages, even though it is idealized in terms of family values. Today, with high percentages of dual-worker families, it is unlikely that we will ever return to the days of Ozzie and Harriet, the quintessential radio family of that era.

Beginning in the 1880s and continuing through the 1950s, the few highly educated, married middle-class women who worked typically withdrew from the workforce when their first child was born. If they returned to work, it was not until the last child was in school full time or out of the home altogether. For most wives at that time, the husband's career took precedence, and the wife's was merely temporary until she took her "proper place" in the home and reared the children.

Nuclear Families—Two Providers

This picture of a single breadwinner changed rapidly beginning in the 1960s. Growing numbers of middle- and upper-middle-class women entered the labor market as the educational level, expectations, and roles of women changed, opportunities increased, and social pressure on mothers to remain at home lifted. Facing family needs in an inflated economy, many more working-class mothers of very young children entered the labor market as well. These situations generated the condition of families with two providers. African American women had been in the labor market, usually as domestics, agricultural, or factory workers, for many decades prior to this time.

By 1991, 48 percent of U.S. families were composed of dual-worker families—families with both parents in the labor force. Barron reports that these changes have paralleled the labor force participation by mothers; 67 percent were employed in 1991, which was 10 percentage points higher than in 1980, and 45 percentage points higher than in 1950 (Barron 1992:789).

Although traditional norms for gender roles are changing, in most two-provider families the overall responsibility for child care and care of the elderly, along with household management, still falls to the mother, at the expense of leisure and sleep time (Bianchi and Spain 1984). Kline and Snow (1994) present an interesting study of working mothers who faced these multiple pressures. A work site skills training program helped to reduce stress on the job, but it was unable to make much impact on stresses at home.

In considering two-provider families, it is useful to distinguish two family forms. First, in two-worker families, jobs for both parents are a necessity rather than an option, particularly in the blue-collar and lower-middle classes. Since the 1960s their numbers have increased sharply as mothers of preschoolers—about 57 percent of them in 1992 (Zlotnik 1995:339)—have entered the labor market because of the rising cost of living and of raising children and because opportunities in service occupations have increased with the advent of affirmative action. Two-worker families will also be true of persons formerly on welfare since minimum-wage jobs may not be enough to support the family. Probably the jobs of most two-worker families are relatively inflexible regarding working hours and individual discretion, so that staying home with a sick child may result in loss of a job. Two-worker families may have to make do with juggling schedules (including working two different shifts), compromising needs, or just letting things slide, all of which imposes stresses on the family.

Second, two-career families with preschoolers, a relatively recent phenomena, is associated with a changing perspective on the status and roles of women brought about by the women's movement. The change is related to greater numbers of women entering higher education and professional education, smaller family size, and women's awareness of their increased life expectancy and of their vulnerability arising from the high rate of divorce. A career presents a new and higher social status and role for middle-class women, many of whom now aspire to both a career and motherhood. Because of an inflated economy and costly lifestyles among young, well-educated adults, many two-career families also feel a financial need for two incomes. Having relatively high financial resources, it is possible for two-career families to purchase quality child care, housekeeping services, and dining out. It may be easier for them to make arrangements with their employers in order to cover unanticipated family emergencies.

Two-career families (and to a lesser extent, two-worker families) may also need to live apart in order to accommodate jobs at distant work sites. Such commuter families miss the innumerable family occasions that one-location families take for granted—what new words the baby has said, the funny ad on TV, the welcomed massage after a sorely trying day. It is not known how many of the 20 million two-career or two-provider families consist of commuter couples, but estimates range from 500,000 to 2 million.

It is important to note that more than 40 percent of full-time homemakers do not wish to work outside the home (Zlotnik 1995). Despite the socioeconomic pressures to do otherwise, full-time homemakers may greatly value the opportunity to raise their children themselves. They find this role to be of enormous social and societal value, whether or not it is recognized fully by contemporary society. Social workers and other service providers have to be careful about promoting their own work-outside-the-home values; they should not assume that a homemaker would rather be working for pay. Taking an ecological perspective on this issue, we need to ensure that both the person and the social environment understand the opportunities and the demands of the dual situation, and accommodate to the mutual satisfaction of each party to the extent possible.

Solo-Parent Families

There have always been some U.S. families headed by a solo parent because of death (especially during the seventeenth, eighteenth, and nineteenth centuries and the early decades of the twentieth), desertion, separation, or divorce. However, in the 1970s and 1980s, the number of solo-parent families in all segments of the population increased at a rapid rate across racial, ethnic, religious, and socioeconomic groups. No longer is death the major cause of solo parenting; divorce, separation, desertion, and unmarried teenage parenthood account for most of it. Zigler and Gilman report some very disturbing facts:

One in 4 children will grow up for some part of their lives in a single-parent home. For black children, this ratio is about 1 in 2. Ninety-six percent of these households are headed by a women. Moreover, the median annual income of young families (headed by people under age 30) has been getting lower in the past few decades. Between 1973 and 1990, the median annual income of these young families fell by 32 percent, and child poverty rates for these families doubled, from 20 to 40 percent. Had women not gone to work, these figures would have been much worse (1996:95–96).

These figures explain the "feminization of poverty" (and the childization of poverty, in Queralt's [1996] apt phrase) since women raising families alone have more limited earning power and fewer economic options than men. Women and their children are often thrust into poverty as a consequence of divorce and separation, while men often benefit financially. Weitzman's (1985) study of divorced families found that in the year after the divorce, the standard of living of the mother and children fell greatly while that of the husband rose considerably. More recent research corrects the details of Weitzman's original findings: it now appears that divorced women's standard of living fell an average of about 30 percent, while men's rose about 10 percent, regardless of whether the divorce occurred under no-fault or fault conditions (Faludi 1996:10). About 45 percent of families enter the welfare system as a result of divorce; another 30 percent enter after having a child out of wedlock (Lieberman 1995), including about 57 percent of black children, 23 percent of Hispanic children, and 17 percent of white children born in 1990 (Bradley 1995).

The most severe impact of divorce was experienced by older homemakers and women with young children. Of noncustodial fathers who are required by the court to pay child support, 55 percent do not pay the full amount, and 25 percent pay nothing at all (Peters 1993:719–720). Five billion dollars in court-ordered support went unpaid (Moral issues 1994:22). Most divorces occur relatively early in marriage (one half in the first seven years), when the children, if any, are very young. (See Stevenson and Black 1996, for recent research on how divorce affects children.)

One-parent families, whether headed by one of 18 million mothers or by one of 1 million fathers, face the same external and internal tasks as two-parent families but without a partner to share them. It is not impossible to perform all these tasks and to perform them very well; it is simply much more difficult to do. Many of the women face additional exceptional tasks posed by poverty, racism, and sexism, by the solo parent's need both to work and to care for children, by the lack of jobs and equitable pay, and by the lack of adequate formal arrangements to support family functioning. Some without informal supports also experience social isolation and loneliness.

Probably most one-parent families adapt by forming friendships and continuing associations with family members and fictive kin, who may be able to provide some of the respite needed by the solo-parenting adult, as well as being role models for the children. Moles concludes his study of the school performance of children from one-parent families by noting that "evidence . . . indicates that children in one-parent families have somewhat lower school performance—especially their grades, achievement test scores, and attendance—but that the family's socioeconomic status has a much larger influence on school performance than the absence of a father" (1992:117).

In a time of rapid social change and with "the end of welfare as we know it," U.S. society is being faced with important challenges in how to enable all children to grow up to be healthy, happy, and productive citizens—what we would term overall personal and social goals. Welfare-to-work may be one path, provided the entire ecology of components are in place: a person trained, motivated, and acculturated to the world of work; an environment sensitive to the strengths and limitations of new workers as well as the ordinary demands of production and distribution. The likely role for social work during this period is to support the range of policies and programs that encourage personal responsibility to the fullest extent possible, family functioning to the highest level attainable, quality day care at affordable costs and accessible locations, adequate health care, suitable education, including adult remediation as needed, and the like. This would be an enormous social program, but "wars on poverty" are not likely to reemerge in the near future. Rather, the helping professions might better address the specific details of a strategy to encourage the strengths of individuals and social environments while seeking to reduce the limitations of both parties so as to attain overall personal and social goals. This would not require national policy developments, but rather state and community action programs. Successful experiments at the state level may eventually influence nationwide actions.

Blended Families

The blended-family form is also referred to as the remarried family, the stepfamily, or the reconstituted family. While it existed over historical time because of shorter life spans, its numbers have grown in recent decades in response to the increasing rates of divorce and the greater social acceptance of divorce and remarriage. About 1 out of every 3 Americans belongs to a stepfamily, and if present trends continue demographer Paul Glick predicts the proportion will increase to almost 50 percent (cited in McCord 1993:156). About 70 to 75 percent of women and 80 to 85 percent of men eventually remarry, most of them rather quickly (five years after their divorce) (Bray 1995:50). Unfortunately, the divorce rate for subsequent marriages is higher than for the first marriage, unless the couple make it through the first year of remarriage, in which case the rate of divorce is about the same as first marriages.

> Typically, men are likely to be remarried seven times faster than women. Indeed, from 1970 [to] 1980 there was a drop of 30 percent in the remarriage rate for women. Three-quarters of women who divorce eventually remarry, but they spend longer periods of time as single parents, and compared to men, fewer divorced women are remarried. The chances for remarriage are significantly reduced as women age. Moreover, black women have fewer chances for remarriage than any other group. (Wattenberg 1986)

It is important to note that only the adult partners get divorced; children remain the children of both parents regardless (Skeen, Covi, and Robinson 1985). Sometimes both partners bring children to the new; sometimes the other partner is childless or the children are in the custody of the other parent. Those children may visit the remarried family either occasionally or not at all, depending on the custodial agreements, proximity, and so on. Children living in the new family not only have a new stepparent but may also have stepsiblings, stepgrandparents, and other adult kin who may or may not accept the new parent or the children as relatives. These children may also have new neighbors, a new school, and perhaps a quite different way of life. To complicate the structure and relationships even more, the new parents may have a child or children together, who are then half siblings to all the other children. On the one hand, possibilities for individual and family identity confusion, jealousy, conflict, and divided loyalties are rife; on the other, the potential exists for extended-kin support, loving relationships, a cohesive family life, and the emotional growth of all members.

The major differences between nuclear families and blended families have been summarized by Wald (1981) and Skeen, Covi, and Robinson (1985): First, the "wicked stepmother" cultural myth persists to some degree and leads to self-fulfilling prophecies that being a stepfamily is somehow less desirable than being a biological family. The very term "step" has a negative connotation. But the facts are not as bleak as the myth suggests for the more than 6 million children under 18 living in blended families. Second, some children tend to fantasize the reunion of their parents, thus leading to resentments of the stepparent. Third, sibling rivalries may be aggravated between stepsibs, since critical decisions have to be made about where to live, what names to call the stepparent, and how to handle loyalties to other relatives. Fourth, in the nuclear family, the marital tie precedes the parent-child tie, whereas in the blended family each adult partner may have children from a previous marriage. Thus there is a built-in imbalance in the ties shared by the newly remarried couple toward the children—his, hers, theirs—that they are to parent. Fifth, the already developed rules, norms, customs, and routines that shaped each family's evolved patterns of relating, communicating, decision making, spending, and disciplining have to be reconsidered in the remarriage. This leads to a potential for clashes in lifestyles. Also, depending on each family's experiences as a solo-parent family before remarriage, there may be other sources of potential conflict. Issues such as whether support continues from the noncustodial parents, custody arrangements and visiting times for all the families and relatives involved, and the possibility of yet other divorces and remarriages lead to many possible supportive resources or problem relationships.

Hetherington, Cox, and Cox (1982) and Skeen, Covi, and Robinson (1985) offered some useful advice for stepparents that we adapt here:

1. Provide some neutral territory so each family member can have a special place he or she can call his or her own.
2. Avoid trying to fit any preconceived role, but be kind, intelligent, and a good sport. Don't expect instant love; earn it; it takes time. Be patient.
3. Parents (and children to the extent possible) should work out the rules of the house that establish rights and responsibilities; these should be enforced and parents should support each other in doing so.
4. Allow children to vent feelings for the natural parent (and against the stepparent), but within reasonable bounds. The child has some responsibilities as well as rights. Expect ambivalent feelings, which are normal.
5. Maintain the primacy of the marital relationship. Some stepparents spend too much time and energy trying to resolve all the blended family problems and neglect their own relationship.

Extended Families

Among immigrant populations in the late nineteenth and early twentieth centuries, extended kin tended to cluster together in one dwelling, as in the case of three generations living together, or in separate dwellings close by in the case of other relatives. To a degree, this pattern continues today among some Italian Americans, Polish Americans, and other white ethnic groups. American Indian and black families typically have extended-kin structures, as do the more recent arrivals: Puerto Rican, Mexican American, and Asian American families. When public housing policies do not permit an extended family to all crowd into one unit, they may preserve safety and sanitation but they undermine significant natural systems of support just when the immigrants are more in need of support for the tasks of cultural and geographical transition. This kind of policy limitation with regard to immigrants is added to racism, poverty, unemployment, and limited culturally congruent formal resources (Mizio 1974).

Spanish-speaking families. Puerto Rican, Mexican American, and Central and South American Spanish-speaking groups are traditionally embedded in kinship systems (including kin and fictive kin) of reciprocal support and obligation. Cubans are less so. Such cultural patterns may be stronger in some families than in others, depending on how long they have resided in the United States (the mainland United States in the case of Puerto Ricans), the nature of their experiences with its culture and its rewards and sanctions, their socioeconomic status, their rural or urban origins, and other variables. In Hispanic cultures kinship consists not only of related kin but also of non-kin tied to the family through custom. For example, in Puerto Rico *Compadrazgo* refers to "companion parents," a ritual kin network

> whose members have a deep sense of obligation to each other for economic assistance, encouragement, support, and even person correction. Sponsors of a child at baptism and confirmation assume the role of *padrino* ("godparents") to the child and compadres to the parents. Witnesses at a marriage or close friends also assume this role. *Hijos de crianza* (children of upbringing) is the cultural practice of assuming responsibility for a child, without the necessity of blood or even friendship ties, and raising this child as if it were one's own. There is no stigma attached to the parent for surrendering his child or to the child who is given up. This may be a permanent or temporary arrangement. (Mizio 1974)

The Puerto Rican family values highly its unity, welfare, and honor, and there is a deep sense of family commitment, obligation, and responsibility:

"Family ties and relationships are intense, and visits are frequent even if family members are not living in the same household. . . . The emphasis is on the group rather than on the individual. . . . The family guarantees protection and caretaking for life as long as the person stays in the system. Leaving the system implies taking a grave risk" (Garcia-Preto 1982:170).

Mexican American families share traditional family values and the extended-family structure with immigrants from Puerto Rico, Cuba, and Central and South America, despite significant differences among them: "Migration and the process of relocation change the family's structure and disrupt the patterns of intrafamilial help and control. Yet there is a tendency among Mexicans in the United States to reconstitute, whenever possible, the original extended family group" (Falicov and Karrer 1980:386). Mexican Americans are the second largest minority population in the United States after the Puerto Ricans, and they may soon become the largest. Some are members of families of Mexican descent and have lived in the American Southwest for several generations. The majority, however, were either born in Mexico or born to parents who were born in Mexico. For the most part, Mexican Americans are from poor or working-class groups, usually rural or semi-rural, and are of mixed Spanish and Indian descent (Falicov 1982).

The generalizations that follow apply only to the poor and working-class families, as middle- and upper-income Mexican families are markedly different in circumstances and value orientations (Falicov 1982). The family of parents and children is embedded in an extended-family network. This family of procreation usually lives in a separate household but near the extended family, thereby preserving its own boundaries and identity. The boundaries are flexible and may permit the inclusion of grandparents, uncles, aunts, cousins, and children whose parents are dead or divorced. Because young adults live with their parents until marriage, boundary problems and loyalty issues sometimes erupt early in the new family's formation. Generally, however, the extended-kin network is characterized by both horizontal and vertical interdependence, with a sharing of child care, financial responsibility, companionship, emotional support, and problem solving. The *compadrazgo* system of compadres is also an important source of support to children and their parents, and may be considered part of the extended family.

Despite proximity and the norm of interdependence, the hierarchical structure of the family is clear. Rules are organized around age and gender as the important determinants of authority in the patriarchal family (Falicov 1982). Because children reside with their parents until their own marriage and maintain an intense connectedness with their parents during adulthood, the parents continue parental and grandparental functions. Hence they may never experience the empty-nest phase of family life. Moreover, "The majority of Mexican families remain two-parent families throughout their lifetimes. The number of divorces is considerably smaller than for Anglo populations. However, common-law marriages and desertions are not infrequent among the urban poor" (Falicov 1982:140).

The terms *Chicano* and *Chicana* refer to those who are part of a social movement that is struggling to be free of oppression and to achieve opportunity and equality as a people. In addition, the Chicana is struggling to change the rigidly prescribed roles of women in the traditional culture. Fimbres described a Chicana as a woman who believes in self-determination and greater equality for Mexican American women in the dominant society and in the Mexican American culture. While bicultural and bilingual, she wants to retain her culture and language but eliminate the double standard between Chicana and Chicano (1982:94). Social workers should be aware of differences within the Mexican American population that arise from generation, education, socioeconomic status, gender, self-identity, and the attitudes and perceptions of the larger society.

Cuban Americans are the third largest Hispanic group in the United States. They, too, place great value on the family. Despite a tradition of paternal authority, derived from the Spanish influence, love of the mother is central. Pampering of children, overprotection, and overdependency are common. Respect for older and deceased family members is important (Queralt 1996). Provision of support by the extended family is probably less among Cubans than among Puerto Ricans and Mexicans. Nuclear families have been the norm among white Cubans since the 1930s, and the nuclear tendency has become more pronounced in the process of acculturation. Cubans may maintain closer ties to the extended family than some other groups, but the ties are evident mostly during crisis periods. The extended-family relationship of *compadrazgo* has lost most of its significance among Cubans in the United States, but friends are still occasionally referred to as compadres (Queralt 1996).

Women's status, always higher in Cuba than in other Latin American countries, has been elevated further in Cuban society since the 1959 revolution. But it is not known to what extent Cuban Americans have been influenced by the changes. It appears that traditional gender-typed roles are still stronger among Cubans in the United States than among Anglos. Machismo (exaggerated masculinity) still prevails (Queralt 1984, 1996).

Black families. Hudgins's (1991–1992) paper on the strengths of black families reviews these controversial issues appearing in the literature over the past 30 years. As we mentioned in chapter 3, initially, Daniel Moynihan's (1967) report based on 1960 census data described the sociological dimensions of the black family as including a large proportion of female-headed households (labeled the "Black Matriarchy") within which many social problems existed (labeled the "tangle of pathology"). In response to this discussion, Robert Hill (1972) countered with a book on "the strengths of black families," including strong kinship bonds, adaptability of family roles, strong work orientation, high achievement orientation, and strong religious orientation, all of which he saw as helping black families survive the many hostile and oppressive conditions prevailing in America since the arrival of the slaves. Hudgins (1991–1992) uses the 1990 census to update this discussion.

Strong kinship bonds. The contemporary African American family should include more attention to networks and extended family experiences. The portion of African Americans living with other relatives exceeds, almost double, those of white persons, thus showing that extended family living arrangements are very real. Extended family networks also provide "a ready source of information on child development, health, food preparation, money management, male-female relationships, and stress management." Teenage mothers who can depend on such family supports are more likely to complete their own education (Hudgins 1991–1992:12).

Adaptability of family roles: egalitarian households. "Role flexibility is the ability of family members to perform both traditional and nontraditional gender-typed family roles." For example, African American women in female-headed households have shown willingness and ability to take on both "father" and "mother" roles, thus contributing to the survival of these families. "The significant tendency for African American women to 'keep' children born out of wedlock reflects a tradition of caring that includes multiple role responsibilities" (Hudgins 1991–1992:13–14).

Strong work orientation, high achievement orientation, resilient children. Data show increasing proportions of African Americans completing college and high school. Surveys indicate that African American families tend to hold higher expectations of their children than comparable classes of white people. Hudgins also reports the high rates of hidden jobs among African Americans, although such day work garners low wages and no benefits. Willingness to work at minimal compensation suggests to Hudgins a very strong work orientation.

Strong religious orientations, steadfast optimism. The black church and the religion presented there has had an important influence on every aspect of African American life. It is personal and expressive, and it shapes people's lives;

the most competent African American families were most involved with religious beliefs and activities, while the least competent were not. The strong religious orientation appears to lead to "steadfast optimism," which would be useful in the worst of circumstances, including in many female-headed households (Hudgins 1991–1992:16–17).

Hudgins ends with the important statement, that policies and programs based on a "tangle of pathology" paradigm are futile, while a paradigm building on the family strengths perspective could be more beneficial to families and more cost effective to government (1991–1992:18). In this time of social change, it would be useful to look carefully at the strengths of individuals, families, neighborhoods, communities, and organizations, rather than having governmental organizations emphasize the limitations of people, especially minority people. It is worth noting that the rate of illegitimacy that so alarmed Moynihan in 1967 among blacks (26 percent) is now almost achieved by whites in 1994 (22 percent) (Robertson 1994:19), but the cry of a white tangle of pathology has not yet been raised.

American Indian families. R. G. Lewis notes that there are 323 American Indian tribes in the lower 48 states, along with 224 tribes of Alaskan Natives (1995:216). These numbers are cited to emphasize the diversity within this one ethnic group and the variety of dialects they speak. Lally and Haynes (1995:195) point out that Alaskan Athabascans can communicate with Arizona Apaches in their own languages, but they must use English to communicate with the Alaskan Tlingit. The story of the contacts between Europeans who came to America and the existing American Indian groups is not a pleasant one. Initial cooperation was soon replaced by the relentless forcing of Indians off their own lands, forced relocations (e.g., the Trail of Tears of the 1830s), deceptions (e.g., the General Allotment Act of 1873, which sold off "surplus Indian lands"), and oppressions (e.g., forced use of Indian boarding schools, often at great distances from the reservations, which tended to break up families). Grim statistics on health, education, and work and welfare often place American Indians and Alaskan Natives at the lowest levels nationwide (Lewis 1995; Lally and Haynes 1995). Current policies of self-determination and assimilation are viewed with suspicion by some American Indians, in light of past experiences with the federal government and American society (Lewis 1995:222–223).

In contrast to a Western view of extended families as three generations living together, Red Horse, a California Cherokee, described Indian family networks as structurally open and village-like. They include several households representing significant relatives along both vertical and horizontal lines . . . accompanied by an additional bonding feature of incorporation by which significant non-kin become family members. . . through formal and informal processes. An individual, for example, may become a namesake for a child through formal ritual. This individual than assumes family obligations and responsibilities for child rearing and role modeling. . . . Structurally, naming ceremonies organize an obligatory, supportive network for children. (1980)

Attneave (1982) stated that among urban Indians, many still adhere to extended-family values and relationships even though contemporary living conditions may change the actual structure. Red Horse and Attneave agree that these values continue even in those instances where present family systems extend over several states. In addition to the importance of family, American Indians also emphasize individualism, a respect for the rights of the person, including children, to have opinions and make their own decisions. Another theme in American Indian culture is the relationship of people to nature. People are thoroughly part of nature and all its creatures and creations; people are to walk in reverential harmony with nature and not seek (in Western fashion) to exploit nature. This indicates a different kind of spirituality that American Indians have, even when it is combined with forms of Christianity. Fasting young people may go into the wilderness for several days on a vision quest for a life direction. Lally and Haynes list these values of Alaskan Natives: respect for elders, love for children, respect for others, respect for nature, domestic skills, humility, sharing, cooperation, hard work, hunting skills, family roles, humor, spirituality, knowledge of language, knowledge of family tree, avoidance of conflict, and responsibility to clan or tribe (1995:198).

The American Indian woman is expected to contribute to the cohesiveness and integrity of the family group and to the tribal group. This expectation is in marked contrast to the general tendency toward rigid gendered roles found in the patriarchal extended-family structures of other cultures (except black families). The socioreligious relational ties of the American Indian woman often place her in decision-making positions that affect the group. Her activities, circumstances, and skills may also lead to her holding significant leadership roles in traditional and contemporary tribal life (Blanchard 1982:100). In 1987, for example, a Cherokee woman, Wanda Mankiller, was elected chief of the Cherokee nation.

Asian American families. The label Asian American is used to describe a large number of different groups. One cluster includes people who came to America from China, Japan, the Philippines, Korea, and the Indian subcontinent. Sometimes a distinction is made with regard to Southeastern Asians—from Vietnam, Cambodia, Laos, Thailand—and "other Asians," which would include people from Bangladesh, Burma (Myarmar), Indonesia, the Malay, Pakistan, and Sri Lanka. Another cluster includes Pacific Islanders from Hawaii, Samoa, and Guam; the U.S. Bureau of the Census describes people of Tongan, Tahitian, Fijian, Northern Mariana Island, and Palauan descent as "other Pacific Islanders" (Balgopal 1995:231).

These many groups have distinctive cultures, but share certain themes or values. Among these are a collectivist orientation. As Balgopal describes it,

> Asians have a collective cultural pattern that focuses on the interdependence of members, harmonious relationships, and the preservation of integrity. It is argued that Asians stress collectivism, rather than individualism, because the individual is expected to make sacrifices for the family [the fundamental and patriarchal unit for Asians] (Segal 1991); the needs of the family take precedence over the needs of the individual; and group cooperation, rather than individual competition, is stressed (Mikler 1993). The emphasis is on restraining the expression of emotion and implicit obedience to family authority and elders are other indicators of collectivism (Sue 1981).
>
> (1995:234)

Both old and new Asian immigrants to the United States place high value on a hierarchical organization of authority and responsibility, and on family obligations based on status and role within the extended family. One's position in the family "defines roles, governs behavior. . . . . Each relationship carries different responsibilities and requires different responses" (Toupin 1981:302). Independence does not have the same value it has in Western society. Rather, interdependence and mutuality are the norms. However, as enculturation takes place, traditional social ties and interactional norms weaken among some younger cohorts.

Asians participate in a variety of formal religions, such as Buddhism, Confucianism, Hinduism, Taoism, Christianity, and Islam (Balgopal 1995:235). Especially among adherents to Confucianism, Buddhism, and Taoism, reverence for the family's past and its ancestors, as well as concern for the family's future status and well-being, provides a strong sense of continuity and obligation. Thus the individual is viewed as the product of all preceding generations. Individual actions reflect not only on the individual and the present family but also on past and future generations. Such a responsibility takes precedence over individual interests (Shon and Davis 1982).

Asian cultures in general prescribe the rules of behavior and conduct in family roles such as husband, wife, child, and in-law to a greater extent than in most other cultures. The extended family, the "clan," is responsible for maintaining the status of the family name or lineage. An individual's adherence to this code of conduct becomes not a reflection of the individual but of the family and kinship network to which he or she belongs. Male offspring are valued more than females, and the expectations of each sex are quite different (Shon and Davis 1982). Shon and Davis describe the family form of the Chinese, Japanese, and Korean peoples. However, the extended-family structure also characterizes Southeast Asians and Pacific Islanders, with differences due to religion (e.g., Hinduism or Islam), social class, war and refugee experiences, and island life. The Hmong extended family, for example, includes all the people who share the paternal grandparents. Thus the extended family is a corporate kinship group that is based in a patrilineal clan system. It may consist of two to ten households in which mutual help is a salient feature (Tou-fou 1981).

Ryan (1982) noted that the traditional values of the Asian cultures have provided the society with a social structure and a strong set of moral values. But they have also fostered great injustices against women, relegating them to a lower status throughout life. This heritage continues to affect the lives of many Asian American women in North America, even of third-generation native-born Asian American women. They face gender stereotyping and racial discrimination in the society and in their ethnic group.

Many Asian American women succeed in adapting to the new culture and in defining new roles for themselves. But the strain of sustaining that new role taxes the coping resources of many others, adding to the life stress generated by poverty, dilapidated housing, poor working conditions, and so on. Role strain is also likely to affect adversely the Asian American family's hierarchical structure and its gendered roles, increasing the stress on all members. Enculturation in the new country may weaken traditional social ties and norms of interdependence and mutuality, especially among young newcomers. In some instances, migrating entails a loss of the extended family and its resources, so that the immediate family of parents and children are alone emotionally, economically, and socially.

Communal families. The communal structure appears to have more similarity to extended-kin structures than to other family forms, although some theorists, notably Kanter (1972), maintain communes are not families but groups, some of which may contain families. Others view communal families—that is, people living as families in a collective—as an experimental family form, different from other families in some important ways. In nineteenth-century America, utopian communes were quite prevalent. They included the celibate Shakers, the polygamous early Mormons, the Oneida community with its "complex marriage" (arranged temporary liaisons, rather than ongoing relationships, with resulting children being raised by the whole community), and the Owenites at New Harmony, Indiana, among many others. Communal structures reappeared during the late 1960s with the student revolt, flower children, hippies, and other countercultural movements. Their members share resources, common facilities, household tasks, and sometimes child rearing. Kanter (1972) pointed out that most of the recent social communes seem to last only four to five years, while those with some core religious or philosophical system seem to survive longer.

There is little current research in this area, but interested readers might like to review papers by Eiduson (1978) on child development in emergent family styles and a chapter by Berger, Hackett, and Millar (1974) that describes the value systems, worldviews, and life styles of rural noncreedal communes as these affected economic arrangements, family structure, sexual relations, and child rearing. The book *Co-ops, Communes, and Collectives* by Case and Taylor (1979) well captures the mood of the late 1960s and 1970s.

Lesbian and gay families. In the Hartman and Laird definition of family presented at the beginning of this chapter, lesbian and gay families perform most of the same functions and tasks that other families do, such as household management, child rearing (where children are present), arrangements for decision making and role allocation, and meeting the emotional needs of all members and the sexual needs of the adult partners. Given current conditions in society, lesbian and gay families do not serve certain other functions, such as legitimizing sexual relationships in the way heterosexual couples may legitimize functions—with recent laws in Hawaii recognizing same-sex marriages being the prominent exception in 1997. Lesbians who choose to may become biological parents, using male friends or artificial insemination procedures. Gay men may take a similar route to become biological parents, but in the nature of the event women are much more centrally involved in the pregnancy. The legal status of the resulting offspring is unclear.

Lesbian and gay couples meet each other's needs for companionship, sharing, support, understanding, and love just as heterosexual couples do. The relationship may involve commitment and mutual responsibility for each other's well-being and not just sexual involvement (Moses and Hawkins 1982). Typically in lesbian and gay relationships, gender-typed roles are replaced by egalitarian roles based on personal interests or ability, although this does not protect partners in either relationship from problematic relationships and even sexual and physical abuse (Leo 1994). Lesbian women have female identities and are socialized as women; gay men have male identities and are socialized as men. With understanding of these facts and the maturing of the gay community, the earlier butch-femme dichotomy modeled on heterosexual gendered roles began to diminish in the late 1960s, especially among lesbians. This freedom from gender role expectations is experienced as a source of strength by both lesbians and gays. Usually both members of the couple work, so that economic dependency is not an issue, although differences in work status and income may pose problems for some (Moses and Hawkins 1982).

Long-term relationships have been more typical of homosexual women than of homosexual men. Many lesbians live in a lifelong relationship until death takes one partner. Unfortunately, because of the legal status of homosexual couples, hospital rules favoring the presence of "family" rather than friends during the terminal dying period has sometimes meant the critical separation of lifelong lovers. The reality of AIDS is changing the sexual promiscuity of many gays, especially younger men who have not yet formed a long-term relationship. Even before AIDS, significant numbers of men maintained long-term and even lifelong relationships.

Issues faced by gay and lesbian families not faced by most other families— or not to the same degree—include reaching agreement on private and shared time and activities; monogamous or nonmonogamous sexual relationships; the coming out of one member that causes internal conflict and possible threats to employment and friendships for the other; separate or shared dwellings; and problems related to child producing, child rearing, and child custody in case of separation. Issues of child custody, foster parenting, or adoption by gay or lesbian parents have legal, emotional, and social aspects. In the case of divorce where one parent is gay or lesbian, the courts have tended to grant custody to the heterosexual parent on the basis of the sexual preference of the other parent and regardless of parenting ability or the wishes of the child. Restrictions have also been applied to visitation and other parental rights. In instances where custody has been granted and the custodial parent is later found to be gay or lesbian, custody has been revoked and granted to the other parent. Some progress is being made in ruling out gay or lesbian lifestyle per se as cause for loss of custody but the future is unclear.

The prevalence of adverse rulings rest on three assumptions that arise from homophobia and associated myths, augmented by the irrational fear of AIDS contagion for the children:

1. The gay or lesbian parent or parent's lover will molest the child. This myth is countered by the fact that 97 percent of child molesters are heterosexual males. There is no evidence that gay parents are more likely than nongay parents either to seduce their children or to allow them to be seduced (Moses and Hawkins 1982).
2. Gay or lesbian parents will try to convert their child to their own sexual preference. This myth is countered by the fact that sexual preference is not a matter of choice. Further, the majority of lesbians and gays have been raised in heterosexual families and not by lesbian or gay parents (Moses and Hawkins 1982).
3. Children of gay or lesbian parents will be ostracized and damaged because of the societal reaction to homosexuality. This myth is countered by the lack of evidence in research that children suffer disproportionately because of their parents' sexual preference.

In all, questions of sexuality strike deep within people's psyche, and we can probably expect this pattern of two steps forward, one step back, to continue, so long as the basic laws of the land remain undisturbed.

Family:Environment

We defined the social ecological perspective of this book to be summarized by the person:environment formulation. We now amend this, in the case of families as persisting and significant units of social life. We suggest it may be useful to conceive of a family:environment formulation as a similar kind of unit of study and action. There is no way we can conceive of the family without its various environmental elements, from the workplace, living community, and culture to the individual actors composing the family itself. And there is no way we can conceive of action with and on behalf of the family that does not take into consideration these same environments.

As with the individual, we can consider parallel terms with regard to the family:environment unit. Early stage theorists have suggested that families go through a universal progression, such as Pollack's (1960) notion of the four stages of a healthy family (viewed as a two-parent and one or more children nuclear family): marriage, child rearing, leaving the nest, and after they are gone. Erikson's model takes us through the life cycle with implications for healthy individuals forming intimacy, generating children and work, and passing on culture to the next generation. Perhaps our earlier discussion of the variety of family forms is sufficient to challenge any such simplistic and universal ideas. A strength in these approaches lay in their purposeful efforts to consider the parallel development of adult and child members of the family as they negotiate their respective life tasks in some tandem fashion. But the absence of attention to differences that arise from ethnicity, socioeconomic status, religion, poverty, family forms, and the historical context of male dominance and female subordination can lead to serious errors in understanding family development and change. It is doubtful that universal, predictable family stages and tasks fit the complexities in family development today, if indeed they ever did. The efforts of Carter and McGoldrick (1980, 1989) come as close as possible in a stage model, to add flexibility necessary to take into consideration all the great number of family forms and variations such as divorce and remarriage. Yet the underlying stages are still present, even though they may not now be universal or inevitable and certainly not sequential.

The position taken in this book is that a conception of family development based on the various common and unique life issues confronting a family over its life course is more dynamic and closer to contemporary families' experiences than constructions based on universal sequential stages. Life issues may be generated by internal pressures arising from members' biological maturational changes, nondevelopmental status transitions, idiosyncratic troubles, external pressures arising from cultural imperatives and the societal context of racism and sexism and the other abuses of power, or from other exchanges between the environment and the family or individual members. In order to cope effectively with such life issues as they come along, the family must modify its form or structure of roles and tasks. Some life events will be stressors, others challenges, and perhaps they may be a mix for different members of the family who have to pull their separate experiences and actions together to act as the family.

Terkelsen (1980) suggested some useful terms that we employ throughout this book. First-order developments are expectable, often challenging events and processes. For example, developmental transitions such as puberty and status transitions such as school entry are expectable in the life course of most families and viewed as positive challenges for which family members have the requisite capacities to resolve. Second-order developments are unexpectable, unanticipated events and processes such as grave injury or illness, job loss, family violence, and bereavement. Some life issues that are first-order developments for most people may be experienced as second-order developments by a few. For example, retirement is a challenging, first-order life issue in most families, but it can be a second-order development and major stressor for others, particularly if it is unwanted or comes too early because of illness or because it is forced.

Families define, experience, and handle challenging or stressful life issues differently according to the meaning that these events have for a particular family. Meaning depends on many factors: the family's worldview; cultural features and individual personality features; the previous experience of the family; the nature of its environment, including the historical, economic, political, and social contexts; the family's internal resources, such as an integration of its values, norms, roles, affectional relationships, and resilience; and its external resources, such as adequate income, housing, health care, and other formal and informal supports for dealing with the issue.

Meaning is especially important because serious discrepancies may exist between the perceived and the actual life issue and between the perceived and the actual resources for dealing with it. Such discrepancies may account, in part, for families with seemingly adequate resources who fall apart when confronting a particular life issue, while others with fewer resources manage a similar issue effectively. What is defined as a stressor by one family may be defined as a zestful challenge by another. Ultimately, all the social ecological terms discussed in chapter 1 may be transferred to the family:environment unit as we do in the following chapters.

7

Genetics/Biology

This chapter addresses the very difficult topic of the place of genetics and biology in the thinking and practice of social work. On the one hand, the great revolutionary thinking of our times appears to be coming from genetics and biology—we have made major strides in understanding the raw materials and some fundamental processes in human beings. On the other hand, extraordinary evils have been committed in the name of genetics, or more specifically, in an early form called eugenics. However, the dividing line between eugenics and genetics/biology may be thinner than realized, which means extra care must be taken in understanding the new knowledge and how we can best apply it in social work.

Outline

Introduction: Social Work and Genetics

A Brief History of Evil: The Misuses of Genetics

Nature: A Review of Genetics for Social Workers

Nature and Nurture in Social Work: A Tentative Balance

Object Lesson: *The Bell Curve: Intelligence and Class Structure in American Life*

Introduction: Social Work and Genetics

The field of biological research has grown enormously in the past few decades, as more powerful methods and ideas have enabled scientists to discover more about the nature of human nature. However, biology as a science has had to separate itself from the travesties that have been committed in its name, from the eugenics and sterilization debacle around the beginning of the twentieth century to scientific frauds in intelligence testing in the early to middle 1900s

(Gould 1981, 1994) to long-standing perpetrations of sexist ideas (Tavris 1992) to the hell of the Nazi Holocaust midcentury to the genetic reductionism and biological determinism of sociobiologists in various guises at the end of this century (Albee 1996; Lewontin, Rose, and Kamin 1984). We briefly review this history of errors and evils, lest we forget.

However, from the social ecological perspective, we want to recognize the potential that is emerging in biological studies of the person—tempered with understanding how the environment may "turn on or turn off" these genetic potentials. While all human life is based on bio-chemical-physical events of which our bodies and their behaviors are ultimately derived, there is a very long and complex path by which these biological potentials interact with other internal events, with interpersonal events, with various kinds of social and cultural events, and with physical environmental events before the genetic possibilities (as modified by all the other intervening influences) are visibly expressed. What exact form a complex social behavior will take—such as those currently identified by words such as "intelligence," "schizophrenia," "delin-quency," or "happiness"—depends on the billions of possible interactions among biological, psychological, social, cultural, and physical environmental events and processes. To say that "intelligence" or "schizophrenia" or whatever social behavior is being considered is genetically caused is highly misleading because it leaves out the large number of postbiological interactions that determines whether and how the complex social characteristic is to be expressed. It also assumes that the target characteristic is itself clearly defined, which is not the case in most complex social behaviors such as those named above or in the various forms of family transformations over the life course, as discussed in part 2.

Some specific gene–specific characteristic connections have been identi-fied, such as the genes that control the color of one's eyes, which means envi-ronmental conditions can do little to control its expression. However, for rea-sons we still do not yet understand, genes may influence different people in different ways: "Because of the complex network of interconnecting steps between a gene and its effects, a change anywhere in the network may influ-ence gene expression" (Rauch and Black 1994:1109–1110). Rauch and Black note that a single gene can have multiple, apparently unrelated effects (this is known as pleiotropy) and that a given outcome (such as mental retardation) may have many possible causes, of which the genetic expression is only one.

Furthermore, with reference to the profession of social work (as contrasted with the profession of genetic counseling), social workers primarily seek to influence psycho-socio-cultural events—like people's reactions to an identified untoward genetic information or with an identified problem with a fetus—and not biological or genetic events per se. Social workers may provide interpretative information, may offer support and understanding, and may connect affected clients to self-help or support groups. Genetic disorders are very complex. As Rauch and Black state:

> In general, a genetic disorder is a condition that is "permanent, chronic, familial, complex, labeling, and threatening" (Schild and Black 1984:53). It is permanent in that the condition is in the person's genes and is an irreversible, fixed attribute. Because genetic disorders are lifelong conditions, they are characterized by chronicity. A genetic diagnosis usually initiates lifelong stress because of the demands of managing the disease; the financial drain; the time, energy, and frustration involved in obtaining needed services; the need to modify goals and aspirations; the difficulty in meeting the needs of all family members; recurrent crises and hospitalizations associated with exacerbation of the condition; and, possibly, death. . . . Many people do not grasp [the abstract language in which genetics are framed]. . . . Some genetic conditions are highly stigmatized [and] . . . may cause social isolation and a poor self-image.   (1995:1112)

What we emphasize in this chapter is an appropriate level of humility in the face of complex biological-psychosocial events. Before generally trained social workers even dream of raising issues about life-relevant interventions—such as what options face a woman considering conceiving a child when there is some evidence of genetic risk in the family—they had better get advanced genetics training or expert advice from genetic counselors as the basis for laying out the full range of options, not only for the sake of the client but also for self-protection in this litigious society. The great majority of social workers will not be adequately trained to make these genetic determinations. Just as we abjure social workers becoming junior psychoanalysts, so we abjure social workers becoming junior genetic counselors. Rather, their training should prepare them to be knowledgeable in referring such questions to genetics experts. On the other hand, social workers may be of great service to those experiencing the powerful emotions surrounding such decisions. These will involve issues of coping with difficult realities, making constructive adaptations so far as possible, and continuing on with the business of life. For these tasks, social workers may be quite helpful. Furthermore, social workers may be useful in primary prevention programs informing people, for example, of the risks of smoking and drinking during pregnancy (May and Hymbaugh 1989) and biochemical hazards in the workplace (Rauch and Black 1994).

We also discuss some difficult ethical issues that have emerged as biological and genetic information has come into contact with the lives of ordinary people. For example, it is now possible to test young persons and accurately predict whether they will succumb to a fatal disease in their adulthood (Huntington's chorea) years in advance of this deadly event. Should we inform the young persons who are so afflicted? Likewise, with AIDS testing, should categorical testing take place—say, all prisoners, all pregnant women, all of some other group wherein the information may help some persons (sexual partners, for instance) and harm others (such as unborn female fetuses in a culture that prefers males)? What is the relationship between our knowledge and our ethical responsibility?

A Brief History of Evil: The Misuses of Genetics

For a variety of reasons, many scientists and other thoughtful people in the late nineteenth and early twentieth centuries—especially those who were white, male, Anglo-Saxon, Protestant, and middle and upper class—believed that the mental and moral traits of human beings were essentially determined by heredity (Paul 1994). The practice involving the selective breeding of cattle to improve the livestock in desired ways was relatively well known, and it was only a short step in (erroneous) thinking that human progeny might likewise be improved. So, it made "good sense"—to those who had achieved social success in a capitalistic society—to propose "improvement" of the human race by selective breeding of the desirable people and selective sterilization—or worse—of the undesirable people, since nature appeared to be so unwise as to make these lower-class undesirables much more fecund and prolific than the elite upper classes.

Charles Darwin (1809–1882), who developed a theory of human evolution, wrote *On the Origin of Species* (1849), introducing concepts like natural selection of superior characteristics in the struggle for survival of the fittest. Later, in *Descent of Man* (1871), Darwin, himself a member of the upper class, warned that if the lower classes continued to outbreed their social superiors, evolutionary regress would result. He thus connected his version of social evolution with what became known as eugenics, which then evolved into organized eugenic movements, first in Germany in 1904, then Britain in 1907, and in the United States around 1910 (Paul 1994:6). Darwin himself did not propose any specific programs to decrease the birth rate of the social inferiors nor to increase the rate for social superiors, and he was skeptical about state intervention. Later Darwinians were not. In 1883 Francis Galton (1822–1911), a major contributor to statistics, proposed the term "eugenics," meaning "good in birth," thus giving a name and an identity to this movement. Heredity was viewed as all-important in determining the nature of humankind, including the mental and moral differences among people; for Galton, environment (nurture) meant nothing (Paul 1994:3, 33–34). *How* we were to obtain the goodness in birth involved various forms of coercion, which eventually spun out of control and devolved into the Nazi Holocaust and Japanese medical experiments in World War II.

Some leaders in the eugenics movement pushed their ideas even further. Some thought the so-called humanitarian actions like indiscriminate charity (or social welfare) and medicine only served to permit the less valuable people and social classes to outbreed the more valuable ones (Paul 1994:29). Society and culture were counteracting the laws of natural selection in which only the fittest survived. This brings eugenics and social welfare ideas on a collision course. Interestingly, Alfred Russel Wallace, who independently originated a theory of natural selection, came to some different conclusions from Darwin. Wallace came from a poor background and by hard work eventually was able to do scientific research among preliterate societies. He found these native peoples and communities quite admirable, especially in comparison with the poverty and inequality in his own dog-eat-dog society (Paul 1994:28; Quammen 1996:20, 40–41). Wallace advocated for social reforms that the social Darwinians of his time condemned as weakening society.

Galton used a family-study statistical method and found that high achievement runs in families, while in the United States other family studies found that major antisocial behaviors also ran in families who have given their names to bad traits: the Jukes family included many criminals, murderers, paupers, and diseased people, while the Kallikaks included one branch of feebleminded persons (Paul 1994:42–44). Since a self-proclaimed moral society cannot ethically kill off its antisocial citizens, its feebleminded members, or its poor, a sophisticated society may find ways for selective breeding, promoting the "desirable" people, discouraging (controlling) the "undesirable" ones.

Early in the twentieth century, in France, Alfred Binet constructed standardized intelligence tests, and others applied his ideas to new areas, such as the mass intelligence tests in the U.S. Army around the time of World War I. People were horrified at the results; many recruits were below normal levels on these IQ tests—they couldn't underline the correct answer in questions like these: "The pancreas is in the abdomen / head / shoulder / neck." Or "Salsify is a kind of snake / fish / lizard / vegetable." Likewise, tests of the poor as well as many groups of foreign-born Americans produced similar results, leading to the conclusion of hereditary inferiority. The statistics were strong and significant; the deductions were logical; but the whole enterprise was a sham, with one leading social scientist faking his data (Gould 1981).

There were other paths toward selective breeding and control of "undesirable" elements that emerged early in twentieth-century America. Immigration laws were written that permitted limited entrance to people, in some rough approximation of the numbers of these nationalities already in place in America. Thus eastern and southern Europeans and most Asian and African immigration levels were sharply limited. The Statue of Liberty in the harbor of New York now said, "Give me only a selected few of your tired, your poor, your huddled masses yearning to breathe free. . . ."

Another path toward selective breeding was the effort to provide birth control methods to all people. This movement presents the most difficult case related to the eugenic philosophy because it ostensibly provides all concerned individuals with the knowledge and tools to control their own reproduction. There was presumably no racist policy or philosophy attached to the movement—but see Turner and Darity (1973) who tested the hypothesis that family planning was seen by black Americans as a form of genocide. There exists the strong presumption that rational people will not knowingly bring children into the world who have physical or mental deficits, and who thus require extraordinary efforts by society to nurture and support them. At a time when the world population explosion may be the number one global problem, it may be the height of political incorrectness to raise some challenging issues about birth control.

Negative eugenics involved preventing breeding of undesirables, while positive eugenics involved promoting breeding of desirables. Negative eugenics appears to involve any kind of force or control with regard to sexual/procreative acts. This may include more than a medical police forcing sterilization on some people. What about high taxes and low social supports for second or later born children? These are legal actions that may have profound influences over the sexual behavior of a married couple, while changes in aid to dependent children may likewise influence intimate actions in the young, unmarried, or noneconomically solvent peoples. Birth control and family planning enable self-control with regard to one's own procreation plans. Birth control information and methods are offered on a voluntary basis, and they depend on inducements to attract people's attention and ongoing participation over the course of a long period of fertility. What defines whether birth control by any of the means described above is positive or negative eugenics? These are challenging questions, especially for social workers who are often in the fore-front of encouraging people to make reasoned plans with regard to their family formation.

The Nazis carried eugenics to its logical conclusion. Compulsory steriliza-tion laws were issued two months after the Nazis came to power in 1933. Peo-ple who were feebleminded, schizophrenic, manic-depressive were sterilized, as were others, including those suffering from severe physical deformity, hereditary blindness, deafness, or severe alcoholism—some 320,000 to 400,000 in all (Paul 1994:84–91). (Scandinavian countries also instituted ster-ilization laws but without linkages to racial discrimination or extermination.)

Sterilization in Nazi Germany was eventually followed by a socially planned program of mass murder involving gas chambers to get rid of "use-less eaters," first defined as mentally ill patients (Paul 1994:90). These murders were followed by mass exterminations of Jews, Gypsies, homosexuals, and other social and political "deviants" who opposed the Nazis. Looking at a recent book on this topic, *French Children of the Holocaust: A Memorial* (Klars-feld 1997), which portrays photographs and brief biographies of 2,400 chil-dren deported to these death camps, we are reminded of one commentator who said in effect that it was wrong to say that 6 million Jews were murdered; rather, one Jew was murdered, then another, then another, then another, 6 million times. In all these Holocaust actions, German biologists and geneti-cists were active, leading members (Paul 1994:91). The Nuremberg War Crimes Tribunal documented horrendous medical experiments on involun-tary subjects, and the world learned the extent of the evil that human beings could inflict on other human beings, all in the name of "good births" and "socially desirable" people inheriting the earth.

At the fiftieth anniversary of the Nuremberg Trials (1994), we once again reflected on these events, wondering not only how they could have happened but also whether they will ever happen again. These reflections took place at a time when evidence is mounting of genocide in Bosnia and in Africa.

Nature: A Review of Genetics for Social Workers

Each human being is composed of billions of cells, grouped as specific clus-ters of tissues, organs, nerves, and other systems, whose interdependent oper-ations represent the biological foundation for all bodily processes, thoughts, feelings, and actions. In the nucleus of each of those cells are tiny paired stringlike structures called chromosomes, one strand coming from each parent in ova and sperm cells. Humans possess 23 pairs of chromosomes in each cell, or 46 chromosomes. The first 22 are matched pairs (autosomes); the 23d is the sex chromosome, in which the female is indicated by XX and the male by XY. Human inheritance involves the combination of male and female chromosomes and the resulting division of cells into specialized groups over time.

Chromosomes are, in turn, composed of genes, which are clumps of deoxyribonucleic acid (DNA) the smallest unit of inheritable information; most human traits are produced by large numbers of genes in combination. There are more than 100,000 human genes. Research is being conducted (at enormous expense) to identify all human genes so as to help scientists understand the genetic contribution to life (Annas and Elias 1992).

Genes are activated to transmit the biological information they hold through interaction with other components in the cell, the dominance or recessiveness of that gene vis-ß-vis others, other events taking place in the body, and how the body responds to various external events (Rauch and Black 1994:1009). Biologically "normal" expression of genes refers roughly to what the average member of a species exhibits; deviant expressions involve nontypical forms, especially those that are dysfunctional to some greater (e.g., mental retardation) or lesser (e.g., color blindness) degree in that society. The meaning of a genetic expression is powerfully influenced by a given culture or society.

The critical interest in genetics for social workers emerges in several situations:

Carrier screening. When a couple are thinking of procreating, they may have questions regarding their personal and ancestral genetic history and the predictions for producing a "normal" child. Certain ethnic groups are at higher risk than others for particular genetic problems, when recessive genes are present in both parents, such as people of northern European ancestry who have a higher probability of carrying genes for cystic fibrosis and PKU, Ashkenazi Jews for Tay-Sachs disease, and African Americans for sickle cell anemia (Rauch and Black 1994:1111).

Prenatal screening. When a woman is pregnant, she and her partner may seek information on risks for fetal disorders, particularly if she has had German measles or has consumed alcohol or other substances during the pregnancy, which increases the risk for retardation. An alphafetoprotein test or an ultrasonograph may be used in such screening. To diagnose the presence of specific inherited diseases or anomalies, amniocentesis may be used (at 16 to 20 weeks of gestation) or chorionic villus sampling (at 10 to 12 weeks). Information at this time permits consideration of various options, from abortion to delivery (Rauch and Black 1994:1111).

Newborn screening and diagnosis. This procedure can identify the presence of serious genetic disorders, even in asymptomatic infants. For example, mental retardation caused by such metabolic diseases as PKU can be eliminated by this early diagnosis through special diets before brain damage occurs (Rauch and Black 1994:1111–1112).

Presymptomatic screening of older children and adults. It is possible to screen for some conditions distant in time, such as Huntington's disease, a neurodegenerative fatal condition that will occur in mid-adulthood.

These four situations may involve social workers, along with specialists in genetic counseling and medical specialists. Most social workers will not have the requisite expertise to deal with the genetics as such, but they may have training in addressing the psychological crises that emerge during these times, perhaps as part of a genetic service team. Rauch and Black point out that clients who receive bad genetic news may need support to help them deal with the emotions and the tasks at hand. A crisis is posed, and many stakeholders—the immediate and extended family in particular—may be involved, at present or in the future. Genetic information is complex, and clients may need assistance in comprehending what they have been told, especially when they view such conditions as stigmatizing or threatening to ordinary functioning or possibly to life itself. Momentous decisions are to be made by the clients; social workers and others may facilitate the range and depth of thinking that is required to make an irrevocable decision that is most nearly acceptable for the present and the future (1994:1112–1113).

Nature and Nurture in Social Work: A Tentative Balance

What is the most useful position for social workers at this time with regard to the nature-nurture controversy? We suggest a position that takes into account the best available information with regard to probable causes and feasible solutions based on ecological theories and research. For example, H. Johnson offers a multifactorial view on the complex topic of violence, arguing that the literature supports two general conclusions: (1) that violence is biopsychoso-cial in origin, and remedies must address biological, psychological, and social factors; and (2) that the relative contributions of biological, psychological, and social factor vary from one situation to the next (1996:6). She notes, how-ever, that the biological contribution to violence (toward others or toward self) has been neglected in the social work literature, and she provides an overview to correct this imbalance. She groups biological factors under a dozen different headings, including neuropathology (brain damage), cogni-tive deficits (such as learning disabilities), neurotransmitter function (such as very low levels of serotonin among people with major depression), mind-altering substances (alcohol, cocaine, crack, and other drugs), mental illness (by subsets within each of the major psychiatric conditions), and endocrino-logical factors (such as studies of men with high testosterone levels correlating with frequency of violent behaviors). Evidence varies for each of these factors; some is indirect, such as in genetics. "Although research does not show that violent behavior is transmitted hereditarily (Mednick and Kandel 1988), sev-eral biological factors that influence violent behavior are related to genetic makeup, for example, anatomic structures of the brain, some types of cogni-tive deficits, endocrine function" (H. Johnson 1996:7).

Other evidence is, as yet, too complex to decipher. For example, with mind-altering substances: "The relationship between alcohol and criminal behavior is highly complex and difficult to evaluate because of methodologi-cal flaws in existing studies, including multiple definitions of alcohol use (dependence, abuse, intoxication, ingestion [and] lack of uniform definitions of crime" (H. Johnson 1996:9). Other evidence seems to stretch beyond the biological to the psychological, if not the sociological: "Violence perpetrated by mentally ill persons often occurs because the individual *believes* him- or herself to be personally threatened. However, the aggressive behavior does not in reality serve a survival function. . . . Violent acts among persons with anti-social personalty disorders include physical fights and assaults, destruction of property, and harassment of others, with no resultant feelings of remorse or guilt" (H. Johnson 1996:11).

Johnson's discussion seems to point to the limits of current categorical sys-tems like biology, psychology, and sociology, and the need to make as many connections between these currently separate domains as possible for the most comprehensive understanding of any complex behavior. Perhaps recent explo-rations in the "person-in-environment" (PIE) approach to systematic describ-ing, classifying, and coding problems of social functioning of adults may be one step in this direction (Karls and Wandrei 1994:1818–1827). PIE is an atheoretical system with regard to causes of behavior. The PIE system looks at both problems and growth in client interpersonal functioning, using four factors: (1) problems in social functioning, (2) problems emanating from the environment, (3) mental health problems, and (4) physical health problems. A complex category system of codes has been developed that supposedly enables the social worker to describe a client's problems in a standardized way. Whether it also enables a worker to indicate areas of strengths and positive (nontherapeutic) goals, and whether this kind of coding will be linked to theoretical and empirical ways of dealing with problems in functioning and their sociocultural contexts, is another story, barely on the horizon. As Karls and Wandrei point out this is only the first step in a journey of a thousand miles (1994:1826).

In general, it seems premature to make any sweeping assertions about genetic determinism or environmental determinism. The more we learn, the more we recognize the usefulness of the ecological principle that both persons and environments must always be considered when acting in any situation. How much of a person's biological makeup is relevant for a social worker to use in actual practice is relatively small, compared to how much psychosocial, cultural, economic, and political information a social worker needs in order to practice in the everyday world.

Object Lesson: *The Bell Curve: Intelligence and Class Structure in American Life*

As a contemporary object lesson in the power of engaging in the politics of genetics, we present a brief review of *The Bell Curve* (Herrnstein and Murray 1994), one of the most controversial books of this decade. Its 844 pages are dressed in professorially conservative style, with 47 pages of bibliography, 220 pages of appendixes and notes, and 22 clear, well-written chapters. For those who haven't time to read every page, the authors kindly present short italicized introductions to each chapter, and snappy boxed discussions of particularly touchy issues, such as "The (Sir Cyril) Burt Affair" (12) (wherein the authors dispute the reports that this eminent psychometrician made up his data, fudged his results, and invented coauthors—see Gould's *Mismeasure of Man* (1981) for a clear statement of the accusation)—or where we are given brief reviews of basic information, such as "A primer on the correlation coefficient" (67). However, this tweedily academic-style book delivers some powerful punches to the body politic—its critics say many of its distorted facts and grossly inaccurate interpretations are delivered below the belt (Fraser 1994)—even while professing worry about how some readers might respond: "We are not indifferent to the ways in which this book, wrongly construed, might do harm" (xxiii).

Let's look at the book. The subtitle *Intelligence and Class Structure in American Life* does not list its major preoccupation, race, though it argues that scientific proof demonstrates the intellectual inferiority of black people compared to whites. The argument begins with the authors' assertion that intelligence is a strong influence in determining one's degree of wealth and social status, and that we are seeing the emergence of a "cognitive elite," with a 14-fold increase in the proportion of people getting college degrees from 1900 to 1990 (24, 29). Then, there was a "cognitive partitioning by occupation" as intelligent people began to dominate in the leading professions and occupations (41, 63), while people with low intelligence are more likely to be found among the poor, the unemployed (163), the divorced (174), those with illegitimate children (180)—in particular, those white women who go on welfare after the birth of their first child (194)—and those white males who get involved with degrees of criminal behavior (246), among other developmental problems (383). (By the way, at this part of the book, the authors speak only of white people.) All these data, the authors suggest, point to the power of intelligence as a variable in American society; we are becoming a veritable intellectual meritocracy.

Herrnstein and Murray choose to use as their measure of intelligence the general intelligence factor, g, as developed by Spearman in 1904 (Gould 1994:16). Then, midway through their book, they introduce a discussion of race and intelligence. This is a complex discussion purporting to present the environmental point of view as well as the genetic point of view. But the upshot of the discussion essentially asserts the intellectual (genetic) inferiority of the population of blacks as compared to whites (276–294). On the other hand, on some studies East Asians (e.g., Chinese, Japanese) score higher on IQ tests than whites, on the order of 3 to 10 IQ points. However, other East Asian/white studies report no significant differences and so the authors conclude we can't be certain if there is a genetic difference at this time (272–276).

With blacks and whites, the matter is entirely different, say Herrnstein and Murray, who report the common findings of 146 studies that show about one standard deviation of difference, about 16 IQ points (226). Is there bias in the tests? Yes. Are the figures changing over time? Yes, the gap is closing by a few points. But the authors suggest suspending judgment at this time to see if the data are real changes or merely a plateau. In general, they stick with this basic

IQ difference between the population of blacks and whites. They assert that "between 40 and 80% of IQ is substantially heritable . . . [i.e.,] is genetic"(298). Remember that IQ is equivalent to general intelligence. The logical conclusion is that blacks as a group have lower intelligence, not just lower IQ scores, than whites as a group. They find it implausible that the environments in which blacks and whites grow are so substantially different as to account for these differences in IQ scores (299), especially when the same racist environments appear not to diminish IQ scores of Jews or Chinese, who have higher group scores than the national average (299). However, bright blacks do as well—even better—than bright whites (324)—a point that only reinforces the authors' argument for the importance of intelligence in the modern world and their assertion that "both genes and the environment have something to do with racial differences" (311). In short, Herrnstein and Murray try to present a persuasive case in favor of genetic influences but modify it slightly to include a little environmental influence as well.

The point for emphasis in this chapter is the assumption by Herrnstein and Murray that race and intelligence are largely attributable to genetics, that they jointly lead to all sorts of important social outcomes (in education, occupation, poverty, unemployment, illegitimacy, crime, etc.), and that there is no compelling evidence that they can be changed by environmental modifications and interventions (such as good nutrition and vitamin supplements—some encouraging studies but too soon to tell for sure [393]; or compensatory education—no evidence at all, after apparently positive studies are carefully examined [398, 402–409]). The American ideal, a meritocracy where all people should be able to go as far as their talents and hard work enable them to go, appears to be coming—even if the intellectual caste at the bottom of the heap, the underclass, grows increasingly miserable. Herrnstein and Murray assert we can't do much about this, particularly for children "unlucky enough to be born to and reared by unmarried mothers who are below average in intelligence—about 20 percent of children currently being born" (419). This includes an emerging white underclass that fits this low intelligence pattern as well (420). They offer a frightening vision of the future, one in which the state becomes custodian for poor children and the homeless, where the underclass will be more concentrated spatially than it is today, and where stricter control of crime will be acceptable, while racism will become more virulent (423–426).

The only way out Herrnstein and Murray can foresee is a kind of return to a kinder gentler world of yesteryear, where there is a valued place for everyone—even those who are not very smart (436–438). They nostalgically discuss a return to a happy neighborhood, where everyone helps everyone to find their valued place and where many perplexing social problems may be mini-mized, if not solved. Oh, brave new (old) world.

Needless to say, this clever and incendiary book did not go unnoticed. We present its argument is some detail in order to jolt social workers into recog-nizing the worldview that challenges their fundamental perspective and their future, a worldview that is shared by a large portion of the populace. Critics attacked the book at almost every point, recognizing some of the reported studies as having serious problems, and rejecting the scientific basis of many of Herrnstein and Murray's interpretations. The arguments are often detailed and technical, but they are necessary to study in order to make a reasoned response to this new form of an old politicalization of genetics. We summa-rize some of these responses and direct interested readers to other resources.

A good place to begin is Fraser's (1994) anthology of critical reviews of *The Bell Curve.* Gould (1994) continues his insightful attack on inappropriate use of intelligence tests that he began in *Mismeasures of Man* (1981). Gould argues that if any of Herrnstein and Murray's four premises are flawed—that intelli-gence must be depictable as a single number [g], capable of ranking people in linear order, genetically based, and effectively immutable (12)—then their entire argument fails. He then points out the flaws. For example, on immutable genetics, Gould notes that a pair of eyeglasses may correct a genetic defect in vision and presumably increase IQ scores, thus making genetics mutable. Gould comments that Herrnstein and Murray downplayed significant contradictory evidence, such as: "the impressive IQ scores for poor black children adopted into affluent and intellectual homes; average IQ increase in some nations since the Second World War equal to the entire fif-teen-point difference now separating blacks and whites in America" (1994:14). Albee (1983) noted that ethnic group immigrants first coming to the United States were usually identified as being of low intelligence, but after one or two generations, these same groups suddenly earned higher IQ scores—surely an effect of learning, not genetics.

Gould (1994:19–20) also notes some statistical problems, such as Herrnstein and Murray's using correlation coefficients (R), rather than the more usual mea-sure of goodness of fit for the many multiple regression results they cite. When the usual measure is employed (R^2), the amount of goodness of fit explained becomes very small. A correlation (R) of .40 becomes an R^2 of .16, which means that this R^2 accounts for very little of the variance in the situation.

H. Gardner disputes Herrnstein and Murray's exclusive use of the common intelligence measure, g: "A growing number of researchers [including Gard-ner himself] have argued that, while IQ tests may provide a reasonable measure of certain linguistic and mathematical forms of thinking, other equally important kinds of intelligence, such as spatial, musical, or personal, are ignored" (1994:29). Gardner cites the important work of Stevenson and Stigler (1992) that is counter to Herrnstein and Murray, showing that Chinese, Japanese, and American children start out at about the same level in school-tested IQ, but that Japanese and Chinese students increase in IQ scores because they attend school more days, work harder in school and at home, have better-prepared teachers, and have parents who encourage and coach them each day and night.

Nisbett (1994:39) critiques Herrnstein and Murray for not including studies of racial ancestry that go against their assumptions, such as the study of the degree of European genes that African Americans have (Scarr et al. 1977). Under a genetic hypothesis, the larger the percentage of European genes African Americans have, the higher their IQ should be. But this is not the case; differences were trivial and nonsignificant. And so on, with critics objecting to about every point Herrnstein and Murray make as well as the way these points are made.

Yet other environmentalist critics of the genetic position attack the heartland of genetic research, identical twin studies of persons with very similar genetic materials who were reared either together or separate from the other twin (Marshall 1996; Poston and Winebarger 1996). For twins reared together, it is difficult to measure the environmental effects of being raised as identical twins, with special efforts at keeping everything exactly alike. However, to the extent that similar environments are generated even for identical twins, the similarity of results on IQ may be derived from the similar environments (as well as identical genetics). For twins reared apart, the environments are different in one sense, but seemingly different social and physical places may still produce similar outcomes. We don't know the active ingredients of how social environments influence IQ. Different school settings produce relatively similar average outcomes. The regularities that do emerge from twin studies, that identical twins score closer to each other on IQ tests than fraternal twins (who are essentially like any other siblings even though born at the same time), can still be considered a complex question since environments may differ in yet unknown ways.

PART II

Tandem Developments of Family Members and Their Environments

The Concept of the Life Course

In part 1, we held up for examination each context or frame of reference for individual and family development. In those 7 chapters, we sketched how society and culture framed events in our lives. Although these large-scale events are often at great distance from our day to day lives, they generate momentous influences to which all must respond. With large-scale organizations, in which most of us live out our lives, other subtle structures and forces shape how we view the world and act in it. We looked particularly at the school and the work site as major organizations that greatly influence what we know and how we engage society. We examined how small groups and families shape the immediate boundaries of our lives and, through their continuous presence, are powerful determinants of what we are today and what we will be like tomorrow. We also reviewed the major changes occurring in the study of biology as potential influences of social work practice, attempting to gain some perspective on the perennial "nature versus nurture" debate.

In the 6 chapters of part 2, we make use of a "life course" model of psycho-socio-cultural development in place of the traditional "life cycle" models based on stage theories such as those by S. Freud, Erikson, Piaget and Inhelder, Kohlberg, and others. (See appendix 1 for a brief description of these theories and some representative current research based on them.) These life cycle theorists have in common the use of various concepts indicating predetermined ages and stages of experience that are fixed, ordered, and universal in nature.

In contrast, the newer "life course" model emphasizes the enormous numbers of life events and life transactions as the substance and outcome of innumerable processes involving persons and environments. Fashioned from the independent but parallel work of psychologists, sociologists, anthropologists, and social historians, newly discovered data bearing on psycho-socio-cultural development (or newly recognized meanings of older data) include cultural differences arising from ethnicity, religion, and socioeconomic status; differences in female and male socialization; variations in sexual orientation; the influence of disability; the effects of powerlessness and oppression; and the far-ranging impacts of environmental pollution. The appearance of new family forms, tremendous shifts in community values and norms, and the critical significance of the physical environment and world peace to continued life on earth add to the need for a new model of human development. (See appendix 2—nonstage theories—and appendix 3—macro theories).

The new data and new meanings cannot be explained by stage models because these models assume uniform pathways of development that lead to fixed, predictable endpoints, without regard for the many powerful differentiating influences. In stage models each stage must be negotiated at some optimal level during a critical period of development in order for the next stage to be addressed successfully. This is an application of the epigenetic principle derived from embryological development. This principle is inappropriate when applied to emotional and social development where there is no inevitability to the order and nature of feelings or social events; the only constant in human life is change. Sometimes this change is slower (giving rise to the illusion of fixed stability); sometimes it is rapid (giving rise to the illusion of total chaos). The truth of the matter is probably somewhere in between: there are islands of temporary orderly change, but such apparent constancy requires eternal vigilance in continuous adaptation.

The older stage models had a limited conception of the environment in which the infant emerged and developed. Writing at a time when fathers worked and mothers stayed home with the children, some stage theorists focused on the environment as consisting only of the baby's mother. The father became significant only toward the end of the first year, and siblings still later. The responsibility for child rearing rested primarily on the mother, and when there were problems, she was faulted by these models. The social and cultural worlds were rarely considered as influences of childhood, and so were absolved from any responsibility—or the need to modify detrimental structures or influences. Massive sets of data have forced the consideration that all psycho-socio-cultural domains as influencing human behavior. For example, in times of economic depression, we observe predictable increases in family violence, substance abuse, and indicators of problems in living. Families in these particular locales have not suddenly all had the same individual epigenetic experience, which has taken a nasty turn toward the destructive. It is clearly a case of the interaction of these persons and the several environments in which they live. How these sociocultural forces are played out in the lives of individuals and families is a major focus in part 2.

The life course model accommodates these new data and new meanings. It acknowledges the self-regulating, self-determining nature of human beings and the indeterminate nature of nonuniform pathways of psycho-socio-cultural development and social life. In fact, diversity of life paths appears to be a prerequisite for social organization in complex societies such as ours (Freeman 1984). As described by Hareven (1982), the life course conception views life events and life transitions not as isolated, separable, fixed stages, but as ongoing processes, occurring and recurring at any point in the life course. They may be expectable or nonexpectable, stressful or challenging depending on uniquely combined influences of personal, social, cultural, and physical environmental features. The life course model also takes account of the merging of individual developmental pathways into collective processes in families, groups, and communities. We described previously these tandem developments in the lives of children and parents, and we expand on the communal and cultural developments in these tandem developments in the following chapters.

A distinctive contribution of the life course model is its time perspective, that is, its notion that psycho-socio-cultural developments and functioning take place simultaneously within what we will term historical, sociocultural, and individual time. For example, periods such as childhood, youth, and old age are to be understood in the continuum of the entire life course, including (1) *historical age:* the effects of the historical configuration of events—those large-scale social changes that influence all individual and collective experience of persons living at that time; these events are indicated by birth date and thus cohort membership; (2) *sociocultural age:* the effects of the particular social and cultural group norms and roles—the socially and culturally constructed meanings for the patterns of life events on family and community life; and (3) *individual age:* the individual life history or life story reflecting chronological age for a particular person.

Historical Time and Cohorts

A *birth cohort* is defined as all persons who were born at a particular historical time and thereby exposed to the same sequence of social and historical changes over their life course (Riley 1978). Members of a birth cohort are likely to experience the developmental process of growing up and growing older differently from the members of every other birth cohort because they live though different historical and social processes or through the same processes but at different chronological ages. The meaning of the Vietnam war era is different for those who were of fighting age in World War II—the "good war"—as compared to those of fighting age in the 1960s and 1970s when the "bad war" was going on, and both these cohorts have had enormously different worldviews than those born after the Vietnam war.

Characteristics of the cohort itself affect individual life conditions.

Cohorts differ in size and sex ratios. Smaller cohorts may have more productive educational experiences, more opportunities in the world of work, and a quicker rise in their economic status. Differences in sex ratios across cohorts affect pairing and parenting opportunities; when combined with cultural oppression and economic status, these events may play havoc with expectable family patterns, such as the Chinese contract laborers who came as male work groups building the railroads in the mid-nineteenth centuries, only to find restrictive immigration rules that excluded Chinese women for many years in America (Hraba 1979).

As the members of the cohort grow up and grow older together, their collective lives can set off social changes that affect different cohorts differently. Riley (1985a) pointed out that the cohort of young women in the later 1960s and early 1970s—responding to many shared experiences—developed common patterns of response, common definitions, and common norms. As a collective force, they pressed for change in social roles and social values. The next cohort of young women and some young men brought the new ideas into the open, institutionalized them, and began the transformation of gendered roles and attitudes in the family and the workplace. This transformation led, in turn, to demands for new social policies and structures, such as expanded child care arrangements, flexible work hours, maternal and paternal leave, laws against sex discrimination and sexual harassment, and equal pay for comparable worth—all of which changed the life patterns of many of today's cohort of young women and men, as well as the developmental experiences of their children. However, there is nothing inevitable or fixed in this process, and there may be changes back to parts of the "good old days," or the "bad old days," depending on one's perspective.

The life patterns of each cohort are influenced by unique sequences of social changes in the family, the school, the workplace, and the community; in ideas, values, beliefs, science, technology, and the arts; and in patterns of migration, fertility, and mortality (Riley 1985b). Within each cohort, however, there are individual differences due to personality and cultural features, as well as different life experiences and life conditions, that are more forceful influences on development than are cohort influences. Different portions of the country may respond differently to the same cohort experience because of their different social and cultural histories. Nonetheless, cohorts add important social and historical dimensions to individual phenomena. Taking account of cohort influences prevents cohort centrism, analogous to ethnocentrism, where we wrongly assume that other cohorts follow the same developmental pathways as our own cohort (Riley 1978).

Social Time, Life Transitions, and Collective Processes

The traditional timetables of many transitions are disappearing. Neugarten captured these crossovers when she wrote: "Ours seems to be a society that has become accustomed to 70-year-old students, 30-year-old college presidents, 22-year-old mayors, 35-year-old grandmothers, 50-year-old retirees, 65-year-old fathers of preschoolers, 60-year-olds and 30-year-olds wearing the same clothing styles" (1978:52). Today, we must add to that list 65-year-olds who are caretakers of their 85-year-old parents and parent substitutes for their 5- to-15-year-old grandchildren in the absence or incapacity of their 35-year-old adult children. More than 3 million children live with grandparents or relatives other than their parents, a 40 percent increase over the last decade (Popiel 1993:9). Clearly, the social timing of many transitions of adulthood is changing markedly. No longer is there a fixed, age-connected time for learning, selecting sexual partners, marrying or remarrying, first-time parenting, second- or third-time parenting, changing careers, retiring, or moving into new statuses and roles. Such transitions are becoming relatively age-independent, contrary to some fixed-stage theories.

Many persons are transcending traditional gender roles heretofore considered unalterable in our society. Examples of gender crossovers include the actual exchange of traditional male and female roles in some families (perhaps because of economic roles accessible to each), solo parenting by fathers—about 1 million by recent counts, compared to more than 18 million women solo parents (Dodd 1988), single-career women having their own children by various means and raising them alone, and the entry of women into previously male occupations and of some men into previously female occupations.

Writing from a different stance, Gilligan (1982) believes human development must be reconceptualized to take into account the differing socialization and life experience of women and men. She points out that women's socialization and life experiences are missing in the traditional stage models of development. When women are measured against criteria for developmental progression in stage models, they are found wanting because the models are based on the study of men and their life experiences in a male-dominated society and culture.

These various age and gender crossovers are said by some to herald new potentials in the life course to be both young and old at the same time and to be both masculine and feminine—if one wishes. These changes are shaping the life transitions and psycho-socio-cultural development of adults and are transforming families. They are also shaping the development of children across the life course in ways that we cannot currently foresee.

Individual Time: The Life Course

Longitudinal research on healthy children and those with disabilities (e.g., Werner and Smith 1992; Murphy 1974; Offer, Ostrov, and Howard 1988; Thomas and Chess 1977) reveals the flexibility of development and the potential for change in children and adults. This flexibility defies the assumption of fixed, uniform, sequential stages, which overlook changing environmental influences. Thomas and Chess believe that the all-important status granted to early life experiences in stage models of development does a disservice to human potential and resilience, and to the significance of the developmental context across the life course:

> In our own New York Longitudinal Study . . . the evolving child-environment interactional process was affected by many emerging unanticipated influences—changes in basic function, new talents, new environmental opportunities or stresses, changes in family structure or attitude, and possibly late-emerging genetic factors. . . . Early life experience may be important in getting a good start in life, but does not fix subsequent development.
> (Thomas 1981)

As we see in the chapters that follow, other researchers in a variety of disciplines also suggest that the emotional and social development of children and adults is not a uniform process. Instead, development reflects the complex interplay from birth to the older years of physical, biological, and cognitive-perceptual maturation; individual potential; cultural influences; environmental constraints and opportunities; and the historical context.

The life course conception provides a fresh vision of life events, life transitions, and other life issues. The emphasis is on human potentialities from birth to the older years and on the environmental "nutrients" needed for their release and continued development. In addition to reflecting the life course conception, part 2 also reflects the view that family members develop simultaneously in continual processes involving both generations, in which parents and offspring are active agents in their own and one another's development. Parents and children develop together in the sense of physical proximity but more importantly in the psycho-socio-cultural sense of becoming who they are through interactions with the others. This tandem development is a neutral concept of simultaneous, reciprocal influence by parents and children on the development of one another and on family transformation in social time. The family transformations brought about by individual, familial, and environmental processes, in turn, influence child and adult development in individual time.

Elder defines the life course as "pathways through the age-differentiated life span, to social patterns in the timing, duration, spacing, and order of events; the timing of an event may be as consequential for life experience as whether the event occurs and the degree or type of change" (1984:180). In part 2 we consider timing, duration, spacing, and the order of events over the life course.

8

Family Formation in a Diverse Society

The various types of family forms and functions we discuss in chapter 6 are now presented in terms of the tandem developments that take place between partners and among members of the family over the life course within our enormously complex and diverse society. We seek to understand the mixing of the bio-psycho-sociocultural strands with the unique experiences of each person and family. Like the warp and woof of weaving, the resultant tapestry of life is extraordinarily rich in colors and textures.

Outline

Love

Marriage

The New Couple
> The Sexual Relationship
> Depth of Commitment
> Level of Intimacy
> Quality of Attachment

Gender Issues: Social Roles of Couplehood

Social Class Differences among Couples

Options Regarding Parenthood

Primary Prevention of Marital Conflict and Divorce: Dawn of a New Day

Love

Freud declared that the major accomplishments of a mentally healthy adult life are loving and working; Alfred Adler (1959) added service to others as a defining ingredient of a mature and effective adult. In this chapter, we consider love as the matrix of living, working, and serving others, all potential parts of family dynamics in a diverse society.

Love is not only a "many-splendored thing" but also an increasingly complex set of feelings, thoughts, and actions displayed between and among people over the life course. We pick up the thread of love at the time of family formation since more than 90 percent of adults in America marry at some time in their lives, and more than 90 percent of these marriages have children (Stevenson and Black 1996). With the many social, economic, and political changes over the past three decades, options for young adults have increased greatly. The same options may be available to people whether they marry, cohabit, or do not marry. All these options may have different patterns of being sexually active or not, and having or not having children. It is unlikely that married people will not be sexually active, but some people may not be able to and others may not wish to. Some married persons may procreate their own children, and others may not, according to their desires and capabilities. These married persons may also choose to have foster children, adopt children, or be the informal family to still other children, whether or not they have their own children. Cohabiting people (heterosexual or homosexual) may also choose whether to be sexually active or not, and whether to have their own children or acquire others through different means. Never-married persons may also be sexually active or not, procreate, or acquire children through other choices. The technology of procreation has also expanded enormously, even though most children are still conceived in the old-fashioned way.

Larson (1991:20) reports that in 1991, 4 percent of the U.S. population aged 19 and over was cohabiting, and 25 percent of Americans have cohabited at some time during their adult lives. Solo parenting is also being deliberately chosen—almost entirely by older, often professional, women. But legal marriage (including remarriage) is still the dominant mode of coming together to form a family. Married and unmarried couples are also deliberately limiting the size of their families; fertility declined from an average of 3.7 children per woman in 1960, to only 2.0 by 1990 (Popenoe 1991:19). This is slightly below the replacement rate of 2.1 children, but the projected population of Americans will continue to rise slightly to at least the mid-twenty-first century. Throughout the balance of this chapter, the term marriage is used whenever the legal institution of marriage is being referred to; otherwise, all the content applies also to all couples in committed relationships, whether heterosexual or homosexual.

What is love? American society appears to subscribe to romantic love, including passion and sexual attraction, as the basis of marriage, in contrast to more traditional societies that view marriage as an institution arranged by the parents of both individuals for economic, political, and social reasons. Freud and others have said romantic love is akin to madness insofar as it leads to irrational views of the beloved, and it is believed by some therefore to be a poor base for a lasting marriage. Others assert that romantic love, passion, and sexual attraction do form an important base, but they yield their salience gradually to a new kind of love that includes mutual affection, caring, respect, and commitment—if the marriage is to be a lasting and fulfilling one for both. In all types of partnerships—married or unmarried, heterosexual or homosexual relationships—being in love and having one's feelings reciprocated by the partner bring joy, elevated self-esteem, and a heightened sense of identity as a person who loves and is beloved.

However, a lasting marriage is not necessarily a measure of fulfillment, as the stigma attached to divorce decreases and women attain more marketable skills to be on their own. About half of all new marriages will end in divorce, although there appears to be a slight downturn in divorce rates in recent years. Rejection and disappointment in love can lead to loss of self-esteem, extreme upset, grief, or depression; however, formal or informal breakups of intense relationships may also clear the way for new beginnings, new relationships of great intensity.

How can it be that two people deeply in love at one point in time will dissolve that loving relationship within a few years of marriage? Is love so blind that it is not aware of problems lying ahead of it? Is scientific understanding and professional helping so clumsy as to not be able to help people foresee and take preventive actions? Given the stakes people have in love and marriage, these are serious questions that we continue to discuss in chapter 12 on family transformations. However, let's begin here with some basic definitions: what is love? It is an interesting exercise to consider how the major theorists might define love, whether or not they ever did so. However, this is not an empty exercise, as we shall see, because such conceptual definitions may be translated into practice strategies to prevent marital problems and to promote happy and constructive marriages (Gottman 1993, 1994a, 1994b; Gottman and Levenson 1992; Markman et al. 1988; Markman et al. 1993). Freud speculated that love was a disguised search for the opposite sex parent, once the object of the child's oedipal/electra complex. This theme was admirably portrayed in the song lyrics, "I want a girl just like the girl who married dear old dad." (The lyrics were modified in World War II by GIs wanting a girl just like the girl who married Harry James [that would have been the actress Betty Grable].)

Jung theorized that a man looks for his opposite half, the illusive anima (while a woman looks for her opposite, the animus), thus resurrecting Aristophanes's presentation in Plato's *Symposium*. In the ancient and much funnier version, the original Being had four arms, four legs, and privy parts to match. But these Beings got too obstreperous, and the gods sliced them in half—now they had two arms, two legs, and a privy part to match. Then these two halves were spun around the world, leaving each person to seek his or her other half. Depending on the slicing, the other half could be a heterosexual or a homosexual partner. Love was the process of finding one's true other half. Winch's (1958) theory of need complementarity of marital partners is yet another modern version of finding that perfect fit between need and need fulfillment.

Skinner might transliterate the passion of love into mutually contingent reinforcers that were generalized to a wide range of interpersonal activities over long periods of time. These reinforcers might include a box of candy—one is reminded of Ogden Nash's poetic pronouncement, "candy is dandy, but liquor is quicker"—but more likely, the personal compliments and subtle strokes for the partner's self-esteem.

Communications and ecological theorists would add yet another perspective to a definition of love. This would consist of mutually satisfying and enhancing exchanges of messages and metacommunications delivered over an intense, long, or long and intense period of time that would result in the persistent development of the system common to them. None of these artificially constructed definitions of love may send shivers up your spine, but they will all prove useful in the coming discussion.

Marriage

"So, who are her people?" your grandmother asks when you announce that you are engaged. Although your grandmother may not have received her doctoral degree in sociology, she is right on the mark regarding the sociological and psychological factors involved in partner selection. General categorical factors, such as residential propinquity, congruency along dimensions of ethnicity, religion, education, and socioeconomic status, as well as shared settings of schooling, work, recreation, and religious institutions all operate to provide a first rough screening of eligible persons. "Oh, yes, I knew her aunt and uncle when they lived on Spring Street; nice family, except she gossiped too much," your grandmother reminisces.

There have been several major demographic trends over the past several decades that are continuing to the end of the twentieth century: Cross-cultural marriages have been increasing; the proportion of white Americans of European ancestry who married a person of an undivided ethnic heritage identical to their own was only 27 percent (U.S. Department of Commerce 1985). Formal marriage across racial lines, although increasing, is still infrequent for both black and white persons. In 1988, of the approximately 956,000 interracial marriages, 218,000 were between blacks and whites, and the remainder between other combinations of interracial couples (Gibbs and Moskowitz-Sweet, 1991:579). About 99 percent of black women and 97 percent of black men married within their race. Nearly 99 percent of non-Hispanic whites married other non-Hispanic whites.

Interreligious marriages have also increased. Religion is not included in the U.S. Census, but according to the National Opinion Research Center, about a third of those Catholics marrying in large urban dioceses marry a non-Catholic. Since 1975, 40 percent of Jewish marriages have been to non-Jews. On the other hand, marriage between persons of quite different socioeconomic levels is less frequent and tends to occur only between adjacent levels and not between widely separated levels. Usually it is the female who marries upward. Detailed statistics are rare for relationships outside of formal marriage.

Many psychological factors are presumed to be related to mate selection, but these are less well understood as related to selecting a particular partner. For example, on a conscious level, people may want to have a close friend with whom to share personal, sexual, and social exchanges; may wish for children; may feel the need to conform to prevailing norms of marriage or local pressures by family and friends; and so on. People may be less aware of their motivations to escape unhappy family situations; they may fantasize rescuing the mate from alcoholism or other difficulties, or of being rescued; they may seek revenge or comfort from earlier love affairs; or they may feel either great dependence or dominance vis-ß-vis the partner; or may deny one's own homosexual tendencies in favor of the protective cover of being married. This batch of misty motivations, if they exist at all, can create unrealistic perceptions and expectations of the partner and self, and may lead to conflicts in the relationship. On the other hand, probably most couples analyze with reasonable clarity the strengths and limitations of their partners, and make rational choices that this set of positives and negatives is acceptable as the basis for marriage, even though they recognize it will take continual efforts to make the partnership or marriage work as well as they hope.

The New Couple

In the case of marriage, the wedding represents a formal joining of two families. In any form of pairing, the new affiliation represents a critical life transition involving a change in status and roles for both partners. It is perceived by many as entering upon "real" adulthood. It may be experienced primarily as a desired challenge with all kinds of wonderful opportunities lying ahead, or primarily as a stressful situation that generates undue anxiety, helplessness, or guilt. Becoming a couple is potentially an enriching arena of adult development, including deepening relatedness, sexual gratification, expanded competence in new social roles, firmer self-concept and self-esteem, and increased self-direction—in tandem with the beloved.

At the beginning, new couples face a dilemma inasmuch as individual needs and the needs of the pair-as-unit are not always compatible. A major task for the pair is to balance individual patterns and traditions with the emerging sense of themselves as a couple whose lives proceed in tandem to an increasing degree. This requires developing a mutually satisfying sexual relationship; sharing responsibilities in household and economic management and trying out various ways of allocating roles and tasks; and becoming aware of the values, norms, rituals, tastes, and preferences that each brings from the past and deciding which will be retained and which discarded while beginning to form new ones as a couple. Other important tasks of beginning together include coping with the inevitable disillusions, differences, habits, and imperfections that tend to appear after a short time of living in close association; reaching agreement about closeness to or distance from family of origin and the friends of each partner; reconciling the job demands of each partner and managing tensions between job and couplehood demands; working out ways to resolve or to manage conflict; and reconciling the idealized view of the partner, and of the relationship, with reality. How the various challenges and tasks are met will depend in large part on the mutuality of the couple's sexual relationship, the depth of commitment to each other, the level of intimacy, and the quality of their attachment—and on the personality and cultural patterns of each partner and the characteristics of their environment. Let's examine each of these factors.

The Sexual Relationship

During the early months of the partners' establishing themselves as a couple, significant factors leading to a mutually satisfying sexual relationship include discovering, meeting, and becoming attuned to the partner's sexual needs and interests, and developing comfort in talking openly about one's own needs, anxieties, and preferences.

Sexual attitudes and behaviors have changed dramatically over the past half century, especially in regard to greater sexual freedom and pleasure for women. Many men and women now enter long-term heterosexual or homosexual couplehood having had previous sexual experience, and thus move easily into establishing a mutually satisfying pattern of sexual activity. However, some may lack accurate knowledge of sexual anatomy and functioning in both sexes or may carry over earlier attitudes and feelings of fear, shame, or guilt about sexuality derived from families of origin, religious teachings, cultural factors, or previous sexual experiences of a disturbing nature (such as rape or having been a childhood victim of incest). These troubling inhibitions require of the partners special patience, sensitivity, and open communication if they are to attain a satisfying sexual relationship. More serious sexual dysfunctions that do not yield to the partners' efforts are now often treatable by qualified sex therapist.

Depth of Commitment

Lauer and Lauer (1986) studied 351 couples with lasting marriages, of whom 300 said they were happily married. Among the common reasons these 300 gave for their satisfaction was a strong sense of commitment based on religious, ethnic, or secular values. The survey described the happily married respondents as people who, among other things, were willing to endure troubled times by confronting problems and working through them.

Critics of the growing trend toward informal living together argue that formal marriage and public marital vows tend to support the couple's commitment to each other and to the marriage over the long run. So, too, do gay and lesbian couples who seek the legalization of homosexual marriages. Critics of marriage, on the other hand, state that true commitment is not ensured by a marriage license and a wedding but is instead trivialized by them. Some take the position that informal living together is a way of testing mutual commitment and the viability of a monogamous choice before undertaking the legal and social responsibilities of marriage (cf. Larson 1991). This implies that the process of living together before marriage is apt to result in a more enduring marriage, although recent research suggests that the opposite is true (Thomson and Colella 1992).

Commitment develops gradually. Yet for some couples, today's easy access to and acceptance of divorce—as important as these are—tend to inhibit the development or to lessen the force of a commitment to work on impasses and relationship problems. There may be cultural changes in the acceptance of divorce as a solution to specific problems; divorce rates peaked in the mid-1980s and have been decreasing very slowly. Although commitment is essential to marital satisfaction, it is not sufficient by itself. Partners must continue to "work" on their relationship; otherwise, commitment tends to be hollow and devoid of intimacy and passion.

Level of Intimacy

Theorists from Freud to Gilligan have noted the difficulty of many men in achieving intimacy either in man-to-man or man-to-woman relationships. The gendered split between the expressive and instrumental functions makes it seem to many men—especially, but not exclusively, working-class men— that expressiveness and the intimacy it supports render them vulnerable and define them as weak and unmasculine. Ginsberg and Gottman don't agree with this blanket interpretation and point to the work of various authors suggesting strong friendships between men, deeply expressed feelings, and even powerful male-male bonds in the organized fighting of wars (1986:241–244).

On the other hand, sharing intimate aspects of self and expressing feelings are regarded by most women as essential to a loving relationship; without such reciprocity, there can be no intimacy. The Canadian researchers Houle and Kiely (1984) studied levels of intimacy, using a Montreal sample of 125 women and men, ages 18 to 43. The women in all age groups achieved higher intimacy scores than their male counterparts. The authors reported that their analysis revealed that, compared to men, "[w]omen are more accessible to their partners, more disposed to respond unconditionally to the needs of the other person, more open, and more committed to resolving problems that arise in the relationship. They also tend to share their emotions almost exclusively with the partner. . . . Men are open to their partners on a selective and conditional basis and are therefore less accessible."

O'Neil (1982) noted that self-disclosure, vulnerability, and trust are essential to the development of intimacy. Yet many men have been socialized not to admit human weakness nor to express intense feelings. Instead, they learn to rely on words, logic, and rationalistic explanations to control situations and explain reality, including the self. O'Neil stated that rigid gender specialization and differential treatment of females and males have "limited the sexes from developing all parts of their personality . . . needed to cope with the complexities of human experience. . . . The psychological, physical, and spiritual costs to humankind have been negative and great" (1982:39).

Balswick (1989) observed that the expectation that men be expressive, together with their early socialization to be tough and to avoid showing emotions, especially tenderness or sadness, constitutes a discontinuity in cultural conditioning. Males are socialized to inexpressiveness as a valued masculine characteristic; yet all married couples are expected to share feelings and to show affections. Balswick adds, "The most serious and destructive effects of male inexpressiveness within marriages may be seen in the accumulating evidence that links inability to express feelings to spouse abuse" (1989:6).

Quality of Attachment

Attachment is an important element in pair bonds, along with commitment and intimacy. Attachment theory is both similarly and dissimilarly expressed in adults and infants. It is similar in displaying a need for ready access to the attachment figure and desiring proximity in stressful situations, displaying heightened comfort and diminished anxiety when in the company of the attachment figure, and manifesting a marked increase in anxiety on discovering the attachment figure to be inexplicably inaccessible. These expressions of attachment are found regularly in well-functioning as well as some poorly functioning marriages (and other pair relationships).

Attachment in adults is dissimilar to attachment in infants in the following ways: Instead of attachment to parental caretakers, adult attachment is to peers of unique importance who are perceived either as sources of strength or as supporters of the person's own capacity for mastery. Adult attachment is usually directed toward a person who is also the object of sexual desire, and sexual contact may itself foster attachment. But adult attachments may not be accompanied by sexual desire. Weiss (1982) believes that attachment is more reliable than sexual desire in pair bonding because of its greater persistence, and it becomes increasingly persistent as the relationship becomes more established. In the face of threat, attachment becomes more powerful, while sexual desire is apt to be suppressed. And while attachment resists redirection to others, sexual desire seems less resistant to attractions of others.

Weiss emphasized that the adult attachment is not found in all the adult's emotionally significant relationships but appears only in relationships of central emotional importance (1982:174). Earlier, Weiss noted that attachment is one component among many that may constitute love, including "idealization of the other, trust, and identification with the other so great that contributions to the other's well-being are felt to be immediately gratifying to the self. . . . And perhaps seeing the other as completing the self by providing capacities or attributes that one lacks oneself" (1973:94) (Shades of Aristophanes!) The various components of love, including attachment, are independent, and their varied combinations differ for different persons and perhaps in different experiences of love for the same individual. Thus attachment is not the same as love. Attachment can also be present in the absence of love; for example, divorced couples sometimes remain attached although they no longer love each other.

Gender Issues: Social Roles of Couplehood

The traditional marriage at the turn of the twentieth century manifested a gender-based division of labor with the male as provider (working in the community and bringing money and resources back to the family) and the female as household manager (running the household—which meant doing or managing the cleaning, preparing food, and socializing—and caring for children and aged parents, as needed). Important changes have occurred in this division of labor, partly in response to the feminist movement and the interdependent social and economic trends, such as the growing numbers of women in the workforce, the increased numbers of women attaining higher education, delayed marriage and childbearing, lowered birth rates, and the increased availability of inexpensive contraception, which gives women more control over their lives.

However, only half the division of labor has really changed. Relatively few men are involved in participating in household management—and these men tend to be younger and better educated. What has been called "modern marriage" (including some people involved in cohabitation) involves a limited reduction in male dominance or power but little real change in household tasks, despite the acceptance of gender equity as an ideal by many of those in such marriages and partnerships.

In contrast, the "egalitarian marriage" (including some people involved in cohabitation) accords equal status and power to the partners, both of whom are usually employed. Household and economic roles are not based on gender stereotypes. Instead, chores are shared equitably according to the partners' interests, abilities, and availability. Roles are interchangeable in the face of the situational needs of the moment, or they are rotated. In some instances, traditional gender roles are actually reversed by the deliberate choice of both individuals. The male partner may remain at home, taking on household and child-rearing tasks while the female partner works or obtains higher education. Egalitarian marriages and informal partnerships benefit from institutional supports (when available) such as part-time work for men and women with full benefits (as when two people share one full-time job); the elimination of policies forbidding nepotism (relatives working for the same employer); paid maternity and paternity leaves (often staggered so that one parent can be home with the infant while the other is working); adequate day care arrangements for children or elderly relatives in the household, including round-the-clock emergency centers for temporary care during crisis, work-related travel, or need for respite; easily accessible medical and dental care, such as mobile neighborhood units; and recreation facilities located in schools-as-community centers for children during after-school hours, for neighborhood forums, and for support groups. These institutional supports for egalitarian couples are equally essential for solo parents and two-provider families.

The egalitarian structure is designed to use the strengths and to reduce the limitations of both partners by eliminating power and status differences, and encouraging individual development as part of the enhancement of the family system. An egalitarian structure is probably found in most lesbian and gay relationships. Egalitarian heterosexual couples are found mainly among educated, liberal young adults, a relatively small percentage of all couples. Even those subscribing to equality may wittingly or unwittingly fall back on more traditional roles when children are born.

Hudgins (1991–1992) and Nobles (1974) pointed out that black family organization has long been egalitarian. In intact black families (which constitute about half of all black families (Jones 1995:154), neither parent is dominant. In the remaining half, which largely comprise female-headed families, Nobles disclaimed the myth of the black matriarch, distinguishing between strength and dominance. The black single mother has needed to be strong in order to maintain the survival of the tribe (family), and she is not necessarily domineering. A review of research findings regarding the socialization of black children reveals that the role behaviors usually defined in the Euro-American culture as feminine or masculine are encouraged in both boys and girls in black families. It is not surprising, then, that role flexibility between the parents in child care and household tasks has long characterized the black family (Hudgins 1991–1992; Hill 1972).

Social Class Differences among Couples

Social class (or socioeconomic status—SES) has been one of the enduring major variables in the sociological literature, even as it has changed over time. (See appendix 3, on macrosocial theorists.) In a general sense, a social class is some large aggregate of people who share a similar socioeconomic status or stratum relative to the various stratifications of people in the whole society. This socioeconomic status implies a relative similarity in economic, educational, and social backgrounds and the subsequent prestige levels, life opportunities, and lifestyles each of these affords the people involved.

Miller and Swanson (1958) made a distinction between entrepreneurial and bureaucratic types of low-income and middle-income households that may become useful once again as large numbers of former welfare families struggle to enter the workforce. Entrepreneurial socioeconomic structures place individual workers against the world, struggling on their own to achieve economic success by their own wits and resources. They have to take chances in risky situations, and learn to trust themselves and be self-reliant (Miller and Swanson 1958:34–42). Farmers and small business owners are quintessential entrepreneurs. In sharp contrast are the bureaucratic structures that involve large organizations that envelop the whole world of its workers in an intricate network of interrelated tasks with coworkers (division of labor) and relatively stable rules and expectations. There is relatively little risk in this bureaucratic world, and the chief values are cooperation (with peers) and obedience (to superiors).

Miller and Swanson make the point that these macrosocial perspectives are transmitted to the children as the nature of the social world and what they need to do in order to succeed in it. Entrepreneurial children are taught to be self-reliant and to distrust the hostile environment, including the government that is seen as exerting controls over them. Bureaucratic children are taught that the world is gentler and more secure, so long as one does not rock the bureaucratic boat and remains loyal and cooperative with others.

However, a half century later, these distinctions have a different ring as layoffs of professional workers and massive "downsizing" of skilled workers occur, so that giant bureaucratic organizations can be more competitive in a world economy. This kind of riskiness in the bureaucratic workplace is more reminiscent of entrepreneurial environments. Moreover, as the end of "welfare as we know it" approaches, because of the Welfare Reform Act of 1996, we can extend Miller and Swanson's conceptual model to another large body of people who have experienced another type of work (or rather, welfare) structure, which provides yet another view of the world and how to raise children to succeed in that world.

Nordheimer (1996) presents some information from sites around the country that welfare-to-work training is going to be difficult to achieve. Looking at the most qualified of the trainees who were then selected for entry-level jobs, anywhere between 25 and 80 percent remain on the job after a short time—no national figures are available. Even so, these are not figures to generate optimism about the success of the new welfare-to-work scene. Why should this be so?

Drawing on Miller and Swanson's orientation, people's work—or now, welfare—experience structures how they see the world and how they convey this to their children so as to prepare them for that expected world. This welfare situation is perceived as hostile, mean spirited, and controlled by distant forces (federal and state legislative initiatives) that appear uninfluenceable—which is like the entrepreneur's worldview. This may be expected to lead to a similar rugged individualism—"Nobody is going to tell me what I can or cannot do." But welfare as a life experience is also overcontrolling, like a bureaucratic structure in which the rules of the game are known and one is forced to play (formally) by the rules in order to receive benefits. This is likely to lead to a welfare-to-work conflict: These people will likely be sensitive to affronts to their autonomy while at the same time they will face ordinary work expectations demanded by bureaucratic employers. This is exactly what Nordheimer (1996) reports: Some trainees quit over "perceived slights to their dignity." "As single mothers, they are on their own and think of themselves as authority figures." Employers note that some new employees "have problems that include absenteeism, lack of discipline about work hours, poor reading and communication skills, and open resentment when given directions." Some trainees felt they were being "talked down to" as if they were children. On the other side, employers value new employees "who show initiative and a willingness to learn, even when that has required training in rudiments like the proper way to answer phones." Some highly successful case illustrations are presented. But, overall, the various incentives do not seem to be enough to get large percentages of new workers to stay on the job. Clearly, social workers and others involved in this massive welfare-to-work transition have to understand the bio-psycho-socio-cultural factors that are pushing and pulling on all parties to this major social change in America.

However, some former welfare people will enter the workforce on a regular basis. What is the effect of working on a person or a couple? Certainly there are more stresses regarding demands of the daily grind, and these may affect women more than men, if employed women continue to do the lion's share of the household and child maintenance. These work-related stresses may put new stresses on the children who also have to adapt to such a significant change in the family dynamics. On the other hand, working may create positive challenges in the lives of the workers and other family members. The nature of their income may likewise be a source of pride, even though the amount may be relatively little. New workers can enter a whole world of acceptable behaviors that are often cut off to people on welfare—from buying whatever they want (if they have the money) to saving for a more nearly attainable future for themselves and their children. They have joined the mainstream of society in holding the American Dream, because working and earning money in a respectable way makes that Dream seem more nearly feasible.

Thus married couples or cohabiting partners in general are likely to reflect in their lives the many influences of social class. Indeed, some argue that in contemporary American society social class has taken over from ethnicity or gender as the dominant variable (Sowell 1994). For example, the marital and child-rearing patterns of most middle-class black and white couples are similar, as are the patterns of most low-income black and white couples. On the other hand, middle-class and low-income black couples are different from each other; so, too, are middle-class and low-income white couples. Single-parent households will also differ on whether the parent is in a low-income situation or is living a middle-class lifestyle. Thus the poor—whether black or white, dual- or single-parent-headed households—have a closer resemblance in lifestyle, life opportunities, and prestige than the middle class—whether black or white, single- or dual-parent-headed households. However, not every low-income couple fits the characteristics of lower socioeconomic status nor does every middle-class couple fit these SES characteristics as described on the following pages because there are many factors that influence life opportunities and lifestyles besides the economic ones.

Options Regarding Parenthood

Most heterosexual couples and some homosexual couples or single individuals face a basic choice: to have a child now or later, to adopt a child or take over ongoing care of a child (as in informal arrangements with members of the extended family or some foster care relationships), or to remain childless. The last option now meets with less disapproval for married couples than formerly. Among couples opting to remain permanently childless or to have no additional children, reliance on female and male sterilization is growing. Sterilization by choice is the second most popular form of birth control for Americans, after the pill (Kantrowitz and Wingert 1993). More than half of all married couples use one form of sterilization or the other. These are tubal ligation for women, which involves severing the fallopian tubes leading from the ovaries to the uterus, or vasectomy for men, which involves removing a small section of the vas deferens near the place where the scrotum is attached to the body. (Neither procedure has any significant effect on either men's or women's ability to perform or enjoy sexual activity.)

The option of parenthood takes place through the physical and psychological communications of a male and a female, either by choice or by accident. In either case, parenthood is an ecological event in its impact, if not in its origin. (Adoption is considered briefly later in this chapter, as is the incredibly complex abortion issue.) An unintended pregnancy that is also unwanted can be a problem for the child and the parents, but many unintended or unwanted pregnancies do become "wanted" before or after the baby's birth.

In any case, expecting a child can be a joyful challenge or a painful source of stress, depending on the couple's emotional and financial readiness, the quality of their relationship, their motivation for and their feelings about children, and the salience of other goals. Other influences are their health status, their cultural values and norms, and the available environmental supports. Some lesbian and gay couples—and some single, career-oriented women— choose to have a baby (through a sperm bank; a male friend, or a female friend in the case of the gay man; or a surrogate mother) although their numbers are not known.

The discussions of pregnancy, birth, and the marvels of child rearing are discussed in the succeeding chapters. We want to present some material on infertility, which is a serious problem for many couples and appears to be on the rise. A couple is considered medically infertile after trying unsuccessfully for a year to have a child. Learning of one's own or one's partner's incurable infertility can be a severe shock to both partners. Some respond to their lost hope for a child with grief; others view the condition as evidence of impaired sexuality that damages their self-concept and identity as a male or a female. However, this information may also transform the couple to consider adoption or other technological options. And other couples simply accept the bad news and move on to other options without disabling or conflicted responses.

Adoption and artificial insemination were the only solutions to infertility until recent technological developments made available additional options: (1)

in vitro fertilization, in which the mother's ova are extracted (a painful and expensive surgical procedure), fertilized in a laboratory dish with her partner's sperm, then implanted in her uterus; (2) embryo transfers involving third-party contributions of ova or sperm; (3) surrogate motherhood, in which a woman impregnated through artificial insemination or an embryo implant carries the child for someone else; and (4) gamete intrafallopian transfer (GIFT), in which the ovum and the sperm are transferred to the recipient's fallopian tubes.

These technological advances also raise all types of ethical issues that are very troubling. Excess embryos may be frozen, to be thawed later and transferred to the same or a different woman, and sperm, donated anonymously or otherwise, may be frozen and kept in sperm banks. Babies developed from frozen embryos have been born, although it is too early to know the possible long-term effects of freezing on genetic material (DNA). When parents of these frozen components of human birth die prematurely, there are questions about disposition of the frozen components and what legal rights they have, if any.

Central regulatory and monitoring structures, as well as medical and psychological screening procedures, are not uniformly in place for the medical, psychological, and legal protection of babies, donors, and donees despite the rapid growth of transfer programs. As a consequence, programs form their own policies, and most transfer centers and many sperm banks limit their services to married couples, thus discriminating against single women and lesbians. In light of the many issues coming to the fore, social workers in family agencies, child welfare agencies, and medical and psychiatric clinics are, or will soon be, helping parents and children with the dilemmas and the unforeseen emotional ramifications arising from the use of the new technologies, as has been the case in the adoption field. Many adults adopted as children conduct a painful search for their biological parents in order to complete their sense of self and to secure knowledge of their cultural, familial, and genetic heritage. How will the children born of the new technologies respond to their situation? How will children react to the knowledge that they were conceived in a laboratory dish? In the case of anonymous donors, how will children respond to the fact that they can never know who their father was? What will be the impact on children born to surrogate mothers when they learn that they were given up for money?

Apart from these personal issues, the public concern about these technological births is very complicated and controversial. For example, fertility drugs occasionally produce multiple fetuses. Moreover, embryo implantation involves the use of as many as four embryos as a means of ensuring against failure, yet sometimes all develop as fetuses. In both situations, some prospective parents have asked for and received abortions of the surplus healthy fetuses in order to ensure the safe development of one or two. This so-called pregnancy reduction is done by inserting potassium chloride by needle into the fetal chest cavity. The heart stops, and eventually the dead fetuses are absorbed. Ethicists and some physicians are raising ethical and moral questions about these procedures.

The second area of controversy concerns infants who survive a late abortion. Should not they have the same rights to neonatal care and support and plans for their future, if they continue to live, as other prematurely born but wanted infants? Fetuses that survive late abortions are usually between 20 and 24 weeks of age. Hence these infants not only are injured by the procedure itself but are at additional grave medical risk because of their extreme immaturity. Viability, or when the baby can survive outside the womb, is being gradually pushed back by technical advances from 28 weeks (cited in the U.S. Supreme Court's *Roe v. Wade* decision of 1973) toward 20 weeks. It now stands at about 24 weeks, but as technology improves, the age will undoubtedly be lowered further.

Some states have set the limiting age for legal abortion at 24 weeks (except where the mother's life is in danger), and some hospitals have set their own cutoff points for elective abortions at 20 weeks in order to prevent such a disturbing event (a live born fetus) and its emotional impact on the mother and the staff. At least one state (New York) requires that another physician be in attendance at the abortion of a fetus of 20 or more weeks of age in order to render care in the event of its survival. Some obstetricians, however, are replacing the saline method of late abortion after 20 weeks with dismemberment of the fetus in the womb (known as dilation and evacuation), thereby ensuring nonsurvival. Others believe this is an unethical and inhumane action, even though it is not illegal.

Few as their numbers are so far, survivors of late abortion are generating difficult ethical, legal, social, and financial issues. The protection of their right to full supportive care and resuscitation is a matter of growing concern to many professionals and others. Kleiman cites a 1984 report of the U.S. Centers for Disease Control which states that 90 percent of abortions are performed before the twelfth week. About 13,000, or 1 percent, are performed after the twenty-first week. Many of these may be carried out on teenagers who were not aware of their pregnancy until quickening (fetal movement), which usually occurs between the seventeenth and twentieth weeks. About 10 percent of late abortions, however, are performed because of serious fetal abnormality. Furthermore, amniocentesis, the most common means of fetal diagnosis for genetic and chromosomal disorders, cannot be performed until the fourteenth to sixteenth weeks of pregnancy. The results take up to four weeks to become available, so an elective abortion following the diagnosis of severe defect may take place as late as the twentieth week. If problems occur in the culturing of the amniotic fluid, the abortion may be delayed still further (Kleiman 1984).

The reproductive technologies described in this section are viewed by many infertile couples, and by those of which one partner is at risk of transmitting a genetic disease, as preferable to adoption, even though only one parent or neither will be genetically related to the child. However, the new technologies are not options for the infertile male; his only choices are childlessness or adoption. Yet less than 1 percent of unwed black mothers and only 12 percent of unwed white mothers now choose adoption for their infants. Hence, nonminority persons seeking adoption have turned to private or international sources. Meanwhile, many minority and disabled infants and older children eligible for adoption languish in long-term foster care, often with many changes of foster home, which may lead to blighted futures (see McDonald et al. 1996; and Barth et al. 1994). This problem is due to policies that do not permit financial subsidies to low-income minority persons interested in adoption and to a concern that cross-racial adoption deprives the child of his or her cultural identity, history, and context. Therefore, it is likely that infertile parents will turn more and more to the new technologies to satisfy their yearning for a child, despite the ethical issues and the possible impact on the children as they grow older.

To look at the birth issue from a larger perspective, we encounter yet other problems. Each child, one by one, adds to the world's population, requires expenditure of various environmental resources to give life and liveliness to the growing person who eventually gives back some contributions to nature and humankind. The ecological perspective requires us to stand back from the particular situation before us and consider the larger impact of this one "vital statistic." While people of North America are not adding disproportionately to the world population explosion, relative to the enormous increases in the developing world, still North Americans take a disproportionate amount of the world resources to satisfy their learned hunger for material goods and a high standard of life, luxury, and comforts. A collection of books on the state of the world are grim reminders of the consequences of population explosions, excessive extraction of limited material and living resources (Brown et al. 1996). The social sciences, let alone the applied social sciences, have not yet come to grips with the megaconcerns nor their responsibilities toward them.

Primary Prevention of Marital Conflict and Divorce: Dawn of a New Day

The rationale for taking primary preventive action *before* a given problem erupts has never been stronger than in the situation of marital conflict and divorce. With a failure (divorce) rate of nearly 50 percent in America and with marital (or partner) conflict practically universal, this problem affects practically every adult. If we knew what were the predictors of marital conflict and divorce, and if these circumstances were modifiable (Markman 1981; Markman et al. 1988; Markman et al. 1993; Gottman 1994a, 1994b; Schinke et al. 1986; Smith, Vivian, and O'Leary 1990), then why would people (including helping professionals) wait until stressful conditions and negative effects had already occurred before "helping"? Some important studies provide information on predictors of marital conflict and divorce; many of these conditions can be identified and resolved to a considerable degree before problems occur. Gottman notes: "Now, after more than a decade of research on divorce prediction, we can predict with over 94% accuracy who will divorce and who will stay married in a short-term, longitudinal study of 3 to 8 years" (1995:103).

We know full well how painful and stressful conflicts in the marriage and subsequent divorce can be. A recent review of the literature by Stevenson and Black (1996) helpfully sorts out this enormous literature on how divorce affects offspring.

There are many efforts aimed at promoting happy marriage, such as the traditional premarital counseling that clergy or lay religious people provide. These usually involve explorations of the couple's religious values often in combination with personality compatibility as derived from inventories or interviews (Markman et al. 1988:210). The assumption that compatibility underlies marital satisfaction or stability has not been supported by research (Gottman 1979). Rather, there is much evidence that it is the quality of the communication between the engaged or untroubled married couple that may be at the core of the matter (Gottman 1994b). Many efforts have been aimed at promoting effective communication and problem-solving skills between engaged or untroubled married people, such as the work of Guerney (1977), Miller, Nunnally, and Wackman (1977), and Markman, Floyd, and Dickson-Markman (1982). Results have been suggestive (Hahlweg and Markman 1988), but these have been short-term studies and they lacked adequate control groups in their design.

Markman et al. (1988) examined a study aimed at correcting these problems. Forty-two couples planning marriage were matched and randomly assigned to a preventive intervention group (E) and a control group (C). These couples participated in a multimodal assessment at pre- and postintervention, and then again at 1.5 , 3, 4, and 5 years (Markman et al. 1993). They had known each other, on average, about 2.5 years; the average age of women was 23 years, and of men, 24 years. Most importantly, the average relationship satisfaction score on the Locke and Wallace Inventory was in the nondistressed range (Locke and Wallace 1959), so these couples fit the primary prevention requirement of addressing a situation before it is problematic.

The preventive intervention consisted of techniques borrowed and adapted from cognitive-behavioral marital therapy (Jacobson and Margolin 1979) and communication-oriented marital enhancement programs (Guerney 1977). It is important to emphasize how these materials were adapted to serve the primary prevention function. The focus is future oriented and not on current problems; for example, skills were taught on how to exit negative affect cycles and how to use active listening and expressive speaking skills. This prevention program also sought to protect and maintain already high levels of functioning, rather than to improve functioning as in the treatment sense. The 5-session program included work on communication skills, problem-solving training, clarification of marital expectations, sensual/sexual education, and relationship enhancement to "make a good relationship better." One note: a major goal of the problem-solving skills was to establish what was called "relationship efficacy," which is a couple's version of Bandura's individual self-efficacy, a point to which we return later.

The results were very interesting. The experimental couples generally maintained high levels of relationship quality, whereas the control couples showed the predictable declines in marital quality found in other longitudinal studies (Markman 1981). Nearly a quarter of the control group couples dissolved their relationship, as compared with 5 percent in the experimental group, a statistically significant finding "suggesting that skill-based intervention programs may not only help couples maintain relationship positivity but may also serve to reduce the probability of relationship dissolution" (Markman et al. 1988:213, 215). Up to 3 years after the program ended, the experimental group couples showed higher levels of marital satisfaction and lower levels of relationship instability than did the control group couples.

In a later portion of this study, Markman et al. (1993) gathered data not only from the experimental and control groups but also from the couples who declined the offer of the program after they had completed the initial pre-assessment session. We'll report their findings on E, C, and D (D=decliners) groups in the fourth and fifth years of the study. Overall, the later years' findings continue the earlier follow-up years but less strongly. Among the important findings relevant to social work concerns is that there were more positive and fewer negative communications in the experimental group, which may lead to their reduced risk of resorting to physical violence (Markman et al. 1993:75). Unlike the control couples, the decliner couples did not differ in positive communications (until 3 years later) or in low levels of physical violence over 5 years as compared with the experimental group. However, the decliners did show a significantly higher rate of breakup before marriage than did the experimental group. This pattern suggests to the researchers that decliners already used constructive communication skills and thought that they did not need the preventive program. However, these decliners did not maintain their positive communications over time as did the experimental couples did.

An important finding is that the preventive program effects seem to be weakening after the fifth year. While there are various interpretations of these results, it seems reasonable to suggest that life conditions are changing and that people need preventive/promotive "booster" sessions to help them adapt old principles to new circumstance, especially, as Markman et al. suggest, at developmentally relevant points in the couple's lives, such as when they are planning their first child (1993:76).

While there are limitations and challenges to this (and all) research, it seems clear to us that there is a reasonable technology available to address important communication and problem-solving concerns before significant problems emerge—and thus to approach that idealistic dream of preventing marital conflict and divorce. We are not there yet, but as Markman et al. say, this work provides a growing conceptual and empirical foundation for future prevention efforts (1993:76). For a popular statement of another approach to helping marriages succeed, see Gottman (1994b); this book is based on his twenty years of research on more than 2,000 couples, as described in Gottman (1994a) and his other papers.

9

Family Transformations: Birth, Infancy, and Language—The Socialization of Children and Parents

This chapter begins a discussion of human growth and development always in the context of the significant environments in which these changes take place. We give special attention to language development as a central feature in the socialization of the child and of tandem developments in the parents and family, as well as in society.

Outline

Introduction

Three-year-old Jan was playing happily with her building blocks and chatting with her London-born father in a kind of stream of consciousness: "what I am doing with this block" and "what this block is"—a double-decker bus now, a big dog later. Her mother walked in with a bag of groceries and her attaché case, greeted them both (in her native language, German), and proceeded to tell them about an old Parisian friend she met whom she had invited for lunch. Later when the friend arrived, the four of them sat down for a meal that was sandwiched by conversations in English, French, and German—and Jan participated in all three languages without missing a beat. Living in a multicultural society (Switzerland) and multilingual household, this was second nature to her. The adults were amused when they asked Jan "what does a dog say? What does a Chein say? What does a Hund say?" and received the culturally prescribed sounds—bowwow, chuffchuff, wauwau.

Jan's American cousin Terri was also three, but had lived her life within an essentially monocultural and monolinquistic environment, and was happily chattering away in English with her parents. Later, Terri will take two years of Latin or German in high school and maybe a year of French in college. When she visits her cousin Jan in Switzerland, they will communicate in impeccable English. Terri will observe Jan talking with friends and store clerks in several languages, with a touch of envy. She is aware she is being shut out of this portion of an interesting world.

However, this linguistic limitation is nothing compared to some of Terri's classmates whose mother tongue was Spanish, which they spoke very well. They too came from a monolingual (Spanish-speaking) household but lived in an English language–dominant society. For some of these classmates, there was a period of difficult transition where they lost content-learning time as they had to scramble to pick up enough English to understand what was going on in class. Some of these students mastered both languages even though they started the second language after almost 10 years speaking Spanish. Others never fully mastered the new language and experienced some difficulties in the mainstream society; they also felt discriminated against because of this linguistic difficulty (Fradd 1985).

In this chapter, we discuss the current state of the arts with regard to some critical events in the lives of newborns, young infants, and children during the first few years of life, including birth and the resulting family transformations, language development, the formation of attachments with the people important in children's lives, and healthy growth and development.

Pregnancy

Different women have different emotional responses to their pregnancy experience. Their emotions may be primarily positive, with happy anticipation of motherhood and child rearing, and pleasure in the attention and support of relatives and friends, or they may be primarily negative, with depressed feelings, especially in the first trimester (when some women experience morning sickness) or worries about bodily functions and feelings of being fat, clumsy, and ugly. Or they may have a mix of positive and negative emotions at seemingly random times.

If they are reasonably well, many pregnant women now remain at their jobs and maintain their exercise regimen almost to the time of birth, in contrast to earlier decades when social disapproval and conventional wisdom directed early withdrawal. In any case, being pregnant represents many changes for the expectant mother and for involved family members. She must give attention to her own and the expected infant's health, including possible changes to a more nutritional diet, increased exercise, and avoidance of tobacco, alcohol, and other drugs that can damage the child in utero or postnatally during breast feeding. The fetus depends on the mother for all its nutrients; therefore her prenatal diet is important for the infant's later mental and physical development. There is some evidence that when the expectant mother is malnourished, the infant's birth weight will be lower and the birth may be premature, both of which present other risks to the newborn.

There are many factors related to preventing birth defects. The March of Dimes has developed a Think Ahead campaign to get women to think about healthy lifestyles even before they get pregnant—especially since more than half of pregnancies in this country are unplanned. Among these lifestyle issues are extremes in the woman's weight; use of alcohol, tobacco, or other substances (including certain medications like aspirin); and taking vitamins (especially folic acid, a kind of B vitamin found in dark green vegetables and orange juice that is vital as the only known preventive of spina bifida), iron, and calcium. Most women wait to see a doctor until after they think they were pregnant, even though momentous growth is occurring in the fetus beginning soon after the first missed menstrual period. In a recent report J. Brody (1996a:C11) notes gum infection (untreated periodontal disease) in pregnant women increases 7 times the risk of a premature and low-weight baby. Other reproductive tract infections (like chlamydia and bacterial vaginosis) produce similar results. These findings, while potentially very grim, offer important preventive opportunities for mothers-to-be and helping professionals.

Recognition is growing that the expectant father has his own set of adaptive tasks, including coming to terms with fatherhood and its personal meaning, especially in regard to early experiences with his own father, making room for the baby in his psychosocial and sexual relationships with his partner, providing emotional support to her during the pregnancy, participating in prenatal classes, and readying himself for his participation in the birth process if this is what the couple wishes. Joint tasks for the couple during pregnancy include anticipatory planning and preparation for the new roles of mother and father, and for reallocating other roles and tasks in their home and work environments; acquiring knowledge about pregnancy, childbirth, and parenting; securing the necessary equipment and clothing for the baby; selecting a name for either sex—assuming they have not taken tests to determine the child's sex; and arranging for safe, consistent child care if the mother and father plan to return to work or arranging for maternal and paternal leaves where available.

Fetal Development

Conception, pregnancy, and birth are parts of a continually unfolding relationship, first between sexual partners, then between mother and fetus, and following birth, among mother, father, and infant; all these unfoldings are viewed within their multiple environments, including the presence or absence of the needed resources, services, and supportive networks and the presence of any noxious or toxic environmental features.

During the first two weeks after conception, the fertilized egg is termed a zygote. About the ninth day it forms two sacs. The inner one is filled with fluid and protects the zygote from injury. The outer one develops tendrils by which the zygote attaches itself to the uterine wall during the second week. Beginning in the third week, it is known as an embryo, and for the next six weeks, it develops all the major organs. The placenta, connected to the embryo's navel by the umbilical cord, develops from the embryo and maternal tissue. By the eighth week, the embryo is about one inch long.

> It has a recognizable brain, a heart that pumps blood through tiny veins and arteries, a stomach that produces digestive juices, a liver that manufactures blood cells, kidneys that function, and an endocrine system. In the male embryo the testes produce androgens. The baby now has limbs and an enormous head with ears, nose, eyes, and mouth. . . . It looks human. . . . It holds its hands close to its face; should they touch its mouth, the embryo turns its head and opens its mouth wide.   (Newton and Modahl 1978)

From the ninth week, when bone cells appear, and until birth, the embryo is called a fetus. From here on it is provided a stable, protected environment by the amniotic fluid that fills the space between the two sacs that developed earlier around the zygote. By the eleventh week and the end of the first trimester, the fetus is able to swallow amniotic fluid and urinates it back about every ninety minutes (Macfarlane 1977).

> Waste products travel from the fluid through the placenta, from which they enter the mother's bloodstream. . . . The fluid is completely replaced every two to three hours. By the end of the third month . . . the fetus has grown to a length of three inches and weighs about half an ounce. . . . It bends its finger when its palm is touched. . . . It has taste buds, sweat glands, and a prominent nose. By now, it has eyelids, but they are sealed shut.
>
> (Newton and Modahl 1978)

The second trimester is generally a time of physical and emotional well-being for the expected mother; the earlier discomforts of nausea, drowsiness, urinary frequency, and so on have lessened or disappeared. Visible and internal signs of the pregnancy are now present. Quickening (fetal movement) is experienced by the mother between the sixteenth and twenty-sixth weeks, although the fetus has been moving spontaneously and has been reactive to touch since the seventh week. The second trimester is also a time of rapid weight gain for the mother. Except for women who were very thin when they became pregnant, a total gain of about 24 pounds is considered desirable for most women at delivery. This represents a combined weight of fetus (7.7 lbs), placenta (1.4 lbs), amniotic fluid (1.8 lbs), uterus (2.0 lbs), water that enlarges the breast tissue (.9 lbs), extra interstitial fluid throughout out the body (2.7 lbs), and extra blood for needed circulation (4.0 lbs). The balance is stored as fat and protein to withstand the demands of the postnatal period (Newton and Modahl 1978).

By the sixth month, the fetus appears fully developed in many ways. Yet most fetuses this age would not be able to live outside the mother because their lungs and digestive system, though well formed, are not yet able to function. The fetus is now about 13 inches long and weights about 1.5 pounds. By the end of the sixth month, the fetus is sleeping and waking; it can open its eyes, look around, and suck a finger; and occasionally it may hiccough or sigh. During the last trimester, the fetus makes heavy demands on the mother for nutrients, minerals, and vitamins. Its rapidly developing brain requires extra protein (Newton and Modahl 1978). Indeed, adequate nutrition is important all through the pregnancy.

The Uterine Environment

Macfarlane presented findings from his and others' research (using such instruments as scanners, microphones, and the experiences of observant mothers) that suggest the fetus lives and floats in a noisy, perhaps rose-tinted, and changing environment. Recordings from tiny inserted microphones reveal a constant, very loud swooshing noise in the uterus that pulses with the mother's heartbeat. It is due to blood flowing through the uterus. Noise also is produced by air passing through the mother's stomach. External noise is muted by the amniotic fluid, but extremely loud noises in the third trimester produce kicking and even violent activity in the fetus. Macfarlane also referred to evidence from several studies suggesting that prolonged severe stress in the expectant mother not only increases fetal movement but results in infant irritability, hyperactivity, and sometimes feeding problems in the postnatal period (1977:9). H. Gardner (1995) emphasizes how uterine environments differ and thus become an early learning experience.

Other adverse changes in the prenatal environment can occur because of damaging substances used by the mother that pass through the placenta to the fetus, such as certain chemicals in tobacco, alcohol, and drugs. The significance of such a transfer was not recognized until the thalidomide catastrophe resulting in the births of severely deformed infants during the 1960s. Not all pregnant women taking the sleeping pill at a critical time in the pregnancy gave birth to a deformed baby. Such variability in the effects of any teratogen (a substance that produces malformation) may reflect genetic differences in susceptibility. By 1977 more than 1,500 substances had been identified as having adverse effects on the fetus (Macfarlane 1977:6)

In the first trimester the fetus is most vulnerable to drugs taken by the expectant mother because all the organs are being formed at this time. For example, the tranquilizer Valium is used by many people. Women who take it during the first trimester of pregnancy are 4 times more likely to have babies with cleft palate or cleft lip than women who do not take it. The drug Accutane, prescribed for severe, disfiguring acne and carrying a strong warning label, has been found to cause serious birth defects if used by pregnant women, most of whom use the drug before they become aware of their pregnancy.

The number of infants born addicted to drugs because their mothers used heroin, cocaine, or crack during pregnancy is increasing at an alarming rate. It is estimated that 100,000 crack-exposed babies are born annually (Gittler and McPherson 1990:3). Such infants can suffer severe withdrawal symptoms and even death. They show behavioral disturbances including irritability, sleep disorders, excessive and high-pitched crying, and tremors. These symptoms disappear within three weeks or earlier, depending on the drug. The long-range effects of infant addiction are not entirely known, however, although some of these babies manifested hyperactivity and attention disorders by the time they entered school or preschool programs. The estimated costs in getting crack babies ready for school is over $40,000 per child per year (Mangano 1990:83)

Most of these infants are at severe psychosocial as well as medical risk. Some remain in hospitals for a long time as "boarder babies" because their addicted mothers are unable to care for them or have abandoned them. In some hospitals, volunteer foster grandparents give essential love and attention to these infants that busy pediatric staff cannot provide. Other babies are placed in foster care, but their difficult drug-induced behaviors render them vulnerable to frequent changes of foster parents. Even healthy infants who return home with their mothers are at risk because the addicted parent(s) may not provide adequate care. The increase in the numbers of addicted babies is also associated with increases in cases of child abuse and neglect. In addition, it is now known that breast milk transfers cocaine and crack to the infant very quickly, causing immediate intoxication and even death.

Fetal alcohol syndrome (FAS), a serious disorder associated with maternal drinking during pregnancy, has been recognized since 1970 (May and Hymbaugh 1989; Alcalay, Ghee, and Scrimshaw 1993). Babies born with this condition are apt to be smaller, with lower birth weight than expected for healthy babies, and to have slight malformations of the face, limbs, and cardiovascular system. Importantly, research on the fetal alcohol syndrome also suggests that pregnant women who drink at are an increased risk of having mentally retarded children (May and Hymbaugh 1989; Alcalay, Ghee, and Scrimshaw 1993). An expectant mother's occasional drink is probably not dangerous to the fetus, but because even moderate drinking can lead to some degree of low birth weight, abstinence is recommended by many authorities.

Smoking one or more packs of cigarettes a day during pregnancy is associated with low birth weight, stillbirth, and early infant mortality. It is thought that these effects are due to a reduced blood and oxygen supply to the fetus, resulting in a deprivation of needed nutrients through the placenta. Smoking is especially dangerous during the second half of pregnancy. Recent research suggests that women who smoked while pregnant were 50 percent more likely to have mentally retarded children, 35 percent if they smoked as few as five cigarettes a week during pregnancy to 85 percent if they smoked at least a pack a day (Smokers 50% more likely 1996).

Awareness of the possible effects of drinking, smoking, and drug use raises a very difficult question: If a pregnant woman has been advised of these dangers but continues to use these substances that may harm her fetus, does this constitute fetal abuse? Does the fetus have a right to be protected from behaviors that threaten prenatal well-being and that may result in postnatal disability or death? If so, should an expectant mother who does not changer her behavior be made to do so? If so, by what means? This is a moral and ethical dilemma for health care providers and the society at large. What is sorely needed are effective ways to help expectant mothers give up their addictions. This raises the question of whether we should extend these effective methods to other addicts, people with AIDS, and others who may be harming themselves and possibly others as well.

Rubella (German measles) is a minor disease in the expectant mother, but if she contracts the disease during the first trimester the effect on the baby can be blindness, deafness, mental retardation, heart disease, so some combination of these disorders. However not all babies of mothers who contract rubella are born with a defect—which complicates the woman's decision on whether to continue the pregnancy.

The AIDS virus in the bloodstream of expectant mothers also passes through the placenta to the fetus, possibly dooming the infant to the disease and painful death in the first or second year of life or later. The presence of antibodies in a newborn's blood indicates its mother is infected with the AIDS virus. In about 40 percent of those cases, the baby is believed to be infected as well. In the other instances, the baby has absorbed only the antibody not the virus. About 7,000 infants are born to HIV-positive mothers, and about 2,000 of these infants are infected with HIV (*AIDS in Children* 1995:205).

Transfers of nutrients through the placenta to the fetus are essential and beneficial. Even antibodies in the mother's blood, resulting from certain infections she experienced earlier, are transferred. The baby is then immune for several months after birth to diseases such as colds, influenza, scarlet fever, whooping cough, measles, and mumps.

Childbirth

Childbirth was a woman-controlled, natural, biological process over the millennia, "a social rather than a medical event, managed by midwives and attended by friends and relatives" (Dye 1980). However, during the late nine-teenth and early twentieth centuries, childbirth was gradually medicalized, as though it were a disease process, and it came under the control of male obste-tricians and hospitals. As late as 1920 almost 75 percent of U.S. births took place at home; by 1960, 96 percent took place in hospitals (Wertz and Wertz 1977). The change was accompanied by the mystification and medical monopolization of knowledge about birthing or what Oakley (1979) pointed to as the claimed superiority of professional knowledge over the expertise of the mothers themselves. It was also accompanied by the psychologizing of such difficulties as multiple miscarriages, late attention to prenatal care, nau-sea and vomiting (early morning sickness), infertility, prematurity, and post-natal depression (also called postpartum depression). Thus these phenomena were viewed as the result of the woman's "problem" with femininity and other intrapsychic issues. No attention was given to the social and economic con-texts. Oakley (1979) commented that few studies of postnatal depression, for example, "consider the impact of sleep disturbance, exhaustion, social isola-tion, work over-load, etc., on the woman's feelings after the birth of the child."

Dye (1980) observed that since the 1920s, when hospitals took control of birthing, it has been viewed as a surgical process. Reliance on forceps, epi-siotomy (surgery to expand the opening to the birth canal, which then requires stitches to help repair the surgery), anesthesia, and the inducing of birth became common. More recently, an alarming increase in Caesarean births has occurred and is thought to be associated with physicians' fear of malpractice suits. The expectant mother, now termed a "patient," is expected to be passive and to submit to professionals' control of her body and the birth. Formal and informal studies reveal that women find the process alienating, isolating, and frightening. Childbirth in the hospital was believed to be safer than at home because the hospital offered an aseptic environment. But Dye's research review shows that mortality remained high until the late 1930s, largely because of the routine use of risky interventions.

The Lamaze model of prepared childbirth appears to eliminate the prob-lems in the medical model of childbirth, at least to some degree. Mothers' and fathers' knowledge of the processes of pregnancy, labor, and birth, gained not only from the instructor but also from listening to the experiences of others, increases self-confidence in the mother, and in the father if he assists at the birth. Most important, the model restores the control of labor and full con-scious participation in the birth to the mother. The classes also include breath-ing exercises that are geared to the stages of labor and that reduce pain: "The informational aspects of the program and the rehearsals for labor seem to reduce the fear of the unknown and the sense of helplessness and isolation for first-time mothers and to give the father a more intimate role in bringing forth the child" (J. Williams 1983:286).

Birthing at home, assisted by a licensed nurse-midwife and, in some instances with backup hospital services if needed, is increasing in the United States. Birthing then becomes a family event. Women deciding on this option report liking the informal, caring qualities of the midwife, who is also more apt than the physician to wait out nature's delays. The few available studies show that home births are just as safe as, and possibly safer than, hospital deliveries for those with uncomplicated pregnancies and the expectation of uncomplicated births (J. Williams 1983). Some hospitals, interested in a more family-oriented birthing process, now provide support groups and programs for expectant mothers who want natural childbirth or who anticipate Cae-sarean sections, as well as for their partners, and the expected baby's siblings and grandparents. The birthing rooms provided by some hospitals and by free-standing birthing centers combine the best features of home and hospital, and offer a desirable option for many couples.

These alternative services are for the most part used by middle-class populations who have private health insurance, as not all centers accept Medicaid. Mothers who are poor may not have access to birthing arrangements other than regular hospital obstetrical care. And indeed, all the adaptive and coping tasks of pregnancy are far more difficult and stressful for poor and solo mothers, and even more so if they are without the support of relatives and friends. Working in Central America, Sosa et al. (1980) created a peer situation involving expectant mothers who lack natural support systems and a doula, a supportive companion previously unknown to the expectant mother. The doula stays with the mother-to-be from admission to the hospital through delivery, providing comfort, conversation, and friendly companionship during this crisis time. Results from this experimental–control group design showed more favorable outcomes when the doula was employed than when she was not.

Implications for such a constructed role are many, from mentors to transfer students who can benefit from learning the local culture to widow-to-widow programs in which a newly widowed person is aided to reenter the social world by a widow, previously unknown to the target person, who has successfully made the transition from wife to widow (P. Silverman 1988). Tadmor (1988) provides an example of empowerment involving a Caesarean birth (CB) population, who are at risk for postnatal depression from this stressful procedure. Hospitals ordinarily structure the treatment of the CB woman as a surgical patient, not as a new mother. Tadmor arranged with the hospital to make structural changes in this birthing process, while she herself provided anticipatory guidance to the CB couple, including the recognized painful aspects. The anesthesiologist lowered the anesthesia level, permitting the mother (and father) to make initial contact with the baby to encourage bonding; then the anesthesia was increased to complete the surgical procedure. Postpartum events included having the CB mother have early contact with the infant for breast-feeding while the pain level was controlled by regional anesthesia. Later, a veteran CB mother visited to initiate contact with a local CB support group. The new mother was encouraged to be a veteran CB mother for others. There were gains all around: in healthier, happier mothers and infants, and in reductions in hospital costs with shortened stays and services.

Infants and Toddlers

The miracle of human birth pales before the spectacular process of becoming a human being, one who walks, talks, and interacts appropriately with a complex symbolic environment. Each of these tasks is highly complex and yet occurs in a being who appears to be totally helpless and without the requisite resources to undertake these tasks. (Remember how difficult it was to dance the tango in high school or to learn a foreign language in your undergraduate years at college?—and you were positively brilliant compared to the very young infant!) However, the young infant is filled with a potential for complex learning of which we are only beginning to understand—or to promote. It is an interesting exercise to develop a chart of developmental changes over the life course (see M. Bloom [1985] as a point of departure). Such a chart would list categories such as physical change; growth in motor skills; affective and cognitive developments; psychosocial, moral, and sexual developments; and indeed, major personality developments, if one accepts a stage point of view (see appendix 1). What we would learn from this exercise is that there is a great deal of information about, and agreement on, physical and motor changes—almost all children crawl before they walk and walk before they run—but there appears to be more variability among people in psychosocial development. Some people appear to learn and act on high moral reasoning compatible with the finest norms of society; others appear stuck at selfish hedonistic levels; and most others fall in between (Arbuthnot 1992). No given set of predictors is fully accurate in telling us which individual will have which level of moral reasoning.

In order to explore these critical events in the lives of young infants and toddlers, we focus in depth on one of the most remarkable stories of human
development, how people learn to understand their "mother tongue" and to
speak it correctly. Each of the other aspects of infancy and the toddler stage
could be discussed in equal detail.

Language Development in the Social Context

*Thomas Carlyle [the famed historian] was only eleven months old and had
never spoken a word when, hearing another child in the household cry, he sat
up and said, "What ails wee Jock?"* —John W. Gardner

Surely the story is apocryphal, since the acquisition of language is a slow and
complex process, not to emerge fully developed overnight. How it takes
place is still a mystery, even though there is a rapidly expanding body of
technical research testing various models. To examine the conflicting types
of theories engaging psycholinguists currently would take us too far afield.
However, when we look for major areas of agreement among biological, psychological (cognitive and affective), and social learning theorists on the
development of the ability to speak and understand a language, we can offer
the following comments as an approximate idea of the state of the art at this
time:

1. Infants are exposed to varying amounts of language, from parents
   and siblings, from the radio and television, from family friends and
   strangers. For example, in a half-hour of interactions, middle-class
   mothers in Lois Bloom's sample ranged from 216 to 579 utterances,
   while low-income mothers ranged from 69 to 513 utterances. Mothers of the poor tend to talk less and sometimes very little compared
   with middle-class mothers, but the ranges may overlap—some low-
   income mothers talking more and some middle-income mothers
   talking less (L. Bloom, personal communication 1997). Out of this
   melange of yet-foreign sounds and silences emerge the units of language for infants to become members of the human community.
   Almost from the moment of birth, the infant is capable of many
   perceptions (sight, sound, smell, touch, and their simultaneous
   occurrences as in the breast-feeding experience). Research is documenting the extent of this perceptual openness to the environment.

2. Infants are no less active in sending information to caretakers and others about their diffuse needs for food, for burping (as an aid to as yet immature digestive processes), relief from discomforts of various sorts. Since infants do not come with an "owner's manual," parents spend considerable time (day and night) learning from the infant what the baby needs based on some very generalized information—crying, odd noises, even periods of silent looking at objects, and eventually social smiles (as contrasted with smiles apparently due to responses to intestinal functioning). What research has emphasized is the wonderful choreography going on between infant and caretakers, the wonderfully synchronized and reciprocal gazing and vocalizing (turn taking) that takes place between caregivers and babies by 3 months of age. However, these interaction patterns occur only in those moments when caregiver and baby are looking at each other. These become the subtle interactions of stimulation and rest that are part of family rituals around regular events like feeding times, baths, and playing (Brazelton 1986; Stern 1985). That is, patterns of taking turns begin to occur in larger social situations. Such interactions lead to learning to communicate; they also influence the forms of thought itself and thus have important social implications (Bandura 1986:498). These interactions also produce significant changes in the adults and the family system they are constructing during this period.

3. One major controversy in linguistics concerns what the infant brings to the communication table, so to speak. Some early behavioral theorists invoke a reinforcement model in which the sounds caretakers use eventually become shaped to be the words the child uses (Skinner 1957). This model does not appear to be adequate to account for children's ability to generate wide ranges of novel and complex sentences, even though it may seem to parents that their responding stimulates the infant to do likewise. In fact, any adult voice responding contingently or noncontingently on what the baby does will elicit vocalizing from the baby. If the parent responds contingently on what the baby is saying, the baby's response will tend to be in a turn-taking mode (K. Bloom 1990).

Other theorists build on the physiological fact that the brain appears to become sufficiently mature to permit children to utter single words somewhere around age 1 and at about age 2 to enable all (normally endowed) human beings everywhere to learn and to speak a language. Chomsky (1965) believes the child only hears sentences, but learns a grammar, that is, a set of rules that can be used to generate new (unheard) sentences. The child—in fact, no one—ever learns a grammar from participating in ordinary language interchanges because ordinary language never includes grammar rules. Thus the child is eventually able to utter a sentence that he or she never heard before and to construct it in an orderly, syntactical way because the child's brain appears to be "hard- wired" to be capable of doing so, that is, the capacity is innate, not learned. A learning theorist might respond by saying the child could infer rules from numerous sentences the child hears and use these learned rules to generate new sentences.

> Chomsky (1957) proposed explicit rules as a way of describing the sentences of a language. Basic sentences (e.g., active, affirmative, simple statements) could be produced, or generated, by a set of phase structure rules, and a different type of rule, the transformation, derived all other sentences (e.g., passive, negatives, questions, complex sentences) from the basic types. This approach became known as transformational generative grammar, and it placed syntax at the center of linguistic investigations in the United States.
>
> (Falk 1994:70)

Not everyone agrees with this assessment of Chomsky's work. Some adhere instead to Piagetian ideas about learning as a form of adaptation (see appendix 1 on Piaget). For Piaget, human development involves adaptation of self and world through two interrelated processes: assimilation, by which information taken in by the child is connected to existing mental images (schemata) representing that child's knowledge of the world, and accommodation, by which these schemata are changed to be sensitive to new kinds of information. At first, this adaptive process occurs through sensorimotor means in the infant, learning through acting on objects. As the child develops, he or she is increasingly able to use mental images in sequentially more complicated logical ways, from which Piaget's later qualitative stages are derived—preoperational, concrete, and formal operational stages. Language is the critical tool.

Piaget noted, but did not pursue extensively, the connection between affectivity and intelligence. L. Bloom quotes Piaget describing affectivity as "the role of an energy source on which the functioning but not the structure of intelligence . . . depend[,] . . . like gasoline, which activates the motor of an automobile but does not modify its structure" (1993:58)

"Actions and feelings in the first year are very much tied to internal conditions and immediately perceivable objects, persons, and events in the environment. In the second year, infants come to think about objects that are removed in time and space when events in the situation cue their recall. And in the third year, infants develop the ability to mentally act on the representations they have in mind, instead of acting on the objects directly" (L. Bloom 1991:4).

L. Bloom (1993) presents an empirically based analysis of how children acquire language. This analysis combines infants' affective, as well as their cognitive, lives. She notes that infants have expressed affect nonlinguistically from birth through cries, smiles, and chortles. But by the end of the first year of life, they want to express much more than displays of affect will permit. What they need is a language to make the contents of their thoughts and feelings public and explicit. Bloom hypothesizes that it is the 1-year-old's intentional states— their immediate thoughts, desires, and feelings—that drive the acquisition of language, so as to be able to express these internal and unobservable happenings to others. Why should infants want to express these? Bloom further hypotheses that infants want to be sociable, to be together with others, to share—this is what drives intentionality.

Let's consider the instrumental function of language for a moment, which includes trying to influence the actions of other people. To do this, there have to be some shared meanings in what speakers intend to say and what listeners understand to have been said. What people intend to say is based on their memory of prior experiences and their current wishes or needs with regard to future happenings—a rather complicated matter for young infants without much prior experience or cognition of wishes for the future. Children learn that words stand for concepts about events or things in the real world. "Words point to and designate the elements in these private mental meanings and make them public, by virtue of shared linguistic meanings invested in them" (L. Bloom 1993:10). As human beings with the innate developmental capacity to use symbols, young children form abstractions of word meanings from recalling prior experience with the word in relation to current circumstances.

In addition to this instrumental view of use of words, language also inherently serves an expressive function—beyond the nonverbal ways to express affect and intention. Indeed, there is no way that what we say (the instrumental side of language) can be separated from how we feel about what we say (the expressive side of language). We can be thankful to Aristotle for many things but not among them is his arbitrary separation of thoughts and feelings; they are intrinsically interrelated, even though there are clear differences between them. However, it is their relationship that is more to the point:

Instrumental language gets things done in the world only because our expressions can influence what others have in mind (as a result of interpretation, the flip side of expression) and hence influence their behavior. There is no way that what we say (the "expression and articulation aspects" of language) can be separated from how we feel about what we say (the "affective" side of language) (L. Bloom, personal communication 1997). The instrumental function of language is more accessible to the public eye, while the expressive function involves subjective attitudes, some of which the speaker may not be aware of, such as biases or stereotypes.

Given this view of young children as having intentionality and sociability, L. Bloom identified three principles of language development. The Principle of Relevance holds that children learn words that have relevance for them. The Principle of Discrepancy suggests that a consequence of a child's developing symbolic capacity is that what is in the child's mind becomes increasingly different from what the child immediately perceives. The Principle of Elaboration states that a consequence of learning more about the world is that the contents of the mind become increasingly elaborated. "The more elements and relations between elements in the intentional states, the more the child will need to know of the language to express and articulate what they are." With these three principles, Bloom describes a variety of language developments, how the changes in language, emotion, and cognition influence each other (1993:15–16).

Learning language occurs within given contexts. Young Kathryn says "Mommy sock" on one occasion (pointing to socks in the clothes basket) and on another occasion (as her mother is putting a sock on Kathyrn's foot). The same words mean different things for Kathryn in the different contexts, although each is used correctly in the given situations. As new contexts emerge in the child's experiences, so language is formed to characterize these experiences and to become part of the child's memory and anticipation.

Stern noted that while significant gains come with the acquisition of language, a great deal of the force and wholeness of original experience is lost or made latent by language. For example, by using language, a split in some preverbal or nonverbal experience of feeling, sensation, perception, or cognition occurs, transforming it into a categorical (linguistic) experience separate from the original person:environment experience. Now a verbal version of an experience exists as well as the original nonverbal version. The words "yellow sunlight" close out all the other preverbal, global experiences of sunlight (1985:174–182).

Stern (1985) also suggests that the ability to narrate one's own life story begins with language acquisition. The child now begins internally to build a story of what her or his life is like and continues the building through the life course. The connections to what actually happened may not be clear and may not even matter. The story is the way one's life is and feels, and it is a metaphor for actuality. (The child's narrative-building gradually forms a life story that later may be shared with life partners, children, in autobiographies, or with a helping professional.) It is not clear how, when, or why the child begins to construct a life narrative but Stern hypothesizes that narrative-making, a universal human phenomenon, may prove to be related to how the human brain is designed—an interesting observation in light of the rising interest in family stories and narratives among social workers who work with families (Laird 1989).

About the age of 3, if playmates are available, friendships become significant features of the social context of language. They provide resources different from but complementary to those provided by the family. For example, friendships shape the social skills of talking, gaining entry into group activities, exercising tact and sensitivity, and extending approval and support to peers. Friendships also shape the sense of identity and foster the sense of group belonging (Z. Rubin 1980). Language is a most important facilitator of social interaction and friendships. They, in turn, contribute to the continuing development of language.

Language thus empowers the child along many dimensions. However, negative influences exerted by the social context operate to make language a means of disempowering large segments of the population and reinforcing oppression. Disempowerment through language begins in the school years or earlier, and continues through adulthood.

Speakers of Spanish

Sotomayer described the consequences of political, social, and economic degradation of the language, culture, and ethnicity of minority groups. She notes that "the 'real world' is reflected and recorded in linguistic symbols, or inventories of experiences, that eventually form the language habits of a group . . . the definition of reality" (1980:51–52). This social function of language is most important to minority groups:

> For the bilinguals of color, such as Chicanos, language has played a most significant social and survival function; for example, . . . in proving the

group feeling of solidarity to deal with the oppressive majority culture. It is a common language that often coordinates the activities of the in-group, by making individuals conscious of the relationships between members and outsiders, thus promoting a sense of belonging . . . over many generations . . . permitting a sense of symbolic continuity and thus survival.

(Sotomayer 1980:53)

When a group's language is devalued by the larger population, the group is disempowered. For Chicano and Chicana adults in this country, language is used as a means of social control. Demanding that groups give up their native language for English is seen by some as disempowering since the language is part of relatedness and provides a sense of community or solidarity in the face of opposition (Fradd 1985). This is not to say, however, that native-language speakers should not also learn English. It is a means of entry into the society's opportunity structure and is therefore empowering.

To provide educational, social, and health services to limited-English or monolingual Spanish-speaking groups is said to be difficult because different varieties of Spanish are used by different groups (Puerto Rican, Mexican American, Cuban, and various South American groups). This may be true where these groups coexist in large numbers in a given area, which is not ordinarily the case, or if written or broadcast materials are to be used across regions.

Speakers of Asian Languages

The observations regarding Spanish speakers hold true for speakers of Chinese, Japanese, Korean, Filipino, and other Asian languages. The elderly or recent immigrants may speak only limited or no English; thus they face serious problems. "The lack of trained personnel who can understand their unique situations, languages, and cultural barriers prevents them from participating in the health and welfare system of the United States in an informed manner" (Owan 1978). The result is underutilization of services, which leads to health and social problems for individuals, families, and the community, especially during the changes in the welfare system of the late 1990s where older persons were rushing to obtain citizenship rather than face the stresses of continuing visitor statuses. Owan pointed out that all ethnic groups have the right to share fully in the benefits of American society while retaining pride in their cultural heritage, their distinctive religion, and their language.

Speakers of Black English

Black English is a separate language, not merely poorly spoken English. Its speakers, like any other speech community, share a set of social conventions about verbal communication and rules about the use of metacommunications (how things are said that qualify, magnify, or deny the verbal or written message) to signify intent, hidden messages, and emotionality. Although it shares some words with Standard English, leading most whites to assume that it is the same language, Black English actually has its own complex history and autonomous rules of syntax, as described by the linguists Dillard (1975) and Smitherman (1986).

Viewed ecologically, any language serves to relate its speakers to one another and to their environment. This is particularly clear in the case of Black English, which serves to strengthen the relatedness among its speakers, enhance their sense of identity and self-direction, and keep firm the boundary between its speakers and the oppressive social context. Draper analyzed the functional aspects of Black English for its speakers as they cope with racism and disempowerment and concluded, "As a boundary-strengthening or distancing device Black English enables its speakers to communicate safely within the group while effectively shutting whites out of the communication process" (1979:271). Draper's work demonstrates the importance of white social workers' respecting and understanding Black English as a separate language and not merely as a distorted version of standard English.

Speakers of American Indian Languages

American Indians have been disempowered in many ways that threaten the survival of their cultures, including denigration of their native languages and being forced to give them up in government boarding schools. One example is the renaming of tribal landscapes and sacred places by the larger society. For three hundred years, a succession of explorers, missionaries, railroad builders, U.S. soldiers, and the federal government have left linguistic and cultural footprints on American Indian lands (Rasky 1988). Keith H. Basso, an anthropologist who has lived and worked among the Apache for thirty years, declared in an interview with Rasky (1988) that superimposing an Anglo language on an Apache landscape is a subtle form of oppression and domination. He is collaborating with Apache leaders in a linguistic remapping that will restore the ancient names used by the Apache ancestors. In "Reflections of an Unremembered Past" Kanani Bell, a social worker, wrote:

> Cheyenne, Crow, Arapaho, Blackfoot, Sious. From days never known and sights glimpsed only indirectly the names crowd my mind more than things merely remembered. Pawnee, Kiowa, Apache, Cree. The names are not reducible to history. They dwell in a different yet not unreachable region. Ogalala, Chicicahua, Cherokee. The names speak within me of the dimly understood. They crowd my world, my being, to the very corners until only the names remain. Or I am the names. . . . In the Navaho, who moved onto the vacated Anasazi lands and named them the Old Ones, the Anasazi live. I am Anasazi . . . Kansas, Iowa, Wichita. . . . Dakota. Names by the tens and hundreds of thousands live through me. Or I live through them and I am the names. (1986)

Social workers function in many of these language domains, and can act to define language-related difficulties experienced by their clients at a sociocultural level, determine who are the decision makers related to this language difficulty, provide information and participate in making a plan to facilitate the language changes, and implement and monitor the processes and outcomes. Owan (1978) described how successful language change in a Social Security Administration office in New York City's Chinatown provided more satisfactory services for clients. It also increased productivity and reduced workload pressures on the staff.

Other Forms of Language-Based Discrimination

Sexist Language

Language has been used as an instrument to disempower girls and women, and to reinforce gender typing. The term "sexist language" refers to the generic use of the male noun and pronouns to denote both males and females (e.g., "Man, being a mammal, breast-feeds his young" [Martyna 1980]); to stereotype people as if only one gender were involved (e.g., businessmen, rather than people in business; chairman, rather than chair or chairperson; authoress, rather than author; Neanderthal man, as if women were not involved in that group of early people); or to stereotype expressions that are commonly used (e.g., Dear Sir, rather than Dear Madam or Sir; Lady Luck, rather than luck; Mother Nature and Father Time, rather than nature and time).

There has been a gradual reduction in sexist language in the publications of the professions, government agencies, and to a far smaller degree, the public media. Despite this advance, sexist language persists in both spoken and written forms, especially in derogatory and obscene terms used to denote women and men. Its significance as an instrument of disempowerment is trivialized by being treated humorously or being ridiculed by men and even by some women. Martyna (1980) observed that when the situation is reversed and the female pronoun is used generically, as in the teaching profession, male teachers have argued for change on the grounds that the female noun and pronouns have resulted in a poor public image and low salaries.

Deaf Speakers

Disempowerment through language follows the deaf over their life course. Often shut out from the world of hearers and speakers of language, they inhabit a world that is the culture of deafness, with its own language and codes of behavior, and deaf friends, organizations, groups, media, sports, commerce, and even street gangs (Walker 1987; Santos 1995; Wax 1995). There are more than 2 million deaf people in the United States, and an estimated 16 million people with some sort of hearing impairment , who face varying degrees of prejudice and discrimination (Santos 1995:685). The extreme social isolation and lack of acceptance and understanding experienced by deaf people are disempowering because they limit participation in community and political life on the basis of a separate language (signing) and hearing (reading lips—which, at best, "reads" only a quarter of what has been said [Walker 1987:19]). These facts lead hearing people to assume the deaf person has a low intelligence—in fact, there is no appreciable difference in intelligence test scores, but reading scores of the deaf are below those of hearing people (Santos 1995:691). Not being able to hear all the nuances of audio cues and taboos, deaf children may pick up a scrambled version of sex education, which may delay their expression of mature sexuality (Fitz-Gerald and Fitz-Gerald 1977).

However, as Wax (1995) points out, the deaf community is becoming a sociopolitical force, asserting that older views of and societal reactions toward the deaf are no longer acceptable: not the ancient biblical view that deafness is a curse, nor the Aristotelian view that deafness indicates senselessness (or low intelligence), nor the medical view that deafness is the deaf person's individual pathology for which a cure should be sought, nor the rehabilitation view that society can help rehabilitate the deaf in employable settings and independent living, nor even the cultural view that the deaf are a victimized minority. Rather, Wax suggests the deaf community is asserting that deafness is one way of being in a diverse society—the deaf are different, not worse than, hearing people. From this perspective, the deaf do not consider themselves as disabled or in need of curing, rehabilitating, or protecting. Deafness requires adaptation in a hearing world. This strong human rights position still faces many challenges before it will be accepted by society.

The deaf community faces some significant choices in terms of teaching communication skills to children (or people who become deaf later in life). Among the deaf and educators of the deaf, the issue of whether to teach signing or to teach lipreading and speaking continues to be controversial, even after the Education for All Handicapped Children Act of 1975 mandated mainstreaming of deaf children. By 1991, 71 percent of deaf students were either partially or fully mainstreamed in public day school programs. Santos suggests that no single approach to educating the deaf can be satisfactory for this heterogenous group, and educators may need to match individual needs with appropriate environments (1995:693–694).

To add to the complexities, different forms of sign language exist. The native language of American deaf persons is American Sign Language (AMESLAN). Deaf people who lost their hearing in adulthood may prefer Signed English (SIGLISH), which follows the syntax and linguistic structure of English (Luey 1980). A report by UNESCO on the education of the deaf concludes:

> We must recognize the legitimacy of sign language as a linguistic system and it should be accorded the same status as other languages. . . . Now that the importance of the national sign languages for deaf education is better understood, it is no longer admissible to overlook them or to fail to encourage their integration into deaf education. The old idea that the use of sign language interferes with the acquisition of spoken and written language is no longer considered valid.   (Lane 1987:35)

The Poor

A group on whom professional language and jargon have a severely negative impact is the poor. Lee (1980) showed that many human service professionals use words that disempower, depersonalize, and dehumanize poor individuals and families. The dis-, un-, and non- words—"disadvantaged," "unmotivated," "nonverbal," to say nothing of "multiproblem family," " dysfunctional," or "resistant'—present a bleak and negative view of people, as if they have only problems and limitations with no counterbalancing strengths and resources (cf. Saleebey 1992; Cowger 1994).

Forms that some clients have to fill out in order to get welfare benefits—ignoring tax forms that are notoriously complicated—are written at a level of language expectation that exceeds what the poor may bring to these agencies. Workers should be sensitive to this kind of language problem.

The Illiterate

Likewise, illiteracy (not being able to read or write at all) and functional illiteracy (being able to read or write a little, but not at an adequate level for ordinary social functioning) is a problem for a large number of people. UNESCO statistics indicate that more than 900 million people are illiterate, and two-thirds of them are women (Werthein 1995:3). More than 10 percent of American adults have an educational attainment of eighth grade or less (*Chronicle of Higher Education* 1997:5). In 1993 the U.S. Department of Education released the most detailed picture ever available on the state of illiteracy in the United States, and the figures are highly problematic as we enter the next millennium. Some 40 to 44 million adults were identified as functionally illiterate, with another 50 million just above this level (Adult literary service 1998). How will these people participate in the computer and space age of the twenty-first century? While there are many programs seeking to provide literacy tutoring, it is still an enormous and hidden problem for many people, which limits their life opportunities in innumerable ways. These people often become skilled in making face-saving adaptations to avoid being detected.

Issues of Linguistic and Cultural Diversity

There is ample evidence that young children can learn two or more languages simultaneously and well, as in the story of Jan at the beginning of this chapter. The older people get, the more difficult it is to learn new languages. The question is how to be able to live and work within a culturally diverse society and world.

The Canadian experience is pertinent to this question. Despite many historical and contemporary similarities between Canada and the United States, they differ markedly in policies regarding language diversity. Equality of English and French has been official Canadian policy since 1867, although English was dominant over French in most situations. In the 1960s a Royal Commission on Bilingualism and Biculturalism was established in response to a rising consciousness and political activity among French-speaking Canadians. The commission documented inequalities between the languages, whereupon the Canadian parliament, reaffirming Canada's bilingual status, initiated a series of changes to overcome inequalities in services and opportunities for French-speaking Canadians.

Fradd notes the long-standing Canadian bilingual policy that views learning the two languages as an advantageous enrichment, not as a meaningless remediation as it is often viewed in the United States. Canadian students maintain their first language, while learning the second, whereas in the United States, adding a second (dominant) language sometimes leads to the loss of the first (native language). Fradd states that bilingualism can enhance the possibility for effective communication and cultural understanding with a larger population of the world's community (1985:58). Others (e.g., Hayakawa 1995) argue that a single language is a unifying force among a nation of immigrants such as American and Canadian societies. Hayakawa does not oppose bilingual education where a child's native language is used to teach him or her English. Rather, Hayakawa argues that trial experiences both in California and elsewhere in the world have not proven helpful when children learn subjects in their native languages for several years before they learn English, by which time, he says, they usually fall behind their English-speaking classmates.

These are difficult issues facing the increasingly multicultural world. Language is the way we express our private feelings and thoughts onto a public stage; language is also the way our parents and teachers convey critical information to us. One way or another, we are our language, and the more able we are to use it (or them) well, the more competent we become as human beings.

10

Family Transformations: Childhood

Following a brief overview of middle childhood, this chapter takes up the impact of school and the child's peer and sibling relationships on the family and on the child's development. First-order changes arising from the smooth developmental transitions of child and parents continue in the school years. However, in its final section, this chapter focuses on unexpected life events such as chronic illness or death of the child.

Outline

Introduction

Do you remember your first day at school? I remember that day as if it were yesterday. I got up very early and was dressed and brushed long before the rest of the family arose. Breakfast seemed to last forever. "Is it time to go? Is it time to go yet?" But just as it was about time to go, I got scared. What if I didn't know enough? Would they kick me out of school? I desperately asked my mother to teach me a hard word so I could make it through the day. She thought a moment and then taught me the word a-n-t-i-c-i-p-a-t-i-o-n. Thus armed, I was ready for anything. I was buttoned up and sent out with my older brother. I remember hopping and skipping all the way to school, and then waiting around outside, very impatiently, until they opened the doors. I rushed in, and then very cautiously made my way to the room I had visited several weeks earlier, the kindergarten room, with its bathtub-size fish pond, its wall of windows looking over the playground, and the various colorful cabinets and cubbyholes where treasure lay.

The kindergarten teacher welcomed me—and a crowd of other little people—who seemed to have emerged from nowhere. I think we had our names pinned onto our shirts, and we sat in a circle while the teacher talked. I don't remember a single word, except it was wonderful. We played with toys and crayons, and went outside to explore the jungle gym and the parallel bars, and then back inside, to a snack of milk and graham crackers. To this day, I still have a childlike love of graham crackers. We then took our naps on big cardboard mats. More play, more sitting in a circle as the teacher read us a story, and then it was time to go home. I wasn't sure I wanted to go home from this magic world, but I was assured I could come back tomorrow . . . and all the tomorrows of my life, whenever I remember the sweet taste of graham crackers and stories and s-c-h-o-o-l.

Middle Childhood

For many children, the middle childhood years are indeed the carefree, golden age of childhood—at least in our adult memory. The social and physical worlds of school-age children expand rapidly and become exciting and challenging arenas of mastery. The physical world exists to be explored, and the sense of adventure is high; the social world of peers is a source of pleasure and sometimes of hurt. Fantasy and daydreams help with feelings of inadequacy, and they stimulate renewed effort through envisioning a competent future. Some of the important influences on the child's ongoing development are family and school; friends, play, and games; collecting and trading treasured objects; identifying with heroes and heroines in sports, entertainment, and storybooks; creating secret clubs, rites, and rituals; and participating in the spiritual life of church or temple and in community youth organizations, settlement houses, and the like.

For many other children, these are not happy years. They face exceptional adaptive tasks imposed by family or neighborhood violence (Hampton et al. 1993; Green 1995), abuse and neglect, chronic illness or disability, parental alcoholism or illicit drug abuse, the loss of a parent by death or divorce, and other griefs. For millions of our children, these years are filled with the horrors of poverty and societal neglect based on color, socioeconomic status, and gender. In a society that believes itself to be child-centered, we do little to ensure for all our children safe housing in a safe neighborhood; a loving, economically secure home, free of abuse and exploitation; adequate health care; and uniformly excellent schooling.

As has been the case since birth, children bring to the experiences of middle childhood differences in genetic potential and temperament that, depending on the environment, will affect how they adapt to the multiple and simultaneous challenges and stresses. Freud viewed middle childhood as a universal period of latency of the sexual drive following a universal oedipal conflict (appendix 1). Recent research suggests that the young child's body is already beginning its growth toward puberty as early as age six. Anthropologists who disagree with Freud report that in other societies with different family structures and kinship systems, neither the Oedipus complex nor the latency period is found. Some suggest that a latency period doesn't exist in Western societies either, as most children continue their sexual play and interests but away from the observation of adults.

In middle childhood, boys and girls grow in physical stature, musculature, and coordination. Facial structure changes as permanent teeth erupt. The pace of cognitive, perceptual, and knowledge development is striking. Socially and emotionally, too, this is a time of change. By now the child has a recognizable and unique personality, that is, relatively predictable ways of behaving and of responding to the environment, as well as characteristic motivational patterns, talents and abilities, and vulnerabilities or limitations. The accustomed ways of coping with stress or challenge that worked in toddlerhood may not suffice in the new environments of school and peer group. Hence, through observing how others achieve desired objectives—like older siblings or classmates at school—expanded facility with language, exploration of the social world, and parental guidance, the child learns new coping methods and new ways of interacting with others and achieves new levels of relatedness, competence, self-esteem, and self-direction.

Moral development is also discernible, and many cultural, familial, and personal values and ideals become part of the self through identification with loving and beloved parents as well as teachers and peers, and through the cultural environment of rituals, religion, and the media. However, whether moral development proceeds in Piagetian stages with inferior outcomes for women is controversial (see appendix 1 on Kohlberg). Pressure toward conformity, however, is exerted by the peer group and by the child's desire to be like her or his peers and to be accepted by them. Thus some of the child's family, cultural, and religious values and norms may conflict with peer standards of behavior (cf. Cherry and Redmond 1994), but most parents help their children begin to take responsibility for their own behavior and impart elements of decision making useful in meeting peer demands (Evans and Raines 1990). This is a time when parents also have an opportunity to teach respect for difference and the rights of others—aided by the child's growing capacity to empathize with the feelings of others (Ponterotto and Pedersen 1993). Similarly, it is an opportune time for parents to provide age-appropriate teaching about sex and reproduction. In many families this began during toddlerhood through the parents' simple answers to the toddler's and preschooler's questions, which are now posed at a higher cognitive level.

Other learning that takes place in the family during these years includes that gained from participation as a responsible family member through assigned chores (Werner and Smith 1992) and from managing an allowance that is unconnected to chores. In many middle-class families, children receive special lessons in dance, art, music, and the like that can enrich their life experience. However, some observers believe that children can be overburdened by too many adult-scheduled activities that leave little or no time for creative child-initiated activity and spontaneous group play free of adult control. Little League baseball may be powerfully stimulated by parents' desires, perhaps as much as the young players. Danish (1983; Danish, Pettipas, and Hale 1990, 1993) argues that sports are useful in the development of competence for the younger child, but that when a child enters puberty, sports detract from the other social lessons that need to be learned.

Worries and Wonders of Middle Childhood

Over the centuries children have devised their own ways of handling fears through games about witches and monsters, chants and rituals, and talismans

(Opie and Opie 1969). However, when an irrational fear persists long after its "proper time," causing pervasive anxiety and interfering with the child's functioning or family life, the child may need professional help. A so-called school phobia, for example, can have the crippling effects of adult phobias (Corville-Smith 1995). In middle childhood, earlier fears give way to very real worries, including concerns about parents' and grandparents' health, school issues, peer friendships, personal appearance, how babies are made, how they are born, and what abortion means. Some children worry about nuclear accidents or a nuclear or biological war, and about being kidnaped, injured, or killed. All these fears may be stimulated to some degree by media reports and TV programming about violence, drugs, explicit sex, computer pornography, and other truly worrisome things. Childhood is no longer a time of innocence, if indeed it ever was. Parents in today's world feel that they must teach protective behaviors to children. Thus children are burdened with precocious knowledge without a mature capacity to deal with it. This circumstance creates confusions, fears, and feelings of incompetence in some children. The parents' dilemma is how to make their children feel safe and protected while teaching them to act safely (Peterson and Mori 1986).

The golden haze through which adults view their own childhood veils the worries and concerns that most school-age children experience. Hence parents are usually unaware of the pervasiveness and intensities of their children's fear. Indeed, Yamamoto et al., who conducted large cross-cultural studies of children, stated, "For two people who have lived side by side for such a long time, the adult and the child appear to know amazingly little about each other! . . . An upshot of this general orientation has been the relative lack of information on how the world actually appears to youngsters themselves"(1988).

In Yamamoto et al.'s study of 1,814 mostly middle-class schoolchildren from the United States, Canada, Australia, Japan, the Philippines, and Egypt, the subjects were asked to rank twenty undesirable events. Their rankings were similar, with high correlations across cultures. All ranked the death of a parent as the most upsetting event and having a baby sibling the least upsetting. School issues ranked high among all. Variations among the grades, sexes, and personal histories of the children were statistically nonsignificant: "Because they are children in a contemporary world, their perceptions and experiences of more or less upsetting life events seem to reveal much that is common, regardless of where they are growing up and/or how" (1988). Still, these are middle-class children. Children in other circumstances might rank undesirable events differently (Hampton and Coner-Edwards 1993). Of interest is the authors' report of large differences in the actual experience of parental death, from 2.8 percent of the Japanese children to 42 percent of the Egyptian children. There were two American groups, whose percentages were 20.2 and 21.6, and in the Canadian group 11 percent had experienced the death of a parent. In the Australian and Philippines groups, the percentages were 16.8 and 16.0, respectively. At first glance, it is surprising that the percentages in the U.S. groups were so high. However, social work studies reveal that growing numbers of schoolchildren and adolescents are experiencing parental death, yet have little or no opportunity to talk about it (Ewalt and Perkins 1979; Cho, Freeman, and Patterson 1982).

Few American families talk together about death or dying or encourage their children's questions about dying. In former times, when most deaths occurred at home, children and adults were involved together in the care of the dying. They grieved together when death occurred. But when hospitals and nursing homes took over the care of dying members from families, death became a taboo subject. Talking about death and talking with dying persons became very difficult for most adults, and parents tended to shield their children from the pain of loss and grief, so the taboo carried over to the home.

Since the early 1970s a change to greater familial and institutional openness about death has begun. Classes in death and dying are offered in colleges, and bereavement groups for adults and for children are provided by social workers. Clinicians now recommend that when the death of someone close occurs, school-age children be encouraged to express their grief, to ask questions about dying and death, and to have their questions answered to the degree possible. Parents can acknowledge that they don't know all the answers.

The hospice movement has put a quite different face on the grim aspect of dying. Hospice refers to "a philosophy of care, value orientation, and service delivery system for people with life-threatening illnesses and their families" (Richman 1995:1359). Hospices serve all ages of persons but particularly the older age group. We introduce the idea of formalized palliative care here, but it will apply through the life course.

Hospice services may be provided in a person's home or in a special institution that does not seek to cure—as does the hospital—but rather to provide coordinated palliative care and supportive services for the dying person and his or her family. There were about 340,000 patients in hospices in 1994; over the previous 5 years, the number of terminally ill people using hospice services increased an average of 13 percent per year (Gillen 1995). The goal of hospice is to help their terminally ill clients achieve a "good or appropriate death" (Richman 1995:1360). By relieving people of as much pain as possible while sustaining their alertness, hospice professionals and volunteers enable the dying clients to communicate the vital messages that need to be conveyed at this critical life moment, not only for the sense of closure for the dying person but also for the betterment of the surviving family.

The Schools and Schooling

Beginning School

Every society, through the elders, prepares its youth for the adult roles it considers necessary to its functioning and survival. Schooling, however, represents learning and socialization processes that take place outside the family in a special, formalized setting—provided, in the case of public schooling, by the community. Starting school is a momentous event for children and parents. For children school is a new and unknown world that most are excited about and eager to enter. A few are initially reluctant to leave the safety and protection of home and family. For parents, the school represents the first real exposure of their parenting abilities—via their child's behavior—to a major community institution. Indeed, developmental and behavioral disturbances are often first recognized by the school. Parents may hold positive expectations and may be pleased about the new transition of school entry for the child and themselves, or they may be fearful of the school's judgment of their parenting and about their child's abilities and deportment.

Parents may have concerns about their child's exposure to values, norms, and lifestyles that vary from their own religious and ethnic values. The caretaking parent may welcome the relief that school entry can bring or may dread the "loss" and loneliness. Poor and minority parents may have had unhappy learning and social experiences in their own schooling and may fear similar experiences for their child. For these and other reasons, first-time school entry is an important life transition for all families with children, and in most instances, it is a smooth and even a happy one. To ease the transition, some school social workers conduct primary prevention programs, such as conducting discussion groups for parents whose children are going to be entering school, alerting parents to school expectations, and learning from parents what schools have to do to be ready for these new students (Felner and Adan 1988).

The school is an environmental force in the life space of its children and their parents. It is also an extension of the family in terms of its educational and socialization functions, but it differs from the family in important ways. The school relates to children on the basis of organizational function and what the child does and achieves in the role of "student," while family members relate to one another on the basis of who one is in terms of kinship, age, and gender. Role relations between teacher and student are formalized and impersonal (less so in kindergarten and the primary grades), while relations in the family are likely to be highly personalized and affectionate. School life is pervaded by competitiveness in which children's performance is continually compared to that of peers (or to national standards) by themselves, the teacher, and others, while family life is not ordinarily conceived of as an arena of competition among the members, although personalized competitiveness may develop between siblings or even between the adult partners. Regular and systematic evaluation is part of the school experience but not of family life. Norms of punctuality, promptness in completing assigned tasks, and compliance with rules are emphasized to a far greater degree in school than in most families.

Coming to terms with these differences is part of the child's adaptive task in the transition to school life. School represents preparatory socialization for adult roles in bureaucratic work settings that are formalized, hierarchical, competitive, and achievement-oriented, and in which worker performance is evaluated. Such settings are also impersonal in that employees are expected to relate to one another only in terms of their formal roles and to restrain the emotionality and spontaneity typical of family roles. (Informal groups and norms also emerge in the workplace, but the major goal of socialization concerns the formal organization.) The school's norms are geared to the workplace norms of punctuality, promptness, compliance with rules, diligence, regular attendance, and so on. One consequence is that when the school is unable to keep some students coming, not only do the students miss out on knowledge acquisition, social experiences, and cognitive development, but they are not prepared for adult working life.

School and Society

Perhaps at no other time since the introduction of public education have the schools been subject to so many demands about what needs to be taught as well as so much criticism about how education is being delivered. For example, the National Commission on the Role of the School and the Community in Improving Adolescent Health suggests that a new kind of health education be taught sequentially, from kindergarten through the twelfth grade, going beyond the food pyramid and personal hygiene. This would include relevant information about disease and accident prevention, family life and sex education, substance abuse, violence, mental health, and nutrition. It would teach skills in effective problem solving, the development of positive values, and the ability to work cooperatively. And it would give young people experiences that would foster lifelong exercise habits (1990:36).

Keniston (1977), Foucault (1979), and others also see the schools as arenas of injustice based on race, ethnicity, socioeconomic status, and power. Today, we add gender and sexual orientation as still other arenas. Keniston acknowledged that schools alone cannot create equality of opportunity, but he added that they can be expected to contribute to the goal instead of perpetuating the status of birth. They can teach all children, regardless of background, the basic cognitive skills for participating effectively in the adult world of jobs, social relations, and civic responsibility. Boyer, president of the Carnegie Foundation for the Advancement of Teaching, warned:

> Unless we find better ways to serve minority students and help those who already have dropped out, the social and economic fabric of the nation will be greatly weakened. . . . The even larger issue is whether this nation can embrace a new generation of Americans and build a renewed sense of national unity while rejoicing in diversity. Our response to this urgent and persistent challenge will have an impact far beyond the classroom and will reach into the future as far as anyone can see. (1984)

Many low-income and minority-group parents feel alienated from and apathetic toward the school as still another impersonal and coercive bureaucracy that dominates their lives (Comer et al. 1996). Most are critical of and deeply concerned about the school's failure to educate their children. Some suburban middle-class parents are also dissatisfied with the public schools, believing them to be stifling children's curiosity and creativity. Many are actively working toward improving the school and the educational processes. Others withdraw their children from public schools. An estimated 10 percent of all schoolchildren now attend private and parochial schools. Some educators argue that middle-class white children in private schools or all-white suburban schools miss out on diverse experiences that will help prepare them for the multicultural character of the real world.

Still other parents teach their children at home. It is estimated that about a million children are taught at home, a practice which is legal in most states (Kaslow 1996). Even though parents may be capable of giving their children an enriched education at home, some educators believe the children may suffer from lack of peer contact, formal credentials for college entry, and exposure to ideas other than those of their parents.

The bilingual education of limited-English-speaking children (LES) and non-English-speaking children (NES) is rapidly becoming a political and emotional issue in a nation that has long been hostile to bilingualism (West 1995; Fradd 1985). For example, a growing "English-only" or "English first" movement now threatens to undermine the educational programs serving LES and NES pupils. Controversy surrounds the question of how the federal government should carry out its charge to educate our non-English-speaking children. About 1 out of 7 children do not speak English at home—about 6.3 million children—but of these most—5.5 million—spoke English well or very well (Garcia 1995). Should the government finance programs that teach children the basic academic subjects in their original language while English is phased in progressively until the children are ready to join regular classes? Or should education be bicultural, preserving the native language and other cultural elements throughout the school years while the children also learn English?

Some opponents of bilingual education attack it on the basis of the myth that it produces cognitive deficits. In fact, the academic skills initially taught in the language of origin transfer to English as it is acquired. The children do not need to learn the same subject twice, once in each language (Hakuta 1988). Hence bilingual education actually advances the learning of LES and NES children instead of defeating their learning at the outset by imposing the unknown English language as the sole vehicle of instruction. Other opponents claim that bilingual education prevents pupils from learning English. Although recognizing that very few bilingual persons ever have native-like control of both languages, Hakuta demonstrated that quality bilingual programs can produce students who are able to speak their native language and also "produce complete meaningful utterances" in English (1988:4). Fradd (1985) compares the Canadian and U.S. bilingual programs. In Canada the rights of both the French minority and the English majority are guaranteed, and all ethnic groups are encouraged to maintain their cultural heritage, including their native languages. Canada's economically advantaged children have been the major participants in the second language program, which is seen as a constructive part of education, in contrast to the focus on disadvantaged or immigrant children in the United States, where there is a remedial orientation.

Hakuta believes that bilingual education is desirable for all English-speaking American schoolchildren—not only for cognitive, linguistic, and cultural enrichment but also to prepare them as citizens of today's world: "Speakers of immigrant languages would then be seen as holders of a valuable national resource to be developed, and they in turn would help in the efforts of monolingual English-speakers" (1988:229–230). However, some issues remain unresolved. Certified teachers, especially for new immigrant and refugee children (e.g., Laotian- and Arabic-speaking) are in short supply. Another issue arises from the fact that the educational system often regards poor black children as unreachable because they do not speak standard English and have trouble learning to read it. The consequence is school failure and dropout, which result in the effective closure of society's opportunity structures of higher education and rewarding work to young blacks. Since the children come to school with a rich and expressive language of their own, which does not prepare them for the expectations and tasks of the school, many linguists have suggested they be taught standard English as a second language, just as Spanish-speaking children receive bilingual education. Stewart (1969), for example, contended that it is important for poor black children to learn to read black English first so that what they see on the printed page corresponds to the speech they hear in their family and community. The transition to learning to read standard English will then be comparatively easy (Smitherman 1986). The recent controversy over Ebonics, as a black language to be taught African American children, shows that the bilingual controversy is continually problematic in American society.

Children with Special Needs

A physical illness or disability may contribute to learning difficulties. For example, limited alertness and stamina, the side effects of medications, prejudice or overprotection on the part of teachers, rejection by peers, inappropriate expectations, excessive illness-related absence, and problems in psychosocial adaptation may create difficulties that aggravate the concerns that all schoolchildren have about their competence and self-worth. On the other hand, high levels of motivation, resilience, persistence, intelligence, and ability to cope with stress contribute to positive educational outcomes for many children with a disability or chronic illness.

Since 1975 the schools have been required to provide appropriate education to children with a functional impairment due to chronic illness or physical and sensory disabilities, and to those who identified as mentally retarded, from severe emotional disturbance or from the so-called learning disabilities.

In 1975 a federal law (P.L. 94–142) mandated equal access to education for these children, including individualized educational programs and related services to meet their unique needs. Parents have the right to participate in the evaluation and placement decisions for their special-needs child and the right to due process in their native language. Children are to be provided with the least restrictive learning environment in a range of alternatives from a regular classroom to special classes, and from part- or full-time to residential treatment, depending on the severity of the problem. Each child is to have a written individual learning plan. Many school social workers, trained in the due process procedures of P.L. 94–142, are serving as mediators in disputes between school and parents regarding the need for special education and the types of services required.

Learning disabilities are not widely understood (Green 1995). The most common one is dyslexia, or the impaired ability to read and write. With appropriate instruction in how to compensate, dyslexic children can succeed academically. Many go on to higher education and the professions. Other learning disabilities are impairment in the ability to speak and in the ability to handle numbers, attention deficit, and hyperactivity. All are thought to be neurological disorders, and some apparently have a genetic base. Learning disabilities are not due to intellectual deficit, although learning-disabled children are sometimes mistakenly assumed to be mentally retarded. Because they may manifest emotional and social distress, they are also frequently misdiagnosed as emotionally disturbed. Their distress, however, is usually due to frustration and low self-esteem as the result of frequent academic failures and social difficulties—before their condition is properly diagnosed. When the diagnosis is accurate and the educational plan sound, beneficial results may accrue. However, the concept of the learning disability is becoming increasingly controversial—most especially in regard to hyperactivity.

Labeling children as hyperactive. For several reasons, controversy is growing over the use of labels by the school. First, labels do not include social and contextual variables. For example, the label "learning disability" is hazardous to the child if it is applied without a skilled, knowledgeable study of the child, the family, and the school. Locating the trouble in the child or the family without considering the impact of the school and the nature of teacher-child transactions can result in viewing a child's unique ways of learning—even her or his creativity—as a problem. Rist and Harrel (1982) contended that social contingencies, such as the time, place, situation, and the professional attributes of the labeler, together with the race, sex, socioeconomic status, religion, and personal attractiveness of the child, operate to bring about the application of a label and the associated segregation and stigma.

The unfortunate negative consequences of labeling include less positive interaction with the teacher, increased levels of peer rejection, and the emergence of "learned helplessness" on the child's part. Teachers and parents expect less, and eventually the children may come to expect less of themselves. Once labeled, children usually retain the label and stigma throughout their school careers, and improved behavior and academic work tend not to be noted in school records. Controversy is especially heated on the issue of labeling children "hyperactive" because the potential for injustice is clear. Several million schoolchildren are so labeled. They are said to be impulsive, noisy, rude, fidgety, sometimes clumsy and accident-prone, and unable to follow directions or to focus on a task. They may show poor judgment, low self-esteem, labile moods, and temper tantrums; they are usually avoided by other children (H. Johnson 1988).

Hyperactivity is attributed to "minimal brain dysfunction," or to the newer "minimal neurological dysfunction" often on what many claim is flimsy evidence. The suggested causes range from genetic factors to prenatal, congenital, and postnatal accidents and conditions. Other observers point to the possibility of gender bias on the part of teachers, who, preferring the docile and conforming behavior believed to be typical of girls, refer many more boys for treatment because of their behavioral styles. (Estimates range up to 12 boys for each girl referred.) Little boys are socialized to reject so-called feminine behaviors. Yet when they enter school they face behavioral expectations of a feminine cast (for example, submissiveness, neatness, and quietness). It is not surprising then that boys are more likely than girls to manifest the male-gendered behaviors experienced by some teachers as a problem and to end up with a label of "bad" or hyperactive. Most of those referred are black males, a circumstance that raises the even more disturbing question of institutional racism.

A variety of treatments have been advanced, including drug therapy, behavioral modification, family treatment, diet, cognitive therapy, and psychotherapy. H. Johnson (1988) stated that stimulant medication (principally the drug Ritalin) is the most effective single treatment, decreasing "motor activity, fighting and provocative behaviors, negativism and argumentativeness, and [increasing] attention span and ability to listen." The use of Ritalin is increasing at an alarming rate, raising another question: Is it a prescribed treatment for an actual disorder or a means of sedating disruptive students, whose culture and behavior are not understood by teachers? Critics assert that improved learning from the use of Ritalin has not been proved. Yet the drug is viewed by teachers as a magic cure-all for management problems in the classroom and is overprescribed by some physicians in response to school pressure. There is some evidence that doses high enough to calm hyperactive children are high enough to inhibit learning capacity. However, H. Johnson (1988) stated that if the correct dosage is prescribed, the lethargy, apathy, overcompliance, and lack of spontaneity reported by many observers do not appear.

A different phenomenon, yet somewhat related to the above discussion, is the continuation of corporal punishment in many schools. The National Coalition of Advocates for Students reported that 5 percent of black children and 2 percent of white children in the United States are physically beaten by their teachers (legally) (Study finds blacks twice as liable 1988). The findings were based on analysis of biennial data published by the federal Department of Education's Office of Civil Rights in 1986. The fact that the rate for black students is more than twice that for white students again reflects institutional racism. Hyman reports that there are more than 2 million incidents each year, with most occurring in southern states. He also reports that boys are punished more often than girls and are usually punished by men (administrators). Punishment is infrequent in the primary grades, but increases with age, peaking in junior high, and dropping sharply for older students (1990:61–62, 65).

We are a society that permits its children, in the 31 states without laws against corporal punishment, to be abused by the very institution designed to educate, protect, and nourish them. Almost all other Western nations and the Soviet Union have laws prohibiting the corporal punishment of children by teachers, parents, and others.

Homelessness. A newly identified vulnerable group of children are the homeless who, with their families, form a large segment of the homeless population. In 1994 estimates of homelessness ranged from 1.7 million to 3 million a year, of which families with children constitute more than 40 percent (Kagan 1994:5). These estimates mean that the number of homeless families with children might vary from between 700,000 to more than a million. About 100,000 are homeless on any given night (Institute of Medicine 1988). It is estimated that half of all homelessness among women and children is caused by domestic violence (Slaughter 1993). About a third of homeless children attend school irregularly or not at all. Some are placed in suburban motels and must commute long distances by county-paid buses or stigmatized "welfare taxis" to whatever school district agrees to take them or to their former city district. They must try to do their homework in one crowded motel room.

While the children fall in the same general scholastic range as other pupils, many are fatigued and depressed, and understandably, some present academic and behavioral difficulties (Schmitt 1987).

In the cities, homeless families and their children live in temporary shelters or welfare hotels, and the children move from school to school as their families move from shelter to shelter. Some school districts refuse to admit homeless children on the grounds that they enroll only children with permanent addresses. Most homeless children, who already feel stigmatized and ashamed, suffer further damage from living in miserable, even corrupting environments. Being denied school admission is a final blow. School is a lifesaver for these children, who desperately need to spend at least part of their day in an ordered nurturing setting (Hechinger 1988).

In July 1987 the Stewart B. McKinley Homeless Assistance Act was passed by the U.S. Congress, largely because of efforts by the National Coalition for the Homeless. It established a national policy and limited funds for the education of homeless children, and it eliminated the residency requirements that exclude homeless children from school. Hechinger (1988) commented that if the children's right to an education is to be protected, progress under the act must be carefully monitored. This is a task that social workers working with the homeless, school social workers, and those involved in policy analysis and program development are in a position to carry out at family and community levels (A. Johnson 1995).

Differences in family forms. Some teachers refer to one-parent families as "broken homes" in considering behavioral and learning difficulties that children may present. They assume erroneously that neglect, lax discipline, and lack of interest in the child's schoolwork typify such families, producing poor grades, delinquency, and so on. Furthermore, most schools do not adjust their procedures to the needs of one-parent families. Solo mothers or fathers must often take time off from work if they are to appear at the times that teacher-parent conferences are scheduled, and not all schools notify noncustody or joint-custody parents about school activities or their child's progress, although the parents have a right to this information under federal law. Also, textbooks tend to show only the two-parent family as "normal" and ignore the growing numbers of other family forms. In fact, the U.S. Census Bureau estimates that more than half the nation's children will spend some part of their dependent years in one-parent families. The implication for the children in a one-parent family is that there is something wrong with their family, as though love and academic success are possible only in two-parent families.

The literature over the past 40 years has had this pathologic orientation toward single-parent families—whereas the majority of divorced people report being better off after the divorce than before (Olson and Haynes 1993). Recent scholarship has pointed out that single-parent families can be successful (Moles 1992; Stevenson and Black 1996), although it requires considerable effort and planning, prioritization of the parental role, a consistent nonpunitive discipline, and open communication, among other skills (Olson and Haynes 1993). Moles (1992) reviews the research literature on the effect of living in a single-parent household on academic performance and notes that when social class is taken into consideration, there are no significant differences as compared to children from two-parent families. On the other hand, Olson and Haynes report research that indicates that children growing up in mother-only families—the vast majority of all single-parent households are headed by the mother—are less likely to complete high school and are more likely to be poor as adults, compared to children raised by two natural parents. Income accounts for part of this difference, but not all (1993: 259–260).

Some teachers hold stereotyped views of maternal employment and attribute poor school performance to the mother's work outside the home. When income level is controlled, many studies show that the children of working mothers do as well as those whose mothers are at home. Etaugh (1984) reported research findings that maternal employment is unrelated to academic achievement for elementary school females and is either unrelated or negatively related for white males but positively related for black males, including those in low-income one-parent families. In a study of 10-year-old French-speaking Canadian children, no relationship was found between maternal employment and school grades, IQ, or academic achievement (Gold and Andres 1980). Some school staffs may reflect societal homophobia, thereby placing the children of lesbian or gay parents at educational risk because of myths about and negative stereotypes of their family life, leading to biased expectations of social and academic performance. The effects are similar to the school experiences of many children in one-parent families.

The School and Sex Differences

The Federal Education Act of 1972 (Title 9) prohibits sex discrimination in federally supported schools but has been poorly enforced. Hence many schools have not yet discarded labeling and other practices that discriminate against either sex. Gendered-role socialization by the school is carried out not only through behavioral expectations but also by the content of texts, classes in cooking and sewing for girls and in shop and woodworking and mechanics for boys, play and games, hair and dress codes, and so on—all of which are educational barriers based on sex. In addition to behavioral preferences and labeling that discriminate against boys, rewarding docility and passivity in girls is restrictive of their full potential and hence is also discriminatory. Moreover the general absence of male teachers in the primary grades results in less access to role models of competence for boys and deprives girls of the option of not identifying with the teacher (Allen-Meares, Washington, and Welsh 1986).

A vast literature on the psychology of sex differences exists that can be only briefly summarized here. Maccoby and Jacklin (1974) reviewed hundreds of studies and concluded that there is no difference between girls and boys in total cognitive abilities such as problem solving, concept formation, memory, learning ability, reasoning, and creativity. Further, the evidence supported only three sex differences in specific cognitive skills: a greater verbal ability in girls and greater spatial and mathematical skills in boys. However, Hyde (1981) reanalyzed the relevant studies and concluded that these differences in boys and girls were so small that the average male's and the average female's scores are likely to be only a few points apart.

It now seems likely that girls' superior verbal skills are related to faster female maturation; boys catch up with girls as they, too, mature. Also, boys tend to regard verbal skills such as writing, reading, and spelling as feminine and so may have less investment in learning them. The hypothesis that boys do better than girls on mathematics tests presents two problems. First, no account is taken of environmental and cultural factors. For example, formal training may be the same for boys and girls, but who helps with homework, what sort of toys and games the children play with, and the expectations of teachers and parents are a few overlooked factors. Second, it has not been established whether test scores measure innate mathematical ability or simply developed ability (Schafer and Gray 1981). Schafer and Gray asserted that environmental factors that act as barriers to the full realization of female students' potential must be removed. Most researchers now agree that children of either sex should not be discouraged from pursuing particular interests and careers on the basis of disproved assumptions about very small sex differences in cognitive areas.

New Directions: Educational Reform

Since the publication in 1983 of the report of the National Commission on Excellence in Education, *A Nation at Risk,* some improvement has occurred. Many state legislatures have appropriated money to raise teachers' salaries. School districts have set new standards in curriculum and teacher competence and have introduced systematic curriculum reviews and teacher training. In an interview, former Secretary of Education Terrel H. Bell stated that such reforms have benefited about 70 percent of schoolchildren, but not the remaining 30 percent, consisting of low-income and minority children (Fiske 1988). Even so, the public is now more aware of the plight of minority and low-income children and of the threat of growing illiteracy and ineffective education to the nation's future. Hence a reform emphasis in the 1990s on modifying the fundamental structure of public education is likely to be supported by a more enlightened citizenry (Fiske 1988).

Educational experts declare that urban schools must be restructured, the control of education being returned to the schools by overgrown, centralized educational bureaucracies. Schools must be smaller or at least must consist of smaller units to foster personal bonds between teachers and children. Teachers must be personally responsible for their students' progress, and principals must share educational decision making with their teachers, while providing educational leadership. Some urban school districts have already moved toward a new management model.

Some observers believe that schools must enhance their contribution to the community by serving also as community centers for after-school and vacation-time play, study, and other activities for all children, especially those who return to unsupervised homes after school because their parents work, and for evening educational, cultural, and civic programs for parents and other community members, especially in poor neighborhoods. Many school districts have already begun such programs (Dryfoos 1994; Zigler, Kagan, and Hall 1996).

School social workers can make important contributions to achieving the needed reforms. The ecological nature of the school makes it a potent site for social work programs, services, and child advocacy to help in the following five areas:

1. preventing negative educational and socialization outcomes among children with a range of vulnerabilities
2. promoting personal capacities for successful learning and socialization for all pupils

3. restoring adaptive social and educational functioning in situations where a good child-school fit is absent
4. facilitating needed policy and procedural changes
5. encouraging parents' participation in school policies and educational matters.

For social workers engaged in policy formation and analysis and in research, school systems are an important arena for policy and program development, and for studies that will contribute to a public understanding of the need for structural change in public education.

Peer Relationships in Middle Childhood

Learning not only takes place in the family and the school but is also imparted by peers, and the groups in which peers interact. Age-appropriate social behaviors learned from peers are as essential as those learned from parents and teachers (Hartup 1979). Children are gradually empowered not only by successful learning but also by successful social relationships. The achievement of friendship and peer group acceptance strengthens the child's self-concept and self-esteem, relatedness, and competence, and after a long period of conformity, contributes to self-direction. Hartup suggested that the egalitarian give-and-take of peer relations, as well as the freedom from constraints imposed by family attachments and hierarchical authority, are responsible for their valuable and unique contribution to the child's social development. The lack of good peer relations in middle childhood is associated with discomfort, anxiety, and a general hesitancy to engage the environment.

The Peer Group

Being part of a peer group provides "a variety of resources that an individual friendship cannot—a sense of collective participation, experience with organizational roles, and group support in the enterprise of growing up. Groups also pose . . . some of the most acute problems of social life—of inclusion and exclusion, conformity and independence" (Z. Rubin 1980:94). Rubin pointed out that peer groups are generally homogeneous and tend to exclude the child who is different in appearance, skills, or temperament. Groups have also practiced exclusion on the basis of race and sex. To the degree that racism abates in society and children have more cross-racial experience in school and possibly in the neighborhoods, peer groups may show a trend toward less exclusion on the basis of race. Similarly, to the degree that parents encourage cross-sex friendships in their preschoolers and schools observe the rights of girls to join boys on athletic teams and in "male" courses (and of boys to join girls in "female" courses), peer groups may show a trend toward less rigid exclusion on the basis of sex. The other bases, particularly that of mental or physical disability and sexual orientation are apt to persist until parental and school efforts to convey acceptance and to teach understanding become more effective. Children may fear what they do not understand.

Across age and culture, boys more than girls tend to congregate in large groups; girls more than boys tend to form pairs (Gilligan 1982). Boys tend to view the group as an entity and to emphasize loyalty and solidarity. Girls tend to view the group as a network of intimate two-person friendships. Boys also have friendships, but they tend to be less expressive and intimate than those of girls. It is probably still accurate to say that, typically, young school-age boys and girls tend to shun and tease each other, to invite and resist attraction, and to express stereotypical taunts such as "girls are silly "or "boys are disgusting." Individual cross-sex friendships occur, but generally the cross-sex friend does not become a member of the other's peer group. In late childhood, as puberty approaches, a less ambivalent interest in the opposite sex appears, although interaction is still strained. These nascent interests help prepare children for romantic interests among teenagers and for the mixed peer groups of adolescence (Z. Rubin 1980).

Typically, elementary schoolchildren have played gender-typed games and sports. Probably the majority still do, despite the integration beginning to occur in organized school sports, Little League, and the like. Girls' games, such as jumping rope, jacks, and hopscotch, tend to be played with one or two well-liked persons. Boys' game are likely to be played in large groups, and they require cooperation regardless of whether are well-liked. Such differences help explain the different models of social relations of boys and girls (Gilligan 1982). That is, boys learn to operate within systems of rules and to cooperate with persons they may not like. They acquire social skills that prepare them for the workplace, but peer socialization for most boys does not lead to an ability to form intimate friendships. On the other hand, peer socialization teaches girls social skills related to intimacy and emotional expressiveness that fit the requirements of personal and familial relationships but not those of the workplace. Thus sex-typed play and social patterns will continue to deprive each sex of learning other important skills for today's world until both have the opportunity to share in the learning experiences of the other (Z. Rubin 1980:109).

Peers are important sources of social comparison; "How am I shaping up?" reflects the universal human need to evaluate oneself by comparison with others. In addition to exclusiveness, peer groups tend to expect conformity as the base for acceptance and evaluation. The tendency is often troublesome to parents because it can stifle individuality. It is especially troublesome when the group's norms, values, beliefs, and expectations differ from those of the parents, and this difference may also be distressing for the child. Pressure toward conformity intensifies in adolescence and is even present to some degree in adulthood (Z. Rubin 1980). Given the significance of peer relations in middle childhood, it is not surprising that social workers find that troubled school-age children respond well to experiences in social work activity groups, "talk" groups, and mixtures of the two (Maguire 1991; L. Brown 1991). Social work groups are also important vehicles for promoting growth for all school-age children in school, at camp, and in neighborhood settings.

Friendships

For most individuals, peer friendships are important throughout the life course from toddlerhood to old age. The school-age child who wants to make friends but does not is likely to be unhappy and distressed, while the child with close friendships is apt to be a happy child (Z. Rubin 1980). By the age of 11 or 12, most children view a close friendship, the "chumship" (Sullivan 1953), as a special, reciprocal relationship of intimacy that develops over time. The preteen's emphasis on psychological compatibility builds on the toddler's emphasis on physical accessibility and the primary-grade child's one-way conception of a friend as a person who does things that please one (Z. Rubin 1980). For the preadolescent, friendship comes to mean appreciating each other's abilities and experiences, trusting each other with one's innermost feelings and private facts, being concerned about the well-being of the other, and accepting reciprocal obligations to each other. Patterns of friendship do vary among individual children: some prefer to have a number of friends; others concentrate on one or two. Conceptions of friendship may also differ across societies and across subcultures within North American society.

Parents and others generally view cross-age friendships and groups as undesirable or at least inappropriate, perhaps because age segregation begins with school entry. Nevertheless, as Z. Rubin (1980) pointed out, the assumption that segregation by age is the only right way is negated by the fact that children in non-Western cultures play and socialize in mixed-age groups.

However, mixed-age relations can have negative aspects, such as bullying of the younger child by the older, rejection of the older child by his or her own age-mates, a younger child's engagement in activities for which he or she is not yet ready, or an older child's sudden loss of interest in and dropping of the younger one. An exclusive preference for older or younger friends may indicate emotional or social difficulties. On balance, however, Rubin suggested that the potential advantages outweigh the negatives. Hartup (1979) cited research findings that younger peer therapists can help withdrawn youngsters. Older peer tutors contribute to the competence and self-esteem of both the tutee and the peer tutor (Allen, Philliber, and Hoggson 1990; Jason et al. 1993; Jason et al. 1993).

The ending of a friendship because of geographic moves or because one of the pair loses interest is a painful stressor. Children differ in how they cope with it. In the case of a move, some respond to the loss of friends and place with sadness and even depression, while others are excited by the newness and opportunity for new friends and experiences. In later childhood, making friends in a new setting is difficult because cliques are already in place. Z. Rubin (1980) believes that most children ultimately succeed in managing the loss and making new friends. Very frequent moves (as in military families and migrant workers), however, appear to have more persistent negative effects on the ability of some children to make lasting friendships. Rubin noted that parents sometimes underestimate the impact of the loss of friendship. They may minimize it with statements such as, "Don't worry, you'll find another friend," as though a friend is like a standardized, replaceable part. It is more helpful to encourage the child to express the attendant feelings and for the parents to verbalize an understanding of how hard the experience is. These important guidelines can also be followed by social workers who work with children.

Sibling Relationships

Goetting (1986) points out that sibling relationships are unique among human ties by virtue of their long duration and the sharing of common genetic and social heritage and a common culture. Such relationships are often egalitarian, and as the family size has dropped over the past century, the importance of siblings has increased in the now-typical two-child families. There is, as readers will appreciate in their own lives, a wide variation in sibling contact and support. Goetting asserts that the sibling bond typically persists throughout the life course, manifesting its positive and negative features in a variety of forms. She offers the following list of developmental tasks of siblings over the life course, in the tradition of Havighurst (1966). We present them all here and remind you of them in later chapters:

Childhood and adolescent sibling tasks: Companionship and emotional support (as intimate friends and confidants); delegated caretaking (as when older children care for younger ones); and direct services (such as forming sibling coalitions for dealing with parents, protection, teaching of skills, help with homework, etc.)

Early and middle adulthood sibling tasks: Continued support, albeit with decreased intensity as adults form their own families and friends; cooperation in care of elderly parents and ultimately the dismantling of the parental home; and direct services (such as at times of crises, baby-sitting, lending of money)

Old age sibling tasks: Continued emotional support, perhaps with more intensity even though with less frequency, which may compensate for loses of other friends and kin; shared reminiscence, based on common biographies; resolution of sibling rivalry, if necessary; direct services, such as aid when ill, financial support, homemaking and repairs, and shopping

Chronic Illness or Disability in Childhood

Among adults, chronic illnesses are few in number but are fairly common. "In contrast, the chronic illnesses of children are relatively rare, and there is a tremendous variety of conditions" (J. Perrin 1985:3). Perrin specified 11 childhood diseases that serve as marker diseases in considering matters of policy, services, the impact on child and family, and so on. That is, they have characteristics that make them representative of all childhood chronic conditions. The 11 are juvenile-onset diabetes, muscular dystrophy, cystic fibrosis, spina bifida, sickle cell anemia, congenital heart disease, chronic kidney disease, hemophilia, leukemia, cleft palate, and severe asthma. Despite their rarity, the illnesses do affect a sizable population. About 1 million American children, or 1 to 2 percent of the total child population, suffer severe chronic illness, and another 10 million, or 10 to 15 percent of the total child population, are less severely involved (J. Perrin 1985:1,3).

Some conditions are genetic or congenital in origin, and others are the result of disease or accident. Some childhood illnesses and disabilities, such as spina bifida, missing or deformed body parts, heart disease, Down syndrome, brain damage, blindness, and deafness, are apparent at birth or during infancy. Others, such as diabetes, cystic fibrosis, leukemia and other cancers, asthma, sickle cell anemia, and chronic kidney failure, may not appear until early or middle childhood. Common issues face all chronically ill children, whatever their particular illness or disability. However, a few differences can exist within a single condition or across conditions that have different impacts on the child's school attendance, peer relations, and adaptation to the illness or disability—just as personal, social, and cultural differences do.

Among such differences are the following: (1) limited mobility in some conditions affects access in the physical environment and may prevent participation in sports and other activities with peers and siblings; (2) the course of any condition may remain stable or may change over time: some conditions may progress toward improvement (as in controlled diabetes) and others toward decline (as in muscular dystrophy), and some are characterized by unpredictable ups and downs (as in asthma) that may be more stressful for a child than a stable yet more severe condition; (3) children with cognitive or sensory impairment have different adaptive patterns and service needs from those without such impairments; and (4) the visibility of the disorder (as in facial or limb deformities) has a significant negative effect on peer relations, with social and developmental consequences for the child (Pless and Perrin 1985).

Chronically ill or disabled children are at higher risk of emotional and social disorders than healthy children. The available evidence suggests that children with mild disabilities suffer as much as, or more, than those with severe disabilities—perhaps because of the invisibility of the symptoms, which enables a child to pass as "normal" and to keep the illness secret. Peers then expect such children to behave in all respects as others do. When, for medical reasons, they cannot, a difficult conflict arises for them (Pless 1984).

Stein (1983) writes: "Diagnosis of a chronically ill child is one of the most severe stresses that a family can sustain, because it involves not only the sudden shock and grief experienced when the child is diagnosed, but also years of multiple traumatic events, constant medical treatment, and continual worry and anxiety." When the chronic illness or disability of a child is severe, it has serious consequences for the family's development and well-being. Indeed, "family members are burdened with caring responsibilities, affected by anxiety and sometimes by guilt, strapped by unpredicted expenses and possible

economic ruin, and facing an uncertain future that may include the premature death of the child" (J. Perrin 1985:2).

Limited finances complicate the situation. One parent, usually the mother,
may have to leave employment for full-time care of the child, and the other
parent may have to work at two jobs. There may be no money or time for
recreation and vacations. Stein (1983) pointed out that insurance policies vary
and that eligibility for public aid is often inconsistent and meager: "There are
also hidden costs: lost opportunities, lost work time, lost chances to advance
in one's career or to go back to school." The parents may not have the time or
energy to maintain their social ties or affiliations with self-help groups, which
could have been very helpful, even essential, to the family's well-being. The
scarcity of community services or difficult access to them also makes life more
difficult. These and other consequences of childhood illness or disability
become enormous burdens for a solo parent.

The late onset of illness or disability implies different developmental and
service needs of the child from those for a child having an early onset: "Children born with a condition affecting their functioning appear to adjust to it
more readily or to develop in the context of their illness in different ways from
those able-bodied children who, having gone through typical developmental
phases, develop permanent conditions later in childhood. . . . Children who
have once had an ability react to its loss differently from those who never had
it" (Pless and Perrin 1985:47).

The tasks faced by the parents and the family during the school years are
somewhat different in the two groups, since the parents in the first group have
had to deal with a grave condition for all the child's life. If they have been relatively successful in meeting the life issues involved and the feelings engen-
dered, the child and the parents will be relatively ready for the transition of
school entry and the many adaptive tasks of the school years. In contrast, the
parents in the second group may still be mourning their child's lost health and
may still be caught up in life-threatening aspects or life issues that the illness
creates for them and the child. In the face of the painful and relative newness
of the illness or disability, they and the child must now meet the demanding
new challenges of school entry and all that follows upon it.

For the school-age child, growing up different may take its toll psychologically and socially: "Handicapped children want a chance to grow, to have
freedom and fun, training and education, and to progress to the extent of
their abilities with help from their family, school, and community" (Bern
1980). Their interests, goals, and concerns are the same as those of other children, and this is a particularly difficult time to be different from one's peers.

The restrictions imposed by disability or chronic illness, such as limited mobility, pain and discomfort, arduous treatment, or parents' and teachers' well-intended but excessive efforts to protect the chid from medical crises, can unduly inhibit the child's desired participation in the play and academic activities that are so important in sustaining relatedness, competence, self-esteem, and self-direction. Weitzman (1984) noted that the school provides "chronically ill children with numerous opportunities to address issues [of independence and social skills. It] is the logical setting in which overdependence can be diminished, negative social behaviors can be unlearned, and social conventions can be assimilated into the child's behavioral repertoire."

It is possible to enhance the lives of disabled children, as well as able children, through designs of environments sensitive to developmental needs. For example, Shaw (1987) designed a playground that was usable by disabled children, including addressing accessibility (for wheelchairs) and activities at different heights (such as raised sandboxes or a chalk wall for drawing). Parallel bars are used to enhance upper-body strength; with creative planning—such as a ladder hung horizontally above a ramp where children pull themselves up to a platform hand over hand—children in wheelchairs can participate in activities. The variety of environments include graded challenges hard enough to be challenging but easy enough to permit accomplishment.

Despite the hazards of growing up different, a serious illness or disability does not have to rule out successful adaptation by the child and family in responsive physical and social environments. For helping professionals, "there are many ways to help in the adaptive process, by being available and supportive, by anticipating, and by advocating the needs of children with physical health problems" (Stein 1983).

Dying in Childhood

Dying in infancy, childhood, or youth is a particularly anguishing experience for the dying young person, the parents, the siblings, and relatives. Not only is it regarded as unfair and inappropriate, but the unique issues in losing a child make parental bereavement an overwhelming assault. This is true at any age of parent and child, as outliving one's child is tragic, untimely, and unnatural. "No matter what the age of their child, [the parents] have lost their hopes, dreams, and expectations for that child, have lost parts of themselves, and their future, and suffer the terrible ordeal of outliving their child" (Rando 1985). Parents who have other children must somehow continue to carry out the parental role they are grieving for and having to relinquish. Additionally "parents must 'grow up with the loss.' It is not uncommon for them to mark [birthdays and] the times when the child 'would have' graduated, 'would have' gotten married. The grieving process is continual. . . . Their grief may continue longer and have more upsurges in it because parents demarcate their lives by events in the lives of their children, whether the children are alive or dead" (Rando 1985).

Rando observed further that because both parents are simultaneously confronted by the same overwhelming loss, the most therapeutic resource—the spouse, to whom one would usually turn for emotional support—is not fully available. Friends who are parents sometimes avoid the bereaved for various psychological reasons, so social supports may not be available. Survival guilt is generated "because this is an era, in comparison to centuries past, when infant and child mortality is at the lowest rate ever, leaving parents unprepared to deal with the loss of their children" (Rando 1985). Grandparents suffer a double loss, for they grieve for their children's loss as well as their own. Self-help groups, such as Compassionate Friends, for parents whose child has died of any cause, and Candlelighters, specifically for parents of children who die of cancer, can be very helpful. Hospital social workers also offer parent support groups.

For the very young dying child, the fears of separation and abandonment are uppermost; hence, the parents must try to assuage those fears in their child at a time when they are dealing with their own fears and grief. A preschooler has similar fears plus the fear of annihilation or mutilation through painful diagnostic and treatment procedures. The school-age child possesses an intellectual comprehension of death to some extent, yet an endless future seemed to stretch ahead for the pleasures of doing and achieving. Dying at this age is therefore an interference with the sense of self and an assault on relatedness, self-direction, and the sense of competence. Some believe that older schoolchildren know intuitively when they are dying and are deeply worried about dying alone. Reassurance that they will not be alone is extremely important. While many terminally ill children die in hospitals, more and more families are arranging for their child to die at home surrounded by the family, with parents holding the child's hand, or holding the child in their arms. Some children, such as Ryan White, the young hemophiliac who died from AIDS after facing much social ostracism, rise to unbelievable heights of altruism in their terminal illness.

Throughout the mourning process and beyond, the work of integrating the loss of the child into the family paradigm goes on. The work can be hampered by a deteriorating relationship between the parents, even though their relationship was satisfying before the death. One or both parents may displace feelings of blame and anger on the other. They may misinterpret each other's grieving behaviors as hostile or uncaring. They may engage in incompatible grieving styles that keep them from comforting and supporting each other. Gender typing can impede the expression of grief in men or the expression of anger at the loss in women. If the mother is a homemaker, she encounters numerous reminders of the child continually, while the father, who is at the workplace, may be distracted by his job activities and experience some relief.

The fear of losing another child may inhibit sexual intimacy, or the depression experienced by one partner may lead to sexual problems for both. The parents may be unable to respond to the questions, fears, and sadness of their other children, so that further tensions develop. Families with these or preexisting difficulties are at risk of physical or emotional disorders, divorce, or disorganization. Social work services, if they are sought or if the family accepts referral, can help to prevent such outcomes by providing emotional and social support in the tasks of reorganization. (See Rando 1985 for further suggestions on working with bereaved parents and families.)

Some families, given sufficient time and adequate personal and formal supports, slowly transcend what is likely to be a permanent sense of loss and anguish, and they turn their attention to meeting the needs of the surviving family members. Physical activity; rituals and ceremonies, including anticipatory planning for anniversary phenomena each year; open communication and expression of feelings, including acceptance of the periodic ups and downs of individual members' emotions in response to the loss; flexibility in roles and tasks; sharing decision making; and making opportunities for recreation appear to be a few of the self-healing processes that families draw on for the work of reorganization. Eventually, they achieve a new view of themselves as a family in which the lost child is now present only in memory. They attain a new view of their relationship to the world and may help other parents facing or experiencing loss, or work with a voluntary health association to raise funds for preventive services or research.

11

Family Transformations: Adolescence

Puberty and adolescence are major expectable transitions, generally calling for moderate and usually nonconflicted changes in most families' organization and worldview. In a relatively small number of young persons, however, the biological and nonbiological transitions may precipitate or may be accompanied by one or more nonexpectable second-order developments, such as "coming out," substance abuse, unintended pregnancy, grave injury, suicide, chronic illness, or terminal illness. These require major family transformations and are addressed in this chapter. Similarly, the developmental transitions of the parents as they leave young adulthood and enter the middle years may represent first- or second-order developments inducing mild or major changes in the family. These, too, are considered.

Outline

Puberty, Adolescence, and the Environment

Entering the Teens: Puberty

Do you remember when you reached adolescence? Finally, you had "arrived," after watching some of your friends get there ahead of you. What were the first signs? Was it some enlargements on your body?—a little posturing secretly in front of a mirror showed the inescapable changes, even though you had a way to go before you modeled publicly. Or maybe it was a few hairs in funny places—why should there be hairs growing there? Was there a change in your voice? Or a new odor? Or something about the way you acted? Did you hope that people would notice? People did seem to look at you any differently—of course, everyone could guess your secret. Is that what those jokes were all about? Why can't people leave you alone? This is a private matter; you'll only tell a few of your closest friends. Remember?

Puberty is a biological process that results in the transformation of the child into an adult. The process is crucial for the survival of the species and momentous for the individual. Puberty begins in most girls at about the age of 10 or 10+, and in most boys at about 12 years, and it takes about 2 years to complete. It involves hormone changes, which in interaction with the hypothalamus (a part of the brain) lead to increased physical size and muscular development, the redistribution of body fat, changes in facial contour, the growth of internal sexual organs and external genitalia, and the appearance of secondary sex characteristics (the female breast and pubic and axillary hair; lowered pitch of the voice and facial hair in the male). Ovulation and menarche in females usually occur at about 12+ years. Early cycles are frequently but not necessarily infertile. In males, the ability to ejaculate may occur as early as 12, but the production of mature sperm usually occurs later, at age 13 or 14.

The rapid physical and physiological changes in both sexes lead to youngsters' preoccupation with body image and physical appearance. Hamburg (1974) noted the different effects on girls and boys of early entry or late entry into puberty. Some individuals complete pubertal changes before other individuals have begun. This is a serious disadvantage and a life stressor for many late-developing boys. They continue to look like elementary-school boys at a time when it is important to look grown up. They have a 4-year developmental lag as compared to the average girl of their age, and perhaps a 2-year lag in relation to the average boy their age. They most likely do not know or believe they will later catch up with their peers. Hence their self-esteem is low and their anxiety is high. Their compensatory behaviors may be maladaptive and may tend to continue even after puberty has been completed.

Early-maturing girls are at some disadvantage compared with late maturing girls; they may be self-conscious and feel "different" from their classmates because of their physical development. As a result, they may lack poise and ease in social interactions. Petersen and Spiga (1982) concluded that while early puberty is better for boys, being on time is best for girls. For both boys and girls, how puberty and its changes are experienced varies according to the timing of the developmental changes, the preparation for them, the meaning attributed to them, individual vulnerabilities, and the nature of the environment, especially the family, the school, and the peer group. Hormonal treatment is now available for children who enter puberty prematurely and for those whose entry is abnormally delayed, thus preventing trauma. Either condition is usually defined medically as being out of average range by a year or more.

Entering the teens represents the acquisition of a new status and social identity as an adolescent—the badge of entry into teenage culture. This can be pleasing or stressful or both, depending on how the individual responds to the need for new behaviors, standards, and role models. Drugs, drinking, and sexual activity now reach down into junior high school, exerting new pressures on the "new" teenager to act wisely, often without preparation or support. Hamburg (1974) contends that youngsters entering the teens and for the next few years want and benefit from the guidance and support of their parents (especially the same-sex parent) in their efforts to cope effectively with this major life transition.

Entering the Teens: Adolescence

In contrast to puberty, which is a biological process, adolescence is a cultural phenomenon that in effect is an "artificial" postponement of adulthood. It is a comparatively recent phenomenon that arose out of late nineteenth-century changes in the economic and social structures of U.S. society (Kett 1977). With industrialization and its growing need for universal education at higher and higher levels and with the reformist definition of child labor as morally wrong, children's dependence on their parents began to lengthen. Gradually, the period between puberty and the time when the individual achieved economic and social independence as a young adult became formally defined and institutionalized as adolescence. For a time, it was assumed to end at about age 18 at the completion of high school. Now, with many women and men completing college and graduate or professional education, often with continuing financial dependence on the parents, the period has lengthened to include the years from 19 to 22 and beyond—at least in the minds of some parents and psychologists, if not in the minds of the young themselves. As the columnist Ellen Goodman once observed, "Adolescence isn't a training ground for adulthood now. It is a holding pattern for aging youth."

In nonindustrial societies, after a childhood of practicing increasingly adult-like tasks, formal ceremonies and rituals mark the smooth transition of the pubescent child into the rights and responsibilities of adulthood. But in Western societies, adolescence segregates youths from the world of adults for a decade or more. Thus adolescents form a separate society, having its own subcultures of norms and values, dress codes, leisure activities, music, food, and language. Dryfoos notes that these have led to the "new morbidities"— young people become victims of unprotected sex, drugs, violence, and depression—in contrast with the old morbidities of malnutrition, chronic diseases, and personal hygiene problems (1994:2). Some adult activities are permitted older adolescent, such as driving, voting, serving in the armed forces, and drinking alcohol. These lead to ambiguity and contradictions in the definition of adolescence. In the absence of alternative rituals, sex, drinking, and drug use become the rites of passage for many youth.

During the past century, psychoanalysts and others viewed adolescence as a time of personality disorganization, severe mood swings, bitter rebellion against the parents, and maladaptive behaviors. The emotional upheaval is said to derive from the upsurge of libidinal and aggressive drives, which weaken the defenses against earlier oedipal strivings. The turmoil is considered necessary, as it propels young people toward separating from their parents, establishing their own identity, and becoming mature healthy adults. These assumptions were based on generalizations made from studies of clinical and correctional populations.

Coexisting with this view is a normative position that youth is a period of physical growth, psychological and social development, and the construction of life plans. It holds that most teenagers and their families cope successfully with the adaptive tasks of puberty and adolescence. These adaptive tasks in the life transition from childhood to adulthood include:

1. Creating an expanded self-concept (including a new body image), which draws on identifications with one's gender, family, and cultural group that began in childhood and became part of the self, and on past experiences and aspirations for the future. The self-concept may now expand to incorporate new feelings of pride, or it may contract with feelings of shame or confusion.

2. Increasing self-direction and independence from the parents while maintaining mutually satisfying relations with them.

3. Establishing same-sex and opposite-sex friendships, and preparing for adult commitment to a sexual partner.

4. Maintaining group affiliations and learning social interdependence.

5. Defining vocational interests and readying oneself for pursuing them.

6. Building on values absorbed from the parents and developing one's own set of moral values, spirituality, and philosophy of life.

Despite occasional tensions and discontents, the successful completion of these tasks and the parents' reciprocal tasks lead to first-order changes in family roles, responsibilities, and relationships consonant with the adolescent's increasing maturity. This is not to deny that among some adolescents and their families the adaptive tasks exceed the resources for coping with them. Rather, it is to say that social, emotional, and behavioral difficulties are neither inevitable nor universal in all adolescents and their families. For some, adolescence may pose stressful life issues, depending on genetic, familial, cultural, societal, and other environmental factors. Before we consider these stressors, the next section considers what is known about normal adolescents.

Studies of Normal Adolescents

Throughout the 1960s, 1970s, and 1980s, Offer and his colleagues studied what normal adolescents think and feel about themselves in psychological, social, familial, sexual, and coping areas (e.g., Offer, Ostrov, and Howard 1981; Offer and Offer 1975). *Normal* was defined not as psychological health but as random groups of adolescents who were representative of a school's student body. Large samples were drawn of male, and later of female, high school students in the United States, and later in the United States, Australia, Ireland, and Israel. The researchers also compared younger teenagers (13 to 15 years of age) and older teenagers (16 to 18 years of age), as well as 2 different cohorts experiencing adolescence in 2 different decades and comparison groups of physically ill, delinquent, and disturbed youth.

The vast majority of those in the normal samples functioned well, maintained satisfying relations with peers and family, accepted the values of the larger society, and were not wracked by emotional upheaval (Oldham 1978). Most had adapted to their bodily changes and emerging sexuality without undue conflict and were making a relatively smooth transition to young adulthood. About 20 percent, however, reported having cognitive or affective problems. A major cohort difference was found in greater self-esteem among the 1960s normals than among those of the 1970s. The difference was attributed to experiences of growing up in the affluence of the 1950s versus growing up in the 1960s with the turmoil of the Vietnam war, Watergate, and economic distress. Likewise, cohorts of youth growing up in the 1980s and 1990s have experienced generally prosperous eras (for the majority of people at least) as well as some momentous political, economic, and scientific events (the dissolution of the Soviet Union, the end of "welfare as we know it," and the exploration of Mars, to mention only some highlights).

The differences between normal adolescents and delinquent, disturbed, or physically ill adolescents were found to be significant in many areas. Delinquent adolescents showed lower self-esteem and were much more hostile, unhappy, suspicious, empty, confused, ashamed, and pessimistic than the normals; their reports about their families were especially negative. The disturbed adolescents were significantly lower in self-esteem than the normals. Disturbed affect, pessimism, poor body image, and interpersonal difficulties were prominent. They felt as negatively toward their families as the delinquent youths did, but instead of rebellion and hostility, they reported deep self-doubt and emotional upheaval. They also felt sadder, lonelier, and more rejected by their parents than the delinquents did. The physically ill were similar to the normals in many ways. Where they differed was where they could be expected to differ. They expressed "sadness, loneliness, and negative feelings about their physical well-being, yet they retain[ed] a sense of optimism and commitment to values and family" (Offer, Ostrov, and Howard 1981:117–118). They felt they were a burden to their families, and they denied the importance of sexuality. The authors suggested that the latter attitude was an adaptive response, inasmuch as its opposite, yearning for the unattainable, would only bring on great pain and despair.

In the early 1980s, the researchers studied 5,938 middle- and upper-class teenagers from the United States, Australia, Bangladesh, Hungary, Israel, Italy, Japan, Taiwan, Turkey, and West Germany. The findings were similar to those described for the normals in the earlier studies. The authors claimed to have found a "universal adolescent," based on agreement (75 percent or higher) across countries in the areas of positive familial relationships, vocational and educational goals, superior coping, satisfying social relationships, and to a limited extent, individual values. However, in a commentary at the end of the book, Harry C. Triandis, a cross-cultural psychologist, notes that a questionnaire limits responses, so "there is no opportunity to inquire about aspects of the subject's world that are specific to particular cultures." Moreover, all the subjects were literate, urban, middle-class, and exposed to the mass media. Thus they may have thought alike, but they may have been "diverging progressively from teenagers in their cultures who are less affluent. Without representative samples we cannot say much about a 'universal adolescent' " (cited in Offer, Ostrov, and Howard 1988:128).

Rutter (1979b) and Thomas and Chess (1984) also rejected the idea of adolescence as a time of emotional turmoil, maladaptation, identity crisis: "Most young people go through their teenage years without significant emotional or behavioral problems. It is true there are challenges to be met, adaptations to be made, and stresses to be coped with. However, these do not all arise at the same time and most adolescents deal with these issues without undue disturbance" (Rutter 1979b:86).

Interviewing the white middle-class subjects in their New York City sample, Thomas and Chess (1984) found that for teenagers with a healthy childhood developmental course, the teen years were a challenging period of psychological growth. They entered adolescence with an optimal level of self-esteem, healthy behavioral patterns, positive relationships with family and peers, and effective coping resources. Others mastered the demands and expectations of adolescence but did so less smoothly. They were, perhaps, rebellious or negativistic, but without social or legal difficulties or evidence of psychopathology. For them, too, it was a positive and healthy developmental period with a successful outcome.

Among those who had suffered behavioral disorders in childhood, some found new coping resources as a consequence of maturation, environmental opportunities, and a supportive family situation that enabled them to master the earlier psychological problems. But among them were a small number in whom the new demands of adolescence were experienced as very stressful, exceeding their resources for coping with them. The result was a behavioral problem or the exacerbation of a previously existing disorder.

These studies are largely of white middle-class groups, except for the study by Rutter (1979b) who reported on disadvantaged youth in Great Britain. Few studies of nonclinical populations of minority and poor adolescents are available. However, over a four-year period during the 1960s, Ladner studied 100 low-income, urban, black female children and adolescents in the United States. Despite the stressors of growing up black and female in a racist and sexist society, most of these youngsters showed adaptive strengths of self-esteem, awareness of the societal sources of their oppressive circumstances, resourcefulness, supportive kin and peer networks, and a generalized hope for improving their life chances through education that would ensure employment (1971:77–108). More recently, Furstenberg, Brooks-Gunn, and Morgan (1987) studied a group of black women who had unwanted pregnancies as teenagers but were able to move out of poverty as young adults, primarily by marrying. Perhaps, like the young (and older) people described in Robert Coles's (1993) autobiographical book *The Call of Service,* some purpose transformed their lives into something of personal and moral value. What this personal affirmation is and how it needs an affirming social context is a central quest for social workers, which leads us to an exciting topic: resilience.

The recent resilience literature reveals some important patterns about normal children and youth growing up in disadvantaged homes and communities. Resilience refers to the fact, as Garmezy (1971) so neatly expressed it, that sometimes healthy children emerge from unhealthy settings. Benard (1992) adopts an ecological-systems perspective in noting that children are embedded in families, which are connected to schools and to the community at large. One cannot look at only one piece of this social fabric because a checks-and-balances system exists among individual, family, peer, neighborhood, and community institutions. Where there is a problem in one sector, other sectors may step in and help achieve balance in the developing person. Benard summarizes the literature to identify what empirically supported factors have emerged that might be the active ingredients to help children at risk—and by implication, all children—achieve a healthy development. She presents the following characteristics (adapted from M. Bloom 1996):

> Characteristics of resilient children: (1) social competence (skills relevant to working, playing, loving and expecting well); (2) problem-solving skills; (3) autonomy (self-efficacy, internal locus of control, impulse control, etc.); and (4) a sense of purpose and future.

> Protective factors within the family that promote resilience: (1) care and support by at least one closely bonded adult—not necessarily a parent, it could also be a relative, older sibling, teacher, minister, or neighbor; (2) high parental expectations (a belief that the child has potential for a successful future); and (3) encouragement of the child's participation in the family, such as having chores even at an early age.

> Protective factors within the school: (1) teachers may provide the caring and support that buffer a child against problematic family or community conditions, as well as offering growth experiences; (2) high expectations from school, along with high level of support for attaining these objectives; and (3) youth participation and meaningful involvement in the school system.

> Protective factors within and beyond the school: Peers may be present to buffer children at risk from harsh family or community influences and may stimulate their constructive growth and development.

> Protective factors within the community: (1) a competent community promotes the social networks and social cohesiveness to provide the support for a lifetime of growth and development; (2) social norms in the community may exhibit high expectations of its young citizens, which along with available resources may enable youth to participate as successful citizens; and (3) the availability of meaningful opportunities in social and economic tasks heightens self-esteem, enhances moral development, and social competence in young persons.

The important point about the resilience literature is that many of these factors may be influenced by professional action—see Cowen et al. (1995) who present a preventive intervention for enhancing resilience among highly stressed urban children. This may become a major avenue of preventive services by social workers and other helping professionals in the coming decades.

The Formal School Environment: Junior High, Middle School, and Senior High

We have seen in earlier chapters that society itself has certain tasks and responsibilities in the support of all its families at points of transition in the life course. In the case of teenagers, however, U.S. society has done little. Instead, we create and tolerate environmental conditions that adversely affect many of our youth. These include intense, pervasive sexual stimuli across all media formats; high levels of violence in families, the streets, and the schools; militarism and the settlement of international political conflict by violence; readily available alcohol, illicit drugs, and guns; a steadily widening resource gap between impoverished and affluent families; and corruption and sleaze in high places. These environmental conditions are societal issues and not psychological ones. If they exceed the coping resources of many teenagers today, the solution is not individual change but societal change.

One major social environment that is an important influence on adolescents is the school system. State and local governments, which control schools, have made some significant changes during the twentieth century.

Junior high schools, consisting of the seventh, eighth, and ninth grades, were introduced in the 1930s as a means of putting together children who were similar biologically and intellectually and separating them from younger and older children. Concurrently with the biological changes of puberty, youngsters leave the elementary school and the security of a self-contained classroom and a single teacher. They enter the larger, more impersonal junior high school, where classes rotate, each with a different teacher and perhaps different students. Academic pressures increase, and there is an emphasis on achievement and an increased threat of failure. This setting is similar to the high school, so that what was expected to result in a smooth transition later simply displaced the transition downward by two years, increasing the stress on the 12- or 13-year-olds (Hamburg 1974). As a means of reducing such stress, middle schools were introduced offering the sixth, seventh, and eighth grades. Students then go on to junior or senior high schools. While larger than the elementary school, the middle school seeks to maintain personal relationships by the use of teaching teams and small units of students.

What was presented in chapter 10 concerning discriminatory practices in the elementary school applies also to the high school experiences of many minority adolescents. Unresponsiveness to cultural diversity, the prevalence of stereotypes, and lowered expectations based on color, language, or both continue. Males, especially, are disproportionately represented in high school dropout rates, non-college-bound tracks, school suspensions, and so on. Urban high schools are often old, poorly maintained, dilapidated, and vandalized. They are usually much too large, often with as many as 5,000 students, and the result is extreme depersonalization, anonymity, and a prison-like atmosphere. Even with systems of guards and ID cards, many schools are plagued by violence from outside. They also suffer from internal violence because some students carry weapons to protect themselves while on the way to and from school and once inside as well. Drugs and drug dealers are easily accessible both inside and outside some schools.

In some suburban districts (and urban ones), parents, colleges, and employers complain that high schools no longer prepare students to successfully meet the demands of higher education or of the world of work. Researchers and academicians report a disturbing degree of illiteracy in one subject after another among the nation's teenagers. Enlightened school districts are initiating changes. Some schools stimulate the aspirations of minority students through the participation of parents, teachers, the school administration, and community experts in the life of the school (Comer 1988; Comer et al. 1996). Some high schools collaborate with local colleges and universities to improve their teaching content and methods. Others interest local corporations in supporting high school enrichment programs to strengthen curricula and stimulate student motivation and interests. Many high schools offer community service programs, believing that helping others builds students' competence and self-esteem and provides important community roles for adolescents. Dryfoos (1994) describes the "full-service school" as one that beings together education, health, mental health, and various social services that may be needed in a given location. Zigler and Styfco (1993) term this the school of the twenty-first century (see also Zigler, Kagan, and Hall 1996, and our discussion in chapter 4).

Adolescent Worries and Wonders

Most teenagers are apt to worry about their physical appearance and sexual attractiveness; their relationships with peers, including finding a romantic partner; their athletic prowess; their relationships with their parents; their academic performance, including future academic or vocational goals and the financial means for achieving them; and the social pressures toward sexual activity and the use of alcohol or illicit drugs. But as they become intellectually better able to grapple with abstract issues, some social, religious, or philo-sophical conflicting ideas may emerge in their consciousness.

Who Am I? Self and Sexual Orientation

Most, if not all, teenagers worry about who and what they are and will become. Theorists and researchers offer us many concepts to understand this self-preoccupation, such as Erikson's (1963) discussion of identity formation (see appendix 1) and Marcia's (1991) studies in coping with identity crisis. For Erikson, the adolescent crisis begins in the inner revolution of puberty as it meets the outer sociocultural demands for adultlike behavior. The integration of an identity that occurs in the course of grappling with these psychosocial forces is characterized as "the accrued confidence that the inner sameness and continuity gathered over the past years of development are matched by the sameness and continuity in one's meaning for others" (Erikson 1963). Marcia (1991) identifies four ways in which people cope with this Eriksonian identity crisis: (1) They may achieve identity by struggling to make some critical deci-sions on personal values and career choices; (2) they may foreclose any ado-lescent struggle by accepting the decisions of others on their values and careers; (3) they may experience identity diffusion by not being able to make any clear value or career decisions; or (4) they may go into a kind of morato-rium on decision making because they continually struggle with critical ideas without coming to any existential choice.

One critical element in one's self-identity is one's sexual orientation. We discuss this in some detail as representative of significant issues of the self. Moses and Hawkins (1982) distinguished between sexual orientation and sex-ual preference, which together with gender identity and gender role behavior constitute one's sexual identity. Sexual orientation refers to (1) the physical; that is, one's past and present gender preference in sexual partners and sexual relationships; (2) the affectional; that is, one's past and present gender prefer-ence in primary emotional relationships; and (3) one's past and present gen-der preference in partners in sexual fantasy. These elements of sexual orienta-tion exist on a continuum from exclusively homoerotic to exclusively het-eroerotic. Being homoerotic does not imply a confused gender identity. Most gay and lesbian persons, like most heterosexual persons, have a gender iden-tity that matches their sex.

Some people may have no gender preference (bisexuality). Others may have a gender preference only in the physical activity, or only in emotional relationships, or only in fantasy, or in some combination. The preference of some is realized, while others may experience life conditions in which their preference is not realizable, although their underlying sexual orientation is not affected. Also, the physical and the emotional components of the sexual orientation may not match. Various differences and similarities can be true of past preferences as well, and there may be differences or similarities between past and present preferences.

Probably many teenagers experience some initial confusion in sexual orientation. Some develop "crushes" on older same-sex peers or on same-sex adults whom they admire. Same-sex chumships and relationships, characteristic of late childhood and early teens, may give rise to homoerotic feelings. And some young teens may have had occasional homosexual experiences, actual or in fantasy, that may have been pleasurable or may have stimulated feelings of shame or guilt. None of these varied experiences necessarily reflect a homoerotic orientation, although they may. But they can lead the teenager to worry, "Is there something wrong with me?" For the great majority of teenagers, sexual identity eventually comes to focus on heterosexuality, a sometimes sweet, sometimes painful, coming of age as a sexual being, ready and able to form intimate relationships with another person that may eventuate in marriage and the birth of a child. The paths on this heterosexual development are quite varied, as the personal experience of the reader likely reveals. An analysis of the development of sexual identity among homosexuals may add some perspective to such developments among heterosexuals.

A small number of teens do become aware of their homoerotic orientation when dating begins. They find that dating the opposite sex is not enjoyable, and they are attracted instead to members of their own sex. This attraction may lead to concerns about their mental health, their gender identity, and the visibility of their difference, in the light of societal attitudes. For adolescents or others who are aware of but conflicted about being different, acknowledging their gay or lesbian orientation to themselves may be a painful struggle. Such acknowledgment to oneself and possible disclosure to others, known as coming out, is a long and difficult process. It may take place at any point in life, from the early teens to young, middle, or older adulthood. Indeed, many adults struggle against self-labeling and even marry and have children—perhaps to prove to themselves and others that they are heterosexual.

There are many complexities in "coming of age in a heterosexist world" for gay and lesbian adolescents (Zera 1992). Moses and Hawkins (1982) specified four steps in coming out: (1) coming out to oneself; (2) identifying oneself to other gay people; (3) identifying oneself to heterosexual others, such as parents, other family members, and friends; and (4) going public at work, school, community, and political levels.

1. Coming out to oneself: The self-labeling of gayness, which seems to require one or two years to accept, means taking a step into a world of rejection, stigma, and isolation. For gay adolescents the step is fraught with additional problems. Teenagers may not know quite what their homoerotic orientation means, but they do sense that they must not talk about it. Hence they are unlikely to obtain positive information, support, or role models and may develop a distorted image of gay people and of themselves. Adolescence is the time when, regardless of one's sexual preference, one searches for a romantic partner and prepares for an adult commitment to a partner in living. These tasks are apt to be much more difficult for the gay teenager. And gay teenagers with physical disabilities face even more difficult tasks in a society that still discriminates against those with disabilities. Religious and cultural homophobic attitudes further complicate matters.

2. Coming out to other gay people: The risks in this and the next two steps are very great for most teenagers, but they are included here in order to present the complete process as it may unfold among adults. Adult gays cannot be helpful to teenage gays because they are underage, and the probability of there being a teenage gay network is low. Among adults, coming out to others is often less a matter of telling than it is of going to places where gay people are found and showing interest in persons of the same gender.

3. Coming out to nongay persons: Coming out to the wider social environment means communicating one's sexual preference and lifestyle to family members and friends. The desired outcome is to have friendly relationships with both gay and nongay people. But such disclosures can be painful because of rejection or insincere acceptance by loved ones—generated mainly by negative societal attitudes. Moses and Hawkins believe the wisest course for teenagers is not to come out to others until they are of age—as painful as it is to pretend to be something one is not. Parents will be shocked and may punish the teenager or take him or her to be "cured" or "saved." Even in late adolescence or early adulthood, parental responses may be harshly negative. Similarly, the adolescent should be cautious about coming out to peers. They may subject her or him to severe ostracism, a

painful experience to face without a supportive network. Rather than take this risk, an unknown number of gay men and lesbian women remain forever silent—also a painful state: "Being in the closet is depressing, exhausting, anxiety provoking, and time consuming. It necessitates continual efforts to dissemble . . . and produces anxiety over the prospect that one will be found out in spite of all that one can do" (Moses and Hawkins 1982:90).

Moses and Hawkins suggested that coming out to one's parents, especially, requires much thought and preparation—and in many instances, it may not be necessary or wise to tell them. In other instances, one or both parents do react positively, or at least they restore their positive relationship with their son or daughter after their initial shock, anger, hurt, and disappointment subside. For the gay or lesbian person, coming out to nongay friends may be less stressful than disclosing to parents because the risks are lower.

4. Going public: This step is the process of coming out publicly to all or most persons in one's life, taking political positions, and being part of the gay and lesbian movement. Acknowledging one's homosexual orientation publicly and politically is an expression of courage and pride and may also reflect the presence of a strong supportive network.

A fifth step is identified by Lee (1991) as self-acceptance and identity synthesis. This refers to the attainment and continued strengthening of a positive, proactive self-concept as a gay person that is integrated with all other aspects of the self. She noted, "There is an externalization of the feelings of oppression . . . . a sense of settling down, being one's self, having a community of friends and chosen family, and a special committed loyal relationship."

Who Are My Friends? Family and Peer Groups

Adolescents learned the importance of family and friends during their earlier years. However, in adolescence, with its pressure to become a separate individual but one who still needs the support and aid of important groups, family and peers become more significant. Special friends become the looking-glass that adolescents use to examine not merely their appearance but their inner thoughts, fears, and dreams. Peer groups add to special friends the power of a small organization, with special roles and responsibilities that provide power and privileges against the seemingly irrational demands of the world (read: parents, school).

Peer groups can serve both positive and negative functions. In the positive sense, they reinforce the common emerging knowledge, skills, and values. When the group values are socially positive and constructive, we see one step in social development as moving into bonding with the conventional (prosocial) society (cf. Hawkins and Weis 1985). When the group values are antisocial, as in a delinquent gang, then the individual members still receive reinforcement that is vital to them as people who may be individually disparaged but who gain some prestige and support as members of a group, even though this puts the individual and the group in opposition to society. (See further discussion of small groups in chapter 5.)

What Will I Do (for a living)? Education and Employment

Adolescents typically perform chores around the house without pay and receive an allowance that is independent of chores. These activities are, in combination, important lessons for adulthood (Werner and Smith 1992). Money is recognized very early as an important token for what it can obtain, even though children are almost entirely supported by their parents. Piggy banks become an introduction to the lifelong task of saving for distant goals. All these lessons come together in adolescence, as young people become increasingly able to perform work that is valued by adults other than their parents—such as baby-sitting, shoveling walks, and cutting lawns. With increased external income comes increased responsibility to save some of it for long-term goals (like going to college) as well as to spend some money for personal choice goals; the bulk of the adolescent's necessities are still likely to be purchased by the parents. Lessons about work, money, and employability come in a variety of packages throughout adolescence.

Education becomes the royal path to employability. Especially for poor families, even those whose parents themselves may not have had extensive schooling or good experiences at school, education holds some cultural magic. The American Dream is alive and well, and is based on obtaining relevant and sufficient education. Unfortunately, the social resources to provide an adequate education are not equally present throughout society, as is discussed in chapter 4.

For those whose social world is limited by poverty and oppression, the vital lessons of adolescent education and employment may not receive the support and reward necessary to move into adulthood with appropriate employable skills. The dropout rate for minority youth is about twice that of majority youth; unemployment of minority youth may run three times that of the majority youth. For these minority young people, the delicious promise of adolescence may have a bitter taste.

What Is in My World? Opportunities and Dangers

The world, for adolescents, is filled with innumerable sources of curiosities to be sampled—despite, sometimes even because of, the prohibitions of adults. There are ample images on television, if not visible images in affluent neighborhoods, of the good life. There are also subterranean messages about pleasures that are off-limits, dangerous, illicit—and thus are to be explored by the risk-takers among the adolescents. Middle-aged parents and older-aged persons in positions of power try to warn adolescents against these risks—often forgetting that they themselves, a generation or so before, pushed the envelope of their environment against the wishes and dictates of their parents. The conservatism of middle and older age has much power to control many of these limit-pushing opportunities, although setting limits can constrict the options of youth facing a new world, different in many respects from their elders. This is a domain of potential conflict even for "good kids" and more so for youth long in conflict with parents and teachers. The challenge for adults is to encourage adolescents in a healthy exploration of the social and physical environment not only for its own sake but also to locate themselves as separate and independent young people, a necessary step before they take up the interdependence that is the mark of adult life, as we discuss in the next chapter.

Part of normal growing up is coming to terms with the larger world. With their growing conceptual abilities, adolescents come to understand more fully the nature of the world, for good and evil. Issues have to be faced, such as the ever-present threat of nuclear annihilation by war, accidents involving nuclear energy plants (such as at Chernobyl in the former Soviet Union and Three-Mile Island in Pennsylvania), and life-threatening environmental contamination caused by the storage of large quantities of radioactive wastes as well as by conventional industries (such as in Bhopal, India, where a gas leak explosion caused much loss of life).

The world that adolescents increasingly come to recognize they share with others is a rapidly changing place. In North America, the liberties that adolescents and adults take for granted are the object of desperate search in other places in the world. The remarkable emergence of political and economic freedom throughout Eastern Europe, South Africa, and other parts of the world is in full sway. Yet along with the rising expectations of freedom come the dreams of nationalism and religious choice, which have produced new world conflicts at the beginning of the twenty-first century. While the possibility of rogue nations and even terrorist groups using nuclear weapons cannot be discounted, the emergence of biological warfare may be taking the place of the nuclear threat.

Thus we need to consider the potential psychosocial consequences for children and youth who have lived with, and thought about, these almost unimaginable dangers that threaten all human and physical life as they know it. For many adolescents, this meant a loss of the stability and the confidence in the parent generation that are crucial for developing values, ideals, commitments, and a philosophy that gives meaning to life and death (Beardslee and Mack 1982). Other researchers and clinicians believe that nuclear and biological fears contributed to the cynicism, disillusionment with family relationships, reckless behaviors, and immersion in sex, drugs, and alcohol observed among some adolescents.

There are also some hopeful signs. A growing number of voluntary groups advocate alternative forms of energy, major cuts in military spending, and a return to supporting social and other domestic programs. Paradoxically, our best hope may lie in the growing worldwide interest in preventing the ecological collapse heralded by acid rain, climate changes, shortages of freshwater, accelerating rates of species extinction, depletion of the planet's rain forests, and the spreading destruction of the protective ozone layer. It is conceivable that cooperation among nations and peoples to save the planetary environment on which all life depends could transcend the economic and military competition that destroys human and other resources (Gore 1992). This is not just a figment of the legendary romantic enthusiasm or fanaticism of youth; this is a world goal that may require the risk-taking, boundary-pushing actions of adolescents in the face of the ineffective status quo of their elders.

Adolescent Health and Illness

Health and Healthy Lifestyle

Health is a state of body, mind, and society. What is healthy depends in part on what beliefs are held at a given age by the individuals who are members of that society. For a variety of complex reasons, economic and political as well as scientific, adolescents are facing a new definition of health and healthy lifestyle that includes a significant component of personal responsibility in the context of an unevenly regulated environment. For example, while the surgeon general requires informational messages about the dangers of smoking to be printed on every package of cigarettes and on all advertising, another part of the government is providing enormous subsidies for tobacco growers. And while hundreds of thousands of dollars of private and public funds are being spent on mass media campaigns to convince youth not to start smoking—as more than 3,000 young people in fact do start every day—the tobacco industry spends millions to "inform" people about the satisfactions of smoking by independent-minded beautiful people who are exuberantly portrayed pushing the limits of physical and social actions (R. Davis 1987).

Healthy lifestyle is a matter of forming healthy habits. These include eating regular meals, especially a healthy breakfast to get one off to an energized start (Perry, Story, and Lytle 1997). One should eat moderate-size meals in order to maintain an optimal weight for one's size. (Carry around a 5-pound bag of flour to see what it feels like to be 5 pounds over the recommended weight range for your size!) Young adults should exercise regularly each day about 30 minutes; exercises should include aerobic, stretching, and strengthening procedures for optimal physical performance the rest of the day (*U.S. surgeon general's report* 1996). Smoking and alcohol (as legal substances) should not be part of a healthy regime for adolescents, and illicit drugs should be completely eschewed. Alternative highs of vigorous activities such as jogging, hiking, swimming, and such should be part of a healthy lifelong style of living. There should be quiet times for contemplation, as with yoga, meditation, or religious or philosophical musings. Sleeping an adequate number of hours each night is also necessary for good health. We have to add, in these days of the new mortalities (Dryfoos 1994), that adolescents who are sexually active should practice safer sex. Childhood injuries have replaced infectious diseases as the leading cause of childhood death. As the former U.S. Surgeon General C. Everett Koop said, "if a disease were killing our children in the proportions that accidents are, people would be outraged and demand that the killer be stopped" (qtd. in Tuchfarber, Zins, and Jason 1997:250). These are but a few of the common-sense ways of maintaining that overflowing cup of health adolescents are given. We also add that good personal health means taking a social interest in the welfare and betterment of others—a partner, one's own family, one's friends, and ultimately all humankind. This gives focus and purpose to an otherwise largely egocentric perspective on health. Otherwise, as George Bernard Shaw observed, "youth is wasted on the young."

Disability and Chronic Illness in Adolescence

As Asch and Mudrick point out, disability is the by-product of social and physical environments that do not accommodate people with different functional abilities of a physical, emotional, or cognitive type (1995:752). From this ecological perspective, we must acknowledge that personal disabilities do pose challenges, but people and environments can mutually adapt to most of these conditions. "The disability rights movement argues that, like many other minorities, people with disabilities are disadvantaged as much or more by discrimination as by their physical limitations"—however well-meaning the "discrimination" is (Asch and Mudrick 1995:753).

Although accidents are the leading cause of death among adolescents, many accidents are not fatal but result in prolonged or permanent disability (including brain damage) in adolescents (and others). Superimposed on the developmental tasks, concerns, and interests of adolescents, disabling injuries cause severe biopsychosocial losses and require new behavior patterns. They represent particularly traumatic second-order developments for youths and their families.

Adams and Lindemann (1974) compared the medical data and life histories of two adolescents, one 17-and one 18-year-old male, who suffered similar severe spinal injuries and permanent paraplegia. Neither young man possessed the range of physical capacities taken for granted in human behavior. They had lost permanently the ability to walk, grasp and release, and many other sensorimotor functions. Despite their similarities, their responses to the physical, social, and psychological rehabilitation processes and those of their families were extremely different. One established a new and apparently quite satisfactory life for himself, while the other made little progress. The latter regarded himself as sick and was regarded by his environment as sick. He therefore exhibited illness behaviors and expected to be cured. He was unable to come to terms with the real issue of being different, which requires a change in self-concept, including a changed body image and changed feelings about oneself, one's world, and one's future. He clung inflexibly to his original vocational goal, no longer realizable, and was reinforced in this inflexibility by his family. Suggestions of more realistic aims by the treatment team were serious threats to his self-esteem, and he angrily rejected them as did his family. Ten years later, despite all the efforts of the rehabilitative team, he remained seriously depressed, excessively dependent, and inactive.

The other teenager, after mourning his massive losses, gradually exhibited awareness and then acceptance of his difference. Despite recurring, severe medical problems and occasional depression, he developed a new self-concept and ways of adapting. He conceived and carried out new plans and new, realistic goals for the future. From the beginning, his family and friends accepted and supported his new self-concept, his changed expectations, and his independent orientation. He subsequently graduated from college and secured a position teaching in a high school.

Similarly, chronic illness is a difficult second-order development. It can undermine adolescent strivings and impose unwanted dependence on the parents and others. It may alienate peers insofar as the adolescent "differs" from the acceptable in appearance, diet, physical stamina, and activity levels. The illness may require a new body image and new feelings about oneself and one's future. It may make dating difficult or impossible or may induce feelings that the illness renders one unattractive as a potential romantic or sexual partner. Chronically ill adolescents face two dangers: "(1) overstressing the limitations and potential interferences of the illness and succumbing to a sense of futility and despair, or (2) denying their realistic limitations, often setting themselves up for great disappointments when their unrealistic goals cannot be achieved" (Perrin and Gerrity 1984).

Failing to follow medical regimens and exacerbating the illness are another hazard. The teenager's opinion about regimens that might interfere with her or his lifestyle need to be listened to and each point addressed. Adolescents must be allowed to make decisions about their illness so they can gain some sense of mastery and control. The particular decisions should be appropriate to the individual's developmental level, and their range should be increased as the teenager continues to develop. Such self-care can help ready the adolescent to function as a competent adult with a chronic illness, even though it may lead to occasional errors or short-term marginal control. The process is more difficult for teenagers who have been chronically ill from early childhood and who have not been encouraged to strive for self-sufficiency. They are at risk of becoming dependent, unproductive, and unhappy adults (Coupey and Cohen 1984). Coupey and Cohen identified chronically ill adolescents who are in need of special counseling: "Those with visible deformities that might interfere with the expression of their sexuality—for example, paraplegic adolescents, those with ostomies, amputations, or abnormal genitalia. The issues of physical sexual expression and reproductive capacity should be addressed during the adolescent years by an informed and sensitive counselor in order to correct misconceptions and avoid unrealistic expectations and later disappointments."

Teenagers with asthma, sickle cell disease, diabetes, scoliosis, or hemophilia, for example, go through the process of coming to terms with their new teenage bodies just as healthy teens do—wanting to be tall, slim, sexy, beautiful, and strong. Since some part of their body is already different, they often experience an intolerable blow to their idealized body image. Coupey and Cohen continued: "It is bad enough to have scoliosis, but then to have to wear a body jacket that flattens your new, normal breasts and makes you look like a shapeless lump is difficult to accept. . . . We assume that the adolescent with scoliosis shares our concern over the progression of her deformity and possible future deterioration of her respiratory function and [we] fail to understand why she will not wear the corset as prescribed."

Substance Use and Abuse

The use of alcohol and illicit drugs becomes abuse when it interferes with an adolescent's social and psychological functioning and development. Substance abuse disrupts the family, leads to poor school performance and dropout, affects cognitive and social development adversely, and can lead to delinquency. It also has a potential for creating chronic illness and increases the risk of accidents, suicides, and homicides among teenagers. Some experts suggest that abuse is a symptom of severe emotional disorder and is a way of avoiding the pain of the emotional stress created by depression, emptiness, rage, and so on. Others believe that alcohol and illicit drug abuse are outcomes of complex transactions among biological, emotional, and such environmental factors as family, peers, school, and societal influences (including availability and easy access). In this view, substance abuse is a maladaptive effort to cope with the stressors that these systems and their interplay present. In turn, substance abuse creates new stressors.

Alcohol. Although teenagers may drink less regularly than older persons, they tend to drink larger quantities and are more likely to become intoxicated. Statistics on alcohol use by youths 12 to 17 years old show that slightly more than half that age group and 92 percent of high school seniors have used alcohol at least once. Among the 12- to 17-year-old group, 7.8 percent (during the prior 4 days) and 37 percent of the seniors (during the prior 2 weeks) had 5 or more drinks at one sitting (NIDA 1988a, 1988b).

Botvin and Dusenbury (1989) describe three stages in research in the substance abuse area that are a good characterization of primary prevention thinking as well as trends in the substance abuse field. The first generation of research in primary prevention practices involved simple, linear thinking that emphasized information about the risks involved that any rational person would use to stop the harmful practice. While student participants in these studies did learn about alcohol and other substances, they did not change their behavior. A second stage was reached in the rigorous research of Evans and his colleagues who studied the psychosocial factors involved in smoking and drinking—peer pressure and mass media instigation. Evans devised methods for students to resist these pressures—and to do so without losing friends (Evans 1976; Evans and Raines 1990). His work encouraged others to construct variations along the lines of Evans's work. The third stage may be represented by the work of Botvin and Dusenbury in which a complex curriculum is systematically delivered, providing information, self-directed behavior change (as in developing a sense of personal control), critical decision making, and skills in coping with anxiety. The entire program is given in 20 sessions in the seventh grade, with a booster set of 10 sessions in the eighth grade, and another set of 5 sessions in the ninth grade, with strong positive results (1989; also Schinke and Gilchrist 1984). This systematic approach will likely become standard as we seek to address the complex problems of adolescence.

Cigarettes and other tobacco products. Sizable proportions of adolescents continue to establish cigarette habits, and many youth are using smokeless tobacco (Evans and Raines 1990), which poses the usual litany of health risks, including cancer of the jaw and mouth region. Cigarettes constitute the class of substance most frequently used on a daily basis by high school students. NIDA (1988b) suggested that almost a third of high school seniors apparently do not believe that cigarette smoking presents a serious health risk. (See also Hooked on tobacco [1995]; Elders et al. [1994].)

Recent legal actions by the states' attorneys general on pressing tobacco companies to pay for medical expenses states incurred due to tobacco-related illnesses has once again ignited the national debate on the harmfulness of using tobacco products. The fate of the multibillion-dollar settlement proposed in 1997 is unclear at this time. Critics argue that it exonerates the tobacco industries from paying the full costs, while allowing them to continue to sell tobacco products, as well as denying government control over tobacco as containing addictive substances.

Valentich (1994) presents a stinging report about social work's minimal involvement in programs and policies related to the reduction or cessation of cigarette smoking. Given the extensive knowledge base on the significant harm smoking causes both the smoker and those subject to side-stream smoke—cigarette smoking has been identified as the single most important source of preventable morbidity and premature mortality in each U.S. surgeon general's report since the first was written in 1964—social workers have had difficulty conceptualizing tobacco as a drug. Valentich speculates whether this is related to social workers' own smoking habits (1994:444). If this is so, North American social workers are going to have to do some significant thinking and attitude change before they can assist their clients in stopping this harmful habit.

Drugs. A drug is any substance that chemically alters the functioning of a person; prolonged use may also permanently alter structures of the brain as well. Drug abuse, therefore, involves such use of a drug (in amount, duration, or both) that the consequences of the use are detrimental to the person's health, to social responsibilities (like doing adequate school work), to social relationships (such as performing social roles at a minimal level of competency), and to society at large (for instance, endangering others by driving while intoxicated).

There are several classes of drugs whose effects are an interaction of the drug itself and the persons or groups involved in taking them. Cannabis family drugs (like marijuana) relax the inhibitions and increase appetite and possibly disoriented behavior; overdoses may lead to slow behavior and fatigue, paranoia, and time disorientation. Nicotine (from tobacco) increases alertness, euphoria, and a loss of appetite; overdoses lead to agitation and insomnia, and for long periods of use, there are an associated host of deadly outcomes, from cancers to heart disease. Narcotics (such as opium and heroin) are likely to produce euphoria and a sense of well-being; overdoses may lead to slow breathing, coma, and possibly death. Depressants (like alcohol, tranquilizers, and barbiturates) disorient and impair reaction time, as well as numb the senses; overdoses may also lead to slow breathing, coma, and possibly death. Stimulants (such as caffeine, cocaine, crack, and amphetamines) increase alertness and euphoria; overdoses may increase agitated behavior, insomnia, and loss of appetite. Hallucinogens (such as LSD) produce often vivid illusions and hallucinations; overdoses may lead to more intense experiences to the point of psychosis and death. Synthetic steroids are a relatively new drug that build muscles, something favored by adolescent males and body builders; overuse leads to a variety of bad side effects, from damage to the heart and kidneys to impotence to liver cancer; once muscles are artificially enlarged, it is difficult to stop using the steroids because flab develops and one feels less powerful.

Most of these drugs are addictive, physically and psychologically, and attempts to stop using them once a person is addicted are often very difficult. Some are associated with enhanced sexual pleasure or with a blissful forgetting of current problems; others have just the opposite effect. Because many are deemed illegal in most countries—England allows drug use by doctor's prescription—an international black market has sprung up; participants often take great risks in order to make enormous sums of money selling drugs. Drug abuse remains a very difficult social and personal problem.

For adolescents, drugs are all too readily available, and large numbers of adolescents have experimented with their use. The use of illicit drugs (alcohol and tobacco are legal substances) was virtually unknown among young persons until the 1960s. By the late 1970s both experimental and frequent use of illicit drugs had spread to teenagers (*Healthy people* 1979). Except for alcohol and marijuana, the rates among youth were low compared to those among adults. Marijuana has been and continues to be the most widely used illicit drug in the United States. In one study, of the 12- to 17-year-old group, 23.6 percent had used the drug at least once, and 12 percent had used it in the prior 30 days. The corresponding figures for high school seniors were 36.3 percent and 21 percent. A strong relationship exists between current use of marijuana and the use of other drugs (NIDA 1988a).

The rates at which youth use drugs has fluctuated over time. In the 1980s it appeared as if rates were falling from the increases of the 1970s, or at least leveling off. More recent evidence in the 1990s suggests that rates of adolescent drug use are increasing again. Inhalant use is highest during early adolescence, especially in the eighth grade, and is second only to marijuana—as many as 1 in 5 or 1 in 6 students has tried an inhalant.

Regular use of illicit drugs by adolescents leads to school dropout, unemployment, and street crime among all ethnic, racial, and economic groups (Fraser and Kohlert 1988). It is important to keep in mind, however, that among the 12- to 17-year-olds in 1985, 70.5 percent had never used any illicit drugs at any time in their lives, and 86.1 percent had not used any illicit drugs within the past month (NIDA 1988a). The findings of Thomas and Chess (1984) on adolescent drug use and those of NIDA appear to be congruent with the percentage of problem-free teenagers found by Offer and his colleagues. Nevertheless, even though the rates of current illicit drug use by high school seniors are small (except for marijuana and the licit drug alcohol), they are not inconsequential. Just 1 percent of the nation's high school senior class of 1987 represented about 26,000 individuals. The use of illicit drugs by high school and college students (and other young adults) remains greater in the United States than in any other industrialized nations (NIDA 1988b).

Newcomb and Bentler (1988) found that light alcohol or drug use (once a month or less) by adolescents at social gatherings does not lead to lasting negative effects. In fact, in later years such teenage users cannot be distinguished from those who had abstained. Heavy use (weekly use or more) by teenagers, however, is associated with serious personal, social, and economic problems in young adulthood whether or not the young person is still taking drugs.

Adolescent Sexual Activity

Sexual norms have changed drastically over the past several decades in the wake of social developments that led to more and earlier sexual activity in male and especially female teenagers. African American youth become sexually active earlier than Hispanic, white, or Asian youth—in roughly that order—and boys at younger ages than girls, but the gaps are narrowing as white youth and girls of every ethnic background are becoming sexually active at younger ages (Sagrestano and Paikoff 1997:79). Earlier onset puts these youths at higher risk for pregnancy and sexually transmitted disease. In 1985 1 out of 4 persons with gonorrhea or syphilis (25 percent) was between 10 and 19 years old. Those 15 to 24 years of age account for 75 percent of all cases of sexually transmitted diseases except AIDS (*AIDS and the education of our children* 1988). Young adolescent girls are likely to be having sex with older boys and men, which puts these young women at high risk for sexually transmitted diseases (Sagrestano and Paikoff 1997:77).

Sexually active teenagers (both heterosexual and gay) and those using drugs intravenously are at risk of contracting and transmitting AIDS. Minority youth are disproportionately affected in the AIDS epidemic; culturally sensitive preventive practices have been explored by several investigators (Schinke et al. 1990; Schilling et al. 1992). A 1989 study of 16,861 U.S. college students who had their blood tested as part of normal medical treatment found that 0.2 percent carried the virus that causes AIDS (Bacon 1989). If that rate were applied to all 12.5 million students, it could indicate that 25,000 college students may already have been infected with AIDS. The incidence among students is slightly higher than the 0.14 percent for military recruits, and about half the 0.4 percent to 0.6 percent rate for the U.S. population as a whole.

Out of the 19 institutions across the country involved in the study, 10 showed no cases, while 5 had rates of 0.4 percent or higher. The highest rate was 0.9 percent or 9 per 1,000.

Parents and schools share the responsibility for teaching teenagers about AIDS, how it is spread, and how risk of the disease can be avoided. Sagrestano and Paikoff (1997:87) summarize relevant literature: "Recent research indicates that adolescents who report discussing sexuality with their parents, including how pregnancy occurs, birth control, and protection from STDs, are more likely to attempt to avoid AIDS through using condoms and having fewer partners (Leland and Barth 1993). Teenagers who perceived their communication with their parents as poor, however, are likely to initiate sex earlier than those who do not (Christopherson, Miller, and Norton 1994)."

While less than I percent of AIDS cases involved adolescents, epidemiological evidence shows that prevalence was much greater among the 20- to 29-year-old group. The majority of these individuals had probably contracted the diseases during adolescence inasmuch as the average length of time between infection and onset is 8 years. Given these facts, it is clear that communication among family members is a vital ingredient for possible primary prevention programs.

Adolescent Pregnancy and Childbearing

More than 1 million U.S. adolescents become pregnant each year. Sagrestano and Paikoff summarize this situation:

> On the basis of 1990 data (Alan Guttmacher Institute 1994), among sexually experienced teenagers, 9 percent of 14-year olds, 18 percent of 15–17-year olds, and 22 percent of 18- to-19-year olds become pregnant each year, which reflects both higher rates of reproductive maturity (fecundity) and higher frequency of intercourse in older teens. Furthermore, among adolescents aged 15 to 19, 19 percent of African American, 13 percent of Hispanic, and 8 percent of White teens become pregnant each year. These ethnic differences reflect differences in rates of sexual experience among ethnic groups. (1997:80)

Of these million pregnancies, about 500,000 give birth, 350,000 obtain abortions, and 140,000 miscarry (Sagrestano and Paikoff 1997:81). While teenage childbearing affects only a small percentage of adolescents each year (6 percent of the 12- to year-old group), the cumulative numbers of adolescent parents and their children represent a major social problem. The human costs are high for the parents and their babies, and the social and economic costs affect society as a whole. Burt (1986) estimated that families begun by teenagers constituted 53 percent of all families receiving Aid to Families with Dependent Children, food stamps, and Medicaid benefits; these needs will not change rapidly, even with the change in welfare laws. Babies of young mothers are at high medical risk of low birth weight, prematurity, mental retardation, and various physical disorders. If their mothers suffer from malnutrition, as many impoverished teenagers do, the infants are at risk of physical and mental disorders and even death. They are also at the social risk of growing up in impoverished one-parent households.

Racial differences in sexual activity and unintended pregnancy rates have long existed. Premarital birth rates among white teenagers doubled between 1980 and 1991, while the rates among blacks went up about 45 percent in the same time period (C. Williams 1995:34–35). Teenage mothers are at social risk of disrupted schooling, dropout, repeated pregnancies, limited employment prospects, and poverty. Adolescent mothers are also at medical risk because sexual intercourse, pregnancy, and childbirth in very young mothers are positively correlated with cervical cancer and with uterine disease requiring hysterectomy. Compared with older groups, young teenagers suffer a higher incidence of anemia, toxemia, labor complications, and maternal and infant death (Gilchrist and Schinke 1983). Poor teenage mothers may not obtain prenatal care or may seek it late in the pregnancy.

The rates of adolescent pregnancy, abortion, and childbearing are higher in the United States than in other industrialized nations, although the age of beginning sexual activity and the rates of frequency are comparable (Sagrestano and Paikoff 1997:80). In 1987 the Alan Guttmacher Institute calculated the number of pregnancies and births for each 1,000 teenagers 15 to 19 years old in major Western countries as follows: USA—96 pregnancies, 54 births; England and Wales—45 pregnancies, 31 births; Canada—44 pregnancies, 28 births; France—43 pregnancies, 25 births; Sweden—35 pregnancies, 16 births; and the Netherlands—14 pregnancies, 9 births. The report concluded that the increasing availability of contraception and sex education had helped reduce the rates in other Western countries. The contrast was even greater for girls under age 15: "The USA rate, at five births per 1,000 girls of comparable age, is four times greater than that of Canada, the only other country with as many as one birth per 1,000 girls under age 15" (cited in Hayes 1987:16).

Canadian policy and programs are instructive. Henshaw and Jones (1988) reported four major differences from the United States that appear to contribute to lower rates of unintended pregnancy: (1) Canada's lower economic barriers to contraceptive services; (2) the provision in family planning clinics of up to one and one-half hours of individual counseling on sexuality and sexual relationships for women when they become sexually active (with an emphasis on avoiding unintended pregnancy, and how to use a particular contraceptive method); (3) encouragement to use oral contraception as the effective reversible method, although others are available; and (4) the referral of high school students for contraceptive services by school nurses placed by public health units in most public schools and many Catholic schools. The clinics also seek to educate the public about contraception and reproductive health. As a consequence of these differences, Canadians appear to be more effective users of contraception than are people in the United States and therefore have lower rates of unintended pregnancy and abortion.

Despite their extent, family-planning services in the United States are not easily available and accessible to young low-income teenagers. Contraceptives are difficult for young female adolescents to use, especially over the long run. Embarrassment in discussing them with the partner and in using them, together with lack of accurate information about pregnancy risk, interfere. For teenagers living in poverty, accurate information is harder to come by than for middle-class adolescents (Moore, Simms, and Betsey 1986). Public opinion about what needs to be done is not unanimous. Hence, a rational policy has been difficult to establish. In addition, "Sex saturates American life—in television programs, movies and advertisements—yet the media generally fail to communicate responsible attitudes toward sex, with birth control remaining a taboo subject. In addition, a deep-seated ambivalence toward sexuality has prevented Americans from responding to the problems of unintended pregnancy as rationally as have other Western nations" (Westhoff 1988).

Despite group and individual differences among teenagers, the National Research Council's Panel on Adolescent Pregnancy and Child Bearing (NRC Panel) observed:

> For every young person, the pathway from sexual initiation to parenthood involves a sequence of choices: whether to begin having intercourse; whether to continue sexual activity; whether to use contraception and, if so, what method to use; if a pregnancy occurs, whether to seek an abortion or carry the pregnancy to term and give birth; whether to marry, if that is an option; and, if a child is born outside marriage, whether to relinquish it for adoption or raise it as a single parent. Whether consciously or unconsciously, actively or passively, all adolescents make choices about their sexual and fertility behavior.   (cited in Hayes 1987:27)

Teens themselves tell researchers and pollsters that peer pressure is the principal reason for opting to begin and then to continue sexual activity. Sixty percent of sexually active teenage girls reported that they did not use any contraception on a consistent basis, and almost 40 percent of young women and men reported that they never used any birth control at all. Most said they did not intend to and did not believe they would become pregnant.

The NRC Panel found that two very different beliefs have existed in the United States over the years: (1) unwanted pregnancy and childbearing are due to a lack of individual responsibility maturity, knowledge, and values; (2) they are the result of pervasive problems associated with poverty, including limited education and employment opportunities and the likelihood of growing up in a fatherless family that is poor. The panel came down on the side of policy efforts to eliminate poverty, strengthen family ties, and enhance youths' perceptions of their future (cited in Hayes 1987).

With respect to perceptions of the future, Moore, Simms, and Betsey (1986) found from their review of the research that youths with high educational aspirations are less likely to engage in sexuality and to become parents. Black and white Americans hold equally high educational aspirations, but blacks are more apt than whites to drop out of school (for reasons shown in chapter 10 and earlier in this chapter). Those who drop out are more likely to become pregnant. The need, then, is to help young black people remain in school and achieve their educational goals.

The NRC Panel's report stated that the highest priority must be given to preventing unintended pregnancy among teenagers. For those who will nevertheless experience unwanted and untimely pregnancy, and who choose to raise their children, supports and services must be available to ensure the children's healthy development. The panel also stated that alternatives to childbearing and child rearing should be available (e.g., see Diliworth-Anderson 1994). The report noted that abortion is a legal option for all women including teenagers under certain conditions, but it acknowledged that abortion is a highly controversial issue and is considered inhumane or morally reprehensible by many people in our society.

Adoption is also an option for those who choose to continue pregnancy but do not wish to raise their child. However, adoptive parents are often difficult to find for minority children and children with disabilities or serious illnesses, and public policy usually does not approve low-income applicants for adoption or provide subsidy payments to them. Among the more than 1 million teenage girls who become pregnant each year, only about 7 percent relinquish their infants for adoption. McLaughlin et al. (1988) did a study of 146 adolescent mothers who had rejected abortion and had chosen adoption for their children and a control group of 123 mothers who had parented their children. Those who had relinquished their children were found to be more likely "to complete vocational training, delay marriage, avoid a rapid subsequent pregnancy, be employed after the births, and live in higher income households" than the parenting mothers. "On several measures of self-esteem, satisfaction with life, and satisfaction with the decision, however, there were few differences between the two groups."

McLaughlin et al. concluded that there are no significant negative effects on teenage mothers who relinquish their children when they are compared with those who parent their children. The authors cautioned, however, that their findings cannot be generalized to all pregnant adolescents because the subjects were clients of a pregnancy counseling service; more than 80 percent were white, reflecting the racial composition of the area; and the service was affiliated with an adoption agency and was therefore apt to attract adolescents who wished to relinquish their babies. These limitations, however, do not affect the conclusion regarding the relative well-being of both groups.

An unfortunate omission in the literature, and therefore one that probably exists in practice and research as well, is attention to the sexual and social developmental needs of adolescents in foster care or of physically or mentally disabled adolescents in institutional care (Barth et al. 1994; Mech and Ryeraft 1995). For example, McDonald et al. (1996) present an important research synthesis on the long-term effects of foster care on young adults who had been foster children. Twenty-nine studies were reviewed; these were all the available reports in English from 1960 to 1992. To simplify a complex report, they found that former foster children were below the general population in 6 areas, including marital outcomes, parenting outcomes, mental health outcomes, as well as educational attainment, housing, and criminal behavior. These former foster children were at the level of the general population on maintaining good contacts with their foster parents, with their biological families (especially their siblings), and with friends; they also showed success in achieving life satisfaction outcomes. Unclear results were reported for the former foster children in employment, chemical dependency, and physical health outcomes. From these synthesized data, we can infer that something is lacking in a variety of areas in foster care as it is currently constituted, including foster children's adult sexual developments, marriage, and parenting. This is an area of need that social workers and others will have to attend to in the next decade. (See also Polit, White, and Morton 1987).

Adolescent fathers. Research shows that the fathers of pregnant teenagers are on average about 5 years older than their partners (Sagrestano and Paikoff 1997:80–81). These authors note that in terms of pregnancy rates, only 4 percent of sexually experienced males aged 15 to 17 impregnate their partners, compared with the female pregnancy rate of 18 percent for this age range. They also note that about 85 percent of teen pregnancies are unintended, but that "intention" is influenced by socioeconomic status, ethnicity, and marital status. Higher income teens are less likely to intend to become pregnant than lower income teens; black and white teens are less likely to intend to become pregnant than Hispanic teens; but the majority of all teens, including married teens, do not intend to become pregnant.

Early studies (e.g., Ladner 1971; Stack 1974) found that the young fathers were usually unable to offer financial help to their partners and babies because of unemployment. But most acknowledged paternity and provided emotional support during the pregnancy. Following the birth, many couples continued their relationships. Some fathers visited regularly, and others lived with the mother and the infant. More recently, Sander and Rosen (1987) cited studies showing that "an adolescent father's involvement in his partner's pregnancy increases the young mother's sense of confidence in her nurturing skills, heightens her sense of security after delivery and raises the father's self-esteem."

McCluskey, Killarney, and Papini (1983) found a tendency for teen parents to marry within the first two years following the birth, usually because the father now had a job. If marriage did not occur within those two years, it was less likely to occur at all. The researchers also reported that the reactions of teenage fathers to pregnancy and birth are similar to those of older fathers when economic and social factors are not overwhelming. When compared to controls, teenage fathers are psychologically normal. However, it is not yet known if teenage fathers influence their children' s development and, if they do, whether this influence is similar to the influence of older, married fathers in their children's development—especially that of their sons.

All adolescent males, including fathers, have been seriously neglected by sex education programs and family-planning services. The NRC Panel underscored the need to include teenage males in the concept of the at-risk population (cited in Hayes 1987). Unwanted childbearing is not a problem only of teenage girls. Boys' attitudes, motivation, and behaviors are as central to the problem as those of girls. Shapiro noted that, contrary to widespread assumptions, not many fathers or mothers talk with their sons about premarital sexual activity nor do they communicate values that counteract the influence of the media and the erroneous information imparted by peers. As a result, adolescent males need accurate information about the "use of birth control, avoidance of exploitation, respect for the relationship, protection and check-ups against sexually transmitted diseases, and consideration for one's sexual partner" (1981:14). Shapiro advocated sex education that includes values and ethical guides, communication skills, decision-making skills, and knowledge about sexuality, parenting, and family life.

Recent research in this area of high-risk sexual behavior shows some encouraging results. For example, the Teen Outreach program involves a school-based approach to promote progress in school and to prevent pregnancy by encouraging other life options (Allen, Philliber, and Hoggson 1990). A two-pronged approach was used involving, first, a weekly small discussion group promoting autonomy and relatedness and second, a volunteering component in the community or in school (as tutors). This program has been used and evaluated nationally and shows positive results in lower pregnancy rates, lower school dropout rates, and fewer school-related problems. What is particularly interesting is that middle school participants benefited from both the autonomy and public service components, while high school students did not, suggesting that Teen Outreach is more developmentally appropriate for middle school students than for high school students (Sagrestano and Paikoff 1997:92).

Adolescent Death

Adolescence is a period of relatively good health as measured by illness and death rates. The death rate is substantially lower than in all other age groups except childhood, being 2.5 times the rate for children. However, various circumstances result in accidental or intended deaths of adolescents.

Accidents. Let's review the leading causes of injury death by several age groups. In the 5- to 9-year group and in the 10- to 14-year group motor vehicle passenger accidents are the leading cause of injury death. However, only in the 10- to 14-year group are homicide and suicide the next leading causes (CDC 1995 cited in Tuchfarber, Zins, and Jason 1997). Seventy-five percent of teenage deaths are caused by accidents (involving automobiles, motorcycles, and farm vehicles; swimming, diving, and other sports; fires, explosions, and firearms), homicide, and suicide. Teens represent two-thirds of all accidental deaths (*Healthy people* 1979).

Fatal accidents in adolescence are attributed to errors in judgment, aggressiveness, and in some instances, ambivalence about wanting to live or die. Alcohol is implicated in about half the fatal driving injuries. Teenagers also place themselves at greater risk while driving under the influence of marijuana and other drugs. Excessive speed is a factor in vehicular fatalities in almost half those involving teenagers 15 to 19 years old (*Healthy people* 1979). Greater risk taking is present during adolescence than during other times of life. It may be a reflection of teenagers' normal striving for independence and exploration of novel experiences and situations. Recent studies provide evidence of the inability of many adolescents to evaluate risk realistically and the limited capacity among younger teenagers to understand the concept of probability. Other adolescents feel invulnerable and may hitchhike or refuse to wear helmets when riding motorcycles. Still others feel the real risk lies in losing status with the peer group if one does not submit to its pressure to engage in what adults define as risky behaviors (*Healthy people* 1979).

Suicide. The suicide rate for adolescents aged 10 to 14 and 15 to 19 increased in the years from 1982 to 1990, 120 percent and 28 percent respectively, while suicides among 20- to 24-year-olds declined about 7 percent (Kalafat 1997:175). Suicide attempts (as contrasted with "successful" completions) are far more numerous—estimates run to more than 400,000—which means that many adolescents sustain serious injury, even if it doesn't result in their deaths. A suicide attempt is also a predictor of a successful future suicide. Suicide cuts across all age, racial, occupational, religious, and social groups. But the greater frequency with which it occurs in some groups suggests that social and cultural factors are significant. While the overall rate of suicide rate remains the same (it is the tenth leading cause of death in the United States), the rate has soared for adolescents. For college students, it is the second most common cause of death. The actual numbers of suicides may be higher, as some suicides may be unrecognized or may be unreported because of the social stigma or for religious or insurance reasons.

Across all age groups, males comprise approximately three-fourths of all who commit suicide, and white males account for 70 percent of that total. Males tend to use the deadliest weapons: firearms (more than 50 percent) and hanging. Women used less lethal methods such as drugs and wrist slashing until recent years, when more than half the 15- to 24 year-old females who have killed themselves have used guns.

In some urban areas, sharp increases in suicides among young black males have outdistanced the rates for white males in the same age group. This is a startling increase, since the overall suicide rate for blacks is traditionally about half that of whites. Blacks aged 15 to 24 now account for 26 percent of all black suicides, a greater proportion than that of whites in the same age group for all white suicides (Berman 1986).

The extent of suicide among other racial groups is not clear because in suicide statistics Hispanics, American Indians, and Asians and Pacific Islanders are subsumed under "other." However, the suicide rate is believed to be high among new immigrants. And young American Indian males are killing themselves at a rate more than twice the average for their age group. The U.S. Indian Service states that the reasons include drug and alcohol abuse, economic distress, and unemployment. But tribal leaders believe that suicide, as one of the leading causes of death among native Americans ever since the development of reservations, reflects broad despair among Indian youth (see also Mauk and Rodgers 1994).

Such suicide clusters also appear among white high school youth of both affluent and working-class families. Clusters are defined as three or more completed suicides closer together in time and space than would be expected by chance in a given community. The federal Centers for Disease Control reported in 1988 that about 5 percent of the 5,000 teenage suicides a year are believed to be a part of clusters. Hearing about a suicide may induce adolescents already at risk to kill themselves, viewing the act as romantic or even heroic.

The trend toward increasing suicide among the young may be linked to:

1. Environmental factors such as the increased availability of firearms, changing family patterns, the declining influence of traditionally stabilizing institutions such as organized religion, the dissolution of a sense of community, rapidly changing social norms that aggravate the developmental tasks of adolescence, and the intensive pressures of competing for limited educational and employment opportunities.

2. Personal factors such as the loss of a parent, the loss of a family member to suicide in the past, a loss of self-esteem because of perceived failure or rejection, and the loss of a sense of security due to disorganized or abusive family situations, including sexual abuse (Pfeffer 1987). Nuclear or biological warfare anxieties may have contributed through creating a sense of hopelessness.

According to Ryerson (1987), suicide-prone teenagers may show signs of feeling sad, hopeless, and worthless and may appear lethargic and withdrawn. But some may be verbally aggressive and physically assaultive and are apt to be viewed as being sullen or troublemakers rather than being suicidal. Suicidal adolescents often show less involvement with school and poor academic performance or underachievement. They may cut classes, be rebellious, and fail to prepare for classes. Those who do well academically tend to perceive their performance as inadequate, a perception that increases their despair. Suicidal adolescents may show changes in peer relationships and may become argumentative or disruptive with peers. They may give away treasured belongings. They report receiving little affection from their parents and little enjoyment from spending time with them. Berman (1986) speculated that this may be the reason why suicidal adolescents have deficient problem-solving skills and lack the needed personal resources for meeting the psychosocial demands of adolescence.

Youth who exhibit accident-prone or excessive risk-taking behaviors, or who talk directly or indirectly about suicide, or who show sudden changes in patterns of school or familial functioning are at high risk for suicide. Those who make multiple attempts are at very high risk for a completed suicide. The suicidologist Berman (1986) believes that preventing teen suicides will require approaches that address vulnerabilities, impulsiveness, and the adolescent tendency to view suicide as the only possible solution. Many school social workers, as well as those in community mental health centers, offer suicide awareness and prevention programs. These may include training teachers in how to discuss the subject with pupils, recognize the warning signs, inform parents, and refer suicidal students to knowledgeable staff members. Other social workers believe it is also important to train teenage peers to recognize warning signals and make referrals to staff because a suicidal teenager is more apt to talk to peers than to parents or professionals. Clinicians appear to use direct interview data to assess suicide potential in clients; Jobes, Eyman, and Yufit suggest that combining these interview data with standardized measures of hopelessness, suicide intent and ideation, etc. would be more helpful in identifying suicide risk (1995:10).

Mauk and Rodgers (1994) present a thorough discussion of a school-based postvention with adolescent survivors of peer suicide who have experienced a major disturbance in their assumption of personal and social equilibrium. The tasks are not only to help them deal with the suicide of their peer but also to assist them in going on with their own lives in a spirit of hope that includes the recognition of this traumatic event in their lives.

Murder. Murder accounts for more than 10 percent of all deaths among adolescents and young adults—just under 7 percent for whites but almost 30 percent for blacks in this age group (*Healthy people* 1979). While automobile accidents are more likely to occur among whites, young blacks of either sex are about 5 times as likely to be murdered. Among young black males 15 to 24 years of age, homicide is the second leading cause of death, and it is the leading cause of death for black males 25 to 44 years of age. Most black homicides are related to drugs or alcohol (see Murray, Guerra, and Williams 1997).

Thus ethnicity becomes an important distinguishing factor. Among black males ages 15 to 44, homicide is a major problem. Black males of this age are 5 or 6 times more likely to die of homicide than their white peers; and black females more than 2 or 3 times more likely than their white peers (Tuchfarber, Zins, and Jason 1997:255). Youth violence, including gang violence, has been escalating rapidly in recent years for both black and white males, but not females. The homicide rates of youth ages 14 to 17 increased by 172 percent from 1985 to 1994. Murray, Guerra, and Williams point out that this increase in youth violence is primarily attributable to an increase in the lethality and not the frequency of violent acts (1997:105–6). The same proportions of youths are committing violent offenses today as in 1980, but a larger proportion of these acts involve handguns that raise the seriousness of the impact. With the projected increase in the proportion of teenage males in the next decade, these trends are expected to get worse. Violence is going to continue to be a major challenge for the helping professions in the immediate and long-range future.

Terminal Illness in Adolescence

Typically, the older adolescent begins a lifelong process of developing a religious or philosophical position on the meaning of life and death that becomes the foundation for optimism about the future. The task of infusing the future with hope is more difficult now because of the increasing complexities and problems of modern life and because of society's attitudes toward illness and death. What is it like, then, for terminally ill adolescents to confront the imminence of their own death? Terminal cancer, while not common in adolescence, symbolizes the quintessence of the teenager's confrontation with an untimely death: "The prospect of one's body killing one presents the patient with a most cruel paradox. It is this tragic quality that predominates or stifles the reactions of a majority of dying adolescent patients, their parents, and the caretaking staff. In our experience most dying adolescents deny their fate, while a more remarkable minority adjust best within the realistic context of their despair" (Schowalter 1977:195).

Schowalter believes that young people's temperament shapes their illness behaviors—along with the type, extent, and rapidity of the disease process. Those teenagers who do not acknowledge that they are dying keep their thoughts and feelings vague. They defend equally against telling or being told about themselves. This reaction contrasts with the rage or the calm seen in those who either actively grapple with or passively submit to the idea of their death. While adolescent patients in general are inquisitive and demanding, teenage cancer victims are typically passive, probably because they know they have a fatal illness, because they have picked up cues that discourage questions, or both (Schowalter 1977).

Among teenagers who acknowledge that they are dying, the most common response is "Why me?" "It is usually inconceivable to the patient that such an unspeakable horror as their cancer is not the fault of something or someone. . . . Self-blame [is] very common. Sexual fantasies or experiences, arguing with parents, getting bruised in fights, and poor physical hygiene have all been suspected by our patients as causing their malignancies" (Schowalter 1977:196–197).

Schowalter added that if blame is missing, the patient must face the awful fact that his or her death makes no sense. Many fatally ill teens are also haunted by the realization that they are dying before fulfillment. They not only mourn the loss of a future but lament that their time spent in growing up was wasted. And finally, being able to grasp the finality of death, teenage patients commonly express anticipatory mourning for the self and for those whom they will lose at death.

Parents' Development and Family Transformations during Their Child's Adolescent Years

The significant factor addressed in this section is the tandem development of parents and children. What happens in the lives of children affects what their parents do; likewise, events in the lives of parents affect their children. Social networks and institutional supports allow for a bit of flexibility in tandem developments—if the child is able to go to a cooperative nursery school, the parent may be able to get a part-time job, or if the parent gets a full-time job in another city, the child will have to start anew with proprietary nursery school, friends, and so on. In the final section of this chapter, we explore some of the major themes and variations in tandem development of adolescents and their parents and families.

There are expectable first-order events in this period, such as adolescents' acquiring greater intellectual capacity, emotional range and depth, and behavioral skills, along with experiencing inevitable physiological changes that are the hallmark of adolescence. Each of these first-order events requires adaptation by the parents and other family members, with the underlying principle being to facilitate the gradual expansion of autonomy of the adolescent. This is not simply helping the youth to be independent—rather, it is a matter of appropriate interdependence. The teenager will usually be financially dependent and socioemotionally attached to the parents for many more years, even though the teenager may begin to get part-time or full-time (and usually low-paying) jobs. The adolescent will expand the range and meaningfulness of peer contacts, including budding intimacy and sexual behaviors, so that pressures to conform to peer standards and demands may increase greatly on day-to-day happenings. However, parents usually maintain considerable influence in long-term values and decisions, such as in advanced schooling and career choices. But fundamentally, parents must gradually relinquish the kind of parental control exerted during childhood and rely more on discussion, negotiation, and mutuality in establishing expectations for conduct. Even if the tensions spark occasional rebellion, parents and teenagers will survive the struggles as long as the parents continue to show love and respect for their child and the child is able to reciprocate. To paraphrase Mark Twain, adolescents often find it remarkable how much their parents learn between the time the teenagers enter and exit adolescence.

Parents are busy during their children's teen years. They face the demands of their work or career, keeping up the household—although with increasing help from their offspring—maintaining ties to extended-family members and friends, and participating in community activities—not only the children's schools but also religious, fraternal, recreational, or service activities. Parents may also have to manage the needs and concerns of younger children and their own parents, so they may not be able to devote themselves exclusively to the preoccupying needs that adolescents experience.

With regard to second-order or unexpected developments, these matters are more difficult to deal with. Yes, adolescents will become sexual beings, a topic that may fascinate parents almost as much as the youths, but when events result in teenage impregnation and pregnancy, and whatever sequelae follow (abortion, miscarriage, or childbirth), then what is a normal first-order life issue of pregnancy becomes a second-order event because it is out of time and place, and it requires a host of unanticipated activities for which the involved parties may not be ready. The life script suddenly gets rewritten, not only for the pregnant girl but also for the father of the child, the families of the teenagers, and the array of medical, health, and social services they will need. Tandem developments now involve a much wider array of persons, including the newborn. While different cultural groups are more accepting than others of "illegitimacy"—the very term has a social class- and culture-related moralism to it—still there is an objective burden imposed on the youth and all the others who choose to remain involved.

When a youth's sexual orientation takes an unexpected direction, such as homosexuality, then it breaks the parents' long-held expectations for dating, marriage, grandchildren, and the like, all of which have to be revised if the relationship between parent and child is to be maintained. Interestingly, the parent/family struggle with the child's coming-out parallels the process of self-awareness, first in a negative or fearful response (and possible denial of the reality), followed by gradual acknowledgment and beginning acceptance. Then parents may make various degrees of public statements to friends and family. Parents may even join self-help groups, such as Parents of Gays or Parents and Friends of Lesbians and Gays (PFLAG), which can be helpful to parents as sources of information, emotional support to ease the stress, and help in dealing with, or taking action against, environmental hostility.

Although adolescents are generally healthy and vital people, accidents do happen and chronic illness and disability do occur in adolescents. Suddenly, the years of hope and anticipation are broken by the realization that these desires will never be able to be fulfilled. Managing difficulties in physical, social, sexual, emotional, educational, and vocational development become unexpected but critical tasks for the involved youth, the family, friends, and a new addition, the health care team, including the social worker. The family and the team must support the ill or disabled adolescent in his or her efforts gradually to achieve a new self-concept, new life goals and plans, and new behavior patterns. At the same time, parents need to manage their own sorrow and possible guilt feelings or anger about the disabling accident or the illness. This is especially difficult if the outcome of the condition is uncertain or has a downward course. There will necessarily be many changes, in communication patterns, role assignments, gaining a new body of knowledge about the condition and its associated complications, and the multiple and diverse transactions with the social and physical environments. Fundamental characteristics of the entire family must change because the family's shared reality has been changed. This is the meaning of tandem development regarding the unexpected.

Many teenagers will experiment with forbidden substances like cigarettes and beer, and most people as adults will continue to drink (but not smoke). However, some adolescents will also begin on the path of substance abuse involving illicit drugs, a troubling second-order development whenever it occurs. Alcohol and illicit drug abuse are associated with school dropout, family conflicts, alienation from peers, malnutrition, health and sexual problems, difficulties in adolescent psychosocial development, crime, driving accidents, and lost potential. Because many adolescent abusers exhibited behavioral or emotional disorders or negative worldviews and school problems before becoming addicted and because many of these adolescents are children of abusers, these second-order changes and needed family transformations often require long-term professional helping (see Meeks 1989; Fraser and Kohlert 1988).

Yes, everyone will die someday, but the death of a teenager has particular poignancy because the youth and his or her parents and friends have glimpsed the beginning realization of the potential in this individual. Death may come to the teenager, as to anyone else, slowly or suddenly, with or without the opportunity for the patient and the survivors to prepare for the many challenges of facing death and experiencing the final moment. The impact of fatal illness and death of young children on their bereaved parents and siblings applies to the loss of a teenager as well: it is an excruciatingly difficult and sorrowful event that requires time to mourn, to adjust, and eventually to create a new family structure.

A slow dying period permits people to make some preparations and to communicate meaningful exchanges of love, but a very long period of time makes managing the lingering illness and death very difficult. A sudden death by accident, suicide, or homicide steals away the opportunity for these emotional preparations, anticipatory mourning, and final communications, and thus makes closure more difficult. For some cultural groups, there is comfort in religious belief; for others in the same cultural group, there may be anger that their child was not protected by their deity. In their anguish, parents and others may ruminate long and hard about what they might have done or should have done to prevent the accident or illness. Social work services in the hospital or community agencies, including bereavement support groups for parents and siblings, are helpful to families in the long and hard tasks of transforming and integrating the new family structure in the face of this overwhelming loss. Parents have to be especially careful about how their relationship with each other is to survive the untoward death of their child, so as not to put the marriage in jeopardy.

Caplan et al.'s (1989) work on crisis intervention may be useful when a medical crisis is present. Lay support groups of various types—such as for families of children who have died of cancer, AIDS, or in an automobile accident—may be helpful for parents and siblings. All the people involved in a life—the youth, the parents, siblings, extended family, and friends—should renew efforts to prevent the preventable and to challenge life to the fullest for whatever time remains, so that if something unexpected occurs, one can say this was the best life it could have been, and will continue to be for the survivors.

12

Family Transformations: Adulthood

Adulthood spans the time from the late teens or early twenties to the early or late sixties, depending on the state of affairs of the person:environment mix. Sometimes late adolescents strike off on their own, working and earning their own keep and perhaps starting a family of their own. Sometimes this movement into full responsibility as an adult is delayed through advanced education supported in part by one's parents or the lack of economic opportunities to go it on one's own. Likewise the end of adulthood and the advent of "old age" is misty. It may be when a person retires from a formal job—if she or he ever does. It may be when Social Security benefits begin (between ages 62 to 67 for different categories of people). It may be when a person defines him- or herself as old. However, throughout this long period of time, adults face challenges of marriage or nonmarriage, health and illness, and ultimately death and bereavement. We seek to provide an overview of this intensely complex period of life.

Outline

Health Changes during Adulthood
    Decrements
    Illness
    Disability
Dying and Death

Introduction

As comedian Lily Tomlin once remarked, "I always wanted to be somebody when I grew up. Maybe I should have been more specific." Ready or not, here we are in adulthood, the time when everything prohibited to children is now permitted, but when all the responsibilities not required of children are presumably carried on our strong, muscular, well-developed backs. Ready or not, here we are in positions of great responsibility, for ourselves, for our mates and children, for our extended family and neighbors, for our workplace activities, for our community and state, to say nothing of our responsibilities to the international community and the planet Earth. Maybe we should have read the fine print in our contract on growing up. But ready or not, here we are in adulthood.

Adults can enter contracts as individuals vis-à-vis other individuals (in marriage, for example) or groups (for instance, as investors). These contracts are public documents declaring and protecting the relationships that they describe. We have discussed a variety of normative or first-order developments in adults throughout this book, and in this chapter we focus on the second-order developments that may or may not occur to a given individual—but that will occur in sizable numbers (and stable proportions) to members of society. For example, we expect certain approximate rates of marriage and divorce, of suicide and homicide, of health and illness, of births and deaths. Sociologists have tried to explain these expectable patterns or rates (see appendix 3), while psychologists and others have tried to account for which specific individuals will become a "statistic" (see appendixes 1 and 2). Practitioners in helping professions make use of all the above information as they try to place unique individuals and groups within the larger set of general forces so as to make inferences of likely future events and behaviors that will guide practice decisions. In contrast to their scientific colleagues, helping practitioners directly add values and norms into the equation of what actions are possible and what actions are desirable.

There have been some major developments in how helping practitioners have added values to theories and empirical facts. We have characterized these developments in terms of a social ecology, a strengths perspective, and a strong recognition that professional helpers should employ the full range of helping modalities as needed, from primary prevention to treatment and rehabilitation. This perspective is intended to raise new kinds of questions and answers with regard to traditional topics. To this end, we begin our discussion of adulthood with a topic that would not even have been considered several decades ago: Is it possible to prevent marital distress and divorce?

Preventing Marital Distress and Divorce: Is This Possible?

Given the state of love and good will that exists between the starry-eyed couple at the beginning of their marriage and the grim statistics that about half all such marriages will end in divorce, is there no way to prevent the escalation of marital distress that leads to this unhappy outcome? We present a preliminary report of some fascinating research and some potentially good news that addresses this issue. Be forewarned, however, that although researchers have been studying this topic seriously for the past several decades, they offer us only some preliminary ideas and evidence on preventing marital distress and divorce. Yet given the nature, breadth, and depth of this problem and the many effects it has on other individuals and groups, it is clear that helping professionals should give great attention to the prevention of marital distress and divorce.

Gottman (1994a, 1994b) and his colleagues and students have been studying marriage and marital stability and change over the past two decades using direct observation and careful methods of sequential analysis of behavior, which are remarkable changes from the ways marriage had been studied in the past. From his various studies, Gottman presents a number of perspectives on the marriage situation and offers some theoretical models that attempt to put all the known facts together.

Successful Marital Styles

First, he notes that there appear to be three types of successful marital styles and two unsuccessful styles (Gottman 1993). Let's begin with the successes. The first successful marital style is termed the "validating marriage." What it is like should be no surprise: The marital partners are able to discuss difficult topics easily and calmly. They are able to listen to and understand the other person's point of view and are able to validate the worth of these views even while disagreeing. The marital partners engage in a problem solving–like approach by hearing out the other person, then attempting to convince the partner of the rightness of their point of view, and finally, they negotiate some compromise with which both can live. Validating couples value open communication, a "we" feeling, being in love, displaying affection, and sharing time and activities with each other.

That there are two other styles of successful marriage may come as a surprise to some readers. The second successful marital style is called the "volatile marriage. " These volatile partners fight with passion—without bothering to listen to the other much—and express considerable anger. However, the volatile couple is also passionate in making up, expressing affection (more than the validating couple), and valuing each other's individuality, personal space, and privacy. The volatile partners have a richly exciting marriage, in part because they relish the intensity of the relationship.

The third successful type of marriage is termed the "conflict-avoidant" style. These couples have a strong sense of shared basic values, and rather than engage in arguments that tend to end in deadlock in any case, they simply agree to disagree and avoid conflicts. These conflict-avoiders accentuate the positive and accept the negative or neutral, which means that their discussions end in each feeling good about the other, even though the problems are not resolved. However, this marital pattern leads to minimal companionship and to less passion than in the other successful marriage styles. They too (like the volatile) value independence and privacy, but in the avoidant situation, this might lead to loneliness. Next, let's turn to the unsuccessful marital styles; both of these make intuitive sense.

Unsuccessful Marital Styles

The first type of unsuccessful marital style is termed the "hostile/engaged." This would be a marital couple who argue frequently and heatedly, and do so in an off-putting manner. They hurl insults at the partner, call names, engage in putdowns and sarcasm—all the while keeping engaged with the partner. The second type of unsuccessful marital type is called the "hostile/detached." There is still the hostile manner like the other unsuccessful marital type, but now the partners rarely listen to one another and are emotionally detached.

Gottman classified his observations regarding the four mechanisms by which marriages seemed to destroy themselves. These are independent mechanisms; no stages or progressions are implied. First and least harmful is criticism attacking a person's personality or character as a global characteristic. On the other hand, complaining is described as voicing anger, displeasure, or other negativity about a specific characteristic; Gottman describes this as one of the healthiest endeavors one can do in a marriage, in part because conflicts are practically inevitable and it is more important to figure out how to deal with them than trying to deny their existence.

Second, there is the destructive mechanism called "contempt," in which the message is delivered by name-calling, hostile humor, and mockery, and by body language expressing contempt for the other person.

Third, the partner may become defensive, as a way to protect him- or herself and to ward off perceived attacked. There are many ways to be defensive, such as denying responsibility or making excuses.

Fourth, and most destructive, one or both parties may stonewall, that is, avoid conflict by removing oneself either physically (leaving) or emotionally (getting involved in some other activity).

By means of one or more of these several mechanisms, the partners begin to enter a negative reciprocity, meaning the tendency on the part of spouses to continue negative behavior once it began (Cordova et al. 1993:559). Marital dissatisfaction increases and begins a possible cascading effect wherein marital dissatisfaction leads to serious considerations of marital dissolution, then to marital separation, and finally to divorce. This cascade model received preliminary support in Gottman and Levenson (1992). In attempting to offer a theoretical account for dissolution, they propose a balance theory that suggests that marital stability requires regulation of positive and negative interactions—this is measured by a complex interaction code and statistical definition, but the practical implication reduces to how spouses talk with each other. The happy stable marriages showed a ratio of 5 positive to 1 negative interaction, whereas the unhappy and unstable marriages had a ratio varying around 1 positive to 1 negative interaction (Gottman 1993:12; Gottman and Levenson 1992:224, 230). Correlational findings do not imply causation, but they may lead us to think about positive interactions as a way to keep out or get out of a negative reciprocity cycle and thus may provide a hint about preventing marital distress that may lead ultimately to divorce.

Techniques for Preventing Marital Distress

Markman and his colleagues conducted some research specifically aimed at preventing marital distress (Markman et al. 1988; Markman et al. 1993). They studied the short- and long-term effects of a cognitive-behavioral prevention program with a group of 42 couples planning to be married, then matched and randomly assigned couples to experimental or control groups. The participants were tested in pre- and postintervention periods, and again in 1.5-, 3-, 4-, and 5-year follow-ups, using marital and premarital adjustment tests, sexual dissatisfaction scales, and some communication tests.

The prevention program emphasized teaching relevant competencies before any need emerged, thus taking advantage of the natural good relationship that existed between the couple. The program had 5 sessions of about 3 hours each and involved 4 elements:

1. Enhancing communication skills focused on maintaining the current high levels of functioning and high motivation to learn preventive/promotive skills, such as how to exit a negative affect cycle before it gets out of hand. These skills also included active listening and expressive speaking skills, using videotapes and feedback on performance.
2. Problem-solving skills were taught, including brainstorming and contracting as a skill for couples, in order to establish what they term "relationship efficacy," which we understand to be a concept parallel to Bandura's self-efficacy idea.
3. Realistic relationship cognitions, that is, expectations of each partner vis-ß-vis the other, were discussed.
4. Training was also given on handling relationship conflicts, as well as sensual/sexual education; these were strategies to prevent dysfunctions and exercises to promote better relationships and sex.

Results were generally supportive of the prevention hypothesis. The experimental group maintained generally high levels of relationship quality, while the control group showed declines (Markman et al. 1988:214). By the third-year follow-ups, nearly 25 percent of the control group couples had broken up, whereas this was true of only 5 percent of the experimental group (Markman et al. 1988:213). This same pattern was maintained in the fifth-year follow-up. The experimental group couples also had higher levels of positive communication skills and lower levels of negative communication skills and marital violence. However, the differences by the fifth year were not as strong as earlier, which leads the authors to recommend that "booster shots" on their training program might be useful (Markman et al. 1993: 72–76).

While these findings are encouraging on the primary prevention of marital distress and, ultimately, divorce, the authors urge caution because of the limitations of the studies, which used self-selecting volunteers, relatively small numbers, and so forth. However, so important are the implications of this kind of applied research that we recommend readers remain alert to new reports on the primary prevention of marital distress and divorce (Smith, Vivian, and O'Leary 1990).

Nonmarriage: Divorce, Separation, or Never Married

We are a marrying people; more than 90 percent of Americans marry at some time during their lives. People who never marry may choose to do so for religious or social reasons, or may not be permitted to marry (as is the current fate of most gay and lesbian couples). The nonmarried are a special type of minority because so much of social life is geared around couples, marriage, and children; more than 90 percent of all married Americans have children. The nonmarried may make parentlike relationships, such as being a favorite aunt or uncle, or a friend of the family (and the family's children). Nonmarried persons can form families, as discussed in chapter 6, or family-like relationships (without any sexual relations or without a common household) as among friends who share selected activities and affective support. These kinds of relationships are functional equivalents of the major type of marital association, and should they break up, the participants probably experience the same kinds of painful psychological dynamics as marriage partners.

Divorce

After almost doubling since 1965, the U.S. divorce rate fell for the first time in 1986 to around 50 percent, but the number of divorces may be rising again. Remarriages occur, more frequently for men then for women, but these second marriages have an even higher divorce rate, of nearly 60 percent (Gottman 1994b:16). These are one of the highest divorce rates in the world. Indeed, some observers note that the United States may no longer be a monogamous society. Instead, it may be tending toward a polygamous society by practicing plural marriages sequentially rather than concomitantly. The high divorce rates notwithstanding, separation and divorce are painful experiences for every member of the family, and the emotional, social, economic, and legal issues accompanying divorce create severe stress. How long the stress continues depends on how well the family restructures itself. Throughout this section the focus is on divorce in families with children. The section begins with separation, usually the preliminary step in the divorce process.

The Separating Family

For many, securing a divorce may take a year or more because protracted disputes over child custody and property settlements clog court calendars. Some places mandate predivorce counseling so spouses will understand the range and depth of matters involved in divorce. Whatever the duration, however, life is on hold for separating spouses, and work, finances, parenting, and plans for the future are permeated by emotional upheaval and uncertainty. On the basis of their research, Bloom, Hodges, and Caldwell (1983) concluded that the separation experience is far more stressful than the actual divorce, which finally comes almost as a relief to the spouses. The research subjects were 50 newly separated white men and women from a nonclinical population, some with and some without children, and a matched group of nonseparating persons. Both groups were well educated, some being in graduate school. The average length of marriage was 8.5 years, ranging from 4 years for male nonparents to 15.5 years for female parents.

The data were derived from initial in-person interviews about 2 months after the separation and a telephone follow-up 6 months after the initial interview. Most of the subjects reported their marriages had been generally good except for a 6-month period before the separation. During this period, slightly more than 25 percent of the subjects had experienced changes in the relationship with the spouses, and in sleeping and eating habits, finances, work responsibilities and hours, and social and recreational activities. Also reported were sexual difficulties, in-law troubles, and physiological and psychological symptoms, such as weight loss, headaches, upset stomach, fatigue, and feelings of an impending nervous breakdown.

The three most frequent marital complaints were communication difficulties, differences in values, and lack of love reflecting "the slow distancing that takes place within a couple as their relationship deteriorates" (B. L. Bloom, Hodges, and Caldwell 1983:224). Complaints of physical abuse were rare, while verbal abuse was common. It was reported more frequently by women than by men and more frequently by parents than by nonparents. The most frequent precipitating events were infidelity; events outside the relationship, such as completing school, changing jobs, taking a trip without the spouse, or the expiration of the lease on the home; and some version of the "last straw," such as prolonged drinking, a second suicide attempt, or continual delays on the part of the spouse in completing graduate school.

The subjects drew readily on formal and informal supports. Nineteen persons had received couples' counseling and 25 had obtained individual counseling before separation, and almost all the subjects reported having someone, a supportive friend or relative, with whom they could talk about their marital problems. However, loneliness was a problem for many, and for some it predated the separation. At the time of follow-up, loneliness was reported as frequently as it had been originally, but the degree of severity had lessened.

Seventeen separation-related problems were reported in the initial interviews. Three were more severe at follow-up: child rearing, career planning, and relationships with parents. At follow-up, the males reported significantly fewer severe problems than the females in four problem areas: guilt and self-blame, feelings of incompetence, homemaking, and relationships with parents. Three problems were less severe among parents than among nonparents: mental health, self-blame, and feelings of incompetence. "In comparison to men, women, prior to separation, have greater dissatisfactions with their marriages and more symptoms, and more commonly initiate the separation. They seek more help and have stronger social supports. . . . At the time of the initial interview, women perceive more benefits from the separation. . . . Women's initial adjustments to the separation appear to be more positive and to be made more easily" (B. L. Bloom, Hodges, and Caldwell 1983:236). By the end of the first eight months, the men had caught up with the women and tended to perceive fewer problems with the separation. For both the men and the women, attachment to the spouse appeared to weaken during the early months of separation.

Custodial parents felt that the problems associated with marital disruption were made greater because of having children. Parents reported changes in their children since the separation; 40 percent of these changes were viewed as positive. About half reported that their children were having interpersonal difficulties in school but felt that these were unrelated to the separation. In regard to work and the workplace, 42 of the 50 subjects were employed at the follow-up. At the initial interview 15 percent of the subjects reported work-related difficulties, such as absenteeism, loss of effectiveness, or conflict with coworkers. At follow-up 90 percent reported such problems.

Initially, the parents were more opposed to separation than the nonparents, but they had fewer postseparation problems—perhaps because they were older than the nonparents. The parents also experienced far more and longer-lasting anger in response to marital disruption than the nonparents. Regardless of their sex, the parents tended to blame their spouses for their difficulties and saw as little as possible of the spouses during the separation. The authors concluded that acceptance of the reality and permanence of the separation was at least partially achieved. Other aspects such as physiological and psychological problems were just as disturbing at follow-up. Work-related and child-rearing problems intensified as time went on (see also Stolberg and Bloom 1992).

The Postdivorce Family

Most of what was noted in Bloom, Hodges, and Caldwell's study of separation also characterizes the first year or two after divorce. Divorce itself, while a major life stressor, is not as important as the postdivorce family environment in determining the mental health of the family members (Goldsmith 1982). The postdivorce family must carry out the same functions as the married family but does so in altered ways. Divorce does not necessarily result in the family's disintegration, nor is it the end of the family. Rather, the family continues but must reorganize its structure of roles, tasks, and relationships following the loss of an adult member. Factors affecting the restructuring process include "the predivorce family situation, sex and age of adults and children, postdivorce quality of family relationships, custody arrangements, and prior mental health of adults" (Goldsmith 1982:298).

The prominent divorce researchers Hetherington, Cox, and Cox (1982) view divorce outcomes as different for each family member. Stressors, supports, and coping abilities vary for the spouses, the parents, and the children. These authors regard divorce not as a single event, but as a complex social, psychological, and economic process over time that imposes different stressors and elicits different responses at different points. During and immediately following divorce, conflict, loss, change, and uncertainty are likely to be prominent. These are usually resolved within a few years if additional, multiple stressors do not appear. The long-term adaptation will depend in large measure on the nature of the custodial family as an environment for its members.

Mourning a death is aided by religious and other ceremonials, but society has not developed rituals, customs, and support systems to assist divorcing parents and their children to move through this second-order development (Elkin 1987). Each family must find its own way of integrating the divorce into its new paradigm. Beal (1980) suggested that couples who work toward maintaining friendly relations during and after the divorce are apt to have a less intense experience of loss. They will also be better able to dissolve the marital relationship while maintaining the relationships between each parent and the children that are so important to the children's well-being. The family transformation is easier to achieve.

Goldsmith (1982) also found that positive feelings toward the former spouse are associated with more effective coparenting, particularly when the feelings are mutual. She declared that positive feelings toward the former spouse should not be confused with continued attachment and inability to separate. Divorced persons who are unable to separate emotionally will be unable to mourn the loss, work through the separation, and move on in their separate lives. In Goldsmith's study, most parents who held positive feelings did not experience themselves as being unable to separate, as is often assumed by clinicians when they observe positive feelings between former spouses.

Effects of Divorce on Children

An important aspect of divorce concerns the effects on children before, during, and after the divorce procedures. However, the literature is filled with contradictory bits of information, based on different definitions of terms and different groups of people studied. Stevenson and Black (1996) have provided a recent review of this literature that is a useful guide to this topic. Stevenson and Black note that "the parental divorce process can be viewed as a series of stressors that are related to inevitable changes in the lives of offspring," even though children within the same family may react quite differently and use different coping mechanisms with regard to these common events (1996:38). Children react differently to the divorce, in part because of their age and, with it, their capacity to understand what is happening. Young infants are relatively unaware of the conflicts, while preschoolers become aware but lack the sophistication to resolve the emotional distress. Young school-age children are deeply affected, but they come to recognize that other children have gone through the same situation as they. Teenagers generally have the sophistication to deal with the divorce process, and they are becoming more independent of the parents and family in any case.

Children from divorced families score lower on school grades and on standardized tests, and they complete fewer years of schooling than do offspring from nondivorced families. However, it is important to note that these differences are small, and Stevenson and Black suggest that they are likely to stem from economic pressures and emotional stress, rather than from the divorce per se (1996:39, 72).

While most theories of human behavior predict that a father in residence is necessary for appropriate gender-role development (especially for boys), analysis of the data suggests that such differences between one-and two-parent families are small for boys and very small for girls (Stevenson and Black 1996:83). These authors continue: "The majority of offspring of divorce will not experience behavior problems" (112). However, these children are more likely to use controlled substances but the available literature isn't clear about causes. Likewise, children of divorce are more likely than children of nondivorce to misbehave or to be delinquent, but these are more likely to be caused by economic hardship, parental conflict or pathology, than by the divorce per se (112). These authors note that unhappy, conflict-ridden homes are more harmful to offspring than are stable single-parent homes (138).

There is no relationship between the parental divorce and the child's sexual orientation—contrary to theoretical predictions that fatherless families will produce more homosexual children. There are few differences in the attitudes of children of divorce and nondivorce toward marriage, even though offspring of divorce are less trustful and less optimistic than offspring of nondivorce (Stevenson and Black 1996:99). Children of divorce get divorced themselves more than children of nondivorce, but that may reflect more the fact that they got married at an earlier age and other economic factors (99).

Custody Issues

During the twentieth century, most custody decisions have been made almost automatically in the mother's favor, probably because of cultural stereotypes that view mothers as uniquely suited to provide care. Today, maternal custody still prevails, although more and more fathers are being granted custody, not necessarily on the grounds of the mother's unfitness but often because both parents wish it for financial reasons or because of the mother's need for education and career planning. Faludi (1996) summarizes research on the economic side of divorce: in general, divorced women's standard of living dropped about 30 percent while men's rose about 10 percent. Goldsmith (1982) reported that the issues for a custodial parent of either sex are generally identical, and there is no evidence that custodial fathers do any worse or better than custodial mothers. But many noncustodial mothers feel stigmatized by friends and relatives because of the cultural stereotypes of motherhood.

In one of the few studies of father custody, Warshak and Santrock (1983) studied 64 white, mostly middle-class families with children ranging in age from 6 to 11. Half the children were boys and half were girls. Approximately one-third of the children were in their father's custody, one-third were in their mother's custody, and one-third were living in intact families having no history of separation. The three types of families were matched for the age of the children, for family size, and for socioeconomic status. The two groups of children from divorced families were also individually matched for sibling status and for age at the parents' separation (which, on the average, preceded divorce by 10 months). Most custody arrangements had been agreed upon prior to the court hearing, and relinquishment of custody by both fathers and mothers appeared to be a matter of not wanting custody or of having no preference rather than issues of unfitness.

The assumption that children of divorce will function less well than children of intact families was not borne out in this study. However, there were differences between boys and girls in father custody; the girls did less well than the boys. In general, the researchers found that children living with the same-sex parent uniformly scored higher than children living with the opposite-sex parent on measures of demandingness, maturity, sociability, and independence. Whether psychoanalytic, social learning, or other theories are used to explain these results, Warshak and Santrock declared that "there is something very important about the ongoing, continuous relationship of a child with the same-sex parent" (1983:259). They added that the findings should not be used to advocate dividing the custody of siblings along sex-related lines, since the importance of the sibling system in postdivorce adjustment is unknown.

The authors also found that in both forms of custody, parental warmth, a clear setting of rules, and extensive verbal interaction were significantly correlated with 6 of the 9 child observation scales: self-esteem, maturity, sociability, social conformity, anger, and demandingness. Custodial fathers used support systems more than custodial mothers did, and children in paternal custody had more contact with the noncustodial parent than children in maternal custody. The most frequent drawback of the divorce mentioned by the children was their reduced access to the noncustodial parent. Eighty-four percent of the children expressed ongoing reconciliation wishes. Two-thirds of the children were positive about the possibility of their custodial parent's remarriage: "Taken together—the focus on parental loss, the reconciliation wishes, and the remarriage endorsement—these findings suggest that children of divorce want to live in two-parent homes, despite the conflict, turmoil, and failure of the predivorce family" (Warshak and Santrock 1983:257).

According to Goldsmith, "In any family, there will be a 'decider system '—that part of the system that maintains control and order" (1982:304). In married families, this is determined internally; in divorced families, it is determined externally. However, in the latter, the legal arrangement is less important than the actual control structure that develops. In either maternal or paternal custody, coparenting may vary from little or no sharing of control and decision making to almost equal sharing. In either case, the former spouses, despite the end of their marriage, continue to be the parents of their children for life. Hence, in any custody arrangement the parents' cooperation and shared decision making in regard to the children are necessary for the children's continued development. The structure of the divorced family, then, consists of the custodial parent-child, noncustodial parent-child, sibling(s), and individual subsystems. In the event of the remarriage of one or both parents, the children and their parents actually remain a continuing interdependent subsystem of a total system that is now much larger. Some problems experienced by the new system may derive from continuing difficulties in the relationships among the original family members, as described in chapter 6.

To ascertain the intrapersonal and interpersonal factors that contribute to successful coparenting, Goldsmith (1982) studied 85 divorced couples with children under 18 years of age. The couples had been separated for from 2 months to 2 years before the divorce. Their names were randomly selected from the court records of Cook County, Illinois. The subjects were white, and all the mothers had legal custody. Interviews took place 1 year after the divorce and again 3 years later. Wherever possible, the former spouses were interviewed individually. Only those couples in which the father had seen the child at least once in the 2 months preceding the interview were included, since the focus of the study was coparenting.

The majority of the couples experienced some conflict or stress in the coparenting relationship, the fathers being more dissatisfied than the mothers. Eleven couples reported a cooperative, supportive, and satisfying coparental relationship. Many others who reported stress as a characteristic of the relationship also said their relationships involved cooperation and mutual support. Most of the couples had maintained direct communication with each other, and this tended to increase in connection with a special occasion or a problem with the child, such as school or medical issues. The majority also reported that they occasionally spent time with each other and the children during birthdays, school events, church functions, visits to grandparents, or outings. The parents generally felt more satisfied and supported when there was a sharing of responsibility and interest: "The noncustodial fathers in these cooperative coparenting couples are more likely to stay actively involved with their children and to achieve emotional separation from their former wives" (Goldsmith 1982:321).

A friendly, cooperative coparenting relationship supports the custodial parent's effectiveness in child rearing and the child's continued development: "Many former spouses . . . were able to relate in friendly ways without becoming involved with one another sexually or romantically, and while continuing to develop new relationships" (Goldsmith 1982:317). Those who did not establish clear boundaries around their parental interaction experienced enmeshment and distress. These contaminated the coparenting, and the couple's ability to separate and develop new relationships was inhibited. Goldsmith suggested that substituting the term "coparent" for the term "ex-spouse" may identify and validate this ongoing, important subsystem of the divorced family. It may also help an enmeshed couple clarify their status vis-ß-vis each other. With a million or more children experiencing divorce each year, their emotional and developmental needs require greater public and professional attention. Joint custody has come to the fore as a means of ensuring children's access to both parents: "Sole custody too often results in the father feeling disenfranchised and divorced from his child, and the mother being overwhelmed by having to assume most of the parenting responsibilities" (Elkin 1987). Some states now have joint custody statutes, although there are many differences among them. Some courts oppose the notion of joint custody; others impose joint custody on parents who do not wish it and who will be unable to coparent because of extensive reciprocal hostility.

Elkin pointed out that in joint custody "both parents are empowered by the court to retain *equal legal rights, authority, and responsibility* for the care and control of their child, much as in the intact family" (1987; italics in the original). Joint custody does not determine physical custody but allows the parents to work out the residential arrangements that will best suit the child's needs. It is an option that is not right for every family. For example, joint custody is not appropriate in the presence of any of the following negative factors: family violence, including, of course, child abuse; child neglect; mental pathology; a family history indicating parental inability to agree on child rearing; the parents' inability to distinguish their needs from those of the children; children who are likely to be unresponsive to joint custody or to rebel against it; a family history of severe disorganization; the unalterable opposition of both parents to joint custody; or logistics militating against a joint custody plan. Elkin's analysis of the assumptions, benefits, and pros and cons of joint custody can be helpful to social workers involved with separating and divorcing families.

Elkin described a kind of divorce mediation that, like joint custody, represents a focus on what is best for the children in divorce. (The mediation process is used to resolve all divorce-related issues not just custody.) As in joint custody, the aim is self-determination: the right of the divorcing families to define the postdivorce structure rules in accordance with the needs of each individual and the family as a whole. Mediation is neither therapy nor arbitration. Rather, it is a short-term, goal-directed problem-solving process in which a trained divorce mediator tries to reach goals that will help the couple disconnect emotionally and reconnect as parents.

Health during Adulthood: Awareness of Expectable Strengths

Most people in adulthood, especially early adulthood, enjoy good health—or rather, because good health is taken for granted, adults rarely think about obtaining and maintaining, or losing, their health and energy. The small decrements that do occur, are, at first, barely noticeable, like holding the book a bit further away as one becomes a little more farsighted. Later decrements become more noticeable and adults usually find ways to compensate for them, such as when having a hard time fitting comfortably into one's good suit leads one to think about the exercise machine sitting unused in the basement.

However, the overwhelming fact is that the long period of adulthood, even divided into young, middle, and several old-age categories (discussed in chapter 13), is still characterized by health and vitality. There are inevitable changes related to age but not to a specific age for every person; people age at different rates, and different parts of people age differentially such as having an "old" skin—too much sun bathing—a "middle-aged lung"—no smoking, but living in a polluted area—and a "young" heart—thanks to a good history of jogging and swimming. Nature provides the basis for reproduction of the species, and society provides the foundation to socialize young children to perpetuate the culture. After children have grown into their own young adulthood, reproduced, and then grown older, nature is essentially done with them, but society is not. A complex society and culture requires much energy and intelligence on the part of adult participants, so that we must inquire into physical and mental health.

With physical health, all systems are go. We don't read in the papers or hear on National Public Radio that Joe's heart is beating well or that Mary's brain is functioning well. Although when an ordinary event, like giving birth, occurs in unusual circumstances, like a 63-year-old woman being the mother, it becomes newsworthy because of its rarity. But all the good features of physical health are operating for the vast majority of adults, although more with the younger than the older adults, so that the tasks of the modern world get performed. Some physical activities improve with age, such as driving skills and fishing—where experience begins to cumulate and more than offsets the decrements in energy and visual acuity that occur with age. However, decrements are occurring even with vigorous middle-aged adults, but their ability to adapt far exceeds the minor and often insidious changes. Sometimes chronic problems begin, such as needing eye glasses or being a bit stiff on getting up on a cold, damp morning. But most adults adapt, and the major message is one of health and strength.

With mental functioning, all systems can be on go if people will exercise their cognitive abilities throughout their lives. Inactive minds are just as likely to go flabby as inactive bodies. Creative work in some occupational fields or professions seems to require time to mature, while other ideas seem to require breaking out of established boundaries that may be overlearned through experience; thus relative youth is a valuable asset. So, for example, writers of distinguished novels are often older than authors of great short stories, who tend to be older than notable poets. The same is true across fields: older for jurists, younger for mathematicians and computer theorists, for example.

It is also true that mature adults process new information against a broader experiential base, and are able to integrate their ideas and experiences to generate perspectives for themselves and others. This, too, is the basis of practical intelligence, on solving the myriad of daily challenges and some of the unexpected ones as well. This broader experience may also lead to tolerance of diverse ideas or to increasing rigidity in the belief that one's ideas are the best—depending on the social contexts of those experiences. Lifelong education is not only possible but is increasingly accessible by adults and older persons.

Adulthood is also the time when mature people are in the cat-bird seat, pulling the levers at whatever level they are at and controlling some portion of the social world. They enter adulthood through some career or occupation and begin their climb to some peak of contribution and reward. This is the time we've all been waiting for, when we make the decisions and we give commands to our family members and subordinates—if we have any—or at the very least, we can command ourselves as free and autonomous adults—if we are free from innumerable bonds. We recognize, sometimes with a bit of a shock, that we are coming to or are at the peak of whatever social power we will be able to command. We have some degree of health, wealth, and options. What shall we do with all these riches? These are the tasks of adulthood.

Health Changes during Adulthood

Physical changes occur throughout our lives and, in given environmental contexts, may prove to be beneficial or not beneficial. Some changes are quite noticeable, such as gray hair, dry and wrinkled skin, a drift upward in weight, a drift downward or outward in body shape, increasing farsightedness, and declines in physical energy and dexterity. Other changes are less visible, such as increased blood pressure that predisposes people to heart attacks and strokes, less resistance to colds, more difficulty in hearing, which may not always be self-observable. It is possible to delay some of these events, although at great cost in time, energy, and resources, so that it becomes a question of how to spend the time and energy most productively—to be what we are or what we would like to be. For other of these events one may compensate by physical prostheses (e.g., a hearing aid), medications (for diabetes), exercise and moderation in eating (for overall health). Others may require psychosocial prostheses, such as a spouse observing first signs of skin cancer on an inaccessible part of a mate's body, writing out lists of daily activities so that none gets forgotten, and so on. Adulthood is not merely a grand engagement with nature, society, and self; it is also a planned adaptation to changes in one's person and one's environment.

Adults are subject to an incredible array of possible problems, decrements, illnesses, and disabilities. Some may be carried over from adolescence, while others emerge new in adults. Each of these problems forms the subject matter of specialties, from the medical arts dealing with physical health problems to the psychological arts dealing with mental health problems; the arts of social workers and others help people engage in social health problems. Students will take specialized classes in the study of these problems and the solutions so far devised; we will not discuss them here in detail. Rather, we will give one instance of each class of change: decrements, illnesses, and disabilities.

Decrements

A professor we know is half-deaf and over the years has become increasingly hard of hearing. His students rarely know this, as he glides around the lecture hall, talking and listening to students, first on this side, then on that side of the room. When he really can't hear, or can't understand what he hears, he will smoothly ask the student to "tell us more about that." And then he asks other students what they think of this—if no one volunteers. He avoids loud noisy gatherings, not because he is antisocial but because such noises blur together and make meaningful conversation difficult. In confidence, he once told us that when he is alone he hears noises that don't exist except as "splashing echos on the shores of my mind." We suggested he not mention this, recalling that the DSM-IV mentions the pathology of hearing voices. When he accidently goes to a loud concert, he turns his deaf ear to the sound and smiles, although if it is too loud, he has to plug up his other ear with his finger. He says he can sleep while his wife listens to the radio by sleeping on his good ear, although sometimes, he confesses, he doesn't hear the alarm clock ringing. In dull committee meetings, we've seen him rest his hand over his good ear and appear totally above the fray. We know that he has also promised his temporal bone to the Deafness Society for study of this condition when he dies; he has shown us the small identification card he always carries. He has adapted well.

Illness

Illnesses can be of an acute or chronic nature. Acute illnesses, like the flu or an appendicitis attack, come rapidly and often painfully, require immediate attention, and usually pass in a relatively brief period of time, after which the person regains his or her former level of functioning. Chronic illness is of a different nature. It may emerge slowly or rapidly, but it remains a long-term uninvited guest in the person's body or mind. It may never leave. Chronic illnesses require the continuing attention of medications or protheses, even though there may be fluctuations in seriousness or periods of remission when the illness seems to have disappeared entirely. Chronic illnesses are difficult to bear because of their longevity; it takes considerable personal strengths and strong social supports to maintain the thrust of an adult life when burdened by such an illness. Yet we marvel at people who do just this, for what is the alternative? To dissolve in self-pity, dependence, and inaction? The pain and misery are still present. To maintain ordinary daily activities, even in the face of pain and difficulty? This requires a great deal of courage and resolve. To excel in spite of the misery? This requires an extraordinary person with extraordinary resolve. Freud, for example, spent the last nine years of his life in constant pain from cancer of the jaw, but refused pain medication because he wanted to be alert enough to complete his thinking and writings. Ryan White, the young hemophiliac who contracted AIDS from a blood transfusion and found that he was ostracized because of the public fear of AIDS, spent the last years of his life trying to be a normal kid, while also going public support on behalf of AIDS victims. These are stories that become legends for the rest of us.

Disability

Aunt Ruth is a walking museum of disabilities. She has visual problems and wears thick glasses. Her hearing aid works reasonably well, but it sometimes picks up the background sounds as foreground sounds and squeals. Her arthritis has bent her over about 15 degrees, which makes it somewhat hard for her to walk. She has to watch what she eats because of some digestive problems whose names she cannot remember. And she has a heart condition that is being controlled by diet and exercise. However, this doesn't slow up Aunt Ruth. She retired early, gave up her home and car, and moved to an adult living center that offers a continuum of opportunities, from private apartments with full kitchens to rooms in a hotel-like independent living quarters where residents can take their meals in a common dining room. There is also a sick bay, where people with temporary problems can go—and later return to their own homes. Visiting nurses don't have far to go to check up on the rehabilitating resident. (For serious illnesses, residents go to the local hospital.) Aunt Ruth is fortunate to have enough money to purchase her apartment and pay a small monthly fee for maintenance and upkeep. Other residents get helping hands from relatives, and a few residents get support from the church that sponsored this center. Aunt Ruth is managing her chronic disabilities on her own but with the help of a variety of professionals nearby. She is active on the welcoming committee at the center, as well as continuing her long-standing participation in several groups, for the "poor folks who can't handle their disabilities very well," she says. She is a ferocious card player and pretty good on the electric organ. Aunt Ruth is much in demand at the center.

Dying and Death

Dying and death are natural occurrences overlain with layers of cultural meaning and social implications. Societies differ as to whether they are death-accepting or death-denying. In death-accepting cultures, such as in old Mexico, death is viewed as a natural occurrence and is celebrated in religious festivals that personify death and bring the idea of death closer to everyday life. Relatives may die at home, in the center of their families in familiar surroundings. In a death-denying culture, such as our own, we disguise dying and death, we use remote institutions with paid workers to literally lay hands on dying and dead persons. We prettify the corpse and leave the funeral ceremonies as soon as possible. And we rarely think about dying or death, particularly our own.

Adults at the height of their power have great difficulties dealing with death, even though they are responsible for the health of their children and probably will be involved in the care of their elderly parents and grandparents. Cultural heros die—old movie stars, baseball players, supreme court judges—and we read their obituaries not merely for facts of their lives but for the reflection of our own life in theirs. We were thrilled to the bone by them in that famous film, or heard about them when glued to the radio as a youth, or benefited from their emancipating decisions. When siblings or near age–peers begin to get sick and die, adults are shocked not only for the loss of relatives and friends but as a memento mori of their own mortality.

Grieving over these losses is an important part of living, and gives us some anticipatory training in dealing with even closer deaths, eventually including our own. There have been several theories about grieving, from Freud's distinction between normal and healthy mourning and unhealthy fixated grief in melancholia to Kubler-Ross's (1969) stage model—denial, anger, bargaining, depression, and acceptance. However, people seem to enter and exit the five stages in no necessary order. Some people may experience all the stages; others may experience only one or two, or something else entirely. Perhaps the important point is that there is enormous sadness for an unreplaceable loss, but dying people need to find some meaningful closure to their life in whatever way it can be expressed, while the survivors must go on living.

Adulthood covers a very long period of time. Dying in adulthood may mean dying before or during the prime of one's life, the highest points in one's social, economic, or personal developments. Dying may rob the person of being able to benefit from his or her labors, to indulge in the rewards of a lifetime. We assign a kind of psychological time line on a death—too early, on time, beyond the right time—and children and young adults are always too early. When we discuss old age, we find that no time is the right time, but some time may be too late, when we have outlived our friends and family, our resources, our reputation (see chapter 13).

In a death-denying culture, how does one relate to a dying person or to the friends and relatives of a dying person? It is always difficult to be a friend or worker in these situations, but it is more difficult for the dying person and their close associates. To be helpful means we are open to their communications—the content and the feelings—to the extent they want to talk about the illness or other matters; they take the lead. Be honest in what you say, but admit ignorance when you don't know. The dying person may be in pain or fearful of the unknown. It is difficult to speak in these situations, but a touch or an arm around the shoulder can be very meaningful and supportive. Support whatever belief systems the dying person and family hold; these are their final moments and they should be helped to make the most of it, through remembering good memories, expressions of shared love, and a meaningful farewell.

13

The Elderly Family and Its Transformations

"How old would you be if you didn't know how old you was?" asks the ageless Satchel Paige, an extraordinary baseball player who outperformed professional athletes half his age. This chapter deals with the aging process, the elderly, and the elderly family. It deals with the changes that occur as people grow older, a situation clouded with many stereotypes. Being older has many potential positives, including life as a couple once again, grandparenthood, retirement in good health, with adequate financial resources, and with an inquiring mind that literally opens up a world of possible good experiences. There is also the fact of life that all people will die, and with this fact come the various ways individuals, cultures, and society have sought to address this final passage.

Outline

Introduction: Aging and the Elderly Family

The Years of Middle Age: 45 to 64

    Physical Changes and Psychosocial Reactions

    Middle-Aged Children in the Middle

    Grandparenting

    Family Transformations: Life as a Couple (again)

Over 65: Growing Older in America

    Societal Attitudes toward Aging

    Demographics

    Economics

    Health Conditions

    Living Arrangements

Rural Life and Aging

Introduction: Aging and the Elderly Family

Growing older is neither a social problem nor a disease but a process of biological and psychosocial change that begins at birth and continues through life. In 1935, with the passage of the Social Security Act, mandatory retirement from the workforce at age 65 became the U.S. marker of old age. Yet there is nothing magical about that age. It had been set arbitrarily by Bismarck in late nineteenth-century Germany when a system of social insurance was instituted. Until 1935 most Americans worked as long as they could. With current laws against age discrimination in the workplace, the new reality is that some now work into their 70s at a high level of productivity, often higher than that of younger colleagues. A few may work productively into their 80s. Some affluent others in their 50s retire voluntarily to enjoy their leisure and good health as long as possible.

Being elderly today is partly a matter of self-definition. Given the extension of the life course and the improved health maintenance during the twentieth century, many people do not consider themselves middle-aged until their mid-50, and they do not consider themselves old until their mid-70s or even their 80s (Rimer 1998, A1). Self-definitions may derive from cultural influences, as some cultures define when one is an elder based on chronological age. On the average, blue-collar groups go through expectable life transitions such as leaving school, first job, marriage, and first child about five years earlier than those in middle-income and professional groups. It is not surprising, then, that working-class persons tend to define themselves as middle-aged and elderly earlier than middle- and upper-class individuals do. Those engaged in hard physical labor, for example, may feel middle-aged at 30 and old at 50.

Various writers have constructed categories that label periods of aging, such as Neugarten's (1978) notions of young-old (55 to 74), old-old (75 to 85), and the very old (over 85); or Hooyman and Kiyak's (1996) the "frisky, the frail, and the fragile." The categorization that we use in this book reflects a view of aging in which older persons are in better health and social functioning, and living longer than did older persons of several decades ago. We define the years of middle age as generally beginning about age 45 to 64, followed by the young-old period, age 65 to 74. We use the term mid-old to refer to people 75 to 84—the middle period of old age—and the old-old as people 85 years and over. These are rough approximations, and we recognize there will be individual variations of striking importance. Such classifications underscore the great diversity among the elderly and the public's view of aging. What people in their mid-60s enjoy, require, and can do—and their adaptive tasks—are quite different from the needs, activities, and life tasks of those who are in their mid-80s. When individual differences in health and self-definition are added, the diversity becomes great indeed, requiring careful attention from policy and program developers and practitioners (Atchley 1994; Hooyman and Kiyak 1996; Kart 1994). The three old-age categories are examined later in the chapter.

Genetic factors operate in biological aging. The timing of such processes as graying hair and skin changes, bone loss and decreasing stature, and diminishing visual and hearing acuity, muscle mass, vigor, and heart and respiratory function is related to genetic inheritance interacting with lifestyle and the environment over the life course. Thus the changes begin earlier in some people than in others. Race and poverty play important roles in aging because the longevity rates among people of color have been much lower and the illness rates have been much higher than those of middle- and upper-class persons and all whites (Stokes 1993). But beginning in the early years of the twenty-first century, the proportion of nonwhite elderly—like nonwhite people in general—is expected to increase at a higher rate than for the white elderly population (Hooyman and Kiyak 1996:19), although the great majority will still be white (Ozawa 1997).

Ideas about declines in cognitive capacities such as intelligence, memory, learning ability, and judgment are controversial. Myths and stereotypes view deterioration in these capacities as inevitable in the elderly. It is more accurate to say that older persons show decline in (timed) performance tests of intelligence (known as fluid intelligence) but maintenance of (untimed) verbal tests of intelligence (crystallized intelligence) (Hooyman and Kiyak 1996:195). A study of 1,000 people age 51 to 92 years in 30 Florida cities found that when 450 of the subjects were retested 10 years later (the rest had died or moved away), their verbal comprehension showed no significant change. Basic arithmetic skills showed only modest declines (Cunningham 1986). The researcher stated that educational level was a better predictor of test performance than age. He, like other investigators, believes that depression, substance abuse, alcohol, and lack of exercise, rather than aging itself, account for some diminished intellectual skills. Other studies have found that developing new means to solve problems is more impaired than knowledge learned in the past. Similarly, memory of the distant past tends to be better than that of the recent past, although this discrepancy may merely reflect the older person's interest in thinking and talking of the past as a means of maintaining self-esteem and a sense of identity and continuity.

The advice "use it or lose it" applies to intellectual as well as physical capacities. Brain research has shown that brain cells are stimulated by use. Also, the brain of a healthy older person maintains its circuits and repairs them if they are damaged (Cotman 1987). Thus the effects of disease should not be confused with normal aging. For example, certain organic conditions, such as stroke, can lead to brain changes due to a gradual loss of cells in the cortex, which affect intellectual capacities. Alzheimer's disease and other forms of senile dementia result in gradual intellectual deterioration to a profound degree. Several of these abnormal conditions are considered in a later section on health.

The Years of Middle Age: 45 to 64

The last chapter ended with the development of the adolescent and the parent(s), presumed to be in their early 40s, and the associated family transformations. This section picks up with the departure from home of the last or only adolescent child, now a young adult. He or she may have departed for marriage, higher education, employment, the armed forces, independent living arrangements and self-support in whole or in part, and so on. The departure may occur at any time from about age 18 years on, depending on circumstances: physical, mental and emotional capacities; cultural, ethnic, and class patterns; and the like.

For many middle-aged parents today, the years from the time of the last child's departure until the death of the spouse may last 30 or 40 years and, in some instances, may be the longest segment of the partners' life together. As the term "empty nest" implies, the parents now reoccupy the earlier status of child-less couple. They may welcome this, or they may need to rediscover and renew their love for, interest in, and attention to each other. Many enjoy their freedom from child rearing responsibilities and provide support to each other for the "losses" involved. They may feel relatively comfortable in their work roles. Some women who began careers after children were in school may find that the pace of the career and their interest in it now pick up. Many men, with a diminished need to succeed, become interested in recapturing the warmth and intimacy of the early marriage years before the arrival of children. Some others, who have gone as far as they can in one particular kind of work, may weigh carefully the idea of career or work changes as a now-or-never possibility. They will face bar-riers to overcome, such as covert age discrimination, the changing economy, financial risk, and the comfort of the status quo. To some extent, such changes are limited to those at the upper levels of the occupational structure. Such a change by either partner also entails extra time and energy that may require shifts in the roles and responsibilities of each partner (Barron 1992).

But for most couples, these years mean they have time at last for each other and for individual and shared activities and friendships. Many, if not most, parents and their young-adult child work out a different, but loving, adult-to-adult relationship. With the child's marriage or other committed relationship, the parents incorporate the partner into the family system and into their own psychic structures as a loved person—not always easy, depending on the cir-cumstances. Also, they are now no longer the "next of kin" to their children, sometimes a wrenching recognition. They must again modify their relation-ship to their adult children, who from now on will be more allied to their part-ner. The parents are no longer needed in quite the same way. But many begin to look forward to new status as grandparents. Meanwhile, they assume as best they can any new responsibilities as the middle-aged children of their own aging parents. Neugarten (1968) found that very few middle-class, middle-aged persons wish to be young again, although they do want to feel young and to have youthful attitudes. Many in their 40s and 50s feel they now know how to manage their lives and to take whatever the future may bring.

Physical Changes and Psychosocial Reactions

Earlier theory, bolstered by folklore, suggested that middle age is especially difficult for women because their major function of child rearing is over, and fertility is lost with menopause, which occurs sometime around ages 45 to 55. It is likely today that neither issue is a significant concern to many middle-aged women. First, almost 50 percent of mothers are in the workforce, and more than half of all women between the ages of 45 and 64 are employed, so child rearing has not been the only or the major function of most of today's middle-aged women. In fact, 20 percent of the preschoolers in the United States whose mothers worked in 1992 had fathers at home as the primary care-taker, 16 percent had grandparents, and 8 percent other relatives as primary caretaker (Mink 1994). Many who did remain at home with their children until the last one departed look forward to returning to work, or obtaining education for new work roles, or taking on community responsibilities. Second, in contrast to the views of male physicians, recent studies indicate that most women experience menopause as a relief. Sexual activity is more plea-surable because the couple is freed from worries about pregnancy or contra-ceptive use: "There is no age limit for female sexuality (that special sense of self through which we express passion, warmth, closeness and affection). Many women in their middle and late years enjoy satisfying physical and emo-tional intimacy. Many others do not because of poor health, negative atti-tudes, or because they have difficulty finding an appropriate sexual partner; still others choose a celibate life style" (*Hot Flash* 1984).

Some women may experience menopausal discomforts such as hot flashes, palpitations, and vaginal shrinkage and dryness because of hormonal changes, but hormone replacement therapy relieves these symptoms in most instances. Hormonal replacement therapy is believed also to protect older women from heart disease and osteoporosis, a bone-thinning disease that leads to fractures. Replacement of estrogen and progesterone in combination is thought to pro-tect against the risk of uterine cancer posed by estrogen replacement alone, but it may increase the risk of heart disease for some. Because of the risks, the matter of hormonal replacement is still controversial within the medical pro-fession (Hooyman and Kiyak 1996:234).

Older men can remain sexually active into old-old age, but the level of per-formance changes. Neither the penis nor the internal sexuality system func-tions as it once did. Erections may take longer to obtain and may not be as large or hard as they once were, and there might not be the same quality to the ejaculation as in younger men. Importantly, older men have a trade-off to consider: Extended time in lovemaking usually leads to a milder orgasm, while a more rapid intercourse (and less foreplay) leads to a stronger orgasm. Since "half the fun is getting there," for both persons involved, older men have to decide on each occasion how to experience sexuality. For both men and women, having regular sexual activities over time will reduce the likelihood of having problems in old age (Klein and Bloom 1997).

What has been noted by several researchers across different cultures, however, is a certain personality change in men and women that begins in the middle years. Men tend to become more nurturant and expressive and to shift from active to passive mastery. Women tend to become more active, assertive, and independent. Gutmann (1977), who developed the hypothesis, explained the shifts as "a return of the repressed." That is, early gender-role socialization represses one side of each gender's total humanness; the relative freedom from stereotyped gender roles in old age permits its reemergence. Cross-cultural studies bear out the tendency among older people to become androgenous (Livson 1980; Sinnott 1986). Riley (1985a) suggested that this capacity to combine traditionally masculine and feminine traits, replacing earlier gendered roles, may be the best means of coping with aging. She believes that if these ideas are corroborated by further research, such a generic role in later life may contribute to the social adaptation of older persons.

Little information is available about the extent of alcohol among midlife and older women, but we do know that "many of the ten million alcoholics in the U.S. are women who began drinking late in life, and, unlike their male counterparts, are closet drinkers" (Blume 1985). Notably, the highest proportion of problem drinkers in men is found in the 21- to 34-year-old group, while in women the highest proportion is found in the 35- to 49-year-old group. Many experts today agree that alcoholism is not willful misbehavior but an illness that has genetic, biological, emotional, and social roots. Yet all alcoholics, including women, bear a stigma. Additionally, women suffer a special stigma because they are expected to follow high moral standards. It is sometimes assumed that women who drink are sexually loose because of the historical assumed link between alcoholism and sexual promiscuity. The stigma and shame women feel make it difficult for them to seek help for alcohol abuse, although there are now many self-help groups available.

Neugarten (1969) noted that the self-concept of middle-aged adults has elements of the past within it. Adults think of themselves in the present in terms of where they have come from, what they have become, and how content they are at 50 compared to when they were 40. For most men and many women, the middle years are a time of stock taking, of coming to terms with what has been achieved in contrast to what was hoped for. It is also a time for self-introspection and couple reflection, with consideration of possible changes to ensure a satisfying life ahead, and rejoicing in the freedom to enjoy it. Neugarten showed that for most people this period is accompanied by a changing time perspective: "Life is restructured in terms of time-left-to-live rather than time-since-birth" (1968:97).

Middle-Aged Children in the Middle

In addition to the departure of the now young-adult child, the couple (as well as childless couples and single individuals) may be faced with the declining health of their own parents. Given the extended longevity and the growing prevalence of four-generation families, they and their aging parents may even be faced with the care of their very old grandparents. They are part of what is called the "sandwich generation," squeezed between attention to their children and grandchildren and the needs of their own elderly parents and very old grandparents. The problem has become a women's issue because most caregivers are women. A 1987 study by the National Center for Health Research of the U.S. Public Health Service found that in 1986 caregiver relatives were 72 percent female, of whom 29 percent were daughters (or daughters-in-law) and 23 percent were wives; the rest were other relatives (siblings, nieces, etc.) or friends. Their average age was 57 years; 25 percent were 65 to 74 years of age; and 10 percent were over 75. Three-quarters of the caregivers shared living arrangements with the recipient relative; one-third also worked; and one-fourth reported their own health as poor. One-third of the caregivers were poor; one-third provided care without any assistance; and only 10 percent purchased formal services. Of the 28 percent who were male caregivers, 13 percent were husbands, and 9 percent were sons; the remainder were other relatives or friends.

On one hand, the need for caregiving is growing because elderly parents or other relatives are living longer. The fastest growing segment of the aged population is the over-85 group, who are more likely to suffer chronic illness or mental impairment and to need care. On the other hand, fewer caregivers are available because more women are working outside the home. The study just cited found that 44 percent of the daughters were employed and had to juggle the demands of working and those of caregiving, perhaps becoming vulnerable themselves to severe stress and consequent physical illness. Also, 14 percent of the wives and 11 percent of the daughters had left their employment to become full-time caregivers. Others had rearranged their work schedules or had changed to part-time jobs.

Some caregivers expressed guilt and resentment because of fear they had neglected their spouse and children or because they could not satisfy the elder's demands. Even in instances where the arrangement had not worked out, mostly because of the relative's deteriorating health, the caregivers expressed satisfaction that they had tried rather than immediately choosing institutional care. Others wept as they spoke of the forced decision to find an alternative arrangement. The researcher concluded, as many clinicians have, that unpaid caregiving relatives must have specialized supports to sustain them so they can continue to provide care (C. Hill 1984). Recognition of this need is growing in North America, and services are being developed such as respite for the caregiver, day care for the elderly, nursing and homemaker services, and referral and information services. Many are staffed by social workers.

Grandparenting

It is widely assumed that grandparents have all the joy that children bring, without the responsibilities and pressures of child rearing. While this is true in many cases, unfortunately, some grandparents have to assume the parenting function once again because of the serious emotional or substance abuse problems of their adult children, which makes them unable to care for these grandchildren (Jendrek 1992; Burton 1992). In the same way, grandparents bring a special joy to their grandchildren that some observers may call spoiling but that to the children means gentleness, patience, love, and unrushed time. Grandparents are living longer today, and many are lucky enough to know their grandchildren as teenagers and even as adults. Some live near enough for frequent visiting; others may live across the country but keep in touch by telephone, mail, email, and vacation visits. Still other grandfathers and grandmothers today may be employed full time beyond age 65 and are unable to be with their grandchildren as much as they would like to be. Many parents of adult children who have delayed childbearing in favor of careers feel that their anticipated grandparenthood is being suspended. For some, the suspension is likely to be permanent, as more young people prefer to remain childless. It may represent a troubling interruption of the emotional transition in the aging process—already labeled "grandparent anxiety" (E. Brody 1984). The basis for such anxiety is not simply the fear of the lost opportunity of the fun of cuddling a baby. Grandchildren are a reassurance to the older couple that their adult children will have fulfilled, secure lives. Even if the suspension is not permanent, delayed childbearing means that the "grandparents will have less time to watch the grandchildren grow up, despite extended life expectancy. On the other hand, when hoped-for grandchildren are finally born, they will arrive closer to the grandparents' retirement. They may then have more time together" (Atchley 1994).

One of the few studies of grandparenthood is more than 30 years old (Neugarten and Weinstein 1968), but it remains pertinent. The authors interviewed both grandparents in 70 white, middle-class Chicago families—the authors recognize the need for more diverse studies—these grandparents lived in separate households from their adult children.

Five major styles of grandparenting were identified: formal, fun seeker, surrogate parent, reservoir of family wisdom, and distant figure. Age differences are of particular interest. The formal style, following the prescribed role of grandparenting and not interfering with the parenting function, occurred significantly more often among those older than 65. The fun-seeker and distant-figure styles occurred significantly more often in those under 65. These represent new, nonauthoritarian styles that may be the consequence of the youthfulness (in actual age and in self-definition) of the grandparents and of their cohort experiences as they grew old in times of changing values. "They may also reflect processes of aging and/or the effects of continuing socialization which produce differences in role behavior over time" (Neugarten and Weinstein 1968:285).

Doka and Mertz (1988) studied great-grandparents in the United States and identified two basic styles: The remote great-grandparent had limited contact, mainly on major holidays and family occasions, while the close great-grandparent had frequent and regular contact. It is a testament to these old-old that they continue to participate in family affairs and transmit an extended sense of cultural roots to the other generations.

Family Transformations: Life as a Couple (again)

Many middle-aged couples (or single parents) perceive the many adaptive tasks of relating to their adult children as challenges or opportunities. These center on the child's departure and subsequent marriage; the couple's new relationship to their child as an adult, to each other, and to in-laws; the new status of grandparent; and the recognition of their own middle age and the old age of their own parents as first-order developments. Most middle-aged couples make smooth first-order changes in statuses, roles, relationships, household routines, and other activities. The family's paradigm may shift so that their worldview includes new goals and reasonably happy expectations of the future.

Others dread the anticipated developments in advance, and their worst fears are realized when these developments actually occur. Perhaps the partners have been estranged for a long time, so that reconciliation and reciprocal support are now impossible. One or both parents may miss the child to a painful, even intolerable degree. Either or both may resent the signs of aging in self or spouse. They may experience their work as unsatisfying, or they may feel overwhelmed by the emerging needs of their elderly parents. The future stretches ahead as aimless, lonely, and dreary. The so-called empty nest, now a trap, represents a second-order development to these couples that leads to mounting tensions, depression, despair, and sometimes to declining health in one or both partners. Some may respond to the intensifying stress by seeking marital or personal counseling, informal support from relatives and friends, or both. They may, with support and professional guidance, redefine their life situation. Some may be helped to recall what attracted them to each other originally, to reflect on earlier happy times, and to make use of environmental resources to bolster their self-esteem and to find some pleasure in their present relationship. As a consequence, they may undertake joint efforts to achieve second-order changes. Over time, they may gradually make modest yet useful changes in the family organization and worldview.

Others respond to the stressor differently. One or both partners may look elsewhere for a sense of fulfillment in a new love, may resort to alcohol or drug abuse, or may undertake hasty, unthinking, disastrous changes in job or lifestyle. These steps can push the family toward disorganization. Divorce is not uncommon among such couples. Elderly Latinos in the United States have a higher rate of divorce or separation (22 percent) than either African Americans (19 percent) or whites (7 percent) (Freidenberg 1995). As with younger women who get divorced, this change often leaves the older woman bereft not only of a mate but of a home and financial support as well (Faludi 1996). As a "displaced homemaker" in her 50s or early 60s, she may need to find work—a dismal prospect if she lacks skills and experience or has neither the money nor the energy to pursue training. She may be cut off from her husband's pension, health insurance, and even his Social Security if he elects to work beyond 65. If he remarries, the new wife can claim inheritance of his assets. If the divorced wife is receiving alimony, it is taxable, but it is tax-deductible for the former husband.

Older displaced homemakers are members of a birth cohort who were raised to believe that marriage was a lifelong commitment. Many feel ashamed and humiliated by their perceived failure and the loss of their primary identity. They may lose married friends they had shared with their spouses and may suffer isolation and loneliness. They experience a double assault of being too old to start over and too young to give up, as one woman put it. Only about 11 percent of women who are divorced when they are over 50 years old remarry. They outnumber men their age by 4 to 1, so many continually hope for reconciliation with the former spouse. Some believe the death of the spouse would have been easier (Displaced Homemakers Network 1989). Widows receive better treatment, and there are also rites and rituals to guide their behavior.

This may be the last cohort to suffer such devastation, as women's attitudes and the norms surrounding marriage and divorce change and as women's presence in the workforce continues to grow. Meanwhile, displaced homemakers are a large proportion of the estimated 11 million women who have lost their source of support through divorce (30 percent), widowhood (67 percent), or the disability of their husbands, and who are unprepared for work outside the home. About two-thirds have inadequate incomes; 70 percent are over 55; and 54 percent are over 65 (Displaced Homemakers Network 1989). Fortunately, some social agencies have established individual and group services for these middle-aged women, including mental health and financial counseling, job referrals, legal assistance, and referral service for shared and alternative housing. Some programs are currently offered under the Vocational Education Act of 1984.

The adult children of the divorcing couple also suffer. They may wonder if the parents stayed together for their sake and their family life was a sham. They may feel disillusionment and shame and may even begin to question their own marriage. Some may side with one parent against the other, may resent the loss of cherished traditions and holidays, or may fear that they will now have to look after the bereft, lonely parent. On the other hand, some may develop more satisfying relationships with each parent separately, particularly if open tensions between the parents had been long-standing.

Conversely, older parents may also suffer when their adult children divorce. In some cases adult children come back to live with their parents; in 1990, 1 in 8 adult children returned to their parents' household because of job loss, divorce, or other setback (*American demographics* 1993). In addition, older persons worry about the impact on their grandchildren. Some may experience the divorce as a mark of their own failure as parents. Others may be resentful because divorce is against their religion. Still others, who became genuinely fond of their child's spouse, are saddened by the loss, especially if their adult child is angered by their wish to remain in contact with the former partner. Grandparents fear the loss of their grandchildren if the custodial parent moves away or is too angry to permit visiting. However, as a consequence of grandparent activist groups, all 50 states now have laws establishing grandparent visitation rights, recognizing how important grandparents are to their grandchildren and how the maintenance of the tie can improve the child-rearing environment and help lessen the trauma of the divorce for the children. Breaking the tie is destructive and devastating for children and grandparents.

In sharp contrast, some grandparents may be physically and emotionally overburdened by the full-time care of grandchildren because of the custodial parent's employment or, more recently, because of parental drug abuse and neglect of the children. Instances of the latter kind of case—the "crack babies"—are growing rapidly in the nation's inner cities (Burton 1992). Most of these grandmothers are poor and infirm. Many of their grandchildren are physically, emotionally, or neurologically impaired because of their mothers' addictions, so the grandmother's tasks are even more difficult.

Over 65: Growing Older in America

We dread becoming old almost as much as we dread not living long enough to reach old age.
—Froma Walsh

Societal Attitudes toward Aging

In general, we are a youth-oriented and ageist society. As Simone de Beauvoir noted (1972), we look on old age as a shameful secret that will never happen to us, only to other people. If older persons manifest common human needs for love, security, sexual expression, and acceptance, they are looked upon as absurd and ludicrous—the dirty old man and the little old lady in tennis shoes. In the aged persons we encounter, we do not recognize ourselves. Almost none of us foresees becoming aged until it is upon us—nothing is more expected, but nothing is more unforeseen. But as the birthday cards declare, growing old is better than the alternative.

We cling to myths and stereotypes of elderly persons as senile, infirm, destitute, unattractive, lonely, a burden to society, and unwanted by their families, who dump them in nursing homes as quickly as possible. Of course, many older people are chronically ill or mentally impaired, and far too many live in poverty. We need more humane policies and programs for their proper care and for the elimination of poverty in all age groups. But the greatest number of older persons have relatively good health, are active in mind and body, and continue to develop and to participate in and contribute to their communities. Indeed, more than 41 percent of people 60 years or over performed some form of volunteer work in the past year (Abercrombie 1993).

Demographics

From 1900 to 1995 the percentage of Americans 65 and older tripled (4.1 percent in 1900 to nearly 13 percent in 1995), and the number increased 10 times (from 3.1 million to 32.7 million) (U.S. Department of Commerce 1995a). The older population is expected to continue to grow in the future. Growth will slow somewhat during the 1990s because of relatively small numbers of babies born during the Great Depression of the 1930s. The most rapid increase is expected in the years from 2010 to 2030, when an estimated 65.6 million baby-boomers reach age 65 (Atchley 1994:30). By year 2030 people 65 and over are expected to represent about 21 percent of the population. The older population itself is getting older. In 1985 the 65 to 74 age group (17.0 million) was nearly 8 times larger than in 1900, but the 75 to 84 group (8.8 million) was 14 times larger, and the 85 and over group (2.7 million) was 28 times larger (AARP 1995).

People are living more years as older persons, defined by convention as 65 years and over; we use the conventional definition in this book. The current life expectancy for persons currently at age 65 is an additional 17 years (U.S. Department of Commerce 1995b). However, this expectancy differs by gender and ethnicity. In 1990 the life expectancy of older American women was 78.3 years; for men it was 71.5. For Japanese women and men, the figures were 81.4 and 75.6 years respectively—highest in the world (Atchley 1994:22). For older African American men, the life expectancy is 66 years, while for older African American women, it is 74.7 (1993 figures from Hooyman and Kiyak 1996:20). Interestingly, at age 75 and over, there is apparently a crossover effect in which African Americans, Pacific Asians, and American Indians have greater life expectancies than white Americans of the same age, which may be due to biological strengths, psychosocial resources, or perhaps some age reporting errors (Hooyman and Kiyak 1996:444). American Indians have a life expectancy of about 64 years (Kart 1994:394), which has implications for what they will get from their Social Security taxes they paid over their working careers.

In 1992 there were 18.6 million older women and 12.5 million older men, or a sex ratio of about 149 women for every 100 men. The sex ratio increases with age; for persons 85 and older, there are about 259 women for every 100 men. This difference emerged between 1920, when women outlived men by only two years, and 1970, when the difference became almost 8 years. What accounts for this striking sex differential in mortality? In a careful study, Waldron and Johnston (1976) analyzed the higher male mortality rates in seven major causes of death, and reported the following:

> Very roughly, we estimate that one-third of the difference between male and female death rates may be due to men's higher cigarette smoking (with the major contribution via increased coronary heart disease, lung cancer and emphysema); one-sixth may be due to a greater prevalence of the aggressive, competitive Coronary Prone Behavior Pattern among men (with the major contribution via increased coronary heart disease); one-twelfth may be due to men's higher alcohol consumption (with the major contribution via increased accidents and cirrhosis of the liver); and one-twentieth may be due to physical hazards related to employment (with the largest contributions via increased accidents and lung cancer).
>
> (Waldron and Johnston 1976:24)

Today, these proportions will have changed because women have been smoking more, have been increasing their Coronary Prone Behavior Pattern or Type A behavior (involving highly competitive, aggressive, and hurried work orientation), and have been slowly obtaining more work positions that had been formerly male domains. Such is the price of social progress. However, it will be still many years before the sex ratios become even approximately equal.

More than half of all older persons are married and live with their spouses in an independent household. However, because of differential longevity, 40 percent of older women are married compared to 74 percent of older men (Hooyman and Kiyak 1996:285). Half of all older women in 1985 were widows (51 percent). Remarriages commonly occur among older widowed or divorced people, but older men are 6 times more likely to remarry than older women in any given year, meaning that older men more often marry women younger than 65 (Kuhn 1993). Five percent of older men and of older women had never married. Although divorced older persons represented only 4 percent of all older persons in 1985, their numbers (more than 1 million) had increased nearly 4 times as fast as the older population as a whole in the preceding 10 years (3.4 times for men, 4.0 times for women) (Profile of Older Americans 1986).

The coming generation of older persons is distinctively different from those who came before. The 65-to 74-year-old group is the best educated generation of elders ever; 2 in 3 finished high school, compared to just over half of those 75 years and over (Treas 1995). Four percent had fewer than 5 years of schooling—the level thought necessary to read a newspaper or the directions on a bottle of medicine. However, this includes Hispanic and African American elderly of whom 27 percent and 12 percent, respectively, had fewer than 5 years of schooling (Treas 1995:21).

In 1990 about 90 percent of persons 65 years of age and older were white; 8 percent were black; and about 2 percent were American Indian, Eskimo, Aleut, Asian, or Pacific Islander. Hispanics, who may be of any race, represented 3.5 percent of the older population. By the year 2030 nonwhite people are projected to be 22 percent of the older population; by 2050 that figure is projected to be 30 percent (Hooyman and Kiyak 1996:19). Research is still limited, but a few studies with an ethnographic emphasis are reviewed.

The idea of double jeopardy, first developed with respect to black women, has been expanded to include other oppressed groups and the notion of multiple jeopardies (such as being an older lesbian of color). While the concept of double jeopardy is important, the 1982 Schaie, Orchowsky, and Parham study demonstrated that the double jeopardy concept must be supplemented by the interaction effects of race with cohort and historical period effects. For example, because marital history affects income status, the higher level of income of elderly white women than that of elderly black women is due not just to racial differences but also to cohort differences in the marital stability and the occupational and wage histories of both women and men at different periods of time (Jackson 1985).

Economics

The median income of older persons (ages 65 and above) in America is $17,160 in contrast to a household income of $35,639 for younger persons (Seidman 1995). Seidman goes on to note that the median income of women 65 years or older is $8,189. From 1989 to 1992, the poverty rate for persons age 65 and above rose from 11.4 percent to 12.9 percent. More than 25 percent of people age 65 and above are near-poor, that is, under 1.25 times the poverty level (Seidman 1995:66).

There is a discussion—some call it a controversy—about the relative status of older persons and children in terms of how much support each group gets.

The economic status of the elderly as a group has improved as a result of federal legislation (Social Security, Medicare, and so forth), even though there are large pockets of poverty still present. Children, especially in one-parent households of nonwhite mothers, are overrepresented in the poverty group. That either group is disproportionately below the poverty line is simply a choice U.S. society has made regarding how it wishes to aid in the development of young people or provide support for old persons. Both could be adequately addressed if society chose to do so (Hooyman and Kiyak 1966:509; Lawlor 1987; Ozawa 1986).

The relative economic position of older Americans has improved considerably from 1959 when more than 35 percent fell below the poverty line to 1990 when 12.2 percent did. However, this 1990 figure has to be compared to the 10.8 percent of persons 18 to 64 years of age who were living in poverty. As mentioned above, for children (under the age of 18), the figure was about 20 percent. More than 9 out of 10 older persons (93 percent) get Social Security and Supplemental Security Income (SSI); without Social Security, the poverty rate for older persons would be 55 percent (Hooyman and Kiyak 1996:367–377).

Ethnicity and gender are two important factors in determining economic status. For example, consider these percentages of older Americans with incomes below the poverty line in 1990: whites, 10 percent; African Americans, 34 percent; Hispanics, 22.5 percent; Asian Americans, 14 percent; American Indians, 35 percent (U.S. Department of Commerce 1991). When gender and old age are considered, the figures become even more extreme: The proportion of older unmarried white women living under the poverty line, 24 percent; older unmarried Hispanic women, 50 percent; and older unmarried black women, 60 percent.

About 61 percent of aged American Indians live below the poverty level, the greatest proportion among all groups (Crowley 1988). Almost one-third (32 percent) of elderly blacks and almost one quarter (24 percent) of elderly Hispanics were poor in 1985, compared to one-ninth (11 percent) of elderly whites. Poverty was probably more extensive among aged Mexican Americans (and Central Americans and South Americans) than among Puerto Ricans and Cubans because many Mexican Americans were undocumented aliens who could support themselves and their families only by part-time work. They are not eligible for Social Security or Medicare and are afraid to apply for welfare for fear of being reported to the Immigration and Naturalization Service and deported (Salcido 1979). These constrictions have changed for some who were eligible and applied for legal resident statuses under the 1986 Immigration Reform and Control Act. But this makes it even more difficult for those without legal residence to secure employment because of employer sanctions, or to obtain health care and social services because of lack of federal reimbursement or the fear of discovery (Gelfand and Bialik-Gilad 1989).

Thus the primary predictors of poverty in American are old age (over 75), gender (female), ethnicity (people of color), and marital status (unmarried, divorced, or widowed). To this can be added people who live alone, and people living in rural areas.

Health Conditions

The young-old, as a group, are healthier than previous generations of elderly persons, but they still have some significant health conditions worth noting. The numbers of heart attacks and stroke rise rapidly with increasing age, which makes cardiovascular (heart) diseases a main cause of death in older Americans and a major cause of disability. About 50 percent of persons 65 years and over die from cardiovascular diseases, while an estimated 300,000 Americans of this age group are in nursing homes as a result of limitations from chronic cardiovascular diseases; this includes about 180,000 people who are admitted because of stroke (U.S. Departments of Labor, Health and Human Services, Education 1994).

Cancer represents another important group of hazards for the elderly. Cancers of all types account for 20 percent of the deaths of older persons, but these occur differentially by gender. For men, cancers account for 24 percent of the deaths, while only 18 percent for women (Kart 1994:71).

Cerebrovascular diseases (strokes) account for about 8 percent of all deaths of older people. Together, heart disease, cancer, and strokes add up to about 70 percent of deaths of older persons and about 50 percent of all deaths of Americans. It is understandable why we, as a society, are focusing preventive and remedial efforts on these big three.

However, many other conditions affect older persons. Rates of disability increase with advancing age. In particular, functional disability rates are 3 times higher for people aged 75 to 84 compared with the population under 65 years of age; 40 percent of those 75 years and over had two or more chronic illnesses (Perspectives on Health Promotion and Aging 1992). Diabetes is prevalent in the elderly American population; 18.7 percent of the population between 65 and 74 have diabetes (Hodes 1995). Approximately 10 percent of persons with AIDS are 50 years or older, and about 2 to 3 percent are 60 or over (Linsk 1994:364–366).

Accidents are another special risk for the elderly, whose vision, balance, and judgment may be reduced. Between one-fourth and one-third of all accidents occur to the elderly. Falls, particularly those that cause hip fractures—about 240,000 occur each year (Cohen 1992)—are very serious for the elderly because of the complications they lead to and the restrictions in mobility they cause. Recent research suggests that an exercise strengthening regimen for the elderly—indeed, with people 90 years of age—can be very helpful in reversing some of the frailty that contributes to falls (Cohen 1992). Injury, mostly falls, is the sixth leading cause of death in persons 65 years and older in the United States, with more than 10,000 deaths annually (Perspectives on Health Promotion and Aging 1991). The death rate from falls increases with age.

Arthritis is not a life-threatening condition, although it is a painful one that may limit the quality of life for the more than 37 million Americans—1 in 7—who have some form of this rheumatic disease (Departments of Labor, Health and Human Services, Education 1990). Osteoporosis is present in epidemic proportions in older persons, afflicting 90 percent of women over 75 and large numbers of older men too, and causing disability or mortality from hip fractures (T. Williams 1990:257–258).

Living Arrangements

About 94 percent of the older population live in ordinary community households; 6 percent in nursing homes, homes for the aged, and other group quarters; and less than 1 percent in mental hospitals, prisons, and the like. It is instructive to look at the age and gender differences in living arrangement. Almost 8 out of 10 men (79 percent) ages 65 to 74 live with their spouses, while 13.4 percent live alone. Even at ages 75 and over, 65.6 percent of men live with their spouses, with 20.8 percent living alone. Contrast these figures to women ages 65 to 74 of whom only half (51.3 percent) live with their spouses and a third (33.7 percent) live alone. At age 75 and older, these figures for women become more extreme: less than a quarter (24 percent) live with a spouse, while more than half (53.2 percent) live alone. The rest in each age and gender group live in homes with relatives or nonrelatives (Atchley 1994:42).

Of the 18.2 million households headed by older persons in 1985, 75 percent were owners and 25 percent were renters. Older male householders were more likely to be owners (83 percent) than were females (66 percent). The housing of older Americans is generally older and less adequate than the balance of the nation's housing. About 36 percent of homes owned by older persons in 1983 were built before 1940 (21 percent for younger owners), and 8 percent were classified as inadequate (6 percent for younger owners). About 83 percent of older homeowners in 1985 owned their homes free and clear.

Researchers find that about 80 percent of the elderly have surviving children, and 80 percent of those see at least one child once a week (Hooyman and Kiyak 1996:291). Most older persons do not want to live with their children and fear being a burden to them. Most like to live near their children but wish to maintain their independence as long as possible. We saw in the prior section that most families regard the nursing home only as a last resort—when the older person is severely impaired or the adult child's personal caretaker resources are depleted. The myth that elderly dependent parents are financial drains on their adult children is false. Although their incomes are limited, most elderly are twice as likely to give regular financial assistance to their children than they are to receive it (Hooyman and Kiyak 1996:291–292).

Many older rural and urban black and Hispanic people live in unsafe, dilapidated housing because they are poor. A report reveals that 15.2 percent of all farm laborers aged 65 and over live in housing without plumbing (18.3 percent of Hispanics and 33.8 percent of blacks). There are relatively few specialized housing projects for farm workers in this country (*After the harvest* 1987). Among elderly American Indians, the situation is even worse: 42 percent of this population have no toilets in their homes and 65 percent have no telephones. Asian and Pacific Islander elderly, in general, do not experience such dire poverty, but many live in unsuitable housing (Crowley 1988). Older persons tend to live in older, poorly insulated homes that are less energy efficient, so these elderly residents tend to have higher heating costs, which is especially burdensome to fixed and low-income households. These people are forced to make difficult decisions, whether to buy food or heating or medicines (Tull 1994).

In addition to traditional "retirement homes" or "homes for the aged" supported by fraternal and religious organizations, a variety of alternate living arrangements have appeared in recent years, often subsidized by public and private funding. These include:

1. Home care (home aides come to the house to perform household chores, personal services, or both, depending on the level of their training and client need)

2. Respite care (family caregivers can place their older family member while they take some time off for their own mental and physical health)
3. Adult day care (an older person can be taken in the day time to be cared for and provided stimulation and structure, then return home at the end of the day)
4. Assisted living (a range of services from moderate levels of skilled nursing to almost full independence in a private apartment, with options that address the needs of the well-but-frail elderly who may need services such as personal care, cafeteria, house cleaning, transportation; some assisted living arrangements have a doctor's office on the premises, a beauty parlor, library, craft areas, and so forth (cf. Regnier 1994)
5. Cooperative group or extended-family-type homes (cooperative living places established and perhaps managed by community organizations or established independently by five or six older people of one or both sexes who want to try shared living [Magan 1989]

Sharing homes with unrelated people is becoming increasingly popular for older persons; there are some 350 organizations that match prospective home sharers, and more than 670,000 older persons were sharing homes in 1980, an increase of 35 percent over 1970 (Magan 1989). Other cooperative homes are small apartment buildings especially designed for elderly individuals and couples, some of which develop strong mutual aid systems that promote relatedness among the tenants and enable frail individuals to avoid institutionalization (Hochschild 1974). Unused college dormitories have been converted into apartments for the elderly and offer a new way of life to them, including taking tuition-free courses and developing friendships with students, to their mutual benefit. In return, the college earns needed income. Such innovative housing developments are still in short supply, although the numbers of elderly needing them are growing rapidly. (Hochschild 1974, 7) Other living arrangements are also available. Affluent older persons who live alone or with spouses or partners may reside in retirement communities of various types, depending on their income, leisure interests, and personal preferences. Some prefer continuing-care communities that are similar to retirement communities but have medical, nursing, and infirmary care on-site. Others may reside in congregate housing that consists of private apartments with central dining areas, housekeeping services, and transportation by vans. Elaborate mobile home parks are another option.

Rural Life and Aging

In general, rural people are fiercely independent, resist outside intervention, and place high value on self-reliance and natural helping provided by kin, friends, and neighbors. Today, these values may be truer of rural elderly than of younger residents. While the elderly comprise about 13 percent of the U.S. population, they account for more than 26 percent of the rural population. About 30 percent of all persons over 65 live in rural areas. Older persons who live in nonmetropolitan areas have lower income and are in poorer health than comparable people living in urban areas. For example, 41.5 percent of rural black elderly have incomes near the poverty level, while only 28 percent of urban black elderly are poor (Hooyman and Kiyak 1996:328)

The rural elderly include many members of racial and ethnic minorities, especially blacks, Chicanos, and First Nations Peoples—American Indians, Eskimos, and Aleuts. The life conditions of rural older persons vary markedly across North America. In the rural northeastern United States, elderly persons who live alone outside a village or town and who are without transportation may be extremely isolated during the snows of winter and the deep mud of springtime. In the Upper Plains, the Far West, and the Southwest, where distances are great and rural towns are far apart, the lack of transportation for health care, shopping, banking, visiting friends, and so on is a very serious problem for older people, especially if they are poor, disabled, or both.

"Rural aged are found to have poorer physical and mental health, more chronic disease, smaller incomes, poorer diets, and homes that are [more] deteriorated and unsanitary than the aged living in urban residences" (Weber 1980:208). At particularly high social and medical risk are older farm laborers who are no longer able to work because of age, illness, or disability. The concept of retirement does not apply to them: most simply work as long as their physical condition permits. They may not qualify for Social Security, or if they do they receive a small amount.

Social, health, and mental health services and skilled practitioners (physicians, nurses, and social workers) have always been in short supply for all age groups in many of the more isolated U.S. rural areas. What services exist often are located centrally in the nearest large town or city. Fortunately, in many rural areas, older persons are embedded in close, supportive relationships with kin, neighbors, and friends, who fill part of the gap and whose help also fits rural values. A sample of 80 older rural natural helpers, within a larger study, were found to be significant sources of relatedness, support, and tangible assistance to their elderly, middle-aged, and younger relatives, neighbors, and friends (Patterson 1987). Advances in communication systems also mean that rural health facilities may have some access to advanced medical knowledge.

The Young-Old: 65 to 74

In the year 2000 people born between 1926 and 1935 will be members of the young-old group. They represent a different cohort from the mid-old and the old-old, with different formative experiences. As mentioned previously, the 65 to 74 cohort is better educated than the two older cohorts. Its members are healthier and more vigorous than the members of the two older cohorts were at their age. They are also active politically and form an important age bloc in local and national politics because of their numbers, interest, and active participation. Many of them constitute a pool of wise, experienced, caring people who make important social contributions through community activities and volunteer work and feel self-fulfilled in return.

Nonetheless, societal attitudes toward, and perceptions of, older people reflect a loss of the dignity and meaning that characterize older people in traditional societies. On the other hand, far greater opportunities for leisure, cultural, and educational activities, health maintenance, and self-realization exist for today's elderly, especially the young-old (Atchley 1994) and those with sufficient incomes.

Retirement

Before the legislation prohibiting forced retirement on the basis of age, many retirees, especially men, found adaptation to a life without work difficult. With the various options now open, and with improved health, men and women can undertake retirement when they are ready. Even some who are financially secure prefer to keep working as long as they can. Others mark a particular age as their retirement time. Many with very limited resources, however, need to work to supplement their small incomes from Social Security, and some of them may be unemployed and seeking work. Among that group are some black men who see themselves as "unretired." They have not held regular jobs and have no pension income. They believe they will always need to work, but it is difficult for them to find employment (AARP 1988).

Retirement had, until about the early 1980s, been viewed mostly in terms of loss—the loss of status, work role, health, spouse, and friends. In particular, retirement was a transition in which the worker exited from the "socially respectable, clearly defined status of work to the amorphous, ill-defined, and rather negatively perceived 'roleless role' of old age" (Nowak and Brice 1984:107). In their extensive review of the research, Nowak and Brice referred to a 1968 study (by Reichard, Livson, and Petersen) that proposed a typology of personality styles predictive of men's responses to retirement. The typology identified three adaptive styles: the "mature," who find satisfaction in activities and relationships; the "rocking-chair men," who welcome freedom from the activity that has interfered with their passive orientation during their working years; and the "armored," who ward off their dread of physical decline by keeping active. Two maladaptive styles were also identified: the "angry men," who have histories of blaming others for their difficulties and are unable to accept their aging, and the "self-haters," who feel depressed, lonely, and worthless in retirement.

Nowak and Brice also found research support for the following predictors of the quality of the retirement years: health, income, the characteristics of the occupation, willingness to retire, and the marital relationship. Atchley described retirement not as an event but as a process involving the interplay of many factors in the preretirement and retirement years. He presented a model of the process that is of particular interest to social workers in practice, programming, planning, policy, and research. It consists of eight interrelated phases of adaptation to retirement: preretirement, honeymoon, the immediate retirement routine, rest and relaxation, disenchantment, reorientation, retirement routine, and termination. Two subphases constitute the preretirement phase: In the remote subphase, one has a vague vision of retirement in the distant future that may encourage financial and other planning well in advance. The near subphase is oriented toward a specific retirement date. Workers may then begin to decrease motivation or performance, and employers may decrease expectations. Workers may also develop preretirement fantasies based on visions of expected health, income, and activity level. Such visions provide a kind of anticipatory socialization. If they are realistic, they are helpful in identifying issues that require advanced decision making. If they are unrealistic, they may contribute to disenchantment with the reality of retirement (1994:300–301).

In active retirement, during the honeymoon phase, those with positive outlooks are likely to experience euphoria for a short or long while, keeping busy in valued activities for which they previously had no time. Depending on personal style, leisure-time options, and degree of flexibility in the face of change, the rapid tempo of activities gradually yields to a more reasonable, stable retirement routine. The immediate retirement routine reflects what the person did with his or her life before retirement; if life was full before, the person will likely be able to realign time to be equally full in retirement. There may be a rest and relaxation phase, rather than the euphoric honeymoon period. But this is usually temporary and eventually the retired person gets restless and resumes various activities.

After these initial "highs," some may experience disenchantment, a letdown, even depression—particularly those who had unrealistic preretirement visions. Even if the visions were realistic, however, the exigencies of fate may bring about changes in health, income, or family status. In this instance, if flexibility is absent or if alternatives are not available the disenchantment may continue indefinitely. When disenchantment sets in, it is necessary for retirees to reappraise their situation and their personal and environmental resources, to reorient themselves, and to reorganize their behaviors and expectations accordingly for a more satisfying life in retirement

In the reorientation phase, the retiree has reached a point where criteria are developed for dealing routinely with physical and social changes. People "take stock" and begin to view retirement in a more realistic view of alternatives within their potential resources. Some individuals move into this phase directly after the honeymoon phase, while others may never stabilize or do so only after repeated efforts at appraisal and reorientation. The retirement routine involves the routinization of activities based on the set of person and environment criteria for making choices "which allow them to deal with life in a reasonably comfortable, predictable fashion." (Atchley 1994:301). The ending or termination phase is part of retirement in Atchley's view. Because retirement is a status, it can be fulfilled only if one has the financial, social, psychological, and health resources for carrying out the retirement routine established in the earlier phases. Without the needed resources to be competent and independent in retirement, the individual transfers into the status of sick person and the role of patient, which have their own set of requirements for reconstituting the lifestyle. This process need not be overwhelming, because in most instances dependence or illness occurs gradually.

Atchley (1994) describes his studies of retirement. In general, married women and men were more likely to retire early, while nonmarried women retire late, because of economic necessity. Because older women tend to have discontinuous and part-time work histories—largely due to their family caregiver roles and gender discrimination—women tend not to have adequate pensions. Belgrave (1988) studied retirement pensions and found that older women received only 60 percent as large a pension as older men received; however, both men and women rated their retirement incomes as adequate.

Older Homosexual People

Older gay and lesbian people are subject to the same culturewide stereotypes and societal attitudes concerning the elderly as other elders are. They also have the same interests and concerns that all older persons have, including love, health, financial security, and acceptance. How these interests and concerns are handled is not entirely clear because of limited research. Moses and Hawkins (1982) and R. Berger (1984) review some studies that suggest that gays and lesbians may have a more successful response to aging than do many nongays. Lesbians holding negative views were concerned about physical appearance (mostly obesity rather than the physical changes due to aging) and loneliness in the later years. Most of the women were more interested in personality, intellect, and health, a finding suggesting they may have less concern about being older than do nongay women, who face a constant emphasis on physical attractiveness and youthful appearance. The minority who worried about loneliness seemed to be expressing concern about being alone rather than being lonely. The small number may reflect a difference between lesbian and nongay women: lesbians may have less difficulty finding partners in their older years than nongay women who are widowed or divorced.

The majority of younger gay men do not report worries about aging, although they do place more emphasis on youthful appearance in their choice of a sexual partner than do lesbian women. Saghir and Robins (1973) reported that 44 percent of the men indicated that they expected to remain involved and interested as older persons. An additional 28 percent expected to grow old in a stable relationship. Among the small number of gay men apprehensive about aging, fears were related to inability to attract a sexual partner because of physical appearance, as well as loneliness and being alone. Moses and Hawkins (1982) believe that as long as the gay community emphasizes youthfulness and the "body beautiful," gay men will continue to worry about physical attractiveness. This worry is positive if it supports interest in maintaining fitness as gay men grow older. It is negative if the preoccupation with physical attractiveness leads to concern about being old.

The few studies of small samples of older gay men reveal that they are neither lonely nor alone. R. Berger (1984) indicates that in urban areas gay rights organizations, social clubs, and gay churches are important places for meeting other gays. Berger and Kelly (1995) describe the gay-organized alternative religious institutions such as Dignity (Roman Catholic), Integrity (Episcopalian), the Metropolitan Community Synagogue (Jewish), as well as the Metropolitan Community Church (nondenominational). While dominated by younger men, these civic and religious organizations attract many older gay men and lesbian women. Berger also mentioned bathhouses, bars, parks, and beaches as sites for meeting others. However. in light of the AIDS epidemic, such places may be of less interest to most gay men, young or old.

About 10 percent of people with AIDS are older persons. It has been said that many of the elderly do not consider themselves at risk, yet some older gays do have more than one partner. It is also conceivable that some older gays may not practice no-risk sex, but compared with younger gays, older gay men have fewer sexual partners and lower frequency of sex, spend less time cruising, and have longer relationships (Lipman 1986). Older gays with AIDS may also suffer from emotional and social isolation. Informing children or grandchildren, for example, may be traumatic.

Moses and Hawkins (1982) suggested that one predictor of the successful aging of gays and lesbians may be their leisure time pursuits during young and middle adulthood. Saghir and Robins (1973) found that gay men are more interested in individual sports and artistic activities and less interested in group sports, while the opposites are true of nongay men. Gays are also more interested in intellectual activities. Similarly, lesbian women are significantly more involved in artistic pursuits and individual sports than nongay women (Saghir and Robins 1973). To Moses and Hawkins, these findings meant that the leisure activities of early and middle adulthood will serve gay men and women well in their older years because they are more appropriate for older persons than the activities of young or middle aged heterosexual men and women. These authors also presented evidence that the successful transcending of the stigma for sexual orientation, the presence of many friends, and retirement's freedom from worry about losing one's job are factors in gays' easier adaptation to the aging process than that of many nongay elderly.

R. Berger (1982) identified unique problems that confront older gay men and lesbian women: The policies of hospitals and nursing homes may refuse to recognize the relationship to one's ill partner when visiting regulations and relatives' consent are at issue. Older homosexual persons may not have wills, so their property may go to emotionally distant, even hostile, kin rather than to the long-term partner. Social agencies may not provide bereavement groups for older gay and lesbian persons who have lost their partners. Many senior citizen centers, day care centers, and the like fail to provide appropriate groups and services to older homosexual people. Services specific to the needs of older gay people, however, are slowly developing in both traditional and new agencies and in churches. One landmark organization is Senior Action in a Gay Environment (SAGE), which encourages active participation by gay seniors (*Practice digest* 1984).

Health and the Elderly

As Neugarten (1978) pointed out, the young-old are distinguished from the mid-old by continued vigor and social involvement. As we have seen, this is only partly the case, insofar as health, vigor, and social involvement vary according to income levels and race. So while it is true for many, others at all income levels do suffer from poor health and often from multiple chronic conditions. Some suffer crippling falls and may incur fractured hips and limbs, especially women who suffer from osteoporosis. Blacks suffer the highest rates of hypertension, with its life-threatening wake of heart disease, stroke, and kidney failure. Among blacks aged 45 to 64, the loss of kidney function associated with hypertension is 10 times greater than among whites the same age. The incidence of cancer is twice that for whites, and death from asthma is 3 times the rate of that for whites. American Indians rarely seek health care, and 80 percent of noninstitutionalized Hispanic elderly report at least one chronic illness.

Many married ill persons are cared for by their elderly spouses. The spouse is not compensated for home care by public or private insurance. Extra costs beyond what Medicare pays for services at home can rapidly drain away the couple's resources. To receive services from Medicaid, the couple must meet a means test that sets very low limits on income and assets. Each state designs its own Medicaid program, so there are many variations in the aspects of home care that are included. Corbin and Strauss related the accounts of 60 ill persons and their spouses, some of whom were young-old, as they struggled together to manage severe illness at home 24 hours a day, every day of the year. In addition to the struggles and pain of the ill spouse in managing the psychological and physical aspects of the illness,

> [t]he well spouse, while indirectly weighing such concerns, also has personal concerns: balancing the value of live-in help against the invasion of privacy that comes with that help; responding to the mate's need for assistance and care yet feeling somewhat resentful that as the caretaking spouse,

one can never become tired or ill because there is no one else to take over; willingly using one's life savings for the medical care of the ill person, while at the same time wondering what lies ahead for one's own future once all that money is gone. (Corbin and Strauss 1988:6)

Another group of older persons, generally neglected by family and social services, are those who are caregivers for their dependent adult children (Jennings 1987). Estimates of older retarded persons range from 50,000 to 315,000. Some are in institutions, but many live at home, where family members are the principal caregivers. Presumably, many caregivers are mid-old or old-old parents, who have had the care of their developmentally disabled children from birth or early childhood. They continue to deal with the issue of "perpetual parenthood," often in the context of social isolation or declining social supports. Jennings pointed out that the emotional and physical care of the adult child are combined with the stresses the parents may be experiencing as they deal with their own declining strength, especially if one or both suffer from chronic illness. The elderly parents face added health costs for themselves and special expenditures for the child in the face of reduced income at retirement. An added persistent worry is the matter of who will provide care and protection after the parents are no longer able to do so because of illness or death.

E. Brody (1981) observed, "Most older people are not sick and dependent. . . . Most do not need any more help than the normal, garden variety of reciprocal services that family members of all ages need and give each other on a day-to-day basis, and in times of emergency or temporary illness." Adult children (mostly daughters and daughters-in-law) "shop and run errands; give personal care; do household maintenance tasks; mobilize, coordinate and monitor services from other sources; and fill in when an arranged care program breaks down." Nonetheless, with advancing age, impairments do increase and lead to a greater need for help from adult children or other relatives. Brody pointed out that while the amount of help needed by noninstitutionalized older persons varies, about 8 to 10 percent are as functionally impaired as those in institutions. Another 10 percent are bedfast or housebound. In addition, 6 or 7 percent can go out, but only with difficulty. These groups, for the most part, live with or are cared for by adult children or other relatives.

Because people are living longer and impairments increase with age, more and more adult children in their late 60s and early 70s will need to provide care and services to their old-old parents. Those young-old children themselves may be experiencing lowered energy levels, interpersonal losses including widowhood, the onset of chronic ailments, reduced incomes, and other pressures. They may have unfulfilled expectations of retirement opportunities such as leisure, freedom, pursuing new interests, and moving to a new climate. As demographic trends continue and inappropriate assumptions about filial piety persist, society must provide supports to the family because it is the only informal support system for mid-old and old-old parents. Brody asked, "At what point does the public and professional expectation of 'filial responsibility' become social irresponsibility?"

The situation is even more difficult for people of color. Between 1970 and 1980, American Indian, Hispanic, and black elderly increased 65 percent, 57 percent, and 34 percent, respectively, compared with an increase of 25 percent of white elderly (Wood 1987). Wood stated: "The situation for middle-aged and older minority caregivers is clearly alarming: Their parents and grandparents suffer more health problems and have fewer financial resources than nonminorities, yet they're often excluded from existing support services or aided only cursorily. As a result, the burden of caring for minority elderly rests primarily on their families—a population that is itself struggling with many of the same problems."

For poor families dependent on public housing, regulations regarding the number of residents in an apartment often make it impossible to share living arrangements with an aged parent. Despite these factors, the extended family serves as a significant support to elderly blacks. Familial support is often reciprocal, as many elderly women and some men help in child rearing and in other ways. On all socioeconomic levels, "extended kin will 'squeeze blood from a turnip' to provide assistance to aged members" (Sussman 1985:431). Generational ties are strong, and elderly members are viewed as having legitimate claims for help. Mexican Americans and Puerto Ricans have a high degree of culturally based family interdependence. A New York study found that Puerto Rican elderly had more social interaction with their adult children than did whites and blacks (Cantor 1979).

A few studies suggest that the traditional Chinese value of filial piety and veneration of the aged may be eroding in some families as young American-born Chinese are influenced by American culture. Chen (1979), for example, found desperate poverty, as well as loneliness, language barriers, physical isolation, and a sense of familial dislocation, in a small sample of elderly Chinese American women and men residing alone in hotel rooms in the Los Angeles Chinatown. In her review of anthropological studies, Keith stated: "In Boston, for example, traditional kinship and inheritance patterns affect care of the elderly Irish and Chinese. In both groups, the child living nearest is likely to become the major caretaker when one becomes necessary. However, among the Irish, this is likely to be a daughter, among the Chinese a daughter-in-law" (1985:247). Nevertheless, Keith cautions that overgeneralizing leads to the false assumption that all elders with obvious ethnic identities are valued and cared for by their extended family. That is no longer the case for many. She suggested that one generalization is appropriate: when younger members of an ethnic group value their ethnic identity, the position of older members as symbols, specialists, or both is likely to be strengthened.

The need to provide outreach and information to elderly refugees and other older persons who do not speak English about their eligibility for programs, services, and benefits is a pressing one. Lack of information is a significant barrier to medical care and social services. Unaware of their eligibility for government assistance of up to three years, many refugees are very dependent for a variety of services on their adult children, of whom they disapprove because they are taking on strange American ways (Eastman 1988). However, eligibility of legal aliens for social and welfare services has recently been called into question in California, often a bellwether state with regard to national trends. At the time of this writing, the matter of services for legal aliens is uncertain.

The Mid-Old (75 to 84) and the Old-Old (85 and over)

"People now, regardless of their age, have more parents, grandparents, and great-grandparents than has ever been true before" (E. Brody 1981). The grandparent generation is providing care for the great-grandparent generation. The squeeze will be even greater because the baby-boomer cohort, when they become young-old, will have fewer children to assist them as they enter the ranks of the mid-old (probably many baby-boomer couples today have more parents than they have children). And with the upward trend in longevity, there will be more mid-old and old-old surviving and needing to be cared for. For example, there are more than 3 million people over 85 years of age, including more than 14,000 people who are over 100 years old.

Persons 85 and older constitute the fastest growing segment of the population in this country, and one of the fastest growing segments worldwide (Crossette 1996:5). The well-known Framingham (Massachusetts) Heart Study has followed a large sample of "normal" men and women over many years. Extensive research into disability among the now older participants was reported in 1983 (Briley 1983). The researchers found that men and women aged 75 to 84 were somewhat more likely to need help with social and physical tasks than the younger participants. Nevertheless, 77 percent of them were able to walk half a mile or more; 85 percent could climb stairs; 50 percent could perform heavy housework; and more than 90 percent were fully capable of carrying out activities of daily living. The researchers believed the group was fairly representative of persons aged 75 to 84 and reflected the better health of contemporary cohorts of the mid-old.

The researchers also remind us that at any given time about 5 percent of the elderly are patients in long-term-care facilities, and another 10 percent living in the community have comparable levels of disability and require assistance. It is these two groups who are of concern to social workers. The first group is considered in the next section. Among the second group are those who live alone. They are mostly women, very old, frail, and living on very low incomes. Older persons living alone constitute 55 percent of all those over 75 and 52 percent of all those over 85. A study of the problems faced by this group, conducted for the Commonwealth Fund Commission on Elderly People Living Alone (1987), found that among the national sample of 2,506 persons, 25 percent were childless, and another 20 percent did not have a son or daughter living within an hour's travel. Because of lack of social supports, the old-old living alone are at high risk for institutionalization. Half of all the respondents had lived by themselves for 10 or more years. Nearly 86 percent of them said they preferred living alone to any alternative they were aware of.

It appears that many of the old-old, who are mostly women, outlive their assets and struggle along on small Social Security benefits based on unskilled work or on their being widows of eligible workers who may have received only small benefits to begin with because of low earnings. Also, half of the women over age 75 and eligible for SSI and Medicaid are not receiving benefits, being unaware of the programs or of their eligibility for them. Both the mid-old and the old-old cohorts grew up in the early years of the twentieth century with an ethos of independence and self-sufficiency, and many prefer to struggle along on whatever income they have.

Despite their own poor health and poverty, more than one-third in the Commonwealth Fund study responded affirmatively when asked if they would accept a 5 percent cut in their Social Security income so that other elderly people would be guaranteed paid medical and nursing-home costs, home health services would be provided for all elderly people in need of such care, and no elderly person would live in poverty.

Health and Care Issues

From the standpoint of the mid-old or old-old parent no longer able to live independently because of infirmities, the move to the adult child's home and family may be perceived as relinquishing her or his independence and self-direction. Sometimes, former tensions between parent and child may resurface; more important, most older persons dread being a "burden" on their children. The literature frequently refers to a "role reversal" assumed to occur between elderly parents and their adult children as the parents become increasingly dependent. This is now regarded as an injustice both to the parents and to the adult children, overlooking the complex development of relationships and roles over time. It is questionable "whether a child can, psychologically, ever really be a parent to his or her parent or that an older adult can renounce or even wish to renounce the parental role" (Harbor Area Geriatric Program Staff 1985:1152). Adult children need, rather, to separate their relationship to the parent from what it was before and to establish a new relationship with new responsibilities. The Harbor Area staff suggests the use of the term "role change" to signify the new responsibilities.

For frail elderly (those at physical or mental risk, or both) who are not fully independent but nonetheless continue to live alone, as well as for many of those living with their adult children, some 1,400 day care programs around the country are a boon. Unfortunately, because most are funded by community sources (and have sliding fee scales) not many communities provide adult day care. Exemplary day care centers provide van transport to and from the center (usually for a small fee), a nutritious lunch, and recreational programming such as painting, crafts, gardening, poetry and music, games, movies, guest lecturers, and field trips. The staffs usually consist of nurses and social workers. Programs operated by hospitals may make medical and rehabilitative services available, including physical, occupational, and speech therapists. As day care programs provide a stimulating, health-oriented environment to their members, they serve to prevent premature institutionalization. They also provide needed relief to family caregivers, even permitting them to work full time. While nursing home costs average about $50 to $90 per day—"national estimates for the cost of one-year stays in a nursing home currently average about $22,000" (*Research Dialogues* 1989)—the average cost of adult day care is about $30 per day and may be met by private or federal insurance programs.

Another positive development for older persons with physical disabilities is that they, like younger people with disabilities, can benefit from increasing numbers of products and housing adaptations designed for their needs. Some products and adaptations are minor and inexpensive (like grab bars on a bath tub), and some are major and expensive (building a ramp to the front door). Home health care agencies may be able to pay for minor adaptations, and various catalogs of products are on the market. For practitioners working with older persons, hospital social workers, occupational therapists, and area agencies on aging can be helpful informants on products, adaptations, and the availability of possible loans and grants.

Mental impairment may accompany physical illness or be disabling in itself. Alzheimer's disease, named for the physician who first described it in 1906, is an irreversible, progressively deteriorating mental disorder. Usually considered a disease only of older persons, it also strikes some in young and middle adulthood, where its course is more rapid and severe. The cause is still unknown but the early-onset cases are believed to have genetic roots because the disease seems to run in families who also frequently have a child with Down syndrome or other chromosomal disorders. The disease that appears in the older years is referred to technically as SDAT (senile dementia, Alzheimer's type). Definitive diagnosis is possible only at autopsy, when the presence in the cerebral cortex of disease-specific neurofibrillary tangles can be established. Hence, differential diagnosis is difficult in cases of senility. The diagnosis of SDAT is made by ruling out other dementias through history, physical and mental examination, laboratory tests, and high-technology testing, which can be inaccurate. Some who are diagnosed as having SDAT may actually be depressed but not demented or may be suffering from fever, infection, cardiovascular conditions, or drug reactions, all of which can affect brain function and are treatable (Butler and Emr 1982).

Approximately 1.5 million Americans over 65, or 5 percent of the elderly population, are thought to suffer from SDAT. The disease is devastating to patient and family, and at least until the final stages, most SDAT patients are cared for at home because Medicare does not pay for long-term care. It is estimated that about half the patients over 65 in nursing homes suffer SDAT (most are on Medicaid). The onset is insidious, with beginning forgetfulness and occasional confusion, depressed mood, or disordered sleep. Many patients recognize that they are functioning less well and may be terrified, or they may deny what is happening. As the months go by, deterioration may be slowed by a stimulating, but not too stimulating, home environment and by keeping the person involved in useful tasks, physical exercise, and social contacts. If still continent and able to leave the house, the person's participation in a day care center is also helpful for patient and family.

As the tangles and areas of brain degeneration (termed *plaques)* increase over time, the symptoms worsen. The cognitive and memory dysfunction and disorientation gradually increase to the point where the individual cannot remember what occurred a few minutes before and does not know where she or he is. Hostile and uncooperative behaviors, wandering, incontinence, failure to recognize spouse or children, and a loss of awareness of the changes in oneself may be exhibited. The rate of decline and the extent of such losses vary in individuals. In the advanced stage, afflicted persons are totally unable to care for themselves and ultimately die. SDAT is now said to be the fourth leading cause of death among the elderly. While incurable, the condition is helped by environmental means to improve the quality of life, as described above, along with counseling for the family. Keeping patients safe by changes in the home to facilitate their functioning and keeping them healthy by careful personal hygiene and treatment are important (R. N. Butler 1975).

Dying and Death

Some of the literature on death and dying implies that the death of an elderly person is less difficult for the family to cope with because the social value of the elderly person is supposedly less, because her or his roles are less critical to family functioning, and because death comes at the age-appropriate time. However, after 40 or more years of a loving and satisfying relationship (or even a not-so-satisfying one), for the surviving spouse the loss may be just as excruciating, as it is for a younger person. Deaths of widowers within a year following the loss of the wife occur at a higher rate than corresponding rate of deaths of widows within a year following the loss of the husband. It is thought that the loss of one's spouse is harder for men to cope with than for women, perhaps because men have less experience in coping with their own basic and household needs and because the social ties of couples are usually maintained by the wife.

Peak (1977) described three general types of responses to dying by elderly persons themselves:

1. Most elderly persons accept dying as part of being old. Their mastery implies that they feel in control of their situation, based on a minimal amount of denial. Many have worked out the acceptance of their inevitable death long before the terminal phase, and many have made

plans for death or are ready to do so. For some in this group, perhaps, the acceptance of dying is facilitated by memories of a life of some satisfaction. The apparently universal tendency of the elderly to recall earlier experiences and to rework their memories in ways that develop a sense of continuity, integrity, and meaning to their life helps prepare them for the inevitability of death as part of life (R. N. Butler 1975). Religious beliefs, cultural patterns, and the love and caring of those held dear help ease the dying elderly person's transition to life's ending.

2. A small group of elderly persons appear to block out the idea of death completely. This reaction prevents their making the plans and preparations that might lead to a sense of closure and peace.

3. A still smaller group comprises those elderly who are greatly disturbed by ideas of death—their own or the death of those close to them. They spend time and energy avoiding the associated fears. It may be that within these two latter groups, the task of the acceptance of death as part of life is made more difficult as they look back upon an unhappy or disappointing past with anger or regrets. Pattison commented that those not ready to die "still question and doubt their existence. Death will be an intrusion unless and until they can affirm that their life was a unique existence to them, that allowed of no other existence" (1977b:26).

Kalish (1968) described a self-perceived social death, where an elderly person feels "as good as dead" and "may as well be dead." Such a self-perception may be precipitated by a terminal diagnosis, by feelings of isolation and helplessness, or by anxiety over increasing dependence. The aged person's loss of statuses and roles, the many personal losses, or indignities imposed by an uncaring institution can lead to these feelings. Kalish also described a category of psychological death in which the comatose, completely drugged, or senile patient is no longer aware that she or he *is*. Since social death and psychological death are reversible in varying degrees, practitioners working with the elderly and the terminally ill need to know how to reverse these conditions and how to prevent them in the first place. What is needed are increased human interaction, cognitive stimulation, and opportunities to function as a mature and responsible adult in whatever ways are still possible: securing information about what is happening to one's physical self; making decisions, however modest in extent; participating in planning next steps; and so on.

Suicide

Those over 65 have the highest suicide rate in the United States, and almost three-fourths of the relatively rare double suicides in Western society are committed by elderly couples. People over 65 constitute a disproportionate number of completed suicides, possibly as much as twice their expected numbers (Koenig and Blazer 1992). These government statistics are based on death certificates. Actual suicides are probably well above that rate, as older persons can easily cover up their suicides. They may stop visiting the physician, starve themselves, deliberately overdose on prescribed medications, or stop taking life-sustaining medications. Thus the cause of death may be listed as heart failure, diabetic complications, and so on. Older persons are more resolute in their desire to take their lives and succeed far more often than teenagers. Their success may indicate that the suicide is not a cry for help, as it is in the teenager who fails in the attempt, but a determination to end what has come be to an unendurable condition.

Older suicidal individuals rarely seek help. For example, only 2 percent of the calls to a Washington, D.C., suicide and depression hotline came from persons 65 and older. Many are reluctant to seek therapeutic help, although if they can be persuaded to go once, many older persons do continue. The reasons for suicide among older persons, especially mates, include the loss of the spouse, the loss of status and organizational affiliation, depression (estimated to be present in 15 to 20 percent of older persons and to underlie two-thirds of older persons' suicides), financial problems, chronic or life-threatening illness, fear of eventual nursing-home placement, or hopelessness and alcoholism.

Situational depression may be helped by support from relatives and friends, supplemented by professional counseling in some instances, but chemically based depression responds best to medication, combined with other forms of therapy. In this connection, a study of suicides in a retirement community demonstrated that elderly married individuals, and not only the widowed, need to be involved in kin networks, friendships, and community organizations such as senior centers or religious and fraternal groups. These social connections counteract the isolation of both widowed men and of married males who have no other social ties. While marriage is a restraining force against suicide, it must be reinforced by other connections if the suicide rate is to be reduced among older married persons. More preretirement counseling, bereavement groups, making sure that every elderly person has a telephone, and stricter gun laws (guns are the primary method of suicide in males) may help reduce the rate. Also, increased dissemination of information about suicide to professionals and the public, including the warning signs of depression (*Useful information on suicide* 1986), and educating older persons and families about hospice as a way to control pain in dying and ensure quality of life to the point of death might be important preventive measures.

In counterpoint to this discussion of preventing suicide is the national debate on doctor-assisted suicide as well as suicide as a personal and rational choice for those who seek release from life for many possible reasons, such as uncontrollable pain, pervasive disability requiring extensive personal aid, the loss of a life partner, and so forth. Opponents of any form of rational suicide bring opposing arguments to each of these reasons. This debate raises enormous ethical and practical issues that will try the values of all people at some point in their lives. All sides of the issue keep a wondering eye on events in Holland, which has legalized doctor-assisted suicide.

Elder Abuse

Another troubling health and social issue is elder abuse in families, nursing homes, psychiatric hospitals, board-and-care homes, and so on. Recognition of the seriousness and extent of elder abuse has been slow, although it is no newer a phenomenon than spousal and child abuse. It can be emotional in nature (verbal assaults and threats), physical (battering, shoving, shaking, tying to a bed or chair, or withholding physical care), medical (oversedating or failing to procure needed appliances such as walkers, glasses, or hearing aids), or financial (misuse of assets, exploitation, and scams). Accurate figures are difficult to obtain, but estimates suggest that 1 million of those 65 or older, or 1 out of 25, suffer abuse. How many at the hands of institutions and non-family individuals and how many at the hands of family members is unknown but one study reported slightly less than 10 percent of 404 clients attending a Cleveland Chronic Illness Center had been mistreated by a family member or a companion (Lau and Kosberg 1979).

The Federal Older Americans Act authorizes ombudsman programs in each state to investigate and act on complaints of abuse in long-term-care institutions. Most states now have laws requiring the reporting of elder abuse by individuals and institutions. In some areas, hospitals have formed interdisciplinary elder abuse teams. Matlaw and Mayer (1986) reported on complex practical, clinical, and ethical dilemmas that surface for social worker team members in the investigation and assessment of suspected elder abuse,

neglect, and mistreatment by families or institutions and in the social consequences of the mandated reporting. It bears repeating that respite services for
family caregivers and day care programs for older persons help alleviate the
intensive stress, frustration, and physical exhaustion many caregivers experience, which leads to abuse by a relatively few of them.

Long-term Institutional Care

While only 5 percent of the elderly are in long-term institutional care at any
given time, it is estimated that 20 percent of the older population are likely to
spend some time in a long-term facility (Atchley 1994). Institutional care
comprises several types, such as nursing homes (intermediate-care facilities),
skilled-nursing facilities, homes for the aged or retirement homes, rehabilitation hospitals, and psychiatric hospitals. This section considers nursing homes
that house the frail elderly (and the young chronically disabled), as these
homes are an important focus of professional and public attention. To a lesser
extent it considers also those homes for the aged that combine many types of
services.

Most patients in nursing homes, but not all, are women. Most are more
than 80 years of age, many have lost their friends and relatives, and some have
even outlived their children. Most frail elderly have multiple physical disabilities, and somewhat more than half suffer mental disability. R. N. Butler
(1975) stated that the rates of organic brain diseases and functional disorders,
such as some depressions and paranoic conditions, increase steadily each
decade after the age of 60. Many older persons with such disorders were discharged from state psychiatric hospitals under the twin policies of deinstitu-
tionalization and short-term treatment. Unable to maintain themselves in the
community without appropriate supports, some have become part of the sin-
gle-room-occupancy and homeless populations; many others have ended up
in nursing homes without any provision for in-house or outpatient rehabilitative mental health services. Professional social workers and other mental
health practitioners are not found on the staffs of most nursing homes. However, the 1987 Federal Nursing Home Reform Act required that by 1990 nursing homes with more than 120 beds have a full-time social worker with at least
a BSW degree.

It is true that some residents without relatives may feel isolated and alone
in the institution, except for possible visits from volunteers. As mentioned earlier, most families regard placement as a last resort when the parent's physical

or mental impairments become severe and deplete the caregiver's emotional and physical resources. Most families visit their parents regularly; bring them home for a weekend or holiday, depending on their condition; take them for outings; and so on. It is harder for families who live at a distance to maintain closeness, but many keep in touch by telephone, cards and letters, and an occasional visit. Increasingly, family agencies and social workers in private practice offer geriatric services to families living at a distance from their relative. These include case management, monitoring of care, visiting the resident, and keeping the family informed.

A serious concern about nursing-home care is a financial one. The cost can range from $22,000 to $35,000 a year or more, which quickly exhausts the personal resources of middle-income persons. Half the couples with a spouse in the nursing home are impoverished within 6 months. The only recourse is to apply for Medicaid, a means-tested welfare program, because Medicare does not reimburse the costs of long-term care (except in a skilled-nursing facility following hospitalization for an acute illness, if ordered by a physician, and then for only 100 days). In some states, Medicaid requires that all property or other assets must be used before aid is given.

A more rational response to the need for long-term care by the elderly is essential. Acute care is said to account for only 10 percent of the catastrophic health care costs of the elderly. Medicare reimbursement for home health care services, adult day care, and respite programs would provide a choice and would very likely prevent the premature institutionalization of many. Another criticism is that Medicaid was established to meet the health needs of poor children and adults of all ages, yet the present arrangement results in approximately 45 percent of Medicaid funds being used for long-term care of the elderly.

A second serious drawback of nursing-home care is environmental. In addition to feeling that placement is the final step before death itself, most elderly—unless they are totally disabled mentally—fear they will lose all sense of independence and self-direction in their lives. And indeed, many nursing homes do fail to provide opportunities for self-regulation, action, decision making, and control over one's life situation to whatever degree the patient's condition permits. At the same time, the elderly also differ from other groups in that sensory, mental, and physical impairments make them more dependent on their environment for well-being than other adults. Yet many nursing homes fail to provide stimulating physical and social settings that nourish the senses, the mind, the social interests, and the other capacities of their patients. The results are devastating, as the patients lose their sense of competence, their self-esteem, their self-direction, and their human relatedness (e.g., Vladeck 1980; Estes and Swan 1993).

In recent years, as a result of media attention and advocacy by families and the human service professions, including social work, some nursing homes have raised their standards of care. They provide recreation, crafts, reality-orientation programs, and outings, and they arrange to bring in pet dogs and cats to visit with the residents (National Institutes of Health 1988). Some have developed affiliations with nearby child care facilities for the exchange of visits for mutual pleasure and benefit. Some provide temporary respite care to relieve family caregivers, although it is expensive. Since 90 percent of nursing homes are for-profit institutions, the extent and rate of change have been limited. Federal standards, inspection, and sanctions have not been entirely successful in eliminating substandard care where it exists, although the ombudsman program and resident councils provide some leverage. With respect to social work, federal regulations do not require that social services be furnished by a professional social worker, but only that such a person serve as a consultant to the individual who does provide them. Such consultations cover many nursing homes, and some tend to define their role solely as that of supervisor of the consultee and not as advocate and consultant to the administration for promoting improved care.

Wells, Singer, and Polgar (1986), Canadian social work educators and researchers, developed an effective model for residents' empowerment in nursing-home care. Its success has led to its spread across Canada. Their demonstration-research projects began in 1970 with a succession of student units in Toronto's municipal system of nursing homes. Working with strengths already in the system, the students achieved remarkable improvements in services and in organizational structures that support the changes (Singer and Wells 1981). By 1982, when that project ended, the links among the residents' kinship, friendship, formal caregiving, and mutual-aid networks had been developed and strengthened; inappropriate staff and resident attitudes about older people and their families had been modified; and policy makers in the institutions had been influenced to provide structures for the continuation of services after the students left (Wells, Singer, and Polgar 1986). Students had also succeeded in supporting residents during the potentially destructive relocation process when one home was closed and the residents were scattered among several others (Singer and Wells 1981). Although the seven homes had previously had no social workers, they obtained funds for social work personnel after the project ended.

Wells, Singer, and Polgar developed an empowerment model that mobilizes the strengths of the residents, the staff, and the organization: "Engaging the clients themselves in the advocacy process helps to empower clients at the same time that it assures quality care" (1986:1). The model is designed to replace the medical and custodial models of long-term care, both of which are known to foster dependence and helplessness. It emerged out of a demonstration-action research project that was tested in two long-term institutions with a matched untreated pair of homes for comparison. Wells, Singer, and Polgar reported, "We were impressed by the capabilities that became evident in the elderly, despite their frailties and physical and mental impairments; we were impressed by the families' interest and dedication; we were impressed by the responsiveness and commitment of staff" (1986:3). The authors provided detailed guidelines for introducing into long-term facilities a process in which the elderly, their families, and the staff participate actively in policy and program development that enhance the well-being and quality of life of the residents and for creating a problem-solving structure to help the institution adapt to changes in the system and in the external environment.

In the United States, the long-term facilities that strive for quality of life, resident empowerment, and staff training tend to be the homes for the aged or home-and-hospitals. They are usually sponsored by religious or other non-profit organizations. While they vary in their mission, the best provide an attractive and functional physical setting and an active social setting. They foster individual choice of programs and activities and avoid rigid routines to the degree possible. Some, certified for Medicaid and Medicare reimbursement, combine several levels of care: hospital (chronic illness) and both skilled-nursing and intermediate care. Some also offer community services such as adult day care and training in gerontology for the service professions, and most have professional social workers, allied health professionals, nurses, and physicians on staff. Some provide rehabilitative services and a rich variety of recreational and cultural programs and activities, including resident councils. Unfortunately, there are some nursing homes that lack all or most of these features and become a living hell for their residents who may have no other alternatives. Helping professionals have an ethical obligation to identify and take action against these inhumane situations.

Adaptations Revisited

Just as people are wonderfully diverse, so, too, are the adaptations they achieve in their passage through time. Simic and Myerhoff (1978) enriched our understanding of growing old under varying circumstances with their suggestion of three universal themes: continuity, sexual dichotomy, and aging as a career. These are inseparable aspects of a single, shared, deep structure of aging, from birth to old age.

Continuity has three aspects. Spatial continuity is people's attachment to certain real, imagined, or mythological spaces that become part of the self or one's identity. Social continuity is the permanency, frequency, and intensity in relationships as they shift over time; some are face-to-face and some are vicarious and symbolic in either life or death. Cultural continuity is contact with and access to a coherent and relatively stable body of ideas, beliefs, values, and symbols. Depending on the society and the culture, and on the exigencies of life, a person may experience more discontinuities or more continuities in life. For example, members of the El Senior Center (Cuellar 1978) in Los Angeles had been cut off from the experiences of their childhood by virtue of their migration from Mexico. There were separated from the culture in which they had been socialized. They were cut off to some extent from their Americanized children and thus had lost a sense of intergenerational continuity. But they found the continuity and strength to structure their old age by turning to each other in their voluntary association. Cultural continuity was restored and savored.

Sexual dichotomy is the disparity in the aging process of men and women, as well as the sex differences in the ways in which older individuals adapt to status and role transitions. In the El Senior Center, female roles appeared to be better defined than male roles. Enjoying the traditional prestige accorded grandmotherhood, the women members easily assumed managerial roles in the center. For the men, masculinity had been defined as physical prowess, now in decline, and was associated with work roles no longer available. Simic and Myerhoff noted that different kinds of power are lodged in male and female statuses and roles: "Power peaks at different times for men and women, and where power declines for one sex, leaving a vacuum, the other frequently steps in to fill it" (1978:240). This statement echoes Guttman's hypothesis that as women age they become more active and dominant, and as men age they become more passive and nurturant.

Simic and Myerhoff view aging across the life course as a career, rather than as a series of losses. They emphasize "old age as a period of activity, participation, self-movement, and purposefulness: [Old age is a kind of work that requires] the constant expenditure of effort for sociocultural and physical survival. To live out each day with dignity, alertness, control over one's faculties, and mobility necessitates the output of tremendous energy." The notion of career also connotes long-term goals, and over the life course the individual "builds, or fails to build, a structure of relationships, achievements, affect, and respect that will give meaning and validation to one's total life at its close" (1978:240). Thus aging as a career represents a storing up of many kinds of resources. While there are inevitable losses, there are also accumulated gains.

As social workers well know, the gains and rewards are differentially distributed in our society because of differing experiences and capacities and, more significantly, because of location in the social structure. Different cultures are also likely to define success differently. A measure of success among the members of the El Senior Center was the skills they had developed in dealing with Anglo institutions and customs: literacy, bilingualism, and some awareness of the basic assumptions of the dominant society.

Thus old age as a career involves processes of construction and reconstruction, both psychologically and socially. Memories, the life story, narrative, autobiography, personal and family history—however such accounts are titled as they are told to others and oneself, they are significant parts of the creativity needed in the work of aging as a career. They are opportunities to relive, affirm, assess, and lend order to the variety of experiences, perceptions, feelings, actions, and relationships over the life course and to reevaluate their significance. They, like myth and ritual, represent the less tangible aspects of continuity. It is no wonder, then, that reminiscence in the "life review" (R. L. Butler 1963) has such therapeutic potency in social work practice with older persons.

Family Transformations: Young-Old, Mid-Old, and Old-Old

The conclusion to be drawn from the data presented in this chapter is that the elderly are extremely diverse: "Because of longer life-histories, with their complicated patterns of personal and social commitments, adults are not only much more complex than children, but they are more different from one another, and increasingly different as they move from youth to extreme old age" (Neugarten 1969). In addition, there are strong cohort, historical period, and cultural effects at work in creating diversity among the old. For most mid-old and old-old persons, the options for managing life events and transitions are apt to be limited because of diminished vigor and the likelihood of chronic illnesses, loss of spouse, dwindling income, and so on. Here the significance of the society and its social and health policies, the family and its capacity for love and caring, and the community and its sense of interconnectedness and communitas comes to the fore.

Walsh (1980) pointed out that while these processes hold potential for loss and dysfunction, they also provide opportunities for transformation and growth. The transitions include retirement, chronic illness or impairment due to physical or mental disability of self or spouse, the death of the spouse or friends and consequent loneliness, and the draining of limited finances and even poverty. For some, one or more of these events and transitions may occur before the age of 75. For others, they may not occur until after that age. Although some of these transitions are expectable, probably many will be experienced by the older person and her or his adult children as second-order developments requiring difficult second-order changes. Because of the great diversity among older persons, it is difficult to generalize the form that the transformations may take among the three age groups. Instead, we present a living example of mid-old and old-old people achieving successful transformations through a combination of individual, collective, and culturally based strengths as they managed many second-order developments. The example itself is a fitting conclusion to this chapter and to the book, for it is a celebration of life.

The example comes from an anthropological study of a group of Jewish mid-old and old-old women and men, immigrants to America from Eastern Europe, carried out by Barbara Myerhoff (1978a). Numbering about 300, they lived in an urban ghetto in Venice, California, isolated from their assimilated, sophisticated adult children by geographic distance. They were poor, frail, lonely, and isolated. They suffered from communal and social neglect, and even from physical abuse at the hands of young thugs who roamed the neighborhood. As members of the dilapidated Aliyah Senior Citizen's Community Center, they transcended the perils of poverty, neglect, loneliness, poor health, substandard housing, and even physical danger through their culture-based personal and collective strengths. The account of their lives, their rituals and celebrations, and their serious troubles and how they managed them is unforgettably moving.

They had migrated to the East Coast of the United States at the turn of the century, working mostly at unskilled and skilled labor. Most had liberal and socialist political beliefs, and many had been active in unions and various workers' movements. When retired, they moved as individuals or couples to California because of the climate and living conditions, leaving their more or less successful children behind. Aliyah's members suffered great discontinuities. Their eastern European *shtetl* (village) culture in which their identity was rooted had been wiped out by the Holocaust, along with the inhabitants. For them there was no way to reestablish the ties of their childhood; their children had not been socialized to the values and norms of the old culture; and even their treasured language, Yiddish, was threatened with extinction. Yet as a collectivity in their voluntary association, the Aliyah Center, they found communitas—a spirit that enabled them to begin to repair the tragic ruptures in their lives. Together, they re-created the environment and the cultural values of their youth by reviving their common language and through culturally based myths and stories, through secular and sacred rituals and celebrations, and even through their sometimes disorderly rivalries and disagreements. Most of the members knew each other well as they had lived in this Yiddish ghetto for two or three decades. Most were in their mid-80s or older.

The subculture they created combined elements from their childhood beliefs and customs with modern urban American practices and attitudes, adapted to their present needs and circumstances and providing them with the essential sense of personal and ethnic worth (Myerhoff 1978b). In a sense, they could reconnect their old age to their childhood because of their common destiny "as poor outsiders and marginal members of society, a situation which did not prevail in their middle years" (Myerhoff 1978b:236). Indeed, their present circumstances recalled *shtetl* life for them. Myerhoff described in detail the incredible odds against which they struggled. Their successes included being able to get up each morning, prepare and pay for food, visit friends, and walk to the beach. These activities required skills of financial management in the face of dire poverty, knowledge of how to survive with little and of how to conserve declining physical energies, knowledge of the available services, and the ability to manipulate their obligations to friends or family.

Their continuing existence was a triumph: "They had outlived all their enemies—Cossacks, Nazis, anti-Semites—and successful defiance of those determined to extinguish them was a conspicuous source of pride" (Myerhoff 1978b:170). Myerhoff wrote of one 95-year-old man that he knew how to look at the inevitability of death without seeking to hasten it, and he knew how to bring the past into the present without remaining fixed on it or using it in negative comparisons with the present. He was able to substitute new standard and desires for himself as old ones were no longer attainable. He generated from within appropriate measures of self-worth in a continuous process of construction and reconstruction. He used thinking, talking, and writing his life story to stave off occasional depression, anxiety, and fear of senility. As the "elder" in their midst, he advised the members on the elements of a positive response to old age: "humor, perspective, the preservation of tradition, the necessity for continual learning, and adapting to change" (1978a:223). He was a symbol to the others of aging as an admirable career. In all these ways, he organized his conception of himself and the meaning of his life, epitomizing the integration of internal and external forces (Myerhoff 1978b).

Like the women at the El Senior Center, the women of Aliyah coped with their difficult circumstances better than did the men. Their skills in establishing social relationships with each other gave them a sense of their own power and meaning, in spite of the environment's negative attitudes toward them and the powerlessness of the traditional female role in their culture. The men, severed from their economically based and intellectually oriented roles, had less adaptability and vitality in the present circumstances than they would have had in the natural course of aging in the original society.

Simic and Myerhoff commented on their collection of cross-cultural studies:

> We have encountered elderly survivors wending their way toward the culmination of life, sometimes following culturally designated routes, and at others traversing terra incognita. For some, this task has met with satisfaction and success, for others it has resulted in misery and failure. Old age has not been the same for everyone. Some have built their future carefully while others have foundered along the way regardless of the cultural context.
>
> (1978:245)

At the close of this book, you, the reader, and we, the authors, may join Simic and Myerhoff in their hope that, "With luck one day we, too, will find ourselves in old age" (1978:245). Yes, a healthy old age, yes; a constructive and contributing old age; a loving and loved old age, yes, yes.

Stage Models of Behavior and Development

Several theories of personality development based on invariant, universal, sequential stages are still used by many social workers and other professionals in the human services. We describe briefly the theories of Sigmund Freud; Heinz Hartmann, Anna Freud, and Erik Erikson; and Jean Piaget and Lawrence Kohlberg. Such brevity fails, inevitably, to do justice to the complexity and richness of the various ideas. Hence, additional readings are suggested, especially more recent research based on these theories. Students might also be interested in the biographies that are available on some of the major theorists.

Sigmund Freud (1856–1939)

Freud sought rational explanations for irrational behavior, such as "glove hysteria" in which only the hand would be paralyzed, whereas the nerves controlling the hand extended into the forearm as well, so there was no physiological way the hand *alone* could be paralyzed. Something in the mind—and for Freud especially the unconscious mind—was at work. He evolved a complex series of explanations and a corresponding practice that focused on unconscious conflicts with the conscious and social realms. We briefly summarize his ideas in terms of five dimensions of personality, work extending over 50 years.

1. Topographic or Depth Dimension: Early in his work, Freud postulated the existence of the unconscious (the largest portion of personality, inaccessible to conscious awareness because it is composed of antisocial wishes that would bring censure if made public; so they are repressed); the conscious (the awareful portion of personality); and the preconscious (that which can be brought into awareness by mental effort).

2. Structural Dimension: Freud expanded this first dimension by postulating several distinct portions of the psyche. The id (the first to emerge and largely unconscious portion of psyche that contains antisocial sexual and aggressive drives), the ego (the second to emerge—out of the id—in order to solve problems and connect the person to reality, and the superego (SE), which splits off of the ego and contains values, expectations, and sanctions internalized from the parents' behavior toward the child—this is the conscience. The ego ideal is the aspiration part of SE, formed from observing various models.

   Id operates on primary process—seeking pleasure, avoiding pain—by imagining what one desires. This imagining doesn't always get what it wants, so the ego emerges and operates on secondary process, a form of rational problem solving, negotiating to meet basic needs. Manifest conflicts occur between the unconscious versus conscious versus superego in terms of how the person ought to behave in given situations.

3. Dynamic Dimension: Freud also discussed the libido, a generalized pleasure-seeking drive, and much later, an aggressive drive (seeking destruction and death). These two forces, in various combinations, energize how the person behaves in the real world.

4. Developmental or Genetic Dimension: This dimension includes Freud's familiar and controversial discussions of the oral, anal, phallic (or immature genital), latency, and mature genital stages of development—each being the temporary focus of pleasure seeking. His discussions of the oedipal-electra complexes occur here, where the child has unconscious sexual wishes regarding the opposite-sex parent and out of frustrated attempts and imagined harms comes to a resolution by identifying with the same-sex parent. Ideas such as penis envy and castration fears also developed in this discussion.

5. Economic Dimension (as in expenditure of energy): Infants form an image of what they desire and thereby invest libidinal energy in that object (cathexis)—usually a person who is a source of satisfactions for the infant. But this energy is not clearly focused in action, so frustration is inevitable. (Hence, ego emerges to try more effective problem solving.) Defense mechanisms are various unconscious mental maneuvers a person takes to deal with experiences of anxiety that signal the emergence of an antisocial impulse. These mechanisms (e.g., denial, projection, reaction formation, etc.) deny aspects of reality and are only partly and temporarily successful in changing the problem.

Therapy

How to make contact with the unconscious and resolve its irrational demands? Freud discovered over time that if patients freely associated whatever thoughts came into their mind, some unconscious ideas as symbols would emerge and could be understood and resolved. Dreams too were a "royal road" to the unconscious, which could be interpreted through dream (symbol) analysis. The patient often formed a transference relationship with the therapist now representing people and forces from early childhood; working through these feelings and symbolic experiences permitted resolution of the underlying unconscious conflict. Freud's entire theory and many of its component concepts have been criticized on many grounds, especially the difficulty of empirically testing the ideas. Some writers find Freud's thinking to be a beginning point for fruitful practice (see L. H. Silverman 1976; Horvath and Luborsky 1993).

Heinz Hartmann (1894–1970), Anna Freud (1896–1982), and Erik H. Erikson (1902–1994): Ego Psychology

Hartmann, Anna Freud, and Erikson were consummate Freudians, true believers in the fundamental position that Sigmund Freud had staked out. But each one chose to expand the ego aspect of Freud's id-ego-superego trilogy, of which Freud had emphasized the id.

Hartmann was concerned with adaptation to social reality (Hartmann 1958). Whereas Freud had viewed the ego as emerging out of id, Hartman assumed that ego has independent energy and is not derived from id nor dominated by sexual and aggressive drives. At birth, the infant has "the primary autonomous sphere of the ego," which contains unconflicted functions such as crying, sucking, the physical skeletal structure that becomes central in movement, and sensory-perceptual and intellectual capacities. The infant is also given the evolutionary genetic inheritance of humankind and is thus able to deal with an "average, expectable environment." There were areas of conflict of id and society (in the form of parents), so that conflicted ego functions did arise out of id ("the secondary sphere of autonomy of the ego"), such as anxiety, reality testing, object relations, and impulse control (which operates on Freud's secondary process thinking and the reality principle). A person's ego is some combination of the primary and secondary spheres, and depending on circumstances (such as severe anxiety or loving supportive family, etc.) one or the other may dominate a person's functioning.

Anna Freud's upbringing was the stuff of which Freudian dreams are made. Suffice to say she had a lifelong quest to attain her father's love. She became a lay analyst, was analyzed by Sigmund, and became a close helper. She became a teacher of children but did lay analysis too (she analyzed Erikson). Her friendship with Dorothy Burlingham (who had brought her children to be analyzed by Sigmund) led to the experimental Jackson Nursery and later the Hampstead War Nursery in London, and to Anna Freud's major contributions to child analysis and ego psychology. Her early work *The Ego and the Mechanisms of Defense* summarized and added to this literature and emphasized a balanced consideration of id and ego forces in analyzing clients. She took on Melanie Klein (the leading psychoanalytic reconstructionist in post–World War II England) and worked with Yale people on a psychoanalytic view of child placement promoting placement with the "psychological parents"—those who truly wanted and valued the children versus the legal "biological parents" (see Goldstein, Freud, and Solnit 1973).

Erikson, as a young man, was an itinerant artist who, by astonishing luck and enormous talents, made contacts with significant people throughout his life—Sigmund and Anna Freud, especially, but also anthropologists, psychologists, sociologists, and political scientists—and developed into a major contributor to psychoanalytic thinking on human development. His *Childhood and Society* interconnected the biological organism, the psychological ego, and the member of society in a universal stage theory. Beyond Freud's psychosexual stages were Erikson's psychosocial stages in which an epigenetic principle was applied: Each stage of bio-psycho-social-cultural growth occurs out of the prior developments. The "eight stages of man" involved genetically determined growth meeting socioculturally determined experiences at various *zones* of the body that challenged the person ("crisis") to develop, to resolve the crisis if possible, ultimately seeking his own identity by incorporating the resolutions of these normal crises into his personality. Erikson wrote many important books, on Luther, Gandhi, identity, and youth and crisis, ending with *Vital Involvement in Old Age* (coauthored with his wife, Joan, and H. Kivnick 1986). He has greatly influenced social work as well as many other areas. Critics point to sexist aspects of his writings, common to psychoanalysis as well.

Jean Piaget (1896–1980) and Lawrence Kohlberg (1927–1987)

Jean Piaget was a "genetic epistemologist," that is, one who studies the genesis of the process of adaptive knowledge. A brilliant student, he had his first paper published at age 10. He was trained in biology and worked with Alfred Binet on intelligence tests but with regard to the cognitive processes that led children to respond (think) the way they did. He evolved his own subjective but innovative methods to test and to understand this process of cognitive development and often studied his own children.

One senses the vitalist biologist behind all his contributions: people adapting to the environment as part of the process of living. For Piaget, knowledge is a process, not a body of information. To know is to act on something, physically or mentally. The purpose of thought and behavior is to adapt to the environment in ever more satisfying ways. Piaget offers a distinctive perspective on mind: People's cognitive structures are called schemata (singular is schema). These are images of actions-with-regard-to-things that people have built up through repetitive experiences. Human development involves acquiring ever greater quantities of interlocking schemata. Piaget's central term is adaptation, which involves the dynamic equilibrium between two major processes: assimilation and accommodation. Assimilation is the process of taking in (understanding) events in the world by matching perceived features of those events with one's existing schemata, when possible. This involves reshaping environmental input to fit existing schemata; this is how people influence (or shape) their environment. Accommodation involves the process of altering existing schemata to permit assimilating events in the world that cannot be ignored and that would be incomprehensible otherwise. This involves reshaping existing schemata to fit environmental input; this is how the environment influences people.

The causes of acquiring schemata include: (1) internal maturation, (2) physical experience (direct interaction with events, which cannot be taught), (3) social experience (i.e., formal teaching), and (4) "equilibrium" (interaction among items 1 through 3). People can be described in terms of the levels and stages of their cognitive development, which are universal, invariant, irreversible, gradual, and consolidating:

Level 1. Sensorimotor—birth to about 2: to know is to sense; object permanence
Level 2. Preoperational—2 to about 7: egocentric speech; start decentering
Level 3. Concrete operational—7 to about 11: mental operations but directly related to visible objects
Level 4. Formal operational—11 to about 15: operate on images of past, present, and future; adult cognitive abilities and logical operations

Lawrence Kohlberg was a Piagetian who focused on moral reasoning and stages of moral development, expanding on Piaget. Levels and stages of moral reasoning (which are universal, invariant, irreversible, etc.):

Level 1. Premoral: Stage 1: punishment and obedience; Stage 2: instrumental behavior

Level 2. Conventional: Stage 3: conformity; Stage 4: law and order

Level 3. Postconventional: Stage 5: social contract; Stage 6: universal ethical principles

People exist predominantly at one stage, but have elements of lower and higher stages. People move to higher stages of moral reasoning by dissatisfaction with existing schemata and attraction to higher ones. Arbuthnot (1992) demonstrates the utility of this approach with a group of delinquent youth who showed both attitudinal and behavioral change in more prosocial directions. Gilligan (1982) criticizes Kohlberg and Piaget for gender bias. Others criticize their subjective methods.

Nonstage Models of Behavior and Development

In this appendix, we offer brief descriptions of theories of human behavior and development that do not assume any necessary sequential ordering among events. Yet these theories have proven to be very useful in a variety of contexts where helping professionals need guidance on the nature of human behavior and how changes might be introduced. We briefly review the work of Albert Bandura, B. F. Skinner, Ivan Pavlov, and a group of communication theorists (Virginia Satir in particular). We also review general systems theory, two theories of oppression (Frantz Fanon and Paulo Freire), and feminist theory.

Albert Bandura's Social Learning Theory and Social Cognitive Theory

Albert Bandura (1925—) combines the methodological rigor of Skinnerian behaviorists with interest in complex human concerns of humanists and psychoanalysts to generate a comprehensive theory of human action that is based on extensive empirical research (see Bandura 1986).

Skinner believed that learning occurs through the direct application of reinforcers to a behavior. For Bandura, such trial and error learning in complex and lethal activities such as crossing a busy street or operating on a person doesn't make any logical sense. Something has to be going on in the learner's mind, based on experiences with other people, to perform such complex behaviors. Bandura's theory suggests that "human functioning is explained in terms of a model of triadic reciprocality in which behavior, cognitive and other personal factors, and environmental events all operate as interacting determinants of each other" (Bandura 1986:19). Human behavior is viewed as an emergent and interactive product of personal factors (cognitive and affective components) interacting with environmental factors (the social and physical environment). Let's examine these three aspects of the theory.

People have the cognitive capability to symbolize, thus potentially creating ideas that transcend sensory experiences. People can generate and test possible solutions to problems symbolically and select the best plan before acting. They are not driven by conflicts from the past (Freud) nor from immediate reinforcers in the present (Skinner). Rather, they are capable of purposive behavior because they can conceive of the future (forethought) and the likely outcomes of their prospective behavior. Thus motivation involves anticipated future reinforcers. The "future" becomes a current motivator by being represented symbolically in the present. The behaviors of other people represent an important part of the environmental context. People from watching what other people do (complex behaviors) and what happens to them (reinforcement/punishment), and thus acquires rules for generating and regulating their own behaviors.

People do not have total free will (as Rogers argues), nor are they totally determined (as Skinner argues). Rather, people are partially free in the positive sense of the "exercise of self-influence," achieved through thought, skills, and motivation within the limits of a given environment. "Partial personal causation of action involves at least partial responsibility for it" (Bandura 1986:39, 40). This idea of self-regulation leads to a critical concept for Bandura, self-efficacy, which mediates knowledge, skills, and motivation on the one hand, and behavior on the other. A person has to know what to do, know how to do it, and anticipate positive reinforcement for doing it—and has to believe that he or she can do it (this is the self-efficacy belief)—in order to perform a particular action. "Perceived self-efficacy is a judgment of one's capability to accomplish a certain level of performance" (Bandura 1986:391). It involves a generative capability in which cognitive, affective (motivational), and behavioral skills are organized into integrated courses of action to serve specific purposes.

Bandura identifies four sources of self-efficacy. First, successful mastery of some part of the task is the most influential source of efficacy information. The second source of self-efficacy information is the vicarious modeling of similar people doing similar things with successful outcomes. A third source of self-efficacy is the verbal persuasion used to talk people into believing they will be able to achieve some task—Bandura notes verbal persuasion alone is limited in its power to create enduring increases in self-efficacy; it also may raise unrealistic beliefs that invite failure. The least influential source of self-efficacy is one's personal readings of physiological arousal (e.g., nervousness may indicate low self-efficacy and become a self-fulfilling prophecy).

B. F. Skinner's Operant Learning and
I. Pavlov's Respondent Conditioning

B. F. Skinner (1904——1990) was a behavioral psychologist whose basic studies in learning were applied in education, therapy, child development and child rearing, and in many other aspects of society; some of his ideas were very controversial. He introduced a large number of terms that have become part of the working vocabulary of psychologists and others. These brief notes describe the background for his work, some of the major ideas he enunciated, and some criticism of his point of view.

Russian physiologist Ivan Pavlov (1849——1936) developed what has been called classical or respondent conditioning, which follows invariably this pattern:

CS (Conditioned Stimulus)————————————➤CR (Conditioned Response)

UCS (Unconditioned Stimulus)————————➤UCR (Unconditional Response)

Pavlov's classical or respondent conditioning pattern:
Time is viewed flowing from left to right as these two
sets of CS-CR and UCS-UCR are paired together.

The CS is introduced slightly ahead of the UCS, which leads to a natural UCR; after a number of paired repetitions (or even once in some traumatic cases), the CR occurs after the CS alone but slightly weaker and slower than the UCR. Second-order conditionings can occur to the prior CS–CR connection, for example, security blankets for a nursing infant. A second signal system involved verbal behavior (symbolic behavior), thus accounting for a full range of human behavior, without assuming invisible entities like minds or souls.

Skinner demonstrated a second kind of conditioning (operant or instrumental). For instance, infantile behavior is freely emitted (no known stimulus causing it). If the parents (or the environment) respond to that behavior in a way satisfying to the infant, this consequence is likely to strengthen the chance that the infant will repeat a similar action. Almost all human behavior is the result of respondent or operant conditions (mostly from operant). Learning occurs by the pattern of consequences the child's behavior receives. Let's look at the logical pattern of the connections between the environment's positive or negative consequence, presented or removed, and a person's desired or undesired behavior, which will either tend to increase or decrease:

The effect on the person's behavior is likely to be a(n):

	Increase	Decrease
If a given type of consequence from the environment (parents, teachers, etc.) is		
Presented	A positive consequence is presented in the presence of desired behavior; this is positive reinforcement.	A negative consequence is presented in the presence of undesired behavior; this is positive punishment.
Removed	A negative consequence is removed in the presence of desired behavior; this is negative reinforcement (or escape behavior).	A positive consequence is removed in the presence of undesired behavior; this is negative punishment (or response cost).

Extinction is the removal of any consequence in the presence of undesired behavior, as in "time out" procedures. Skinner asserts that planned environmental consequences can lead to desired behaviors, as in his utopian novel *Walden II*. We can break down complex tasks into simpler ones and reward each step of mastery (programmed learning). We can give positive or negative consequences to a person's behavior, which will tend to make him or her behave as we wish (e.g., parental discipline and child rearing, teaching, law, therapy, etc.). Some critics find this approach mechanistic (Rogers); others consider it unable to handle innate generative behaviors (like language learning; Chomsky) or complex behaviors (Bandura).

Communication Theories

Virginia Satir (1916–1988) was a social worker who collaborated with psychiatrists Don Jackson, Jay Haley, Paul Watzlawick, and others on a communication theory for work with families and groups. We use her writings as accessible materials on this model. The basic terms for communication theory are

One party (S/R) sends a message (output) across a channel (air, print, etc.) to the other party (R/S) who receives the input, processes it (for meaning, etc.), and makes a response (output) across some channel to the original party.

Two - Party Communication System

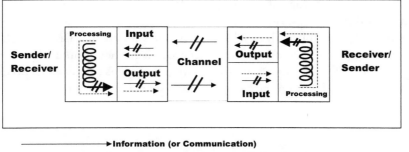

———————————→ Information (or Communication)

- - - - - - - - - - - - - - →Metacommunication (often nonverbal communication
which always flows with the verbal/written communication,
qualifying it, either enhancing or negating part or all of the
communication.)

// = Noise, which may <u>potentially</u> influence (distort or make unuseable)
any or all components of the social communication system.
(This is indicated by an arrow and two (2) hatched lines, —//——→)

This constitutes one communication circuit. In addition to the message (content-bearing information) there is a metamessage or metacommunication that qualifies the message in some way, extending it, modifying it, or even denying it. Metacommunications tend to be nonverbal (intonations, gestures, etc.). Every message has a metacommunciation, involving affective as well as cognitive content. The main issue is potential discrepancy between messages and metamessages. To which should the receiver respond? Noise (interference with clarity of message) can occur at any place throughout the circuit (e.g., hearing difficulty, aphasia, bad phone connection). As communication circuits are continually repeated over the life course, especially among people in families, friendship, and work groups, information cumulates and becomes the memories of the past and expectations about the future. These common and shared memories and expectations become the norms or rules of the group. All social life depends on these collective memories.

"Family homeostasis" (D. D. Jackson) refers to behaviors in which the family acts to achieve a balance in relationships, whether healthy or not. For example, a "family secret" might involve what we all do and say—even without being aware that we are doing this—to make excuses for dad's alcoholism, or what we do and say that puts junior in a double bind (defined below). Workers may discover these family secrets by looking at the group's repetitive, circular communication patterns and may therefore bring out the (unhealthy) pattern for public scrutiny and change. These family rules may be dysfunctional for one or more members of the family ("identified clients"), even though all members are party to the rules. It is often difficult for the others to think of themselves as part of the family problem.

In general, people with problems are people with communication problems. It is the communication system that needs fixing, not the individuals per se. The identified patient is simply one party to the whole, all of which needs understanding. Focus on the communicating system, not the individuals.

Double Bind

A problematic double bind is a "damned if you do; damned if you don't" situation. If a person is locked into that situation without escape, he or she may be literally driven mad because of contradictory demands (e.g., "stick up for your rights, but don't talk back to me"). A therapeutic double bind is a form of prescribing the symptom; if a person can do/not do what is problematic, then he/she is in control of that problem and it isn't a problem. (E.g., "You say you think you're going crazy; OK, go ahead. You're in a doctor's office and it's safe. Go ahead.") Therapy involves many ways of helping people with communication problems back to healthy communications. "A mature person is one who, having attained his majority, is able to make choices and decisions based on accurate perceptions about himself, others, and the context in which he finds himself; who acknowledges these choices and decisions as being his; and who accepts responsibility for their outcome" (V. Satir 1967:91).

General Systems Theory

At an epistemological level, general systems theory (GST) was a response to (1) new ideas in the physical sciences that emphasize patterns, processes, relativity, and uncertainty, over the earlier Newtonian, mechanistic laws thought to govern the physical world; (2) new ideas in the biological sciences that emphasize a holistic understanding of living organisms in their environments; and (3) new ideas in the philosophy of science that question the assumption of objectivity, the separateness of the observer and the thing observed, while recognizing the social construction of reality and the operation of personal and society values in science.

In GST a *system* is construed as an organized whole, usually defined as a set of interacting parts enclosed within a *boundary* that separates the system from its *environment,* which is everything outside the boundary. Some systems have visible boundaries, like skin or fences; other systems have less clearly demarcated ones or changing ones, for instance the boundaries of a family or community. Membership requirements in a group form another kind of boundary, as does a language that is used to "keep out" the uninitiated, such as medical jargon for the specialist that is unintelligible to the lay person.

GST proposes that biological and social systems are *open,* in contrast to mechanistic or physical systems (such as machines or a rock), which are *closed systems.* Being open means there are continuous interchanges with the environment across their boundaries, which support survival and development. *Inputs* into the system from the environment include information, matter, and energy. Open systems are made up of matter and energy; they are organized by information. Thus throughout the life course of the system, it exchanges any or all of these inputs with the environment by a process termed *input-transformation-output.* For example, human beings need nutrients, such as food, that are ingested to add to the body's matter and to supply energy. Eating a wholesome diet, such as low-fat, low-sodium, low-cholesterol foods, provides positive feedback by creating a healthier system.

GST describes a system of nested systems. That is, the individual is a complete system in his or her own right but is also composed of biophysiological subsystems that are complete in their own right, such as an organ or even a cell. Likewise, the individual is a subsystem to larger sociocultural systems. Some GS theorists look for common principles across all systems, such as various system-level responses to information overload (J. G. Miller). Because the system is composed of interacting parts, what happens in one part of the system reverberates through all its parts, influencing them to some degree. The boundaries between systems and their environments vary in degrees of permeability, but all living systems have permeable boundaries so as to stave off entropy, which besets closed systems. *Entropy* refers to the fact that closed systems inevitably run down, become disorganized, and then are unable to transform energy, matter, and information, or produce further work. Open systems can, up to certain limits, store energy, matter, and information to stave off disorganization, like refrigerating food, keeping an address book, or storing fat in our tissues.

Open systems grow, develop, and change over time and space, and maintain a dynamic or changing equilibrium, rather than a static one such as closed systems maintain. By virtue of open systems' continuous input-transformation-output processes, these systems oscillate due to the adjustments in these processes. To survive, an open system must keep these oscillations within normal limits for its kind of system. So-called normal limits are often referred to as a system's characteristic steady state.

To keep within system limits, the system must draw on internal feedback processes to inform it about the relationships among its parts and on external feedback processes to inform it about the environment and its own relationships with the environment. Internal feedback includes biological, physiological, and psychological processes. External feedback includes such processes as the verbal and nonverbal expressions, perceptions, attitudes, expectations, and behaviors of other individuals; the sanctions exerted positively or negatively by social systems; the reactions and responses of physical settings; and many other kinds of information.

Inputs from the environment influence, shape, or alter the system; outputs from the system influence, shape, or alter the environment. This is a metaphor of the reciprocal, transactional life processes of human adaptation described in chapter 1. GST is necessarily more abstract because it refers to specific properties that are common across the tremendous range of open systems, from cells to society. It may be that insights from one level may lead to thinking and solutions for other levels.

Theories of Oppression

Theories of oppression are likely to consider several major topics: What is oppression (to those oppressed)? What is in it for the oppressors? How can oppression be eliminated and not restarted in a new form or by new people? We consider just two theorists of oppression, both of whom have had enormous impact throughout the world.

Frantz Fanon (1925–1961) was born in Martinique, West Indies, a French overseas department (state), and was thus officially French. His family was upper middle class in a society divided between rich and poor, but his experience with colonialism began when white French sailors were blockaded on the island by the British in World War II as the enemy (i.e., troops of the Nazi-controlled Vichy government). These sailors took over the island and exploited the black natives, especially the women. Fanon eventually volunteered for the Free French movement and served in Morocco, observing more French colonialism. After the war, he trained as a doctor, later psychiatrist (a mixture of Freud and Marx). He interned under a doctor using a therapeutic milieu concept in Algeria. About 1954 the Algerian Liberation Movement began (against France), and the police and military fought these groups, torturing them and killing them with impunity. Fanon was in the strange situation of being psychiatrist to victims and oppressors. He became increasingly revolutionary and was at risk of arrest (as many doctors and nurses had been). He began to work as publicist for the revolution, as well as writing his major books, including *The Wretched of the Earth, A Dying Colonialism, Black Skins, White Masks.* He died of leukemia.

The oppressor gains an enhanced sense of self through exploitation of others. Repeated exposure to oppression may lead vulnerable individuals to internalize the negative images projected by oppressors; this leads to a distinction between the oppressor without and the oppressor within (victims oppressing themselves). Oppressed peoples may develop adaptive paranoia so as to be continually on the alert. The danger of the end of foreign colonialism is that some native leaders may take over roles (and oppression) from the foreigners. The real basis for racism was economics and politics.

Paulo Freire (1922–1997) was a Brazilian educator who developed a successful literacy program for slum dwellers and peasants, which also involved addressing their learned helplessness. He challenged them to learn as a cultural-political act so as to take control of their own lives. He was so successful in empowering these poor that the Brazilian military forced him into exile, where his work has been a catalyst for community development, education, and health worldwide.

Education is never neutral; it is always in a cultural-political context that influences the process. Education begins with the experiences of the people and either challenges or reinforces the existing social structures, such as the ones that made and are keeping some people poor. Invited into a village to teach literacy, Freireans would list common local terms, *povo* (people), *fome* (hunger), *voto* (vote), and so on, whose syllables would be broken down and regrouped to form other word sounds. Teaching these syllables and the emerging new words, the peasants learned political expressions (e.g., *o voto e do povo* [the vote belongs to the people]) and political consciousness. The small group process was a dialogue, student and teacher as colearners (you can't have authoritarian instructors teaching democratic content), with the goal of critical thinking (conscientization) about the basic causes of conditions in society and how to change them, gaining control over one's own life. This is also termed liberatory teaching, a theory of learning combined with egalitarian social change. Freire greatly influenced the U.S. civil rights movement (see Shor 1987).

Feminist Theory

There are many writers in feminist theory and many points of view. In reviewing this literature, we note some common themes and concepts. Feminism emerged as a social movement at the 1848 Seneca Falls conference with its Declaration of Sentiments: "We hold these truths to be self-evident: that all men and women are created equal." What feminists (both women and men) were seeking was redress of discriminations against women (no legal status, no vote, no advanced education, etc.) and progress in full citizenship for women (performing any job of which they were mentally and physically capable, enjoying all civil and human rights, and accepting their responsibilities, etc.). Contemporary feminists seek similar goals against subtler discriminations. Many, but not all, feminists share the following principles and values.

Empowerment

Seek egalitarianism (equality of all people); use nonhierarchical social arrangements to achieve social goals; enable/empower people to be all they can be; engage in nonviolent problem solving; be inclusive (of all who wish to participate).

Value the Process (as well as the product)

Even good ends cannot justify the use of bad means (Kant); develop a process of goal seeking through education and democratization of members.

Unity

No one is free until all are free; encourage sisterhood and solidarity (against the enemy of equality in all matters); have respect for differences while preserving uniqueness; be nonjudgmental of others; diversity is a source of strength.

Conflict

Conflict is inevitable (Marx) and peace is achievable; be assertive rather than passive or aggressive; seek the end of patriarchy as a system of subordination of women and privilege of men; individual problems (such as psychological depression) always reflect sociopolitical conditions as well individual conditions.

Openness to Different Ways of Thinking

Be open to nonlinear, holistic thinking and multidimensional thinking; accept that there may be many "truths"; be open to spirituality.

Consciousness Raising

Rename and re-create social reality—tell and value "her-story" rather than "his-tory" (Boulding), both for individual women and women in general; seek liberation through one's own actions—self-reliance (Emerson) rather than dependency on men; having responsibility is good, but sharing responsibility is better; use support groups (e.g., in domestic violence, rape, but also math anxiety support groups).

Interrelatedness of All Things

Eschew false dichotomies between men and women because the potential for similar psychosocial behavior/achievement is greater than the differences that are biologically based; have androgynous skills (e.g., be able to be both tough [when necessary] and caring [whenever possible]).

Values

Emphasize caring and concern, but don't neglect task achievement; place emphasis on health rather than preoccupation with pathology; remove sexist language that reifies the cultural status quo; recognize freedom as double-edged sword (e.g., no-fault divorce versus facts of relative economic loss for women/gain for men), but seek freedom for all.

Examples of Feminist Theories of Human Behavior

Neo-Freudian (e.g., N. Chodorow's revised oedipal/electra theory: adult women find comfort in connectedness and are threatened by separation; men find comfort in independence and are threatened by intimacy)

Neo-Marxist (e.g., Z. Eisenstein: women's oppression stemming from both economic and patriarchal oppression)

Neosocial development (e.g., C. Gilligan: alternative moral development: highest value for women is sensitivity to others' needs, care and responsibility, versus men's highest value of abstract fairness and rights (Kohlberg)

Microsocial and Macrosocial Theories of Human Behavior

In this appendix, we briefly summarize some microsocial, or small group, theories and some macrosocial, or large group (organizations, community, society), theories because these provide a broader context within which individuals and families grow and develop. Both types of theories have their own unique background. They are brought together here to demonstrate the commonalities of microsocial and macrosocial events, especially in the context of human behavior. We look at microgroup theories by Kurt Lewin, as well as by Rensis Likert who considers small groups in large bureaucratic settings. And we consider the classical macrosocial theories of Karl Marx, Emile Durkheim, and Max Weber.

Kurt Lewin (1880–1947): Small Group Theory

Kurt Lewin's field theory and the extraordinary series of research studies he and his colleagues conducted essentially put "groups" on the conceptual map in the social sciences and greatly influenced practice with and through groups. Lewin did this by demonstrating that groups (and specific properties of groups) had demonstrable effects. One instance of this was the famous studies in democracy and autocracy conducted just before World War II. Lewin and his students assigned boys to different groups in a boys club where the common task was to make masks out of papier-mâché, paste, yarn, and other materials. In the autocratic group, the adult leader came into the room and essentially ordered the boys to do certain things. The results were a high quality mask but a very low level of satisfaction among the boys. In the laissez-faire group, the adult leader came into the room and did nothing; the boys were on their own, and the results produced a poor quality mask and low levels of satisfaction among the boys. In the democratic group, the adult leader came into the room and essentially worked with the boys, soliciting their ideas and energy and cooperating in all phases of mask making. The results were a good quality mask and high levels of satisfaction. What is important to note is that the adult leaders for the three groups were, in fact, the same person. What was different was the "climate" the leader constructed in the group and the demonstrable effects following from that constructed group attribute.

Field theory refers to a translation of new relativity thinking from physics into the psychological field. Lewin's general formula (B=P,E) is very close to the ecological and social work axiom that any observed social behavior is a function of the person in some environment. For Lewin the environment was phenomenologial; what existed was what the person was aware of. Let's look at the way Lewin conceptualized P and E. A person exists in a *life space,* those aspects of the world the person conceives as relevant and noticed. That life space has a *boundary* that contains some number of regions through which the person has to go (locomote) in order to reach some desired objective (a *goal* having a positive or *attracting* valance); a negative goal would be one that repelled the person. Life is made up of these attracting and repelling factors, and what one actually chooses to do is the product of a *resultant of action,* which is a kind of balance between the forces that are pushing toward or pulling away from some objective. The boundaries of these internal regions are permeable to a greater or lesser degree, and sometimes the person has to figure out alternative paths toward a given goal. A *value* operates to guide behaviors by determining which activity has the positive valence and which the negative for a given person in a given situation.

After Lewin's death in 1945, his students set up an institute for group dynamics at the University of Michigan and developed applications of this model for various groups, including businesspeople who went to a beautiful retreat in Bethel, Maine, so as to learn sensitivity in groups, to the end of being a more effective leader. In working with individuals and groups, Lewin thought it was important to unfreeze the current but unsuccessful patterns of behavior, move them to some new, desired pattern, and then refreeze this new pattern of behavior so the members could maintain their level of success. This method has been widely used at many levels of society where *change agents* are involved in unfreezing, moving, and refreezing (see, for example, Lippitt, Watson, and Westley).

Rensis Likert (1903–): The Human Relations School

Rensis Likert is part of a long line of theorists working in large-scale organizations, such as businesses, universities, religious organizations, essentially to address the issue of increasing productivity while also ensuring worker satisfaction. The Industrial Revolution had greatly increased productivity at the expense of worker satisfaction. William Morris (1834–1896) and others urged a return to the good old days when workers were craftsmen making beautiful artifacts for a living. But this avenue was open to very few in a modern society.

Some, like Frederick Taylor at the beginning of the twentieth century, pushed productivity to new heights with their ideas on scientific management, using time and motion studies to extract the most from any human labor. This view was satirized by Charlie Chaplin in the movie *Hard Times,* where the worker was reduced to being a cog of a machine. Some have fought the machine, from the eighteenth-century Luddites (who destroyed industrial machines in a belief that they undermined the employment of human beings, a view many contemporary downsized workers will understand) to the legendary John Henry (pitted against mechanical track-laying equipment) to Gary Karpov in our own day (playing chess against computers with their implication for artificial intelligence).

Others examined the nature of the work organization and discovered the unexpected power of informal groups to influence, sometimes negatively, sometimes positively, the workings of the formal organization. For example, in the famous Hawthorne studies, researchers varied the physical conditions for a group of telephone relay workers—they turned the lights up brighter, and productivity increased; they turned the lights down lower, and productivity increased. In fact, almost anything they did seemed to lead to increased productivity, until they comprehended a vital point, that the increased productivity was related to the attention the workers received.

In a classic Lewinian field study, Coch and French (1948) studied productivity in an automobile factory when various social arrangements were modified. In some work groups, the workers participated in the decisions for their section of work, while in other work groups, the workers simply took orders as usual. It became very clear that when workers participated in their own fate to some degree, both productivity and satisfaction increased. This was a critical indicator for much research that followed.

Likert, who was a well-known researcher and pioneer of the Likert scale—you have seen it in many places: very much; much; some; little; very little—turned his interests to the workplace and the productivity-satisfaction balance. He first studied successful leaders and unsuccessful ones to identify what factors distinguished them and found that modifying Weber's classical bureaucratic structure was the critical ingredient. When workers participated with their immediate supervisor in making local decisions and when these supervisors participated with their superiors in the bureaucratic organization—Likert called this linked multiple overlapping groups—then workers at all levels had trust and loyalty within the work group, which became effective an problem-solving unit. The workers became highly motivated to achieve organizational goals (which were, in part, their own goals). Communication is vital for effective and efficient work activities. Interestingly, to make this set of ideas and actions work successfully, at each level administrators had to give up some of their power and share it with subordinates, who were participating in local decisions. The administrators who were able to share power—some leaders could do this; others could not—operated in what Likert described as a System 4, while those who retained all the power and did not involve workers in their own work decisions were described as Systems 1, 2, and 3 (sharing none or some of the participatory model).

Karl Marx (1818–1881) and Friedrich Engels (1820–1895)

Western Europe in the early nineteenth century was moving toward the zenith of the Industrial Revolution and to the nadir of the human condition for the masses of workers. There was brutal exploitation of workers, who were alienated from their humanity by being cogs in a large machine; the cash nexus replaced human relationships in the economic world. Misery was rampant among the working class. Marx sought to understand how these conditions came about and what could be done to change them. His analysis and the action programs stemming from it did in fact change the course of history, although perhaps the lasting contribution is his extraordinary analysis of society.

Marx revised Hegel's view of evolutionary history in which ideas moved through inevitable phases of the dialectical process: thesis, antithesis, synthesis. Marx viewed history from a materialistic dialectic: history as the story of the haves (masters, landlords, bourgeois capitalists) and have-nots (slaves, serfs, proletarian workers), with wives and children taking the status of the husband/father. All history involves this class struggle, but the then-current struggle would be the final one where "the expropriators would be expropriated" and a state of pure communism would (eventually) emerge triumphant.

For Marx, economic structures are the foundation of all other aspects of society. Personal identity comes from one's economic status; ideas and values reflect people's relationship to the means of production: the bourgeoisie control these means, while the proletariat do not. Religion, morality, law (and mass media and social work such as they were at that time) are merely "handmaidens" serving the economic structure, serving to keep workers under control in this life, while promising a better afterlife. (Religion is the "opiate" of the people.)

Why should capitalism, which produces so much wealth, create misery for the workers? Marx uses the labor theory of value, adapted from classical economists: In a monopoly situation, employers hired laborers from large pools of job seekers, whose work produced products that were sold for cash. From the sale of goods, the employers paid wages that were only enough to enable the worker to reproduce new generations of workers, while the rest of the profit (the surplus) from the sale of worker-produced goods went to the capitalist. There were no unions in the early nineteenth century to protect workers from this exploitation. Revolting workers have "nothing to lose but their chains."

The economic system is itself organized around property, which defines a person's economic class; this private property system is supported by the state. However, there is a major internal contradiction in the capitalistic system, which Marx predicts will lead to its downfall: Laborers produce goods from raw materials that are eventually sold for profits, but periodically, markets dry up, and capitalists have to scale back production. This involves firing workers, who then enter the pool of available laborers, but without work or welfare, misery soon escalates. Sparked by the intelligentsia who help to raise workers' consciousness to the nature of their problems, economic crises may spill over into revolts. These are usually put down by police and armed forces (also under the control of the capitalists), but eventually a revolt will reach revolutionary proportions and will lead to the overthrow of the capitalist system. Time is required before the state "withers away" leaving the basis of society "to each according to his need, from each according to his ability." Details are vague.

Engels continued to write after Marx's death. His book on the family from the communistic perspective is interesting, even though his anthropological history is incorrect: The original state of human beings was an economic and sexual communism. However, private property emerged from surplus goods and profits. These eventually created social classes and private sexual property, enforced by dominant males who wanted to see their progeny inherit what they accumulated. Women's status declined as men took over the major economic functions. Women had no property to exchange, and they were vulnerable to the forces of nature. Women had to survive under these changing conditions. So the family emerged as an economic trade: security and status (from the male) for sex and family (from the female). The revolution will change all that, giving women parity with men and changing the nature of sex and family.

Emile Durkheim (1858–1917): Functionalism in Sociology

Durkheim lived at a difficult time in French history—the Franco-Prussian War and World War I—and was very concerned about social instability and the future of society. Unlike Marx, who saw conflict as inevitable, Durkheim saw society as being temporarily out of balance and needing some conceptual understanding to put it aright. The conceptual perspective he provided has set the terms of much contemporary (and conservative) sociological thought, though he has also been strongly criticized (Gouldner 1973).

Sociological Method

Durkheim was determined to view society as its own entity, not as reduced to some collection of reductionistic component parts. Although individual people were real, society was more than the sum of its members and was qualitatively different as well. This is the critical point in Durkheim's thought: society is an emergent phenomenon, a purely social entity, with its own structures, functions, and laws. Society exists independently of its members. The society exists before a given person is born; it exists during his or her lifetime; it continues to exist after that person's death.

Moreover, various *social facts*—patterns of thought and action that are observable within collections of individual actions in a society—also exist independently of the members who contribute to them. For example, in one early empirical study, Durkheim analyzed a large group of data on suicide rates from many countries and districts within countries over long periods of time. What could be a more individual act than suicide? But Durkheim convincingly demonstrates that suicide rates (as well as birth rates) are the collective results of many individual actions but appear to have a pattern separate from the mere sum of these actions. For example, suicide obviously involves different people over time, but the rate of these events are approximately stable over many years. What can cause such a pattern as this? There must be some common social level force (a social fact) creating these stable statistical patterns. This is what Durkheim studies. Durkheim also suggests some ideas regarding other social facts that can be used to address destabilizing events such as high suicide rates.

Society, for Durkheim, is a moral order, a community of moral ideas, even if it is undergoing rapid social change. Morality, as a society-level function, enables people to live together without destructive conflicts. Modern society is formed by a *division of labor*—people working on coordinated parts of some whole task—which leads to greater interdependence and mutual responsibility for one another—rather than the class conflict that Marx finds. This solidarity of interests is based on economic facts, that people are really dependent on one another for the world of goods we enjoy. To reverse the anarchy he saw all around him, Durkheim proposed reintroducing an occupational corporation or guild that would provide the basis of some secular moral and legal principles according to which relations among the various occupations and classes would be regulated.

Durkheim viewed human history as illustrating two kinds of social solidarity that bind a people together and to society at large: The first kind he called *mechanical solidarity*, where the individual is bound to society without mediation, as if the person were a mechanical part of the whole. Laws of such states (usually small and less advanced societies) are repressive so as to punish criminals for their offenses against society. The *collective consciousness* of the society is defined as the totality of beliefs and sentiments common to the average member of that society. The second kind is called *organic solidarity*, which binds the individual to others through the interdependence of their efforts. This division of labor generates cooperation, not conflict. Laws of these states are restitutive, not punitive, so as to restore the status quo. The collective consciousness grows weaker in organic solidarity, just as division of labor generates stronger ties.

Now we return to Durkheim's analysis of the social facts involved in rates of suicide. His master hypothesis is that both the extremes of solidarity or social cohesion will cause high suicide rates. There are two dimensions of social cohesion: integration and regulation. Where people are integrated into society, they receive attachments that supply purpose and ideals to those people. People's worst evil, for Durkheim, was their uncontrolled individual desires that cannot be satiated. Where people are regulated by society, they are involved in the social control of their insatiable desires. This generates a model of four types of suicide:

Integration into society	High: Altruistic suicide, where an individual's life in controlled by allegiance and sacrifice to a higher cause	Low: Egoistic suicide, where strong social changes force the person onto his or her own resources
Regulation by society	High: Fatalistic suicide, where there is excessive regulation of people whose future is blocked and feelings are repressed	Low: Anomic suicide, where norms disappear in sudden social change and no longer function as social controls

Durkheim holds that all social facts contribute to society in some way (a conservative idea), even criminal or deviant behavior since they function to make society think about the nature of decisions and feelings, and thus contribute to the solidarity of society (Abrahamson 1990:196). Durkheim also studied religions and provided the basis of a sociology of religion. He distinguishes the sacred from the profane; religion is the totality of beliefs and practices concerned with the sacred—things set apart and forbidden. Durkheim examined a primitive group in Australia, the Arunta, who gather once a year from their nomadic existence in great excitement and share rituals involving an object that symbolizes their identity—a totem. They can take the totem with them for the rest of the year to remind them of their common symbol of a divine force, which Durkheim sees as society itself. Gods and society are one. The experience of one's society gives rise to what Durkheim calls a *collective representation,* which is a collective intuiting of the divine. This same experience with the group also gives rise to conceptions of time, space, class, logic, and so forth—all social facts.

Max Weber (1864–1920)

Weber lived a half century after Marx and was a contemporary of Durkheim. The essential question for Weber concerned the origins of modern capitalism (a Marxian question). His answer led him through exhaustive studies of ancient cultures, Asian and Western, to emphasize the contribution of ideas (especially religious ideas) in producing fundamental changes in society (a somewhat Durkheimian answer).

Weber introduced several "appropriate" methods for the then-new social sciences. One was the ideal-typical analysis, which involved abstracting elements from real events and synthesizing them into concepts—such as the concept of "bureaucracy." ("Ideal" does not mean "good." It means the scientific essence of a class of events.) The second method dealt with meaningfully comprehending some social event through *Verstehen,* or the interpretive understanding of the subjective meaning of the event to the persons involved. A third was his position on values in science; he proposed the necessary objectivity of the social scientist—conducting value-neutral scholarship even with value-laden topics.

Among Weber's many contributions were some that influence sociological thought today. Weber amplified Marx on the concept of class to include three independent dimensions: *Class,* a determiner of life chances and common fate among members who either own property (bourgeoisie) or do not (proletariat). *Status,* which is the prestige associated with the lifestyle of a group, may differ from class. For example, a bureaucrat may accumulate more money than a landowner thus giving the nonlandowner more prestige than the property owner. *Power or party* involves the ability to influence another person's actions against her or his own will. This power is also independent of class or status, such as the bureaucrat who is able to influence the political process more than a landowner, whether the bureaucrat has money or status.

Weber's enduring contribution involved his analysis of the then-rising bureaucracies, which he saw as an ideal type of a rational problem-solving machine. The bureaucracy was composed of a hierarchy of positions intentionally interrelated and based on specialized skills. Workers had fixed areas of jurisdiction, were recruited on the basis of specialized skills, and held full-time salaried positions in the company to which they owed allegiance (rather than to any individual, as in feudal times). The bureaucracy ran based on formal rules, written on multiple copies, and stored in files; these procedures oriented workers to "go by the book" to serve everyone equally and, as an unintended consequence, led to "red tape"—required procedures that interfered with the task.

Ancient cultures such as the Chinese had elaborate bureaucracies, but only when these were combined with certain religious ideologies in the presence of certain economic events did fundamental changes occur in society. The Protestant ethic, particularly the Calvinistic variety, included worldly activity as the (only) sign of divine election and asceticism as a sign of grace, combined synergistically at this particular moment in history with political-economic events that Marx had described to give rise to modern capitalism. People worked like the devil was after them, and plowed back the profits into their companies. Conspicuous consumption (Veblen 1922) came much later, when religious ideology drifted apart from economic activity.

REFERENCES

AARP (American Association of Retired Persons). 1988. New focus on minority aging. *News Bulletin* January, 6.

———. 1995. *A profile of older Americans: 1995.* Washington, D.C.: AARP.

Abercrombie, N. 1993. National Service Trust Act of 1993. *Congressional Record,* Daily Edition, 21 July, pp. H4886–4950.

Abrahamson, M. 1990. *Sociological theory: An introduction to concepts, issues, and research.* 2d ed. Englewood Cliffs, N.J.: Prentice Hall.

———. 1996. *Urban enclaves: Identity and place in America.* New York: St. Martin's Press.

Adams, J. E., and E. Lindemann. 1974. Coping with long-term disability. In G. V. Coelho, D. A. Hamburg, and J. E. Adams, eds. *Coping and adaptation,* pp. 127–138. New York: Basic Books.

Adler, A. 1959. *The practice and theory of individual psychology.* Totowa, N.J.: Littlefield Adams.

Adult literary service. 1998. A United Way agency [on line]. http://www.indian-river.fl.us/living/service/als/scope.html.

After the harvest. 1987. A report examining the lives and prospects of older farm laborers, prepared jointly by the Housing Assistance Council and the American Association of Retired Persons.

AIDS and the education of our children: A guide for parents and teachers. 1988. 3d ed. Washington, D.C.: U.S. Department of Education.

AIDS in children. 1995. Departments of Labor, Health and Human Services, Education . . . . Appropriations for 1996. Part 4. Hearing. Washington, D.C.: GPO.

Alan Guttmacher Institute. 1994. *Sex and America's teenagers.* Washington, D.C.: Alan Guttmacher Institute.

Albee, G. W. 1983. Psychopathology, prevention, and the just society. *Journal of Primary Prevention* 4 (1): 5–40.

———. 1996. The psychological origins of the white male patriarchy. *Journal of Primary Prevention* [*Special issue: Social Darwinism and political models of mental/emotional problems* (special issue editor, G. W. Albee)] 17:1, 17 (1): 75–98.

Albee, G. W., J. M. Joffe, and L. A. Dusenbury, eds. 1988. *Prevention, powerlessness, and politics: Readings on social change.* Newbury Park, Calif.: Sage.

Alcalay, F., A. Ghee, and S. Scrimshaw. 1993. Designing prenatal care messages for low-income Mexican women. *Public Health Reports* 108 (3): 354–362.

Alexander, D. 1992. Departments of Labor, Health and Human Services, Education . . . Appropriations for 1993. Part 3. Hearing. Washington, D.C.: GPO.

Allen, J. 1986. Achieving primary prevention program objectives through culture change systems. *Journal of Primary Prevention* 7 (2): 91–107.

Allen, J. P., S. Philliber, and N. Hoggson. 1990. School-based prevention of teen-age pregnancy and school dropouts: Process evaluation of the national replication of the Teen Outreach Program. *American Journal of Community Psychology* 18 (1): 505–524.

Allen-Meares, P., R. O. Washington, and B. L. Welsh. 1986. *Social work services in schools.* Englewood Cliffs, N.J.: Prentice-Hall.

Altman, I. 1975. *The environment and social behavior.* Monterey, Calif.: Brooks/Cole.

American demographics. 1993. Special report: The future of households. 15 (12): 27–40.

Annas, G. J., and S. Elias. 1992. *Gene mapping: Using law and ethics as guides.* New York: Oxford.

Anderson, S. C. 1995. Alcohol abuse. In R. L Edwards et al., eds. *Encyclopedia of social work,* pp. 203–215. 19th ed. Washington, D.C.: NASW Press.

Arbuthnot, J. 1992. Sociomoral reasoning in behavior-disordered adolescents: Cognitive and behavioral change. In J. McCord and R. E. Tremblay, eds. *Preventing antisocial behavior: Interventions from birth through adolescence,* pp. 283–310. New York: Guilford Press.

Aronson, E. 1995. *The social animal.* 6th ed. San Francisco: W. H. Freeman.

Aronson, E., and D. Bridgeman. 1979. Jigsaw groups and the desegregated classroom: In pursuit of common goals. *Personality and Social Psychology Bulletin* 5 (4): 438–446.

Asch, A., and N. R. Mudrick. 1995. Disability. In R. L. Edwards et al., eds. *Encyclopedia of social work,* pp. 752–761. 19th ed. Washington D.C.: NASW Press.

Atchley, R. C. 1994. *Social forces and aging.* 7th ed. Belmont, Calif.: Wadsworth.

Attneave, C. 1982. American Indians and Alaska Native families: Emigrants in their own homeland. In M. McGoldrick, J. Pearce, and J. Giordano, eds. *Ethnicity and family therapy,* pp. 55–83. New York: Guilford Press.

Auletta, K. 1982. *The underclass.* New York: Random House.

Bacon, K. H. 1989. Nearly 0.2% of college students in U.S. who were tested carry the AIDS virus. *Wall Street Journal,* 23 May, B4.

Badgett, M., and M. V. Lee. 1995. The wage effects of sexual orientation discrimination. *Industrial and Labor Relations Review* 48 (4): 726–739.

Bales, R. F. 1950. *Interaction process analysis: A method for the study of small groups.* Reading, Mass.: Addison-Wesley.

———. 1955. How people interact in conferences. *Scientific American* 192 (3): 31–35.

Balgopal, P. R. 1995. Asian Americans overview. In R. L. Edwards et al., eds. *Encyclopedia of social work,* pp. 256–260. 19th ed. Washington D.C.: NASW Press.

Ball, D. W. 1974. The family as a sociological problem: Conceptualization of the taken-for-granted as prologue to social problems analysis. *Social Problems* 19 (winter): 295–305.

Balswick, J. 1989. *The inexpressive male: A study of men who express love too little.* Lexington, Mass.: Lexington Books.

Bandura, A. 1986. *Social foundations of thought and action: A social cognitive theory.* Englewood Cliffs, N.J.: Prentice-Hall.

Banta, W. F. 1988. *AIDS in the workplace: Legal questions and practical answers.* Lexington, Mass.: Lexington Books.

Barbarin, O. A. 1981. Community competence: An individual systems model of institutional racism. In O. A. Barbarin, P. R. Good,, M. Pharr, and J. A. Siskind, eds. *Institutional racism and community competence,* pp. 6–19. Rockville, Md.: NIMH Center for Minority Group Mental Health Programs, DHHS Publication No. (ADM) 81–907.

Barker, R. L. 1987. *The social work dictionary.* Silver Spring, Md.: NASW Press.

Barnett, W. S. 1993. Benefit-cost analysis of preschool education: Findings from a 25-year follow-up. *American Journal of Orthopsychiatry* 63 (4): 500–508.

Barratt, M. S., M. A. Roach, and K. K. Colbert. 1991. Single mothers and their infants: Factors associated with optimal parenting. *Family Relations* 40:448–454.

Barron, W. G. 1992. Department of Labor, Health and Human Services, Education . . . Appropriations for 1993. Part 1. Hearing. Washington, D.C.: GPO.

Barth, R. P., M. Courtney, J. D. Berrick, and V. Albert. 1994. *From child abuse to permanency planning: Child welfare services pathways and placements.* New York: Aldine de Gruyter.

Baumer, D. C., and C. E. Van Horn. 1985. *The politics of unemployment.* Washington, D.C.: Congressional Quarterly Press.

Beal, E. W. 1980. Separation, divorce, and single-parent families. In E. A. Carter and M. McGoldrick, eds. *The family life cycle: A framework for family therapy,* pp. 241–264. New York: Gardner Press.

Beardslee, W., and J. Mack. 1982. The impact on children and adolescents of nuclear developments. In R. Rogers, ed. *Psychosocial aspects of nuclear developments (Task Force Report No. 20),* pp. 64–93. Washington, D.C.: American Psychiatric Association.

Beatrice, D. K. 1979. Divorce: Problems, goals, and growth facilitation. *Social Casework* 60 (March): 157–165.

Beauvoir, S. de 1972. *The coming of age.* New York: G. P. Putnam's Sons.

Begab, M. J. 1974. The major dilemma of mental retardation: Shall we prevent it? (Some social implications of research in mental retardation). *American Journal of Mental Deficiency* 78 (5): 519–529.

Begley, S. 1996. Born happy? *Newsweek,* 14 October, 78–80.

Belgrave, L. L. 1988. The effects of race differences in work history, work attitudes, economic resources, and health in women's retirement. *Research on Aging* 10 (3): 383–398.

Bell, K. 1986. Reflections of an unremembered past. Typescript.

Bell, P. A., J. D. Fisher, A. Baum, and T. C. Greene. 1990. *Environmental psychology.* 3d ed. Forth Worth, Tex.: Holt, Rinehart and Winston.

Benard, B. 1992. Fostering resilience in kids: Protective factors in the family, school, and community. *Prevention Forum* 12 (3): 1–16.

Bendix, R. 1960. *Max Weber: An intellectual portrait.* New York: Anchor.

Bereuter, D. 1992. Homelessness in America. *Congressional Record,* Daily Edition, 25 September, pp. H9450–9495.

Berger, B. M., B. M. Hackett, and R. M. Millar. 1974. Child rearing practices in the communal family. In A. Skolnick and J. H. Skolnick, eds. *Intimacy, family, society,* pp. 441–464. Boston: Little, Brown.

Berger, R. M. 1982. The unseen minority: Older gays and lesbians. *Social Work* 27 (May): 236–242.

———. 1984. Realities of gay and lesbian aging. *Social Work* 29 (January–February): 57–62.

Berger, R. M., and J. J. Kelly. 1995. Gay men overview. In R. L. Richards et al., eds. *Encyclopedia of social work,* pp. 1064–1074. 19th ed. Washington, D.C.: NASW Press.

Berkman, L. F,. and S. L. Syme. 1979. Social networks, host resistance, and mortality: A nine-year follow-up study of Alameda County residents. *American Journal of Epidemiology* 109:186–204.

Berman, A. L. 1986. Healing suicidal adolescents: Needs and responses. In C. A. Corr and J. N. McNeil, eds. *Adolescents and death,* pp. 151–166. New York: Springer.

Bern, J. H. 1980. Grandparents of handicapped children. *Social Work* 25:238–239.

Betts, H., and P. Thomas. 1992. Departments of Labor, Health and Human Services, Education . . . Appropriations for 1993. Part 8A. Hearing. Washington, D.C.: GPO.

Bianchi, S. M.. and D. Spain. 1984. *American women: Three decades of change.* Rev. ed. U.S. Bureau of the Census, Special Demographic Analysis, CDS-80–8. Washington, D.C.: GPO.

Blackwell, R. 1996. Forum: Does America still work? *Harper's Magazine,* May, 35–47.

Blanchard, E. L. 1982. Observations on social work with American Indian women. In A. Weick and S. T. Vandiver, eds. *Women, power, and change,* pp. 96–103. Washington, D.C.: NASW Press.

Blanchard, E. L., and S. Unger. 1977. Editorial notes: Destruction of American Indian families. *Social Casework* 58 (May): 312–314.

Bloom, B. L., W. F. Hodges, and R. A. Caldwell. 1983. Marital separation: The first eight months. In E. J. Callahan and K. A. McCluskey, eds. *Life-span developmental psychology: Nonnormative life events,* pp. 217–239. New York: Academic Press.

Bloom, K. 1990. Selectivity and early infant vocalization. In J. Enns, ed. *The development of attention: Research and theory,* pp. 121–136. New York: Elsevier North-Holland. Cited in L. Bloom 1993, 73.

Bloom, L. 1975. Language development. In F. D. Horowitz, ed. *Review of child development research,* pp. 245–303. Vol. 4. Chicago: University of Chicago Press.

———. 1991. *Language development from two to three.* New York: Cambridge University Press.

———. 1993. *The transition from infancy to language: Acquiring the power of expression.* New York: Cambridge University Press.

Bloom, M. 1985. *Life span development: Bases for preventive and interventive helping.* Tables, pp. 3–17. 2d ed. New York: Macmillan.

———. 1996. *Primary prevention practices.* Thousand Oaks, Calif.: Sage.

Bloom, M., K. Wood, and A. Chambon. 1991. Six languages of social work. *Social Work* 36 (6): 530–534.

Blume, S. B. 1985. Alcohol and the older woman. *Hot Flash* 4 (spring): 2–6.

Bodmer, W., and R. McKie. 1995. *The book of man: The Human Genome Project and the quest to discover our genetic heritage.* New York: Scribner.

Borders, W. 1980. Away-on-work husbands and marital stress. *New York Times,* 11 November, B12.

Bott, E. 1972. *Family and social network.* 2d ed. New York: Free Press.

Botvin, G. J., and L. Dusenbury. 1989. Substance abuse prevention and the promotion of competence. In L. Bond and B. Compas, eds. *Primary prevention and promotion in the schools,* pp. 146–178. Newbury Park, Calif.: Sage.

Botvin, G. J., and S. Tortu. 1988. Preventing adolescent substance abuse through life skills training. In R. Price, E. Cowen, R. Lorion, and J. Ramos-McKay, eds. *14 ounces of prevention: A casebook for practitioners,* pp. 98–110. Washington, D.C.: American Psychological Association.

Boulding, E. 1976. *The underside of history: A view of women through time.* Boulder, Colo.: Westview Press.

Bowlby, J. 1969. *Attachment and loss.* Vol. 1. *Attachment.* New York: Basic Books.

———. 1973. Affectional bonds: Their nature and origin. In R. S. Weiss, ed. *Loneliness: The experience of emotional and social isolation,* pp. 38–52. Cambridge: MIT Press.

Boyer, E. L. 1984. The test of growing student diversity. *New York Times,* 11 November, sect. 12, p. 63.

Bradley, B. 1995.Statements on introduced bills and joint resolutions. *Congressional Record,* 16 February, pp. S2823–2889.

Bray, J. H. 1995. Successful stepfamilies. In W. J. O'Neill Jr., ed. *Family: The first imperative.* Cleveland: O'Neill Foundation.

Brazelton, T. B. 1973. *Neonatal behavioral assessment scale.* London: Heineman.

———. 1985. *Working and caring.* Reading, Mass.: Addison-Wesley.

———. 1986. Issues for working parents. *American Journal of Orthopsychiatry* 56 (1): 14–25.

Brenner, H. 1984. *Estimating the effects of economic change on national health and social well-being: A study prepared for the Subcommittee on Economic Goals and Intergovernmental Policy of the Joint Economic Committee, U.S. Congress.* Washington, D.C.: GPO.

Briley, M. 1983. Over 80 and doing fine. A report of the research of L. G. Branch and A. M. Jette. *Modern Maturity,* October–November, 96–97.

Brilliant, E. L. 1995. Voluntarism. In R. L. Edwards et al., eds. *Encyclopedia of social work,* pp. 2469–2482. 19th ed. Washington D.C.: NASW Press.

Brody, E. 1981. "Women in the middle" and family help to older people. *Gerontologist* 21 (May): 471–480.

———. 1984. Report of an interview. *Modern Maturity,* January, 33.

Brody, J. 1995a. Fighting pain with child's play and imagination. *New York Times,* 1 November, C13.

————. 1995b. Hormone replacement for men: When does it help? *New York Times,* 30 August, C6.

————. 1996a. Gum disease in pregnancy linked to premature low–birth weight babies. *New York Times Health Section,* 9 October, C11.

————. 1996b. In search of a healthier old age for women. *New York Times,* 8 May, C10.

————. 1996c. Life in womb may affect adult heart attack risk. *New York Times,* 1 October, C1, C6

Brown, S. V. 1983. The commitment and concerns of black adolescent parents. *Social Work Research and Abstracts* 19 (spring): 27–34.

Brown, L. N. 1991. *Groups for growth and change.* New York: Longman.

Brown, L., et al. 1996. *State of the world.* New York: W. W. Norton.

Buckley, W. 1968. *Modern systems research for the behavioral scientist.* Chicago: Aldine.

Burt, M. R. 1986. Estimates of public costs for teen-age childbearing. Paper prepared for the Center of Population Options, Washington, D.C.

Burton, L. M. 1992. Black grandparents rearing children of drug-addicted parents: Stressors, outcomes, and social service needs. *Gerontologist* 32:744–751.

Butler, R. N. 1963. The life review: An interpretation of reminiscence in the aged. *Psychiatry* 26:65–76.

————. 1975. Psychiatry and the elderly: An overview. *American Journal of Psychiatry* 132:893–900.

Butler, R. N., and M. Emr. 1982. Alzheimer's disease: An examination. *TWA Ambassador,* November, 69–71.

Butt, J., ed. 1971. *Robert Owen: Prince of cotton spinners.* Newtown Abbot, Devon, UK: David and Charles Publishing.

Byrne, D., K. Kelley, and W. Fisher. 1993. Unwanted teenage pregnancies: Incidence, interpretation, and intervention. *Applied and Preventive Psychology* 2:101–113.

Calvert, R. 1996. What is a school-based health center? *Child and Family Agency of Southeastern Connecticut* (winter): 3.

Cantor, M. H. 1979. The informal support system of New York's inner city elderly: Is ethnicity a factor? In D. E. Gelfand and A. Ketzik, eds. *Ethnicity and aging,* pp. 153–174. New York: Springer.

Caplan, R. D., A. D. Vinokur, R. Price, and M. van Ryn. 1989. Job-seeking, reemployment, and mental health: A randomized field experiment in coping with job loss. *Journal of Applied Psychology* 74:759–769.

Caring about kids: Talking to children about death. 1979. Rockville, Md.: National Institute of Mental Health, DHEW Publication No. (ADM) 79–838.

Carmody, D. 1988. Head Start gets credit for rise in scores. *New York Times,* 21 September, B9.

Carpenter, E. M. 1980. Social services, policies, and issues. *Social Casework* 61 (October): 455–461.

Carter, E. A., and M. McGoldrick. 1980. *The family life cycle: A framework for family therapy.* New York: Gardner Press.

————. 1989. *The changing family life cycle.* 2d ed. Boston: Allyn and Bacon.

Case, J., and R. C. R. Taylor. 1979. *Co-ops, communes, and collectives: Experiments in social change in the 1960s and 1970s.* New York: Pantheon Books.

Cattan, P. 1991. Child-care problems: An obstacle to work. *Monthly Labor Review* 114 (10): 3–9.

Cauce, A. M., J. P. Comer, and D. Schwartz. 1987. Long-term effects of a systems-oriented school prevention program. *American Journal of Orthopsychiatry* 57:127–131.

Chadiha, L. A. 1992. Black husbands' economic problems and resiliency during the transition to marriage. *Families in Society* 73 (9):542–552.

Chavis, D. M., P. E. Stucky, and A. Wandersman. 1983. Returning basic research to the community: A relationship between scientist and citizen. *American Psychologist* 38 (4): 424–434.

Chen, P. N. 1979. A study of Chinese American elderly residing in hotel rooms. *Social Casework* 60 (February): 89–95.

Cherry, L., and S. P. Redmond. 1994. A social marketing approach to involving Afghans in community-level alcohol problem prevention. *Journal of Primary Prevention* 14 (4): 289–310.

Chess, S., and A. Thomas. 1986. *Temperament in clinical practice.* New York: Guilford Press.

Cho, S., E. Freeman, and S. Patterson. 1982. Adolescents' experiences with death: Practice implications. *Social Casework* 63 (February): 88–94.

Chodorow, N. 1978. *The reproduction of mothering: Psychoanalysis and the sociology of gender.* Berkeley: University of California Press.

Chomsky, N. 1957. *Syntactic structures.* The Hague: Mouton.

————. 1965. *Aspects of a theory of syntax.* Cambridge: MIT Press.

Christopher, W. 1994. Departments of Commerce, Justice, and State, the Judiciary . . . Appropriations for 1995, Part 3. Hearing. Washington, D.C.: GPO.

Chronicle of Higher Education. 1997. Almanac issue. 44 (1): 5, 6.

Coates, T. J. 1990. Strategies for modifying sexual behavior for primary and secondary prevention of HIV disease. *Journal of Consulting and Clinical Psychology* 58 (1): 57–69.

Coch, L., and J. R. P. French. 1948. Overcoming resistance to change. *Human Relations* 1:512–532.

Cohen, G. O. 1992. Department of Labor, Health and Human Service, Education . . . Appropriations for 1993. Part 3. Hearing. Washington, D.C.: GPO.

Coles, R. 1993. *The call of service: A witness to idealism.* Boston: Houghton Mifflin.

Collins, A. H., and D. L. Pancoast. 1976. *Natural helping networks: A strategy for prevention.* Washington, D.C.: NASW Press.

Comer, J. P. 1988. Educating poor minority children. *Scientific American* 259 (5): 42–48.

Comer, J. P., N. M. Haynes, E. T. Joyner. 1996. *Rallying the whole village: The Comer process for reforming education.* New York: Teachers College Press.

Commonwealth Fund Commission on Elderly People Living Alone. 1987. Data from a survey conducted by Louis Harris and Associates for the commission.

Consortium on the School-based Promotion of Social Competency. 1994. The school-based promotion of social competence: Theory, research, practice, and policy. In R. Haggerty, L. Sherrod, N. Garmezy, and M. Rutter, eds. *Stress, risk, and resilience in children and adolescents: Processes, mechanisms, and interventions,* pp. 268–316. New York: Cambridge University Press.

Coontz, S. 1996. Where are the good old days? In search of the American family. *Modern Maturity,* May–June, 36–43.

Corbin, J. M., and A. Strauss. 1988. *Unending work and care.* San Francisco: Jossey-Bass.

Cordova, J. V., N. S. Jacobson, J. M. Gottman, R. Rushe, and G. Cox. 1993. Negative reciprocity and communication in couples with a violent husband. *Journal of Abnormal Psychology* 102 (4): 559–564.

Correa, A. 1991. Child Labor Amendments of 1991. Hearing. Washington, D.C.: GPO.

Corville-Smith, R. 1995. Truancy, family processes, and interventions. In B. A. Ryan, G. Adams, T. Gullotta, R. Weissberg, and R. Hampton, eds. *The family-school connection,* pp. 270–287. Thousand Oaks, Calif.: Sage.

Cose, E. 1994. Drawing up safer cities. *Newsweek,* 11 July, 57.

Cotman, C. 1987. From a paper presented at a conference, The promise of productive aging, Washington, D.C., and reported in *AARP News Bulletin,* September, 2.

Cotton, N. S., and R. G. Geraty. 1984. Therapeutic space design: Planning an inpatient children's unit. *American Journal of Orthopsychiatry* 54 (4): 624–636.

Cottrell, L. 1976. The competent community. In B. H. Kaplan, R. N. Wilson, and A. H. Leighton, eds. *Further explorations in social psychiatry,* pp. 195–209. New York: Basic Books.

Coupey, S. M., and M. I. Cohen. 1984. Special considerations for the health care of adolescents with chronic illnesses. *Pediatric Clinics of North America* 31 (February): 211–219.

Cowen, E., P. A. Wyman, W. C. Work, and M. R. Iker. 1995. A preventive intervention for enhancing resilience among highly stressed urban children. *Journal of Primary Prevention* 15 (3): 247–260.

Cowger, C. D. 1994. Assessing client strengths: Clinical assessment for client empowerment. *Social Work* 39:262–268.

Cox, T. 1978. *Stress.* Baltimore: University Park Press.

Coyne, J. A., and K. Holroyd. 1982. Stress, coping, and illness: A transactional perspective. In T. Milton, C. Green, and R. Meagher, eds. *Handbook of clinical health psychology,* pp. 103–127. New York: Plenum.

Coyne, J. C., and R. S. Lazarus. 1980. Cognitive style, stress perception, and coping. In I. L. Kutash and L. B. Schlesinger, eds. *Handbook on stress and anxiety,* pp. 144–158. San Francisco: Jossey-Bass.

Cranor, C. F., ed. 1994. *Are genes us? The social consequences of the new genetics.* New Brunswick, N.J.: Rutgers University Press.

Crossette, R. 1996. The "oldest old," 80 and over, are on the increase globally. *New York Times International,* 22 December, p. 5.

Crowley, S. 1988. Report of minority contributions to a Washington, D.C., conference on the needs of the elderly. *AARP News Bulletin,* December, 2.

Cuellar, J. 1978. El senior citizens club: The older Mexican American in the voluntary association. In B. G. Myerhoff and A. Simic, eds. *Life's career—aging: Cultural variations in growing old,* pp. 207–230. Beverly Hills, Calif.: Sage.

Cunningham, W. 1986. Older persons stay intellectually sharp. *AARP News Bulletin,* October, 2.

Curriculum policy statement for the master's degree and baccalaureate degree programs in social work education. 1992. Alexandria, Va.: Council on Social Work Education.

Curtis, P. 1981. Animals are good for the handicapped, perhaps all of us. *Smithsonian,* July, 49–57.

Daly, A., J. Jennings, J. Beckett, and B. Leashore. 1995. Effective coping strategies of African Americans. *Social Work* 40 (2): 240–248.

Dana, R. H. 1981. Epilogue. In R. H. Dana, ed. *Human services for cultural minorities,* pp. 353–354. Baltimore: University Park Press.

Danish, S. J. 1983. Musings about personal competence: The contributions of sports, health, and fitness. *American Journal of Community Psychology* 11 (3): 221–240.

Danish, S. J., A. J. Pettipas, and B. D. Hale. 1990. Sport as a context for developing competence. In T. P. Gullotta, G. R. Adams, and R. Montemeyer, eds. *Developing social competence in adolescence,* pp.169–194. Newbury Park, Calif.: Sage.

Davis, L. 1979. Racial composition of groups. *Social Work* 24 (May): 208–213.

Davis, M. E. 1977. Occupational hazards and black workers. *Urban Health* 6:16–18.

Davis, R. M. 1987. Current trends in cigarette advertising and marketing. *New England Journal of Medicine* 316 (19 March): 725–732.

DeJong, G. 1979. Independent living: From social movement to analytic paradigm. *Archives of Physical Medicine and Rehabilitation* 60 (October): 435–446.

Delgado, M. 1995. Puerto Rican elders and natural support systems: Implications for human services. *Journal of Gerontological Social Work* 24 (1–2): 115–130.

Delgado, M., and D. Humm-Delgado. 1982. Natural support systems: Source of strength in Hispanic communities. *Social Work* 27 (January): 83–89.

DeLone, R. 1979. *Small futures: Children, inequality, and the limits of liberal reform.* New York: Harcourt Brace Jovanovich.

De Long, A. J. 1970. The micro-spatial structure of the older person: Some implications of planning the social and spatial environment. In L. A. Pastalan and D. H. Carson, eds. *Spatial behavior of older people,* pp. 68–87. Ann Arbor, Mich.: University of Michigan Press.

Demos, J. 1974. The American family in past time. *American Scholar* 43 (summer): 422–446.

DeWeaver, K. L. 1995. Developmental disabilities: Definitions and policies. In R. L. Edwards et al., eds. *Encyclopedia of social work,* pp. 712–720. 19th ed. Washington, D.C.: NASW Press.

Diliworth-Anderson, P. 1994. The importance of grandparents in extended–kin care giving to black children with sickle cell disease. *Journal of Health and Social Policy* 5:185–202.

Dillard, J. L. 1975. General introduction: Perspectives on black English. In J. L. Dillard, ed. *Perspectives on black English,* pp. 9–32. The Hague: Mouton.

Displaced homemakers network. 1989. A status report on displaced homemakers and single parents in the United States. A study by the network, Washington, D.C. (July).

Doka, K. J., and M. E. Mertz. 1988. The meaning and significance of great-grandparenthood. *Gerontologist* 298 (2): 192–197.

Drachman, D. 1996. Immigration statuses and their influence on service provision, access, and use. In P. L. Ewalt, E. Freeman, S. Kirk, and D. Poole, eds. *Multicultural issues in social work,* pp. 117–133. Washington, D.C.: NASW Press.

Draper, B. J. 1979. Black language as an adaptive response to a hostile environment. In C. B. Germain, ed. *Social work practice: People and environments,* pp. 267–281. New York: Columbia University Press.

Drezen, W. 1985. Psychotropic drug use in midlife and older women. *Hot Flash* 4 (spring): 3.

Dryfoos, J. G. 1993. Preventing substance use: Rethinking strategies. *American Journal of Public Health* 83 (6): 793–795.

———. 1994. *Full-service schools: A revolution in health and social services for children, youth, and families.* San Francisco: Jossey-Bass.

———. 1997. The prevalence of problem behaviors. In R. P. Weissberg et al., eds. *Enhancing children's wellness,* pp. 17–46. Thousand Oaks, Calif.: Sage.

Dubos, R. 1968. *So human an animal.* New York: Scribner's.

Dunlap, A. 1996. Forum: Does America still work? *Harper's Magazine,* May, 35–47.

Dunn, J. 1985. *Sisters and brothers.* Cambridge: Harvard University Press.

Durkheim, E. 1952. *Suicide.* New York: Free Press.

Dye, N. S. 1980. History of childbirth in America. *Signs: Journal of Women in Culture and Society* 6 (autumn): 97–108.

Eastman, P. 1988. Report of a symposium at Georgetown University, Washington, D.C., on the plight of refugees. *AARP News Bulletin,* September, 1.

Economist. 1995. American survey: Next year's campaign theme: It's the values, stupid. (11 November): 23–29.

Egan, T. 1988. Despairing Indians looking to tradition to combat suicide. *New York Times,* 19 March, 1:54.

Eiduson, B. T. 1978. Child development in emergent family styles. *Children Today* (March–April): 24–31.

Eisenstein, Z., ed. **[need date]** *Capitalist patriarchy and the case for socialist feminism.* New York: Monthly Review Press.

Elder, G. H., Jr. 1984. Families, kin, and the life course: A sociological perspective. In R. D. Parke, ed. *Review of child development research,* pp. 80–136. Vol. 7. Chicago: University of Chicago Press.

Elder, J. P., M. Wildey, C. de Moor, J. Sallis, L. Eckhardt, C. Edwards, A. Erickson, A.

Golbeck, M. Hovell, D. Johnston, M. Levitz, C. Molgaard, R. Young, D. Vito, and S. Woodruff. 1993. The long-term prevention of tobacco use among junior high school students: Classroom and telephone intervention. *American Journal of Public Health* 83 (9): 1230–1244.

Elders, M. J., C. L. Perry, M. P. Eriksen, and G. A. Giovino. 1994. The report of the surgeon general: Preventing tobacco use among young people. *American Journal of Public Health* 84:543–547.

Elias, M., and J. F. Clabby. 1992. *Building social problem-solving skills: Guidelines from a school-based program.* San Francisco: Jossey-Bass.

Elkin, M. 1987. Joint custody: Affirming that parents and families are forever. *Social Work* 32 (January–February): 18–24.

Encyclopedia of social work. 1995. Ed. R. L. Edwards et al. 19th ed. Washington, D.C.: NASW Press.

Erikson, E. H. 1963. *Childhood and society.* 2d ed. New York: Norton.

Erikson, E. H., J. M. Erikson, and H. Q Kivnick. 1986. *Vital involvement in old age.* New York: Norton.

Escamilla, K. 1994. *Hearing on bilingual education.* Washington, D.C.: GPO.

Estes, C., and J. Swan. 1993. *The long-term care crisis: Elders trapped in the no-care zone.* Newbury Park, Calif.: Sage.

Etaugh, C. 1984. Effects of maternal employment on children: Implications for the family therapist. In S. H. Cramer, ed. *Perspectives on work and the family,* pp. 16–39. Rockville, Md.: Aspen Systems.

Evans, R. L. 1976. Smoking in children: Developing a social psychological strategy of deterrence. *Preventive Medicine* 5 (1): 122–127.

Evans, R. L., and B. E. Raines. 1990. Applying a social psychological model across health preventions: Cigarettes to smokeless tobacco. In J. Edwards, R. Tindale, L. Heath, and E. Posavac, eds. *Social influence processes and prevention.* New York: Plenum.

Ewalt, P., and R. M. Honeyfield. 1981. Needs of persons in long-term care. *Social Work* 26 (May) 223–231.

Ewalt, P., and L. Perkins. 1979. The real experience of death among adolescents. *Social Casework* 60 (November): 547–551.

Eyer, D. 1992. *Mother-infant bonding: A scientific fiction.* New Haven, Conn.: Yale University Press.

Falicov, C. J. 1982. Mexican families. In M. McGoldrick, J. Pearce, and J. Giordano, eds. *Ethnicity and family therapy,* pp. 134–163. New York: Guilford Press.

Falicov, C. J., and B. M. Karrer. 1980. Cultural variations in the family life cycle: The Mexican American family. In E. Carter and M. McGoldrick, eds. *The family life cycle: A framework for family therapy,* pp. 383–426. New York: Gardner Press.

Falk, J. S. 1994. To be human: Language and the study of language. In V. P. Clark, P. Scholz, and A. Rosa, eds. *Language: Introductory readings,* pp. 49–75. 5th ed. New York: St. Martin's Press.

Faludi, S. 1996. Media matters: Statistically challenged. *Nation,,* April, 10.

Fanon, F. 1963. *The wretched of the earth.* New York: Grove Press.

———. 1965. *A dying colonialism.* New York: Monthly Review Press.

———. 1967. *Black skin, white masks.* New York: Grove Press.

Felner, R. D., and A. M. Adan. 1988. The school transitional environment project: An ecological intervention and evaluation. In R. H. Price, E. L. Cowen, R. P. Lorion, and J. Ramos-McKay, eds. *14 ounces of prevention: A casebook for practitioners,* pp. 111–122. Washington, D.C.: American Psychological Association.

Felner, R. D., S. Brand, K. E. Mulhall, B. Counter, J. B. Millman, and J. Fried. 1994. The parenting partnership: The evaluation of a human service/corporate workplace collaboration for the prevention of substance abuse and mental health problems and the promotion of family and work adjustment. *Journal of Primary Prevention* 15 (2): 123–146.

Fimbres, M. M. 1982. The Chicana in transition. In A. Weick and S. Vandiver, eds. *Women, power, and change,* pp. 89–95. Washington, D.C.: NASW Press.

Fine, M., S. Akabas, and S. Bellinger. 1982. A culture of drinking: A workplace perspective. *Social Work* 27 (September): 436–440.

Fiske, E. B. 1988. 35 pages that shook the educational world. *New York Times,* 27 April, B10.

Fitz-Gerald, D., and M. Fitz-Gerald. 1977. Deaf people are sexual, too! *SIECUS Reports* 6 (2): 1, 13–15.

Forsyth, D. R. 1990. *Group dynamics.* 2d ed. Pacific Grove, Calif.: Brooks/Cole.

Foucault, M. 1979. *Discipline and punishment: The birth of the prison.* New York: Vintage Books.

Fradd, S. H. 1985. Governmental policy and second language learning. *Educational Forum* 49 (4): 431–443.

Fraser, M., and N. Kohlert. 1988. Substance abuse and public policy. *Social Service Review* 62 (March): 103–126.

Fraser, S., ed. 1995. *The bell curve wars: Race, intelligence, and the future of America.* New York: Basic Books.

Freeman, M. 1984. History, narrative, and life span development knowledge. *Human Development* 27: 1–19.

Freedman, J. L. 1975. *Crowding and behavior.* New York: Viking.

Freidenberg, J. N. 1995. Growing old in Spanish Harlem: A multimedia, bilingual exhibition. *Migration World* 23 (1–2): 34–38.

French, J. R. P., and B. Raven. 1959. The bases of social power. In D. Cartwright, ed. *Studies in social power.* Ann Arbor, Mich.: Institute for Social Research.

Freud, A. 1967. *Ego and the mechanisms of defense.* Rev. ed. New York: International Libraries Press.

Freud, S. 1953–1974. *The standard edition of the complete psychological works of Sigmund Freud.* Trans. James Strachey. London: Hogarth Press.

Friedman, E., A. Katcher, J. L. Lynch, and S. A. Thomas. 1980. Animal companions and one-year survival of patients after discharge from a coronary care unit. *Public Health Reports* 95 (July–August): 307–312.

Furstenberg, F. F., Jr., J. B. Brooks-Gunn, and S. P. Morgan. 1987a. Adolescent mothers and their children in later life. *Family Planning Perspectives* 19 (July-August): 142–151.

———. 1987b. *Adolescent mothers in later life.* Cambridge: Cambridge University Press.

Gamble, T. J., and E. Zigler. 1986. Effects of infant day care: Another look at the evidence. *American Journal of Orthopsychiatry* 56:26–41.

Garcia, E. 1995. Departments of Labor, Health and Human Services, Education. Appropriations for 1996. Part 5. Hearing. Washington, D.C.: GPO.

Garcia-Preto, N. 1982. Puerto Rican families. In M. McGoldrick, J. Pearce, and J. Giordano, eds. *Ethnicity and family therapy,* pp. 164–186. New York: Guilford Press.

Gardner, H. 1993. *Multiple intelligences: A theory in practice.* New York: Basic Books.

———. 1995. Cracking open the IQ box. In S. Fraser, ed. *The bell curve wars: Race, intelligence, and the future of America,* pp.23–35. New York: Basic Books.

Gardner, J. W. 1984. *Excellence: Can we be equal and excellent too?* 2d ed. New York: W. W. Norton.

Garmezy, N. 1971. Vulnerability research and the issue of primary prevention. *American Journal of Orthopsychiatry* 41 (1): 101–116.

Gary, L. E. 1980. Role of alcohol and drug abuse in homicide. *Public Health Reports* 95 (November–December): 553–554.

Gary, L. E., and B. Leashore. 1982. High-risk status of black men. *Social Work* 54 (January): 54–59.

Gelfand, D. E., and R. Bialik-Gilad. 1989. Immigration reform and social work. *Social Work* 34 (January): 23–28.

Gerard, D. 1985. Clinical social workers as primary prevention agents. In C. B. Germain, ed. *Advances in clinical social work practice,* pp. 84–89. Silver Spring, Md.: NASW Press.

Germain, C. B. 1981. The physical environment and social work practice. In A. N. Maluccio, ed. *Promoting competence in clients,* pp., 103–124. New York: Free Press.

———. 1984. *Social work practice in health care: An ecological perspective.* New York: Free Press.

———. 1985. The place of community work within an ecological approach to social work practice. In S. H. Taylor and R. W. Roberts, eds. *Theory and practice of community social work,* pp. 30–55. New York: Columbia University Press.

———. 1991. *Human behavior in the social environment.* 1st ed. New York: Columbia University Press.

———. 1994a. Emerging conceptions of family development over the life course. *Families and Society* 75 (5): 259–268.

———. 1994b. Using an ecological perspective. In J. Rothman, ed. *Practice with highly vulnerable clients,* pp. 39–55. Englewood Cliffs, N.J.: Prentice-Hall.

———. 1997. Should HBSE be taught from a stage perspective? No. In M. Bloom and W. C. Klein, eds. *Controversial issues in human behavior in the social environment,* 40–46. Needham Heights, Mass.: Allyn and Bacon.

Germain, C. B., and A. Gitterman. 1995. Ecological perspective. In R. L. Edwards et al., eds. *Encyclopedia of social work,* 816–824. 19th ed. Washington, D.C.: NASW Press.

———. 1996. *The life model of social work practice: Advances in theory and practice.* 2d ed. New York: Columbia University Press.

Gerstel, N., and H. Fross. 1985. *Commuter marriage.* New York: Guilford Press.

Getzel, G. S., and R. Masters. 1985. Social work practice with families of homicide victims. In C. B. Germain, ed. *Advances in clinical social work practice,* pp. 7–16. Silver Spring, Md.: NASW Press.

Gibbs, L. M. 1983. Community response to an emergency situation: Psychological destruction and the Love Canal. *American Journal of Community Psychology* 11 (2): 116–125.

Gibbs, J. T., and G. Moskowitz-Sweet. 1991. Clinical and cultural issues in the treatment of biracial and bicultural adolescents. *Families in Society* 72 (10): 579–592.

Gilchrist, L. D., and S. P. Schinke. 1983. Teenage pregnancy and public policy. *Social Service Review* 57 (June): 307–322.

Gilder, G. 1996. Forum: Does America still work? *Harper's Magazine,* May, 35–47.

Gillen, G. 1995. HMO: Aging population results in more deaths, fewer births. *Thanatos* 20 (4): 28.

Gilligan, G. 1982. *In a different voice: Psychological theory and women's development.* Cambridge: Harvard University Press.

Ginsberg, D., J. M. Gottman, and J. Parker. 1986. The importance of friendship. In J. M. Gottman and J. G. Parker, eds. *Conversations of friends: Speculations on affective development,* 3–48. Cambridge: Cambridge University Press.

Gittler, J., and M. McPherson. 1990. Prenatal substance abuse: An overview of the problem. *Children Today* 19 (4): 3–7.

Gliedman, J., and W. Roth. 1980. *The unexpected minority: Handicapped children in America.* New York: Harcourt Brace Jovanovich.

Gluckman, A., and B. Reed. 1993. Culture: The gay marketing moment: Leaving diversity in the dust. *Dollars-and-Sense,* no. 190 (November–December): 16–19, 34–35.

Goetting, A. 1986. The developmental tasks of siblingship over the life cycle. *Journal of Marriage and Family* 48 (4): 703–714.

———. 1994. The parenting-crime connection. *Journal of Primary Prevention* 14 (3): 169–186.

Gold, D., and D. Andres. 1980. Maternal employment and development of ten-year-old francophone children. *Canadian Journal of Behavioral Science* 12:233–240.

Goldsmith, J. 1982. The postdivorce family system. In F. Walsh, ed. *Normal family processes,* pp. 297–330. New York: Guilford Press.

Goldstein, J., A. Freud, and A. J. Solnit. 1973. *Beyond the best interests of the child.* New York: Free Press.

———. 1979. *Before the best interests of the child.* New York: Free Press.

Googins, B., and J. Godfrey. 1987. *Occupational social work.* Englewood Cliffs, N.J.: Prentice-Hall.

Gordon, W. E. 1969. Basic constructs for an integrative and generative conception of social work. In G. Hearn, ed. *The general systems approach: Contributions toward an holistic conception of social work,* pp. 5–12. New York: Council on Social Work Education.

Gore, A. 1992. *Earth in the balance: Ecology and the human spirit.* Boston: Houghton Mifflin.

Gottman, J. M. 1979. *Empirical investigations of marriage.* New York: Academic Press.

———. 1993. The roles of conflict engagement, escalation, and avoidance in marital interaction: A longitudinal view of five types of couples. *Journal of Consulting and Clinical Psychology* 61 (1): 6–15.

———. 1994a. *What predicts divorce? The relationship between marital processes and marital outcome.* Hillsdale, N.J.: Lawrence Erlbaum.

———. 1994b. *Why marriages succeed or fail. . . . and how you can make yours last.* New York: Fireside Books.

Gottman, J. M., and R. W. Levenson. 1992. Marital processes predictive of later dissolution: Behavior, physiology, and health. *Journal of Personality and Social Psychology* 63 (2): 221–233.

Gould, S. J. 1981. *The mismeasure of man.* New York: W. W. Norton.

———. 1995. Curveball. In S. Fraser, ed. *The bell curve wars: Race, intelligence, and the future of America,* pp. 11–22. New York: Basic Books.

Gouldner, A. W. 1973. Anti-minotaur: The myth of a value-free sociology. In A. W. Gouldner. *For sociology: Renewal and critiques in sociology today,* pp. 3–26. New York: Basic Books.

Gray, M. C. 1995. Drug abuse. In R. L. Edwards et al., eds. *Encyclopedia of social work,* pp. 795–803. 19th ed. Washington, D.C.: NASW Press.

Greeley, A. 1995. Concern about AIDS in minority communities. *FDA Consumer* 29 (December): 11–15.

Green, R-J. 1995. High achievement, underachievement, and learning disabilities: A family systems model. In B. A. Ryan, G. R. Adams, T. P. Gullotta, R. P. Weissberg, and R. L. Hampton, eds. *The family-school connection,* pp. 207–249. Thousand Oaks, Calif.: Sage.

Guernery, B. G. 1977. *Relationship enhancement.* San Francisco: Jossey-Bass.

Gutmann, D. 1977. The cross-cultural perspective: Notes toward a comparative psychology of aging. In J. E. Birren and K. W. Schaie, eds. *Handbook of the psychology of aging,* pp. 302–326. New York: Van Nostrand and Reinhold.

Hage, J., and M. Aikin. 1970. *Social change in complex organizations.* New York: Random House.

Hahlweg, K., and H. J. Markman. 1988. The effectiveness of behavioral marital therapy: Empirical status of behavioral techniques in preventing and alleviating marital distress. *Journal of Consulting and Clinical Psychology* 56:440–447.

Hakuta, K. 1988. *Mirror of language: The debate on bilingualism.* New York: Basic Books.

Hall, E. H., and G. C. King. 1982. Working with the strengths of black families. *Child Welfare* 61:536–551.

Hall, E. T. 1966. *The hidden dimension.* New York: Doubleday.

Hall, P. 1988. *Cities of tomorrow.* Oxford, UK: Basil Blackwell.

Hallahan, D. P., and J. M. Kauffman. 1994. *Exceptional children.* 6th ed. Boston: Allyn and Bacon.

Hamburg, B. A. 1974. Early adolescence: A specific and stressful stage of the life cycle. In G. V. Coelho, D. Hamburg, and J. Adams, eds. *Coping and adaptation,* pp. 101–124. New York: Basic Books.

Hampton, R., and A. S. W. Coner-Edwards. 1993. Physical and sexual violence in marriage. In R. Hampton, T. Gullotta, G. Adams, E. H. Potter III, and R. Weissberg, eds. *Family violence: Prevention and treatment,* pp. 113–141. Newbury Park, Calif.: Sage.

Hampton, R., T. Gullotta, G. Adams, E. H. Potter III, and R. P. Weissberg, eds. 1993. *Family violence: Prevention and treatment.* Newbury Park, Calif.: Sage.

Harbor Area Geriatric Program Staff (Erich Lindemann Mental Health Center, Boston, Mass.). 1985. Letter to the editor. *Hospital and Community Psychiatry* 35 (November): 1152–1153.

Hareven, T. K. 1982. The life course and aging in historical perspective. In T. K. Hareven and K. J. Adams, eds. *Aging and life course transitions: An interdisciplinary perspective,* pp. 1–26. New York: Guildford Press.

Hartman, A. 1978. Diagrammatic assessment of family relationships. *Social Casework* 59 (October): 465–476.

Hartman, A., and J. Laird. 1983. *Family centered social work practice.* New York: Free Press.

Hartmann, H. 1958. *Ego psychology and the problem of adaptation.* New York: International Universities Press.

Hartup, W. W. 1979. Peer relations and the growth of competence. In M. W. Kent and J. E. Rolf, eds. *Primary prevention of psychopathology.* Vol. 3. *Social competence in children,* pp. 150–170. Hanover, N.H.: University Press of New England.

Havighurst, R. 1966. *Developmental tasks and education.* New York: David McKay.

Hawkins, D. 1996. Homeschool battles. *U.S. News and World Report,* 12 February, 57–58.

Hawkins, J. D. 1997. Academic performance and school success: Sources and consequences. In R. P. Weissberg et al., eds. *Enhancing children's wellness,* pp. 278–305. Thousand Oaks, Calif.: Sage.

Hawkins, J. D., and J. G. Weis. 1985. The social development model: An integrative approach to delinquency prevention. *Journal of Primary Prevention* 6 (2): 73–97.

Hayakawa, S. I. 1995. Bilingualism in America: English should be the *only* language. In G. Goshgarian, ed. *Exploring language,* pp. 230–235. 7th ed. New York: Harper Collins.

Hayes, C. D. 1987. *Risking the future: Adolescent sexuality, pregnancy and childbearing.* Vol. 1 of *National Research Council, Panel on Adolescent Pregnancy and Childbearing.* Washington, D.C.: National Academy Press.

Headden, S. 1995. Tongue-tied in the schools. *U.S. News and World Reports,* 25 September, 44–46.

Healthy people: The surgeon general's report on health promotion and disease prevention. 1979. DHEW (PHS) Publication No. 79–55071.

Hechinger, F. M. 1988. Toward educating the homeless. *New York Times,* 2 February, C11.

Henshaw, S. K., and E. F. Jones. 1988. The delivery of family planning services in Ontario and Quebec. *Family Planning Perspectives* 20 (March–April): 80–87.

Herrnstein, R., and C. Murray. 1994. *The bell curve.* New York: Free Press.

Herzberg, F. 1982. *The managerial choice: To be efficient and to be humane.* 2d ed. Salt Lake City: Olympus.

Hetherington, E. M., M. Cox, and R. Cox. 1982. Effects of divorce on parents and children. In M. Lamb, ed. *Nontraditional families: Parenting and child development,* pp. 233–288. Hillsdale, N.J.: Erlbaum.

Hill, C. J. 1984. Caring for an elderly relative. *Canada's Mental Health* 32 (March): 13–15.

Hill, R. 1972. *The strengths of black families.* New York: Emerson Hall.

Hochschild, A. R. 1974. Communal life styles for the old. In A. Skolnick and J. H. Skolnick, eds. *Intimacy, family, and society,* pp. 565–578. Boston: Little, Brown.

———. 1997. *The time bind: When work becomes home and home becomes work.* New York: Metropolitan Books.

Hockenberry, J. 1996. *Moving violations: War zones, wheelchairs, and declarations of independence.* Westport, Conn.: Hyperion.

Hodes, J. R. 1995. Departments of Labor, Health and Human Services, Education . . . Appropriations for 1996. Part 4. Hearing. Washington, D.C.: GPO.

Hodson, R., and T. A. Sullivan. 1995. *The social organization of work.* 2d ed. Belmont, Calif.: Wadsworth Publishing.

Hoffman, L. W. 1984. Work, family, and the socialization of the child. In R. Parke, ed. *Review of child development research,* pp. 223–282. Vol. 7. Chicago: University of Chicago Press.

Hoge, D. R. 1990. Religion in America: Catholics in the U.S.: The next generation. *Public Perspective* 2 (11): 11–12.

Hooked on tobacco: The teen epidemic. 1995. *Consumer Reports,* March, 142–147.

Hooyman, N., and H. A. Kiyak. 1996. *Social gerontology: A multidisciplinary perspective.* 4th ed. Boston: Allyn and Bacon.

Horvath, A. V., and L. Luborsky. 1993. The role of the therapeutic alliance in psychotherapy. *Journal of Consulting and Clinical Psychology* 61 (4): 561–573.

Hot Flash: Newsletter for Middle and Older Women. 1984. Editorial. 3 (spring): 1.

Houle, J., and M. C. Kiely. 1984. Intimacy: A little-understood stage of development. *Canada's Mental Health* 32 (March): 7–11.

Howell, J. C. 1995. *Guide for implementing the comprehensive strategy for serious, violent, and chronic juvenile offenders.* Washington, D.C.: Office of Juvenile Justice and Delinquency Prevention.

Hraba, J. 1979. *American ethnicity.* Itasca, Ill.: Peacock Publishers.

Hsia, J., and M. Hirano-Nakanishi. 1989. The demographics of diversity: Asian Americans and higher education. *Change* (November–December): 20–27.

Hudgins, J. L. 1991–1992. The strengths of black families, revisited. *Urban League Review* 15 (winter): 9–20.

Hulley, S. B., and N. Hearst. 1989. The worldwide epidemiology and prevention of AIDS. In V. May, G. Albee, and S. Schneider, eds. *Primary prevention of AIDS,* pp. 47–71. Vol. 12. Newbury Park, Calif.: Sage.

Humphreys, N., and J. Nol. 1997. Can a feminist perspective in HBSE exist without "blaming the aggressors"? In M. Bloom and W. C. Klein, eds. *Controversial issues in human behavior and the social environment,* pp. 272–276. Boston: Allyn and Bacon.

Hurst, J. B., and J. W. Shepard. 1986. The dynamics of plant closings: An extended emotional roller-coaster ride. *Journal of Counseling and Development* 64 (5): 401–405.

Hyde, J. 1981. How large are cognitive gender differences? *American Psychologist* 36 (August): 892–901.

Hyman, L. A. 1990. *Reading, writing, and the hickory stick: The appalling story of physical and psychological abuse in American schools.* Lexington, Mass.: Lexington Books.

Iaffaldano, M. T., and P. M. Muchinsky. 1985. Job satisfaction and job performance: A meta-analysis. *Psychological Bulletin* 97:251–273.

Institute of Medicine. 1988. *Homelessness, health, and human need.* Washington, D.C.: National Academy Press.

Ittelson, W. H., H. M. Proshansky, G. G. Rivlin, G. H. Winkel, and D. Dempsey. 1974. *An introduction to environmental psychology.* New York: Holt, Rinehart and Winston.

Jackson, D. D. 1968. *Communication, family, and marriage: Human communication.* Vol. 1. Palo Alto, Calif.: Science and Behavior Books.

Jackson, J. J. 1985. Race, national origin, ethnicity, and aging. In R. Binstock and S. Shanas, eds. *Handbook of aging and the social sciences,* pp. 164–303. 2d ed. New York: Van Nostrand Reinhold.

Jacobson, N. S., and G. Margolin. 1979. *Marital therapy: Strategies based on social learning and behavior exchange principles.* New York: Brunner/Mazel.

James, F. E. 1988. Office pariahs. *Wall Street Journal,* 22 April, sect. 3.

Jason, L. A., J. Johnson, K. Danner, S. Taylor, and K. Kurasaki. 1993. A comprehensive preventive, parent-based intervention for high-risk transfer students. *Prevention in Human Services* 10 (2): 27–38.

Jason, L. A., K. S. Kurasaki, L. Neuson, and C. Garcia. 1993. Training parents in a preventive intervention for transfer students. *Journal of Primary Prevention* 13 (3): 213–227.

Jay, K., and A. Young. 1979. *The gay report.* New York: Summit Books.

Jendrek, M. P. 1992. Grandparents who provide care to grandchildren: Preliminary findings and policy issues. Typescript. Cited in Atchley.

Jennings, J. 1987. Elderly parents as caregivers for their adult dependent children. *Social Work* 32 (September–October): 430–433.

Jeppsson-Grassman, E. 1986a. *After the fall of darkness: Three studies of visual impairment and work.* Stockholm Studies in Social Work 3. School of Social Work, University of Stockholm, Sweden.

———. 1986b. *Work and new visual impairment: A study of the adaptive process.* Stockholm Studies in Social Work 2. School of Social Work, University of Stockholm, Sweden.

Jobes, D. A., J. R. Eyman, and R. I. Yufit. 1995. How clinicians assess suicide risk in adolescents and adults. *Crisis Intervention and Time-Limited Treatment* 2 (1): 1–12.

Johnson, A. K. 1995. Homelessness. In R. L. Edwards et al., eds. *Encyclopedia of social work,* pp. 1138–1346. 19th ed. Washington, D.C.: NASW Press.

Johnson, H. C. 1988. Drugs, dialogue, or diet: Diagnosing and treating the hyperactive child. *Social Work* 33 (July–August): 349–355.

———. 1996. Violence and biology: A review of the literature. *Families in Society* 77 (January): 3–18.

Jones, R. L. 1995. Poverty in the African American community: Perspectives and approaches. In W. J. O'Neill Jr., ed. *Family: The first imperative,* pp. 153–164. Cleveland: O'Neill Foundation.

Journal of Primary Prevention. 1994. 15 (2).

———. 1996. 17 (1).

Justice, B. 1987. *Who gets sick: Thinking and health.* Houston: Peak Press. Cited in L. N. Brown.

Kagan, S. L. 1994. Families and children: Who is responsible? *Childhood Education* 71 (1): 4–8.

Kalafat, J. 1997. Prevention of youth suicide. In R. P. Weissberg et al., eds. *Enhancing children's wellness,* pp. 175–213. Thousand Oaks, Calif.: Sage.

Kalish, R. A. 1968. Life and death: Dividing the indivisible. *Social Science and Medicine* 2:249–259.

Kanter, R. M. 1972. "Getting it all together": Some group issues in communes. *American Journal of Orthopsychiatry* 42 (July): 632–643.

Kantrowitz, B., and P. Wingert. 1993. The Norplant debate. *Newsweek,* 15 February, 36–37, 40–41.

Karls, J. M., and P. Wandrei. 1995. Person-in-environment. In R. L. Edwards et al., eds. *Encyclopedia of social work,* pp. 1818–1827. 19th ed. Washington, D.C.: NASW Press.

Kart, C. S. 1994. *The realities of aging: An introduction to gerontology.* 4th ed. Boston: Allyn and Bacon.

Kaslow, A. 1996. Learning at home. *Christian Science Monitor,* 26 February, 9–11.

Katz, A. H. 1993. *Self-help in America: A social movement perspective.* New York: Twayne.

Katz, D., and R. L. Kahn. 1978. *The social psychology of organizations.* 2d ed. New York: Wiley.

Keith, J. 1985. Age in anthropological research. In R. H. Binstock and E. Shanas, eds. *Handbook of aging and the social sciences,* pp. 231–263. New York: Van Nostrand Reinhold.

Kellam, S. G. 1975. *Mental health and going to school: The Woodlawn Program.* Chicago: University of Chicago Press.

———. 1977. Family structure and the mental health of children: Concurrent and longitudinal community-wide studies. *Archives of General Psychiatry* 34 (September): 1012–1022.

Kellam, S. G., and G. W. Rebok. 1992. Building developmental and etiological theory through epidemiologically based preventive intervention trials. In J. McCord and R. E. Tremblay, eds. *Preventing antisocial behavior: Interventions from birth through adolescence,* pp. 162–195. New York: Guilford Press.

Kellam, S. G., G. W. Rebok, N. Ialongo, and L. S. Mayer. 1994. The course and malleability of aggressive behavior from early first grade into middle school: Results of a developmental epidemiologically based preventive trial. *Journal of Child Psychology and Psychiatry* 35:259–281.

Keniston, K., and the Carnegie Council on Children. 1977. *All our children.* New York: Harcourt Brace Jovanovich.

Kerson, T. S., and L. A. Kerson. 1985. *Understanding chronic illness: The medical and psychosocial dimensions of nine diseases.* New York: Free Press.

Kett, J. F. 1977. *Rites of passage: Adolescence in America, 1790 to the present.* New York: Basic Books.

Kinzel, A. 1970. Body buffer zone in violent prisoners. *American Journal of Psychiatry* 127 (July): 59–64.

Kirk, S. A., and H. Kutchins. 1992. *The selling of DSM: The rhetoric of science in psychiatry.* New York: Aldine de Gruyter.

Klarsfeld, S. 1997. *French children of the Holocaust: A memorial.* New York: New York University Press.

Klein, W., and M. Bloom. 1994. Social work as an applied social science. *Social Work* 39 (4): 421–431.

————. 1997. *Successful aging.* New York: Plenum.

Kleiman, D. 1984. When abortion becomes birth: A dilemma of medical ethics shaken by new advances. *New York Times,* 15 February, B1, B4.

Kline, M. L., and D. L. Snow. 1994. Effects of work site coping skills intervention on stress, social support, and health outcomes of working mothers. *Journal of Primary Prevention* 15 (2): 105–121.

Koenig, H., and D. Blazer. 1992. Mood disorders and suicide. In J. E. Birren, R. B. Sloan, and G. Cohen, eds. *Handbook of mental health and aging..* San Diego: Academic Press.

Kohlberg, L. 1964. The development of moral character and moral ideology. In M. Hoffman and L. Hoffman, eds. *Review of child development research.* Vol. 1. New York: Russell Sage Foundation.

Kopels, S. 1995. The Americans with Disabilities Act: A tool to combat poverty. *Journal of Social Work Education* 31 (3): 337–346.

Kubler-Ross, E. 1969. *On death and dying.* New York: Macmillan.

Kuhn, D. R. 1993. Late-life marriages, older stepfamilies, and Alzheimer's disease. *Families in Society* 74 (3): 154–162.

Ladner, J. A. 1971. *Tomorrow's tomorrow: The black woman.* New York: Anchor Books.

Laird, J. 1989. Women and stories: Restorying women's self-constructions. In M. McGoldrick, C. Anderson, and F. Walsh, eds. *Women in families,* pp. 428–451. New York: Norton.

Lally, E. M., and H. A. Haynes. 1995. Alaska natives. In R. L. Edwards et al., eds. *Encyclopedia of social work,* pp. 194–202. 19th ed. Washington, D.C.: NASW Press.

Lane, H. 1987. Listen to the needs of deaf children. *New York Times,* 17 July, p. 35.

LaPlante, M. P. 1992. How many Americans have a disability? In *Disability Statistics*

Abstract No. 5. San Francisco: Disability Statistics Program, University of California. Cited in Asch and Mudrick.

Larson, J. 1991. Households: Cohabitation is a premarital step. *American Demographics* 13 (11): 20–21.

Lau, E., and J. Kosberg. 1979. Abuse of the elderly by informal care providers: Practice and research issues. *Aging* nos. 299–300 (September–October): 10–15.

Lauer, J. C., and R. H. Lauer. 1986. *Til death do us part: How couples stay together.* New York: Haworth Press.

Lawlor, E. F. 1987. The intergenerational debate. *Public Policy and Aging Report* 1 (2): 1–3, 8–10.

Lazarus, R. S. 1984. The costs and benefits of denial. In S. Brenitz, ed. *Denial of stress,* pp. 1–30. New York: International Universities Press.

Lazarus, R. S., and S. Folkman. 1984. *Stress, appraisal, and coping.* New York: Springer.

Lazarus, R. S., and R. H. Launier. 1978. Stress-related transactions between person and environment. In L. A. Pervin and M. Lewis, eds. *Perspectives in interactional psychology,* pp. 287–327. New York: Plenum.

Lee, J. A. B. 1980. The helping professional's use of language in describing the poor. *American Journal of Orthopsychiatry* 50 (October): 580–584.

———. 1981. Human relatedness and the mentally impaired older person. *Journal of Gerontological Social Work* 4 (winter): 5–15.

———. 1986. No place to go: Homeless women. In A. Gitterman and L. Shulman, eds. *Mutual aid groups and the life cycle,* pp. 245–263. Itasca, Ill.: F. E. Peacock.

———. 1991. Teaching lesbian and gay identity formation content in human behavior and methods courses. In N. J. Woodman, ed. *Lesbian and gay lifestyles: A guide for counseling and education.* New York: Irvington Press.

———. 1994. *The empowerment approach to social work practice.* New York: Columbia University Press.

—, ed. 1989. *Group work with the poor and oppressed.* New York: Haworth Press.

—, ed. 1991. *An annotated bibliography of gay and lesbian readings for social workers, other helping professionals, and consumers of services.* 2d ed. East Rockaway, N.Y.: Cummings and Hathaway.

Lenrow, P. B., and R. Burch. 1981. Mutual aid and professional services: Opposing or complementary? In B. H. Gottlieb, ed. *Social networks and social supports,* pp. 233–258. Beverly Hills, Calif.: Sage.

Leo, J. 1994. Is it a war against women? *U.S. News and World Report,* July 11, 22.

Lerner, G. 1971. Women's rights and American feminism. *American Scholar* 40 (spring): 235–248.

Levenstein, P. 1988. *Messages from home: The mother-child home program and the prevention of school disadvantage.* Columbus: Ohio State University Press.

Levine, R. 1988. More infants showing signs of narcotics. *New York Times,* 1 April, B1, B3.

Levine, R. S., D. Metzendorf, and K. A. Van Boskirk. 1986. Runaway and throwaway youth: A case for early intervention with truants. *Social Work in Education* 8:93–105.

Lewin, K. 1951. *Field theory in social science: Selected theoretical papers.* Ed. D. Cartwright. New York: Harper and Row.

Lewis, M. 1996. The rich: How they're different . . . than they used to be. *New York Times Magazine,* 19 November, 65–69.

Lewis, R. G. 1995. American Indians. In R. L. Edwards et al., eds. *Encyclopedia of social work,* pp. 216–224. 19th ed. Washington, D.C.: NASW Press.

Lewontin, R., S. Rose, and L. L. Kamin. 1984. *Not in our genes: Biology, ideology, and human nature.* New York: Pantheon.

Lieberman, J. 1995. *Congressional Record,* 16 February, pp. S2823–2889.

Likert, R. 1961. *New patterns of management.* New York: McGraw-Hill.

Linsk, N. L. 1994. HIV and the elderly. *Families in Society* 75 (6): 362–372.

Lipman, A. 1986. Homosexual relationships. *Generations* 10 (4): 51–54.

Lippitt, R., and M. Gold. 1959. Classroom social structure as a mental health problem. *Journal of Social Issues* 15 (1): 40–49.

Lippitt, R., J. Watson, and B. Westley. 1958. *The dynamics of planned change.* New York: Harcourt, Brace.

Lisansky-Gomberg, E. 1981. Alcohol and drug abuse. Paper presented at the Stony Brook Conference, Health Issues of Older Women, April.

Litwak, E., and I. Szelenyi. 1969. Primary group structures and their functions: Kin, neighbors, and friends. *American Sociological Review* 34:465–481.

Livson, F. B. 1980. Sex typing over the life span: His, hers, and theirs. Paper presented at the annual meeting of the Gerontological Society of America, San Diego.

Locke, H., and K. Wallace. 1959. Short mental adjustment and prediction tests: Their reliability and validity. *Marriage and Family Living* 21:251–255.

Luepnitz, D. A. 1989. *The family interpreted.* New York: Basic Books.

Luey, H. S. 1980. Between worlds: The problems of deafened adults. *Social Work in Health Care* 5 (spring): 253–265.

Maccoby, E., and C. N. Jacklin. 1974. *The psychology of sex differences.* Stanford, Calif.: Stanford University Press.

Macfarlane, A. 1977. *The psychology of childbirth.* Cambridge: Harvard University Press.

Maguire, L. 1991. *Social support systems in practice: A generalist approach.* Silver Spring, Md.: NASW Press.

Magan, G. S. 1989. A new kind of matchmaking: Make yourself at home: By sharing. *AARP News Bulletin* 30 (10): 1, 16.

Mangano, M. F. 1990. Drug treatment issues. Hearings. Washington, D.C.: GPO.

Marano, H. E. 1997. Puberty may start at 6 as hormones surge. *New York Times,* 1 July, C1, C6.

Marcia, J. E. 1991. Identity and self-development. In R. M. Lerner, A. Petersen, and J. Brooks-Gunn, eds. *Encyclopedia of adolescence.* Vol. 1. New York: Garland.

Marciniak, E. 1991. The ecumenical task, 1991: All ecumenism is local. *Commonweal,* 25 January, 44, 48–52.

Marin, V. M., and E. F. Vacha. 1994. Self-help strategies and resources among people at risk of homelessness: Empirical findings and social service policies. *Social Work* 39 (6): 649–668.

Markman, H. J. 1981. Prediction of marital distress: A 5-year follow-up. *Journal of Consulting and Clinical Psychology* 49:760–762.

Markman, H. J., F. J. Floyd, and F. Dickson-Markman. 1982. Toward a model for the prediction and prevention of marital and family distress and dissolution. In S. Duck, ed. *Personal relationships.* Vol. 4. *Dissolving personal relationships,* pp. 231–261. London: Academic Press.

Markman, H. J., F. J. Floyd, S. M. Stanley, and R. D. Storaasli. 1988. Prevention of marital distress: A longitudinal investigation. *Journal of Consulting and Clinical Psychology* 56 (2): 210–217.

Markman, H. J., M. J. Renick, F. J. Floyd, S. M. Stanley, and M. Clements. 1993. Preventing marital distress through communication and conflict management training: A 4- and 5-year follow-up. *Journal of Consulting and Clinical Psychology* 61 (1): 70–77.

Marshall, J. R. 1996. Science, "schizophrenia," and genetics: The creation of myths. *Journal of Primary Prevention* 17 (1): 99–115.

Martin, P., and E. Midgley. 1994. Immigration to the United States: Journey to an uncertain destination. *Population Bulletin* 49 (2): 2–45.

Martyna, W. 1980. Beyond the "He/Man" approach: The case for non-sexist language. *Signs: Journal of Women in Culture and Society* 5 (spring): 482–493.

Marx, K., and F. Engels. 1848. *The Communist manifesto.* New York: Appleton-Century-Crofts.

Masi, D. A. 1984. *Designing employee assistance programs.* New York: American Management Association.

Maslow, A. H. 1971. *The farther reaches of human nature.* New York: Viking.

Massey, D. S., and A. Singer. 1995. New estimates of undocumented Mexican migration and the probability of apprehension. *Demography* 32 (2): 203–213.

Matlaw, J. R., and J. B. Mayer. 1986. Elder abuse: Ethical and practical dilemmas for social work. *Health and Social Work* 11 (spring): 85–94.

Mauk, G. W., and P. L. Rodgers. 1994. Building bridges over troubled waters: School-based postvention with adolescent survivors of peer suicide. *Crisis Intervention and Time-limited Treatment* 1 (2): 102–123.

May, P. A., and K. J. Hymbaugh. 1989. A macro-level fetal alcohol syndrome prevention program for Native Americans and Alaska Natives: Description and evaluation. *Journal of Studies on Alcohol* 50 (6): 508–518.

McClusky, K. A., J. Killarney, and D. Papini. 1983. Adolescent pregnancy and parenthood: Implications for development. In E. J. Callahan and K. A. McClusky, eds. *Life-span developmental psychology: Nonnormative life events,* pp. 69–113. New York: Academic Press.

McCord, H. R., Jr. 1993. Families today: Many faces, many voices. *Catholic World,* July–August, 154–159.

McDonald, T., R. I. Allen, A. Westerfelt, and I. Piliavin. 1996. *Assessing the long-term effects of foster care: A research synthesis.* Washington, D.C.: CWLA Press.

McGuffin, P., and R. Murray. 1991. *The new genetics of mental illness.* Boston: Oxford, Butterworth-Heineman.

McKenry, P. C., D. H. Browne, J. B. Kotch, and M. J. Symons. 1990. Mediators of depression among low-income, adolescent mothers of infants: A longitudinal study. *Journal of Youth and Adolescence* 19:327–347.

McLaughlin, S. D., S. E. Pearce, D. Manninen, and L. Winges. 1988. To parent or relinquish: consequences for adolescent mothers. *Social Work* 33 (July–August): 320–324.

McNeil, J. 1993. Census Bureau data on persons with disabilities: New results and old questions about validity and reliability. Cited in Asch and Mudrick.

Mech, E. V., and J. R. Ryeraft. 1995. *Preparing foster youths for adult living: Proceedings of an invitational research conference.* Washington, D.C.: CWLA Press.

Mednick, S. A., and E. S. Kandel. 1988. Congenital determinants of violence. *Bulletin of the American Academy of Psychiatry and the Law* 16:101–109.

Meeks, D. E. 1989. Substance abuse disorders. In F. J. Turner, ed. *Child psychopathology: A social work perspective,* pp. 317–350. New York: Free Press.

Melvin, A. G. 1946. *Education: A history.* New York: John Day.

Milgram, D. 1994. Hearings on H.R. 2884, School-to-Work Opportunities Act of 1993. Hearing. Washington, D.C.: GPO,

Miller, D. R., and G. E. Swanson. 1958. *The changing American parent: A study in the Detroit area.* New York: Wiley.

Miller, J. G. 1978. *Living systems.* New York: McGraw-Hill.

Miller, S., E. W. Nunnally, and D. Wackman. 1977. *Alive and aware: Improving communications in relationships.* Minneapolis: Interpersonal Communications Programs.

Mink, P. 1994. Welfare reform: The gender issue. *Congressional Record,* Daily Edition, 11 March, pp. H1310–1314.

Mizio, E. 1974. Impact of external systems on the Puerto Rican family. *Social Casework* 55 (February): 76–83.

Moen, P. 1983. The two-provider family: Problems and potentials. In M. E. Lamb, ed. *Changing families,* pp. 13–43. New York: Plenum.

Mogelonsky, M. 1995. Asian-Indian Americans. *American Demographics* 17 (8): 32–36, 38–39.

Moles, O. C. 1992. School performance of children from one-parent families. In M. Bloom, ed. *Changing lives: Studies in human development and professional helping,* pp. 110–120. Columbia: University of South Carolina Press.

Moore, K. A., M. Simms, and C. Betsey. 1986. *Choice and circumstance.* New Brunswick, N.J.: Rutgers University Press, Transaction Books.

Moos, R. H. 1976. *The human context.* New York: Wiley.

Moral issues of our times: Reaffirming the family. 1994. *Christian Science Monitor,* 2 February, 22.

Morton, A. L. 1969. *The life and ideas of Robert Owen.* New York: International.

Moses, A. E., and R. O. Hawkins. 1982. *Counseling lesbian women and gay men: A life-issues approach.* St. Louis, Mo.: Mosby.

Moynihan, D. 1967. *The Negro family: The case for national action.* Washington, D.C.: U.S. Department of Labor.

Munoz, F. U. 1976. Pacific Islanders—A perplexed, neglected minority. *Social Casework* 57 (March): 179–184.

Murphy, L. B. 1974. Coping, vulnerability, and resilience in childhood. In G. V. Coelho, D. Hamburg, and J. Adams, eds. *Coping and adaptation,* pp. 69–199. New York: Basic Books.

Murray, M. E., N. G. Guerra, and K. R. Williams. 1997. Violence prevention for the twenty-first century. In R. P. Weissberg et al., eds. *Enhancing children's wellness,* pp. 105–128. Thousand Oaks, Calif.: Sage.

Myerhoff, B. G. 1978a. *Number our days: A triumph of continuity and culture among Jewish old people in an urban ghetto.* New York: Simon and Schuster.

———. 1978b. A symbol perfected in death: Continuity and ritual in the life and death of an elderly Jew. In B. G. Myerhoff and A. Simic, eds. *Life's career—aging: Cultural variations in growing old,* pp.163–230. Beverly Hills, Calif.: Sage.

Naditch, M. P. 1985. Industry-based wellness programs. In D. Myers, ed. *Employee problem prevention and counseling.* Westport, Conn.: Quorum Books.

Nash, K. B. 1989. Self-help groups: An empowerment vehicle for sickle cell disease patients and their families. *Social Work with Groups* 12:81–91.

National Center for Health Research. 1987. Report of a study in the *NASW Newsletter.*

National Commission on Excellence in Education. 1983. *Nation at risk: The imperative for educational reform.* Washington, D.C.: GPO.

National Commission on the Role of School and Community in Improving Adolescent Health. 1990. *Code blue: Uniting for healthier youth.* Alexandria, Va.: National Association of State Boards of Education.

National Institute on Drug Abuse (NIDA). 1988a. National household survey on drug abuse, main findings, 1985. Washington, D.C.: DHHS Publication No. (ADM) 88–1586.

———. 1988b. Illicit drug use, smoking, and drinking by America's high school students, college students, and young adults, 1975–1987. Washington,D.C.: DHHS Publication No. (ADM) 89–1602.

National Institutes of Health. 1988. Health benefits of pets. Washington, D.C.: GPO.

Neugarten, B. L. 1968. The awareness of middle age. In B. L. Neugarten, ed. *Middle age and aging,* pp. 93–98. Chicago: University of Chicago Press.

———. 1969. Continuities and discontinuities of psychological issues into adult life. *Human Development* 12 (2): 121–130.

———. 1978. The future and the young-old. In L. F. Jarvik, ed. *Aging into the Twenty-First Century,* pp. 137–153. New York: Gardener Press.

Neugarten, B. L., and G. O. Hagestad. 1976. Age and the life course. In R. H. Binstock and E. Shanas, eds. *Handbook of aging and the social sciences,* pp. 35–55. New York: Van Nostrand Reinhold.

Neugarten, B. L., and K. K. Weinstein. 1968. The changing American grandparent. In B.

L. Neugarten, ed. *Middle age and aging,* pp. 280–285. Chicago: University of Chicago Press.

Newcomb, M., and P. Bentler. 1988. *Consequences of adolescent drug use: Impact on the lives of young adults.* Newbury Park, Calif.: Sage.

Newcomb, T. M., R. H. Turner, and P. E. Converse. 1965. *Social psychology: The study of human interaction.* New York: Holt.

Newman, O. 1972. *Defensible space.* New York: Macmillan.

Newsletter of the Child and Family Agency of Southeast Connecticut. 1996.

Newton, N., and C. Modahl. 1978. Pregnancy: The closest human relationship. *Human Nature* 1 (March): 39–49.

NIDA Capsules. 1988. Facts about drugs in the workplace. Rockville, Md.: National Institute on Drug Abuse.

Nisbett, R. 1995. Race, IQ, and scientism. In S. Fraser, ed. *The bell curve wars: Race, intelligence, and the future of America,* pp. 36–57. New York: Basic Books.

Noble, D. N., and A. K. Hamilton. 1983. Coping and complying: A challenge in health care. *Social Work* 28 (November–December): 462–466.

Nobles, W. 1974. Africanity: Its role in black families. *Black Scholar* 9 (June): 10–17.

Nordheimer, J. 1996. Welfare-to-work plans show success is difficult to achieve. *New York Times,* 1 September, A1, A18.

Notman, M. 1981. Abstract of a lecture on menopause. Cited in *Hot Flash* 1 (fall): 3.

Nowak, C. A., and G. C. Brice. 1984. The process of retirement: Implications for late-life counseling. I S. H. Cramer, ed. Perspectives on work and the family, pp. 108–123. Rockville, Md.: Aspen Systems.

Oakley, A. 1979. A case of maternity: Paradigms of women as maternity cases. *Signs: Journal of Women in Culture and Society* 4 (summer): 607–631.

Offer, D., and J. B. Offer. 1975. *From teenage to young manhood: A psychological study.* New York: Basic Books.

Offer, D., E. Ostrov, and K. Howard. 1981. *The adolescent: A psychological self-portrait.* New York: Basic Books.

———. 1988. *The teenage world: Adolescents' self-image in ten countries.* New York: Plenum.

O'Hare, W. P. 1995. Race/ethnicity and child poverty: A closer look. *Population Today* 23 (3): 4–5.

Oldham, D. G. 1978. Adolescent turmoil: A myth revisited. *Journal of Continuing Education in Psychiatry* 39 (3): 23–32.

Olson, M. R., and J. A. Haynes. 1993. Successful single parents. *Families in Society* 74:259–267.

O'Neil, J. M. 1982. Gender-role conflict and strain in men's lives: Implications for psychiatrists, psychologists, and other human-service providers. In K. Solomon and K. N. Levy, eds. *Man and transition,* pp. 5–44. New York: Plenum.

Opie, I., and P. Opie. 1969. *Children's games in street and playground.* Oxford: Oxford University Press.

Orlandi, M. A. 1986. Community-based substance abuse prevention: A multicultural perspective. *Journal of School Health* 56 (9): 394–401.

Osborn, A. E. 1957. *Applied imagination.* New York: Scribner.

Owan, T. C. 1978. Improving productivity in the public sector through bilingual-bicultural staff. *Social Work Research and Abstracts* 14 (spring): 10–18.

Ozawa, M. N. 1986. The nation's children: Key to a secure retirement. *New England Journal of Human Services* 6 (3): 12–19.

———. 1997. Demographic changes and their implications. In M. Reisch and E. Gambrill, eds. *Social Work in the Twenty-First Century.* Thousand Oaks, Calif.: Pine Forge Press.

Pancoast, D. L. 1980. Finding and enlisting neighbors to support families. In J. Garbarino and S. H. Stocking, eds. *Protecting children from abuse and neglect,* pp. 109–132. San Francisco: Jossey-Bass.

Parkes, C. M., J. Stevenson-Hinde, and P. Marris, eds. 1991. *Attachment across the life cycle.* London: Tavistock/Routledge.

Patrick, L. F., and P. A. Minish. 1985. Child-rearing strategies for the development of altruistic behavior in young children. *Journal of Primary Prevention* 11 (1): 19–35.

Patterson, S. 1987. Older rural natural helpers: Gender and site differences in the helping process. *Gerontologist* 27 (May) 639–644.

Patterson, S., and E. Brennan. 1983. Matching helping roles with the characteristics of older natural helpers. *Journal of Gerontological Social Work* 5 (4): 55–66.

Patterson, S., E. Brennan, C. B. Germain, and J. Memmot. 1988. The effectiveness of rural natural helpers. *Social Casework* 69 (May): 272–279.

Patti, R. J. 1980a. Social work practice: Organizational environment. In H. Resnick and R. Patti, eds. *Change from within: Humanizing social welfare organizations,* pp.46–56. Philadelphia: Temple University Press.

———. 1980b. Organizational resistance and change: The view from below. In H. Resnick and R. Patti, eds. *Change from within: Humanizing social welfare organizations,* pp. 114–131. Philadelphia: Temple University Press.

Pattison, E. M. 1977a. The dying experience. In E. M. Pattison, ed. *The experience of dying,* pp. 303–316. Englewood Cliffs, N.J.: Prentice-Hall.

———. 1977b. Death throughout the life cycle. In E. M. Pattison, ed. *The experience of dying,* pp. 18–27. Englewood Cliffs, N.J.: Prentice-Hall.

Paul, D. B. 1995. *Controlling human heredity: 1865 to the present.* Atlantic Highlands, N.J.: Humanities Press.

Paul, M., C. Daniels, and R. Rosofsky. 1988. A study of employers' practices and reproductive health. Massachusetts Department of Health and University of Massachusetts Occupational Health Program.

Peak, D. T. 1977. The elderly who face dying and death. In D. Barton, ed. *Dying and death: A clinical guide for caregivers,* pp. 210–219. Baltimore: Williams and Wilkins.

Perlman, D., and L. A. Peplau. 1984. Loneliness research: A survey of empirical findings.

In L. A. Peplau and S. E. Goldston, eds. *Preventing the harmful consequences of severe and persistent loneliness,* pp. 13–46. Washington, D.C.: Public Health Service. DHHS Publication No. (ADM) 84–1312.

Perrin, E. C., and P. S. Gerrity. 1984. Development of children with a chronic illness. *Pediatric Clinics of North America* 31 (February): 19–31.

Perrin, J. M. 1985. Introduction. In N. Hobbs and J. M. Perrin, eds. *Issues in the care of children with chronic illness,* pp. 1–10. San Francisco: Jossey-Bass.

Perry, C. L., M. Story, and L. A. Lytle. 1997. Promoting healthy dietary behaviors. In R. P. Weissberg et al., eds. *Enhancing children's wellness,* pp. 214–249. Thousand Oaks, Calif.: Sage.

Perspectives on Health Promotion and Aging. 1991. 6 (3): 1, 3, 7.

———. 1992. Tertiary prevention: Essential to health promotion for older adults. 7 (1): 1, 3, 7.

Peters, H. E. 1993. Enforcing divorce settlements: Evidence from child support compliance and award modifications. *Demography* 30 (4): 719–735.

Petersen, A., and R. Spiga. 1982. Adolescence and stress. In L. Goldberger and S. Breznitz, eds. *Handbook of stress: Theoretical and clinical aspects,* pp. 515–528. New York: Free Press.

Peterson, L., and L. Mori. 1986. Training preschoolers in home safety skills to prevent inadvertent injury. *Journal of Clinical Child Psychology* 15 (2): 106–114.

Pfeffer, C. R. 1987. Families of suicidal children. In R. R. W. Diekstra and K. Hawton, eds. *Suicide in adolescence,* pp. 137–138. Hingham, Mass.: Kluwer Academic Publishers.

Piaget, J. 1955. *The child's construction of reality.* London: Routledge and Paul.

Pinderhughes, E. 1979. Teaching empathy in cross-cultural social work. *Social Work* 24 (July): 312–316.

———. 1983. Empowerment for our clients and for ourselves. *Social Casework* 64 (June): 331–338.

Pless., I. B. 1984. Clinical assessment: Physical and psychological functioning. *Pediatric Clinics of North America* 31 (February): 33–45.

Pless, I. B., and J. M. Perrin. 1985. Issues common to a variety of illnesses. In N. Hobbs and J. M. Perrin, eds. *Issues in the care of children with chronic illness,* pp. 41–60. San Francisco: Jossey-Bass.

Polit, D., C. M. White, and T. D. Morton. 1987. Sex education and family planning services for adolescents in foster care. *Family Planning Perspectives* 19 (January–February): 18–23.

Pollack, O. 1960. A family diagnosis model. *Social Service Review* 34 (March): 1–50.

Ponterotto, J. G., and P. B. Pedersen. 1993. *Prevention of prejudice: A guide for counselors and educators.* Newbury Park, Calif.: Sage.

Popenoe, D. 1991. The American family beleaguered: Flight from the nuclear family: Trends of past three decades. *Public Perspective* 2 (3): 19–20.

Popiel, L. A. 1993. More grandparents face cost of raising their children's kids. *Christian Science Monitor,* 2 November, 9.

Poston, W. S. C., II, and A. A. Winebarger. 1996. The misuse of behavioral genetics in prevention research, or for whom the "Bell Curve" tolls. *Journal of Primary Prevention* 17 (1): 133–147.

Practice digest. 1984. Issue on working with gay and lesbian clients. (summer): 7.

Pressler, L. 1993. Alcohol problems facing Native Americans. *Congressional Record,* Daily Edition, 20 May, pp. S6159–6163.

Profile of older Americans. 1986. Administration on Aging and American Association of Retired Persons. Brochure.

Quammen, D. 1996. *The song of the dodo.* New York: Touchstone.

Queralt, M. 1984. Understanding Cuban immigrants: A cultural perspective. *Social Work* 29 (March–April): 115–121.

————. 1996. *The social environment and human behavior: A diversity perspective.* Boston: Allyn and Bacon.

Rando, T. A. 1985. Bereaved parents: Particular difficulties, unique factors, and treatment issues. *Social Work* 30:19–23.

Rasky, S. F. 1988. Fort Apache journal: What's in a name? For Indians, cultural survival. *New York Times,* 4 August, A12.

Rauch, J. B., and R. B. Black. 1995. Genetics. In R. L. Edwards et al., eds. *Encyclopedia of social work,* pp. 1108–1116. 19th ed. Washington, D.C.: NASW Press.

Redefining "overweight." 1995. *Harvard Women's Health Watch.* (April): 8, 7.

Red Horse, J. G. 1980. Family structure and value orientation in American Indians. *Social Casework* 61 (October): 462–467.

Regnier, V. 1994. *Assisted housing for the elderly.* New York: Van Nostrand Reinhold.

Rehnquist, W. H. 1997. Excerpts from Chief Justice Rehnquist's majority opinion . . . upholding state laws prohibiting assisted suicides. *New York Times,* 27 June, A18.

Reich, R. 1996. Forum: Does America still work? *Harper's Magazine,* May, 35–47.

Reiss, D. 1982. The working family: A researcher's view of health in the household. *American Journal of Psychiatry* 139 (November): 1412–1420.

Renzulli, J. S. 1973. Talent potential in minority group students. *Exceptional Children* 39:437–444.

Research Dialogues. 1989. Long-term care: A national issue. TIAA/CREF, April, 9.

Richards, L. N., and C. J. Schmierge. 1993. Problems and strengths of single-parent families: Implications for practice and policy. *Family Relations* 42:277–285.

Richman, J. M. 1995. Hospice. In R. L. Edwards et al., eds. *Encyclopedia of social work,* pp. 1358–1364. 19th ed. Washington, D.C.: NASW Press.

Richmond, J., E. Zigler, and D. Stipek. 1980. Head Start: The first decade. In M. Bloom, ed. *Life span development: Bases of preventive and interventive helping,* pp. 133–145. New York: Macmillan.

Riessman, C. K. 1989. From victim to survivor: A woman's narrative reconstruction of marital sexual abuse. *Smith College Studies in Social Work* 59 (June): 232–251.

Riley, M. W. 1978. Aging, social change, and the power of ideas. *Daedalus* 107 (fall): 39–52.

———. 1985a. Women, men, and the lengthening life course. In A. S. Rossi, ed. *Gender and the life course,* pp 333–347. New York: Aldine.

———. 1985b. Age strata in social systems. In R. H. Binstock and E. Shanas, eds. *Handbook of aging and the social sciences,* pp. 369–411. 2d ed. New York: Van Nostrand Reinhold.

Rimer, S. 1998. As centenarians thrive, "old" is redefined. *New York Times,* 22 June, A1.

Rist, R. C., and J. E. Harrel. 1982. Labeling the learning disabled child: The social ecology of educational practice. *American Journal of Orthopsychiatry* 52 (January): 146–160.

Robertson, B. 1994. In academia, new praises for the nuclear family. *Insight* 10 (14 March): 198–200.

Robins, L. N., and M. Rutter, eds. 1990. *Straight and devious pathways from childhood to adulthood.* New York: Cambridge University Press.

Robins, L. N., and E. Wish. 1977. Childhood deviance as a developmental process: A study of 223 urban black men from birth to 18. *Social Forces* 56 (2): 448–471.

Roethlisberger, F. J., and W. J. Dickson. 1939. *Management and the worker.* Cambridge: Harvard University Press.

Rogers, C. R. 1974. In retrospect: Forty-six years. *American Psychologist* 29 (2): 115–123.

Rokeach, M. 1973. *The nature of human values.* New York: Free Press.

Rook, K. S. 1984. Interventions for loneliness: A review and analysis. In L. A. Peplau and S. E. Goldston, eds. *Preventing the harmful consequences of severe and persistent loneliness,* pp. 47–79. Washington, D.C.: Public Health Service. DHHS Publication No. (ADM) 84–1312.

Roppel, C. E., and M. K. Jacobs. 1988. Multimedia strategies for mental health promotion. In L. A. Bond and B. M. Wagner, eds. *Families in transition,* pp. 33–48. Newbury Park, Calif.: Sage.

Roscoe, B. 1994. Sexual harassment: Early adolescents' self-reports of experiences and acceptance. *Adolescence* 29:515–523.

Rosen, S. M., D. Fanshel, and M. E. Lutz., eds. 1987. *Face of the nation 1987: Statistical supplement to the 18th edition of the encyclopedia of social work.* Silver Spring, Md.: NASW Press.

Rubin, L. 1976. *Worlds of pain: Life in the working-class family.* New York: Basic Books.

Rubin, Z. 1980. *Children's friendships.* Cambridge: Harvard University Press.

Rutter, M. 1979a. Protective factors in children's responses to stress and disadvantage. In M. W. Kent and J. E. Rolf, eds. *Primary prevention of psychopathology: Social competence in children,* pp. 49–74. Vol 3. Hanover, N.H.: University Press of New England.

———. 1979b. *Changing youth in a changing society.* London: Nuffield Provincial Hospitals Trust.

———. 1981. *Maternal deprivation reassessed.* 2d ed. New York: Penguin.

Ryan, A. S. 1982. Asian American women: A historical and cultural perspective. In A. Weick and S. Vandiver, eds. *Women, power, and change,* pp. 78–88. Washington, D.C.: NASW Press.

Ryerson, D. C. 1987. ASAP—an adolescent suicide awareness programme. In R. F. W.

Diekstra and K. Hawton, eds. *Suicide in adolescence,* pp. 173–190. Hingham, Mass.: Kluwer Academic Publishers.

Sacks, O. 1985. *The man who mistook his wife for a hat.* New York: Harper and Row.

Saghir, M., and E. Robins. 1973. *Male and female sexuality: A comprehensive investigation.* Baltimore: Williams and Wilkens.

Sagrestano, L. M., and R. L. Paikoff. 1997. Preventing high-risk sexual behavior, sexually transmitted diseases, and pregnancy among adolescents. In R. P. Weissberg et al., eds. *Enhancing children's wellness.* Thousand Oaks, Calif.: Sage.

Salcido, R. M. 1979. Problems of the Mexican American elderly in an urban setting. *Social Casework* 60 (December): 609–616.

Saleebey, D. 1997. Is it feasible to teach HBSE from a strengths perspective, in contrast to one emphasizing limitations and weaknesses? In M. Bloom and W. C. Klein, eds. *Controversial issues in human behavior in the social environment,* pp. 16–23. Boston: Allyn and Bacon.

—, ed. 1992. *The strengths perspective in social work practice.* New York: Longman.

Sales, E. 1995. Surviving unemployment: Economic resources and job loss duration in blue-collar households. *Social Work* 40 (4): 483–494.

Sander, J. H., and J. L. Rosen. 1987. Teenage fathers: Working with the neglected partner in adolescent childbearing. *Family Planning Perspectives* 19 (May–June): 107–110.

Santa-Barbara, J. 1984. Employee assistance programs: An alternative resource for mental health service delivery. *Canada's Mental Health* 32 (September): 35–38.

Santos, K. D. 1995. Deafness. In R. L. Edwards et al., eds. *Encyclopedia of social work,* pp. 685–703. 19th ed. Washington, D.C.: NASW Press.

Satir, V. 1967. *Conjoint family therapy.* Palo Alto, Calif.: Science and Behavior Books.

Scarr, S., S. Pakstis, H. Katz, and W. B. Barker. 1977. Absence of a relationship between degree of white ancestry and intellectual skills within a black population. *Human Genetics* 39:73–77, 82–83. Cited in Nisbett.

Schafer, A. T., and M. W. Gray. 1981. Sex and mathematics. *Science* 2216 (16 January): 231.

Schaie, K. W., S. Orchowsky, and I. A. Parham. 1982. Measuring age and sociocultural change: The case of race and life satisfaction. In R. Manuel, ed. *Minority aging, sociological and social psychological issues,* pp. 223–230. Westport, Conn.: Greenwood Press.

Scherz, F. H. 1967. The crisis of adolescence in family life. *Social Casework* 48 (April): 209–215.

Schiele, J. H. 1990. Organizational theory from an Africentric perspective. *Journal of Black Studies* 21:145–161.

Schild, S., and R. B. Black. 1984. *Social work and genetics: A guide for practice.* New York: Haworth.

Schilling, R., N. El-Bassel, Y. Serrano, and B. Wallace. 1992. AIDS prevention strategies for ethnic-racial minority substance users. *Psychology of Addictive Behaviors* 6 (2): 81–90.

Schinke, S. P., G. Botvin, M. Orlandi, R. Schilling, and A. Gordon. 1990. African American and Hispanic American adolescents, HIV infection, and preventive intervention. *AIDS Education and Prevention* 2 (4): 305–312.

Schinke, S. P., and L. Gilchrist. 1984. *Life skills counseling with adolescents.* Baltimore: University Park Press.

Schinke, S. P., M. Orlandi, and G. Botvin. 1988. Preventing substance abuse among American Indian adolescents: A bicultural competence skills approach. *Journal of Counseling Psychology* 35:87–90.

Schinke, S. P., R. Schilling, R. Barth, L. Gilchrist, and J. Maxwell. 1986. Stress-management intervention to prevent family violence. *Journal of Family Violence* 1 (1): 13–26.

Schinke, S. P., R. Schilling, and L. Gilchrist. 1985. Preventing substance abuse with American Indian youth. *Social Casework* 66 (April): 213–217.

Schmitt, E. 1987. Ordeal for homeless students in suburbs. *New York Times,* 16 November, B1–2,

Schowalter, J. E. 1977. The adolescent with cancer. In E. M. Pattison, ed. *The experience of dying,* pp. 195–202. Englewood Cliffs, N.J.: Prentice-Hall.

Schweinhart, L. J., and D. P. Weikart. 1986. Early childhood development programs: A public investment opportunity. *Educational Leadership* 44 (3): 4–13.

Seidman, B. 1995. H.R. 4245, H.R. 4275 . . . To restore the long-term solvency of Social Security. Hearing. Washington, D.C.: GPO.

Selye, H. 1976. *Stress in health and disease.* Reading, Mass.: Butterworth.

Shapiro, C. H. 1981. *Adolescent pregnancy prevention: School-community cooperation.* Springfield, Ill.: Charles C. Thomas.

Shaw, L. G. 1987. Designing playgrounds for able and disabled children. In C. Weinstein and T. David, eds. *Spaces for children,* pp. 187–213. New York: Plenum.

Shilts, R. 1987. *And the band played on: Politics, people, and the AIDS epidemic.* New York: St. Martin's Press.

Shon, S. P., and Y. J. Davis. 1982. Asian families. In M. McGoldrick, J. Pearce, and J. Giordano, eds. *Ethnicity and family therapy,* pp. 208–228. New York: Guilford Press.

Shor, I., ed. 1987. *Freire for the classroom: Source book for liberatory teaching.* Portsmoutn, N.H.: Boynton/Cook.

Shure, M. B., and G. Spivack. 1988. Interpersonal cognitive problem-solving. In R. H. Price, E. L. Cowen, R. P. Lorion, and J. Ramos-McKay, eds. *14 ounces of prevention: A casebook for practitioners,* pp. 69–82. Washington, D.C.: American Psychological Association.

Silberman, C. E. 1978. *Criminal violence, criminal justice.* New York: Random House.

Silverman, L. H. 1976. Psychoanalytic theory: "Reports of my death are greatly exaggerated." *American Psychologist* (September): 621–637.

Silverman, P. 1988. Widow-to-widow: A mutual help program for the widowed. In R. H. Price, E. L. Cowen, R. P. Lorion, and J. Ramos-McKay, eds. *14 ounces of prevention: A casebook for practitioners,* pp. 175–186. Washington, D.C.: American Psychological Association.

Simic, A., and B. Myerhoff. 1978. Conclusion. In B. Myerhoff and A. Simic, eds. *Life's career—aging: Cultural variations in growing old,* pp. 231–246. Beverly Hills, Calif.: Sage.

Simmel, G. 1950. *The sociology of Georg Simmel.* Trans. and ed. K. H. Wolff. New York: Free Press.

Singer, C., and L. M. Wells. 1981. The impact of student units on services and structural changes in homes for the aged. *Canadian Journal of Social Work Education* 7 (3): 11–27.

Sinnott, J. D. 1986. *Sex roles and aging: Theory and research from a systems perspective.* Farmington, Conn.: S. Karper.

Skeen, P., R. B. Covi, and B. E. Robinson. 1985. Stepfamilies: A review of the literature with suggestions for practitioners. *Journal of Counseling and Development* 65 (2): 121–125.

Skinner, B. F. 1957. *Verbal behavior.* New York: Appleton-Century-Crofts.

Slater, P. 1955. Role differentiation in small groups. *American Sociological Review* 20:300–310.

Slaughter, L. M. 1993. Domestic violence awareness month. *Congressional Record,* Daily Edition, 19 April, P.E. 937.

Smith, D. A., D. Vivian, and D. O'Leary. 1990. Longitudinal prediction of marital discord from premarital expressions of affect. *Journal of Consulting and Clinical Psychology* 58 (6): 790–798.

Smitherman, G. 1986. From Africa to the new world and into the space age. In G. Goshgarian, ed. *Exploring language,* pp. 278–288. 7th ed. New York: Harper Collins.

Smokers 50% more likely to bear retarded child. 1996. *New York Times,* 10 April, B7.

Sommer, R. 1969. *Personal space.* Englewood Cliffs, N.J.: Prentice-Hall.

Sonenstein, F. L., J. H. Pleck, and L. C. Ku. 1989. At risk of AIDS: Behaviors, knowledge, and attitudes among a national sample of adolescent males. Paper presented at the Annual Meeting of the Population Association of America, 31 March, Baltimore.

Sosa, R, J., M. Kennell, S. Klaus, S. Robertson, and J. Urrutia. 1980. The effect of a supportive companion on perinatal problems, length of labor, and mother-infant interactions. *New England Journal of Medicine* 303:597–600.

Sotomayer, M. 1980. Language, culture, and ethnicity in developing self-concept. In M. Bloom, ed. *Life-span development: Bases for preventive and interventive helping,* pp. 50–55. New York: Macmillan. First published in *Social Casework* 58 (April): 195–203.

Sowell, T. 1994. *Race and culture.* New York: Basic Books.

Spaid, E. L. 1994. The family room is the classroom. *Christian Science Monitor,* 11 October, 10–11.

Spiegel, D. 1982. Self-help and mutual-support groups: A synthesis of the recent literature. In D. E. Biegel and A. J. Naparstek, eds. *Community support systems and mental health,* pp. 98–118. New York: Springer.

Spinetta, J. J., D. Rigler, and M. Karon. 1974. Personal space as a measure of a dying child's sense of isolation. *Journal of Consulting and Clinical Psychology* 42 (December): 751–756.

Stack, C. B. 1974. *All our kin: Strategies for survival in a black community.* New York: Harper Colophon.

Stein, R. 1983. Growing up with a physical difference. *Children's Health Care* 12 (February): 53–61.

Steinfels, P. 1992. Jewish intermarriage is big concern. *Ann Arbor News,* 3 November, D3.

Stellman, J. M., and S. M. Daum. 1973. *Work is dangerous to your health.* New York: Pantheon Books.

Stern, D. 1985. *The interpersonal world of the human infant.* New York: Basic Books.

Stevenson, H., and J. Stigler. 1992. *The learning gap: Why our schools are failing and what we can learn from Japanese and Chinese education.* New York: Summit Books.

Stevenson, M. R., and K. N. Black. 1996. *How divorce affects offsprings: A research approach.* Boulder, Colo.: Westview Press.

Stewart, W. A. 1969. On the use of Negro dialect in the teaching of reading. In J. Baratz and R. W. Shuy, eds. *Teaching black children to read,* pp. 156–219. Washington, D.C.: Center for Applied Linguistics.

Stokes, L. 1993. The Minority Health Improvement Act of 1993. *Congressional Record,* Daily Edition, 22 November, pp. H10980–10981.

Stolberg, A., and M. Bloom. 1992. Child development and functioning during the divorce adjustment process: Bases of preventive helping. In M. Bloom, ed. *Changing lives: Studies in human development and professional helping,* pp. 274–281. Columbia, S.C.: University of South Carolina Press.

Strauss, A. L., and B. G. Glaser. 1975. *Chronic illness and the quality of life.* St. Louis: Mosby.

Study finds blacks twice as liable to school penalties as whites. 1988. *New York Times,* 12 December, A16.

Sullivan, T., and M. Schneider. 1987. Development and identity issues in adolescent homosexuality. *Child and Adolescent Social Work* 4 (1): 13–24.

Sullivan, H. S. 1953. *The interpersonal theory of psychiatry.* New York: Norton.

Sussman, M. 1985. The family life of old people. In R. Binstock and E. Shanas, eds. *Handbook of aging and the social sciences,* pp. 419–449. 2d ed. New York: Van Nostrand Reinhold.

Tadmor, C. S. 1988. The perceived personal control preventive intervention for a Caesarean birth population. In R. H. Price, E. L. Cowen, R. P. Lorion, and J. Ramos-McKay, eds. *14 ounces of prevention: A casebook for practitioners,* pp. 141–152. Washington, D.C.: American Psychological Association.

Tavris, C. 1992. *The mismeasure of woman.* New York: Simon and Schuster.

Terkelsen, K. G. 1980. Toward a theory of the family life cycle. In E. Carter and M. McGoldrick, eds. *The family life cycle: A framework for family therapy,* pp. 21–52. New York: Gardner Press.

Theodorson, G. A., and A. G. Theodorson. 1969. *Modern dictionary of sociology: The concepts and terminology of sociology and related disciplines.* New York: Thomas Y. Crowell.

Thomas, A. 1981. Current trends in developmental theory. *American Journal of Orthopsychiatry* 51:580–609.

Thomas, A., and S. Chess. 1977. *Temperament and development.* New York: Brunner/Mazel.

Thomson, E., and U. Colella. 1992. Cohabitation and marital stability: Quality or commitment. *Journal of Marriage and the Family* 54:259–267.

Toffler, A. 1980. *The third wave.* New York: Bantam.

Tou-fou, V. 1981. The Hmong of Laos. In *Bridging cultures: Southeast Asian refugees in America,* pp. 73–82. Los Angeles: Asian American Community Mental Health Training Center.

Toupin, E. S. W. A. 1981. Counseling Asians: Psychotherapy in the context of racism and Asian American history. In R. H. Dana, ed. *Human services for cultural minorities,* pp. 295–306. Baltimore: University Park Press.

Treas, J. 1995. Older Americans in the 1990s and beyond. *Population Bulletin* 50 (2): 2–43.

Trost, C. 1988. Occupational hazard. *Wall Street Journal,* 22 April, 25R–26R.

Tuchfarber, B. S., J. E. Zins, and L. A. Jason. 1997. Prevention and control of injuries. In R. P. Weissberg et al., eds. *Enhancing children's wellness,* pp. 250–277. Thousand Oaks, Calif.: Sage.

Tuckman, B. W., and M. A. C. Jensen. 1977. Stages of small group development revisited. *Group and Organizational Studies* 2:419–427.

Tull, A. W. 1994. Departments of Labor, Health and Human Services, Education . . . Appropriations for 1995. Part 7. Hearing. Washington, D.C.: GPO.

Turner, C., and W. A. Darity. 1973. Fears of genocide among black Americans as related to age, sex, and region. *American Journal of Public Health* 63 (12): 1029–1034.

U.S. Department of Commerce, Bureau of the Census. 1991. *Poverty in the United States: 1990.* Current Population Reports, Series P-60, No.l 1k75. Washington, D.C.: GPO.

———. 1993. *Statistical abstract of the United States, 1993.* 113th ed. Washington, D.C.: GPO.

———. 1994. Two-thirds of U.S. households with children were maintained by married couples. *Census and You* 29 (March): 8.

———. 1995a. USA statistics in brief. Statistical abstract of the United States [on line]. http://www.census.gov/stat'abstract/brief.html.

———. 1995b. *Sixty-five plus in the United States.* Statistical brief. Washington, D.C.: U.S. Department of Commerce, Bureau of the Census.

———. 1997. *Statistical abstract of the United States, 1997. [see 1993 citation—add edition number?]* Washington, D.C.: GPO.

U.S. Departments of Labor, Health and Human Services, Education. 1990. Appropriations for 1991. Part 4B. Hearing. Washington, D.C.: GPO.

———. 1994. Appropriations for 1995. Hearing. Washington, D.C.: GPO.

———. 1995. Appropriations for 1996, Part 3. Hearing. Washington, D.C.: GPO.

U.S. surgeon general's report on physical activity and health. 1996. Washington, D.C.: GPO.

Useful information on suicide. 1986. Rockville, Md.: DHHS Publication No. (ADM) 86–1489.

Valentich, M. 1994. Social work and the development of a smoke-free society. *Social Work* 39 (4): 439–450.

Valentine, B. L. 1978. *Hustling and other hard work.* New York: Free Press.

Valentine, C. A., and B. L. Valentine. 1970. Making the scene, digging the action, and telling it like it is: Anthropologists at work in a dark ghetto. In N. E. Whitten and J. F. Szwed, eds. *Afro-American anthropology,* pp. 403–418. New York: Free Press.

Veblen, T. 1922. *The theory of the leisure class, an economic study of institutions.* New York: B. W. Huebsch.

Vicary, J. R. 1994. Primary prevention and the workplace. *Journal of Primary Prevention* 15 (2): 99–104.

Vinokur, A. D., and R. Caplan. 1987. Attitudes and social support: Determinants of job-seeking behavior and well-being among the unemployed. *Journal of Applied Social Psychology* 17:1007–1024.

Vinokur, A. D., R. Caplan, and C. Williams. 1987. Effects of recent and past stress on mental health: Coping with unemployment among Vietnam veterans and nonveterans. *Journal of Applied Social Psychology* 17:708–728.

Vinokur, A. D., M. van Ryn, E. M. Gramlick, and R. H. Price. 1991. Long-term follow-up and benefit–cost analysis of the Jobs Program: A preventive intervention for the unemployed. *Journal of Applied Psychology* 76 (2): 213–219.

Vladeck, B. 1980. *Unloving care.* New York: Basic Books.

Wald, E. 1981. *The remarried family: Challenge and promise.* New York: Family Service Association of America.

Waldron, L., and Johnston, S. 1976. Why do women live longer than men? Part 2. *Journal of Human Stress* 2:19–24.

Walker, L. A. 1987. *A loss for words: The story of deafness in a family.* New York: Harper and Row.

Wallerstein, J. S. 1984. Children of divorce: Preliminary report of a ten-year follow-up of young children. *American Journal of Orthopsychiatry* 54 (July): 444–458.

———. 1985. The overburdened child: Some long-term consequences of divorce. *Social Work* 30 (March–April): 116–123.

Wallerstein, J. S., and S. Blakeslee. 1989. *Second chances: Men, women, and children a decade after divorce.* New York: Ticknor and Fields.

Wallerstein, J. S., and J. B. Kelly. 1980. *Surviving the breakup.* New York: Basic Books.

Walsh, F. 1980. The family in later life. In E. Carter and M. McGoldrick, eds. *The family life cycle: A framework for family therapy,* pp. 197–220. New York: Gardner.

Warren, R. 1963. *The community in America.* Chicago: Rand McNally.

Warshak, R. A., and J. W. Santrock. 1983. Children of divorce: Impact of custody disposition on social adjustment. In E. J. Callahan and K. A. McClusky, eds. *Life span developmental psychology: Nonnormative life events,* pp. 241–263. New York: Academic Press.

Wattenberg, E. 1986. The fate of baby boomers and their children. *Social Work* 31 (January–February): 20–28.

Wax, T. M. 1995. Deaf community. In R. L. Edwards et al., eds. *Encyclopedia of social work,* pp. 679–684. 19th ed. Washington, D.C.: NASW Press.

Weber, G. K. 1980. Preparing social workers for practice in rural social systems. In H. W. Johnson, ed. *Rural human services,* pp. 203–214. Itasca, Ill.: F. E. Peacock.

Weber, M. 1948. *The Protestant ethic and the spirit of capitalism.* New York: Charles Scribner's Sons.

Weiss, R. S. 1973. *Loneliness: The experience of emotional and social isolation.* Cambridge: MIT Press.

———. 1982. Attachment in adult life. In C. M. Parkes and J. Stevenson-Hinde, eds. *The place of attachment in adult life,* pp. 171–183. New York: Basic Books.

———. 1984. Loneliness: What we know about it and what we might do about it. In L. A. Peplau and S. E. Goldston, eds. *Preventing the harmful consequences of severe and persistent loneliness,* pp. 3–12. Washington, D.C.: Public Health Service. DHHS Publication No. (ADM) 84–1312.

Weissberg, R. P., T. Gullotta, R. Hampton, B. Ryan, and G. Adams, eds. 1997. *Enhancing children's wellness.* Thousand Oaks, Calif.: Sage.

Weissberg, R. P., A. S. Jackson, and T. P. Shriver. 1993. Promoting positive social development and health practices in young urban adolescents. In M. J. Elias, ed. *Social decision making and life skills development: Guidelines for middle school educators.* Gaithersberg, Md.: Aspen Systems.

Weitzman, L. J. 1985. *The divorce revolution: The unexpected social and economic consequences for women and children in America.* New York: Free Press.

Weitzman, M. 1984. School and peer relations. *Pediatric Clinics of North America* 31 (February): 59–69.

Wells, L. M., C. Singer, and A. T. Polgar. 1986. *To enhance quality of life in institutions: An empowerment model in long-term care: A partnership of residents, staff, and families.* Toronto: Faculty of Social Work, University of Toronto and University of Toronto Press.

Werner, E. E., and R. S. Smith. 1992. *Overcoming the odds: High risk children from birth to adulthood.* Ithaca, N.Y.: Cornell University Press.

Werthein, J. 1995. UNESCO's role in international education. *Access* no. 125 (February): 3–4.

Wertz, R. W., and D. C. Wertz. 1977. *Lying-in.* New York: Free Press.

West, W. 1995. The last word: Bilingual education spells failure in any language. *Insight* 11 (1 May): 40.

Westhoff, C. F. 1988. Unintended pregnancy in America and abroad. *Family Planning Perspectives* 20 (November–December): 254–261.

Wetzel, J. W. 1978a. Depression and dependence upon unsustaining environments. *Clinical Social Work Journal* 6 (2): 75–89.

———. 1978b. The work environment and depression. In J. Hanks, ed. *Toward human dignity,* pp. 236–245. Washington, D.C.: NASW Press.

White, R. W. 1959. Motivation reconsidered: The concept of competence. *Psychological Review* 66 (September): 297–333.

Wilkerson, I. 1988. Farms, deadliest workplace, taking the lives of children. *New York Times,* 26 September, A1, A21.

Wilkinson, G. T. 1980. On assisting Indian people. *Social Casework* 61 (October): 451–454.

Will, O. A. 1959. Human relatedness and the schizophrenic reaction. *Psychiatry* 22 (August): 205–223.

Williams, C. W. 1995. Adolescent pregnancy. In R. Edwards et al., eds. *Encyclopedia of social work,* pp. 34–40. 19th ed. Washington, D.C.: NASW Press.

Williams, J. 1983. *Psychology of women: Behavior in a biosocial context,* 2d ed. New York: Norton.

Williams, T. F. 1990. Departments of Labor, Health and Human Services, Education . . . Appropriations for 1991. Part 4B. Hearing. Washington, D.C.: GPO.

Winch, R. 1958. *Mate selection.* New York: Harpers.

Windsor, R. A., J. Lowe, L. Perkins, D. Smoth-Yoder, L. Artz, M. Crawford, K. Amburgy, and N. Boyd. 1993. Health education for pregnant smokers: Its behavioral impact and cost benefit. *American Journal of Public Health* 83 (2): 201–208.

Winters, W. G., and F. Easton. 1983. *The practice of social work in the schools, an ecological perspective.* New York: Free Press.

Wong, J. 1981. Appropriate mental health treatment and service delivery for Southeast Asians. In *Bridging cultures: Southeast Asian refugees in America,* pp. 195–223. Los Angeles: Asian American Community Mental Health Center.

Wood, J. 1987. Labors of love. *Modern Maturity,* August–September, 28–34, 90–94.

Wuthnow, R. 1978. Peak experiences: Some empirical tests. *Journal of Humanistic Psychology* 18 (3): 59–75.

Yamamoto, K., A. Soliman, J. Parson, and O. L. Davies Jr. 1988. Voices in unison: Stressful events in the lives of children in six countries. *Journal of Child Psychology and Psychiatry* 28 (March): 855–864.

Zambelli, G. C., and A. P. DeRossa. 1992. Bereavement support groups for school-age children: Theory, intervention, and case example. *American Journal of Orthopsychiatry* 62:484–493.

Zera, D. 1992. Coming of age in a heterosexist world: The development of gay and lesbian adolescents. *Adolescence* 27 (108): 849–854.

Zeisel, H. 1982. *The limits of law enforcement.* Chicago: University of Chicago Press.

Zigas, B. 1993. Homelessness in America. Hearing. Washington, D.C.: GPO

Zigler, E. F. 1985. Assessing Head Start at 20: An invited commentary. *American Journal of Orthopsychiatry* 55 (4): 603–609.

Zigler, E. F., and E. Gilman. 1996. Not just any care: Shaping a coherent child care policy. In E. F. Zigler, S. L. Kagan, and N. W. Hall, eds. *Children, families, and government: Preparing for the twenty-first century.* Cambridge: Cambridge University Press.

Zigler, E. F., S. L. Kagan, and N. W. Hall, eds. 1996. *Children, families, and government: Preparing for the twenty-first century.* Cambridge: Cambridge University Press.

Zigler, E. F. and S. J. Styfco. 1993. *Head Start and beyond: A national plan for extending childhood intervention.* New Haven, Conn.: Yale University Press.

Zigler, E. F., and J. Valentine, eds. 1979. *Project Head Start: A legacy of the war on poverty.* New York: Free Press.

Zill, N., and J. Robinson. 1995. The generation X difference. *American Demographics* 17 (4): 24–29, 33.

Zlotnik, J. L. 1995. Families in the 1990s—the changing picture of who we are. In W. J. O'Neill Jr., ed. *Family: The first imperative,* pp. 333–344. Cleveland: O'Neill Foundation.

Zoucha-Jensen, J. M., and A. Coyne. 1993. The effects of resistance strategies on rape. *American Journal of Public Health* 83 (11): 1633–1634.

NAME INDEX

Abercrombie, N., 355
Abrahamson, M., 33, 42, 414
Adams, J. E., 297
Adler, A., 205
Albee, G. W., 55, 181
Alcalay, F., 26, 232
Alexander, D., 156
Allen, J., 54–55, 140
Allen, J. P., 271, 310
Allen-Meares, P., 266
Altman, I., 37
Annas, G. J., 187
Arbuthnot, J., 236, 394
Aristophanes, 208, 214
Aristotle, 240
Aronson, E., 101–102
Asch, A., 70, 297
Atchley, R. C., 344, 351, 355, 360, 364, 365–366, 380
Attneave, C., 172
Auletta, K., 111

Bacon, K. H., 303
Badgett, M., 72
Balgopal, P. R., 173
Balswick, J., 213
Bandura, A., 10, 22, 25, 31, 395–396, 398
Banta, W. F., 124
Barbarin, O. A., 67
Barnett, W. S., 71, 107
Barron, W. G., 160, 161, 346
Barth, R. P., 222, 308
Basso, K. H., 244–245

Baumer, D. C., 111
Beal, E. W., 329
Begab, M. J., 71
Belgrave, L. L., 366
Bell, K., 245
Bell, T. H., 267
Benard, B., 285
Bendix, R., 76
Bereuter, D., 92
Berger, R. M., 72, 367–368
Berkman, L. F., 143
Berman, A. L., 312
Bern, J. H., 274
Bianchi, S. M., 161
Binet, A., 184
Black, R. B., 71, 181–182, 187–188
Blanchard, E. L., 60, 91, 172
Bloom, B. L., 327–328, 329
Bloom, Lois, 23, 237–242
Bloom, K., 238
Bloom, M., 5, 26, 37, 51
Blume, S. B., 348
Botvin, G. J., 111, 300
Boulding, E., 405
Bowlby, J., 105
Boyer, E. L., 258
Bradley, B., 163
Bray, J. H., 165
Brazelton, T. B., 71, 105–106, 238
Brenner, H., 126
Briley, M., 373
Brilliant, E., 81
Brody, E., 350
Brody, J., 228, 370–371

SUBJECT INDEX